"Written with a fine edge of crazy wisdom detail, this book is a treasure-house of insight and humor. It's so accessible—Chadwick really knows how to invite the reader in."
> —Joan Halifax, author of *The Fruitful Darkness*

"Totally delightful—fantastic couch potato Zen. Chadwick saves you the trouble of going to Japan by making all the mistakes for you."
> —Jack Kornfield, author of *A Path with Heart*

"I love this book!"
> —Ken Wilber, author of *Grace and Grit*

"The famous 'punk monk' has given a sense of Zen, a sense of Japan, and a sense of himself as seeker and wanderer which is sweet, full of good information, and . . . funky. Thank you and okay!"
> —Herbert Gold, author of *Bohemia*

"The results of Chadwick's cultural collision with Japan are funny, insightful, and revelatory."
> —Peter Coyote, actor and writer

"I loved this book—touching, funny, knowing—I couldn't put it down."
> —Robert Whiting, author of *You Gotta Have Wa*

ARKANA

THANK YOU AND OK!

David Chadwick, a Texas-raised wanderer, college dropout, bumbling social activist and hobbyhorse musician, began his formal Zen study under Shunryū Suzuki Roshi in 1966 at the age of twenty-one. Many years later, Suzuki's successor, Zentatsu Richard Baker Roshi, shaking his head, said of Chadwick: "Years of expensive Zen training gone to waste." In 1988 friends and supporters underwrote Chadwick's journey to Japan so he could begin an open-ended period of voluntary exile and remedial education. In Japan he practiced more Zen, got married, studied Japanese language and culture, and taught English. With his wife Elin and toddler Clay, Chadwick now lives in Northern California, where he reads, writes, walks, sits and studies.

THANK YOU AND OK!

AN AMERICAN ZEN FAILURE IN JAPAN

DAVID CHADWICK

PENGUIN/ARKANA

ARKANA
Published by the Penguin Group
Penguin Books USA Inc., 375 Hudson Street,
New York, New York 10014, U.S.A.
Penguin Books Ltd, 27 Wrights Lane,
London W8 5TZ, England
Penguin Books Australia Ltd, Ringwood,
Victoria, Australia
Penguin Books Canada Ltd, 10 Alcorn Avenue,
Toronto, Ontario, Canada M4V 3B2
Penguin Books (N.Z.) Ltd, 182–190 Wairau Road,
Auckland 10, New Zealand

Penguin Books Ltd, Registered Offices:
Harmondsworth, Middlesex, England

First published in Arkana 1994

1   3   5   7   9   10   8   6   4   2

The chapter "Driving Me Crazy" first appeared in slightly different form
in *Tricycle*.

LIBRARY OF CONGRESS CATALOGING IN PUBLICATION DATA
Chadwick, David.
Thank you and OK! : an American Zen failure in Japan / David Chadwick.
p.   cm.
ISBN 0 14 019.457 6
1. Chadwick, David.   2. Spiritual life—Zen Buddhism.   3. Zen
Buddhism—Japan.   I. Title.
BQ946.A334A3   1994
294.3'927'092—dc20
[B]   93-48049

Printed in the United States of America
Set in Garamond No. 3
DESIGNED BY CLAIRE NAYLON VACCARO

TO

AHDEL

AND

KELROY

MY

PARENTS

Once when I was driving Suzuki Roshi to Zen Center from Tassajara, after we'd stopped at the original Thunderbird Bookstore in Carmel Valley and he'd had three cups of coffee and I two, we got back into the car and I was all jacked up and driving down the road and I said, "Suzuki Roshi, may I ask you a question?" and he said, "Yes," and I proceeded to beg him to tell me what it is that I should do to understand reality, to get enlightened. I told him that I was totally dedicated to the Way and that whatever he told me, I would do, no matter what it was. I went on and on making sure that he was thoroughly aware of my sincerity and devotion. I turned to him for an answer. He was sound asleep.

PREFACE

In 1987 I received no calendar for Christmas. On New Year's day I took down the old one and looked at the empty space. I felt like mold growing on the wall and went out to buy a calendar with new scenery. As I walked down the San Francisco sidewalk, the scenario of another year of running the Zen Center's kitchen flipped by in my imagination. I returned to my room with a plane ticket to Japan.

The strings of attachment had been loosened already. My ex-wife had just moved away to the northwest with our fourteen-year-old son, Kelly. My ladyfriend, Elin, would soon go to her mother's house in Atlanta to finish her college thesis and consider her future.

Elin and I spent February and March of 1988 moseying to Georgia, and then, after visiting my mother and son, my long-held dream of seeing the country of my spiritual teachers and many good friends took flight.

The 747 descended through the crystal clean, post-rain April night into the glistening, brightly colored lights of Osaka. I was forty-three and had been associated with the San Francisco Zen Center since I was twenty-one. I studied for five years with Shun-ryū Suzuki Roshi, who ordained me as a priest, and then for another five with Zentatsu Richard Baker Roshi, Suzuki's heir. (*Rōshi*, literally "old priest," is a title that we often translate as "Zen master" in America.) After that I mainly lived outside of the institution and was less of a company man and, though I continued my involvement with the Zen Center, easily half of my activity for the next decade was away from it.

During this whole period, a special teacher and friend was Dainin Katagiri Roshi. He had come to San Francisco in 1965 to assist Suzuki in ministering to the transplanted Japanese-American Soto Zen community and in guiding the zealous non-Japanese devotees of Zen practice. Before Suzuki's death Katagiri went out to start his own group, though he would return at times to help out. I always kept up with him. He was like my Zen uncle.

Once in Japan I hit the ground running. After a couple of weeks visiting friends in Kyoto and elsewhere, I entered a small mountain temple I will call Hōgoji. I went there because Katagiri was in residence for six weeks and had suggested I come join him. He thought it would be good for me to get a taste of monastic life in Japan before I got tied down to some routine or devoured by the complexity of things.

After my stay at Hōgoji I started looking for a place to settle down. Kelly came to visit and he and I traveled around in the summer, and then Elin came to join me in the fall. We traveled for three weeks and, just before our money ran out, moved in next door to a large temple that I will call Daianji in the suburbs of a city I will call Maruyama, a metropolis in western Japan on the main island of Honshū. We got married and spent a wonderful three and a half years there.

This book has two main threads. One is the story of my stay at Hōgoji. It gives the day-to-day of that remote mountain temple, the monks who were there, and Katagiri—how he affected me and how I felt about him. The other story is my life with Elin in Maruyama and our exploration of modern Japan, a place full of wonders, delusion, tradition, pretense and the dance of life—just like the States, only completely different.

I have shuffled the two parts together so the narrative periodically moves back and forth from the isolated Hōgoji experience to my family life and lay Zen practice in the following years. To help keep the reader oriented, I note locations and dates at the beginning of each chapter.

Almost all the proper names have been changed. I did some combining and dividing of characters to protect people's privacy. Left intact are most U.S. and some famous Japanese place names, the names of members of my immediate family, and Shunryū Suzuki Roshi, Dainin Katagiri Roshi and Zentatsu Richard Baker Roshi.

I've tried to define every Buddhist or Japanese term as briefly and gracefully as possible so that those not versed in the subject will not be handicapped or bogged down, while those familiar will not be unduly distracted from the story. There is a short glossary at the end of the book.

I remember Masako-san, a premed student with a thirst for knowledge and experience—a bright and nervous English student of Elin's. She found me in a cozy upstairs blues bar in downtown Maruyama one night listening to Lightnin' Hopkins and going through a stack of notebooks and letters.

"Excuse me," she said, with her hands held together pressed against her black skirt and her head tilted down.

"Oh, hi, Masako," I said in English. "How are you?"

"I am fine thank you. And how are you doing?" she answered carefully.

"I'm fine too, thank you. Sit down, please."

"Oh no. You are busy."

"Then join me for three minutes."

"Thank you," she said and sat down. "What are you doing?"

"I'm going over some notes."

"Are they notes of Buddhist lectures?"

"No."

She was smiling intently as she had been since she said hello. She was looking right at me. I always hear that Japanese don't look at each other, that eye contact is considered rude, but I see them look at each other all the time. I looked back at her.

"Is it Japanese language study?" she tried again after I failed to tell her what it was.

"No," I repeated, "It's notes for a book."

"A book? Are you writing a book?"

"Yes."

"Are you an author?"

"If I finish this."

"That's very interesting," she said.

"I hope so."

"Is it about America?"

"No it's not," I looked at her sternly—play sternly. "Come on, Masako."

She wasn't intimidated. I could see she knew but didn't want to say. "What are you writing a book about?" she asked, inching toward the answer with a touch of worry in her voice.

"About my experiences in Japan."

Her expression turned pensive. The smile was gone. She looked down stiffly and then quickly squeezed her hands before her mouth and stared at me entreatingly.

"Oh please, please be good to us," she said intensely.

—David Chadwick
from back in the States

ACKNOWLEDGMENTS

The kindness, generosity and skill of others have made this book possible.

I am exceedingly indebted to my Zen and non-Zen colleague, friend and tennis-buddy Michael Katz for calling me up in Japan and suggesting that my letters to friends and family could well be the beginnings of a book. I am further indebted to him for buying me a computer, printer and software as a sign of his confidence and then for following up on his initial interest with years of guidance, support and minute attention to the text as it evolved, the title (which he suggested), even the cover—all far beyond the call of duty of an agent.

I am grateful beyond measure to my wife Elin for her constant encouragement, clear judgment and discriminating taste, and for her hard work and endless patience in her wise and merciless editing of and comments on every part of this book at every stage.

A few people read the entire manuscript at one time or another and gave me sound, well-considered advice. Thanks to Jisho Cary Warner for going over it a number of times, making extensive suggestions and comments, and for the copy editing. Thanks to Jane Hirshfield for detailed and carefully chosen comments and to Taigen Dan Leighton for going over the manuscript for some of the historical Buddhist angles. Thanks to David Stanford, my editor at Viking Penguin, for his attentive reading of the manuscript and his valuable suggestions, and to his assistant, Kristine Puopolo, for her worthy recommendations, and thanks to both of them for being so pleasant to work with. Also in this regard, many thanks to Susan Silk, Nonin Chowaney and Jean Leyshon.

I am grateful to many friends, neighbors and teachers in Japan, who were always so generous helping me and my family, answering my questions, forgiving my social blunders. In particular I would like to mention Shōdō Harada Roshi, Daichi-Priscilla Storandt, Hōitsu Suzuki Roshi, Shin Yoshifuku, Kunitomi-san, Nakahara Sensei, Jay Gregg and Kyoko Maeda, Ann Overton, Daijō, Fukiko and Kenji Numoto, Teresa Stockwell and Hashimoto-san for the open-ended use of her tatami room overlooking the vegetable garden at the edge of the woods.

Thanks to the staff of the Pondok Impian in Ubud, Bali, for a blissful transitional space between Japan and the States in which to work and play—and thanks to Kutut for bringing tea in the middle of the night.

In Santa Fe (where we lived for a year upon our return), I would like to thank Russell Smith, Jason Flores, Ron Strauch and Melissa White, and Dan Welch for their kind assistance. Thanks to the Santa Fe Public Library and the First Presbyterian Church for the quiet, rich environments in which to work.

Thanks to Steve Tipton for the word "hobbyhorse," to Neil Rubenking for help with software, to *Womansword* by Kittredge Cherry for the backup on weddings, and to Lois Anne Smith for being such a wonderful English teacher. Thanks to Paul Discoe for the insight, to Philip Whalen for the giraffes, to Brother David Steindl-rast for falling into heaven, to Jerry Brown for the Latin, and to JALT for the advice on contracts in Japan. Thanks to Helen Tworkov and Carol Tonkinson of *Tricycle, the Buddhist Review*, and to Laurie Schley and Michael Wenger of the *Wind Bell* (publication of the San Francisco Zen Center) for publishing excerpts and for skillfully editing them.

Eternal thanks to Daya Goldschlag, Liz Tuomi, Susan Chadwick and my son Kelly, who gets extra credit for noticing the "92."

Nine bows to Shunryū Suzuki Roshi, Dainin Katagiri Roshi,

Richard Baker Roshi, Kobun Chino Roshi, Yoshimura Sensei and many others who have been such great spiritual friends.

Thanks so very much to Yvonne Rand, Bill Sterling, Tom Silk and Susan Silk of the Callipeplon Society for sponsoring my sojourn to Japan (with the understanding that I had to write back) and endless gratitude to the sixty folks who responded so generously to the Callipeplon Society's solicitation. And finally, thanks to the person who anonymously answered with, "You've got to be kidding!"

A NOTE ON APPROXIMATE JAPANESE PRONUNCIATION AND CURRENCY

In Japanese pronunciation:

a   is similar to the   "a" in father
i   is similar to the   "ea" in eat
u   is similar to the   "oo" in look
e   is similar to the   "e" in egg
o   is similar to the   "o" in go, said quickly

Macrons (overlines) indicate the vowel sound is extended.

Examples taken from *An Introduction to Modern Japanese* by Osamu and Nobuko Mizutani, Tokyo, the Japan Times, Ltd., 1977.

This book is about events that took place between April 1988 and April 1992. The value of the yen fluctuated in that period, but think of a thousand yen as worth roughly eight dollars.

CONTENTS

CONTENTS

xx

V · LOOKING

VI · DANCING

CONTENTS

VII · GOING

VIII · GONE BEYOND

EPILOGUE

PART ONE　　COMING

AWAKE IN THE DARK

I was awakened this morning by a disturbing sound. My mind groped at it. In my dream it had been a baby crying. Then it changed to a woman calling in distress from a distance. She stood alone on a vast plain. I moved toward her. Her dress was a robe and she was a he. It was Katagiri Roshi crying out and I was trying to get to him, but I couldn't —I couldn't move closer or open my mouth. I awoke and lay there with an uncomfortable feeling. Still the sound. I sat up staring at nothing, hearing that irritating noise. It came from the darkness in front of me—from the closet. A thick-headed moment passed and then I knew that it was the alarm clock.

I remembered Suzuki Roshi's advice: when the bell rings, get up. Moving forward, clumsily climbing out of the covers, I got up. I reached into the blackness and found the clock, fumbled with it and turned it off. Release. I climbed back in bed and gave Elin a hug and a kiss, to which she responded with a sweet faint sigh. I held her for a second and then, with some additional effort, got out of bed again into the cold air and put on the pair of red plaid undershorts and white V-neck tee shirt that were sitting on a low table waiting for that moment.

The kitchen clock said 3:45. I put the kettle over a flame and walked out to the sink by the washer. I stopped for a minute, stared blankly, went back to the kitchen, took the kettle off the fire and shook it, added a bit more water, put it back on the burner and went out again to brush my teeth and wash my face.

The bell tolled from Daianji—the temple is right next door —calling the monks and students to morning service, to the chanting of *sūtra, dhāranī* and *gāthā*, calling me and penetrating gently into the houses of our sleeping neighbors. I flossed my

3

teeth mechanically and again the bell pealed a gentle, resounding F above middle C. I know because I checked it on an old organ we have in the front hall.

I went into the living room, which is what we call the front tatami room off the kitchen. I was dangerously near somnambulation but could direct myself to the sliding closet door, the thick paper-covered *fusuma* behind which were my robes. The door was off the track and wouldn't budge. I kicked it on the bottom and it slid back with ease.

Reaching in I pulled out a white *juban*, a waist-length underkimono. I put it on, tying its thin strips of white cloth together at my side. Then on went a grey kimono, the left side crossed over the right, and over it a wide, white sash—an *obi*—wrapped firmly three times around my waist below the belly button. In the layers of robes that make up a Japanese monk's outfit, the kimono is a sort of underwear even though it's the second or third layer.

Again the distant bell sounded, keeping me on the move and undistracted. Next I slid into a dark blue, thick cotton robe with long hanging sleeves. It is called a *koromo* and dates back to the early Chinese Zen garb. Quite often they're black but some Rinzai Zen monks wear these blue ones in the winter. We picked up on them years ago at Zen Center. They feel like soft denim. This outer robe is cinched with a loop of black cord that gets doubled up and goes twice around my waist. I used to tie the two ends off right about where my kidneys are when I was younger, but now, alas, I can barely tie it off at all at middle front, and not because the cord has shrunk. This robe, and even more so the next one, which is draped over it, are the sacred robes. They greatly circumscribe one's conduct. I only wear robes for formal practice like *zazen* (Zen meditation) and services over at the temple.

At this point I could put on that final robe, called the *okesa*, or *kesa* to be less deferential to it. It's the most formal robe, the monk's robe of ordination, the one that goes back to the beginnings of Buddhism in India, when it was the only layer. It's the same as the robe that's saffron in the more traditional Buddhist countries like Thailand. Mine's black. There are yellow and brown and purple ones too, but they're for priests with high status. The original kesa were made from discarded rags or the clothes of the dead. They are large rectangles made up of many smaller rectangular pieces sewn together with connecting strips. The pattern is representative of a rice field. Although the color and size differ, the method of sewing and the relationships of the parts are very similar in various Buddhist countries. At the San Francisco Zen Center, as in a few places in Japan, we sew our own by hand. It takes a long time.

The kesa I have here in Japan was a gift to me from sweet, wonderful, deceased Joshin-san, a sewing nun with a partially missing ring finger on her left hand. She cut it off one day when she was younger—to prove the sincerity of her request to change teachers. Her kind tiny hands had cut and sewn my kesa while I was the head monk at Tassajara, a Zen monastery in the mountains near Big Sur. That was fifteen years or so back. It's like having a flag sewn by Betsy Ross. I treasure it, but I don't wear it now. I leave it in the back of the closet. I couldn't tell you how many rules and regulations there are for this robe in the Sōtō-shū, the largest sect of Zen—like not keeping it beneath other garments in the back of the closet, for one.

I maintain a more low-key posture and wear a *rakusu* instead. It looks like a black bib but is actually a miniature kesa that straps around the neck. It's less formal but it does the job. It's old, tea stained and in need of mending. On the back side are some *kanji*, Chinese characters, written by Katagiri about twenty years ago. Suzuki was dying when he ordained me, so he couldn't do the ceremony. Katagiri officiated for him and also wrote on the back of my rakusu. On the time-soiled white backing it says "no end" in the center, up to down. To the left is written "enlightenment" and to the right, "delusion." I looked at this old rakusu while I was standing by the closet in the dimness of the living room, light coming in from the kitchen where the teakettle

5

was puffing out the first hints of a whistle. No end to delusion. That sounds right. No end to enlightenment. That's good to hear. Suzuki used to say that there was no end to suffering, which made sense to me as I plodded back into the kitchen.

I poured boiling water into the small ceramic teapot that held last night's *genmai cha*, green tea with some roasted brown rice in it. I stood waiting for the tea to steep and reached into my kimono sleeve to make sure I had my sutra book down in it. It was there. I poured the tea into a big blue porcelain sushi restaurant cup. The clock said six till four—time to go. I added some cold water to the tea and gulped it. It was warm and felt good on the way down.

Twisting around I adjusted my robes. A thought occurred to me and I laughed. No matter how ridiculous my feeble efforts, by wearing these robes I am participating in an ancient tradition that goes all around the world and back for at least twenty-five hundred years. The outer layer is from India, the next was added a millennium or so later by the Chinese, further in are the Japanese kimono and juban, and below it all is my American underwear.

An international outfit, I mused, heading off to the temple in the darkness.

SULFUR IN THE AIR

KIKUOKA, APRIL 28, 1988

There's a hot springs resort town named Kikuoka on the rising edge of the wooded low mountains of central Kyūshū, the southernmost island of the big four that comprise Japan. Kikuoka is a modest place with no national treasures or famous sites that would bring in the droves.

6

It nonetheless has a dependable flow of Japanese tourists and businessmen taking a break. The hot tubs are amply peopled and keep this town's water trade (night life) going year round into the wee hours.

I'd only been in Japan for fifteen days when I arrived in Kikuoka, en route to a temple in the nearby mountains, and my curiosity for every little thing Japanese was still in full force. I stepped off the bus from Beppu at about two in the afternoon and decided to hang around for a day before heading off to the temple. I left my bag at a small hotel and went out to see the place.

As I walked around that town of twenty thousand or so with a notebook and wide eyes, my thoughts were like energetic spring sparrows flying from one place to another looking for seeds. I had absolutely no sense of what to write and what not to write and so I wrote everything. I noted the size and composition of bricks in building walls and the arrangement and character of stones on creek sides and how carefully they were set and how mysterious their pores and I noted every tiny irregularity and I tried but couldn't describe the moss growing on the stones. I scribbled rapidly about a piece of tissue paper clinging to a beam in a temple bell tower and the small yellow butterfly on it.

I copied kanji from the signs in the hilltop shrine above the low-lying town. I looked down over the buildings, out into the valleys beyond, and drew a hurried and artless sketch of the streets and roofs with steam rising here and there into the slanting rays of the late-day sun. Descending from the shrine, I counted the seventy-two worn stone steps leading back to the town and smelled a few pines to see if the aroma was the same as their cousins' in Big Sur. In the Western-style toilet of the largest hotel, a five-story light green cement affair, I pulled the toilet paper and it activated a music box in the roll that played a squeaky version of "When Irish Eyes Are Smiling." I wrote that down. I wrote everything down.

Back out on the streets as the sun was setting, I walked around and looked around, eyeballing the storefronts and peeking inside.

The streets were fairly uncrowded. I passed an old lady pushing what looked like an empty baby carriage and a mother walking with a real baby bundled on her back. A few schoolgirls in black uniforms giggled when they saw me. I studied the goods that were for sale. Many shops were wide open in front with plain wooden display tables covered with enamel tea cups or bins full of shirts or racks of shoes. At night everything is moved inside and a sliding metal door is brought down.

I'm not a shopper. I didn't want to buy anything much and was as likely to look at the floor as the goods. The floors might be cement, as they were in a hardware store, or wood, as in a kimono shop. One place had packed earth that led to elevated tatami mats. I took it all in and chewed it up like a goat, tin cans with the grass.

Structures amuse me: how high the doors, how wide the windows. I peered at the dark ceilings and noticed the grain of the wide overlapping boards—planed thin on the overlapping edge so that they look as if they butt together. I stacked it all in my eyes as high as it would go. Sometimes I like to see what sort of hinges are on the doors before I meet the people inside. Up and down the street were friendly old wood beam and mud wall shops with tile roofs, and newer flimsy flat-roofed buildings with a thin coat of cement for outer walls. The former made me sigh and the latter made me sad.

Why, I wondered, comparing the new with the old, would anyone build a plain and hopeless building like this when they probably already had a sturdy noble place like that. I looked from one to the other. Does not compute. I shook my head and lamented the aesthetics of the present. And then I wondered what it had been like at that spot ten years before, and right after the war, and hundreds of years before that. I looked down the street and imagined it lined with thick-straw-roofed, blackened wood buildings faced with *shōji*—latticed wood sliding doors covered on the inside with translucent sheets of handmade rice paper. I saw dirt streets full of people wearing straw hats and sandals and here and there a sword swinging from a waist sash. I saw that old world now preserved in samurai movies and wondered what it was really like. I had an idea of what it would be like for me. They'd take one look at me and cut my head off.

I stopped to ask directions from a man who was sweeping the sidewalk with a bamboo twig broom in front of his drug store, which was in one of the old-style buildings. I wanted to find a coffee shop to sit, read and write in. There are coffee shops everywhere—finding one on my own wouldn't have been a problem. I just happened to like the way he looked and wanted to chat in my primitive Japanese. The old pharmacist told me I was on the right track.

"There's a good place right around the corner," he said. We got to talking and I said he had a charming building and he said apologetically that it was old and small. He told me that just eight years before, almost all the buildings in that area had been old-fashioned like his and had been replaced one by one by the new models.

"Isn't it a shame," I said, and he agreed with me, but I couldn't tell if he cared or not. I thought that maybe he yearned for one of those new bland buildings himself. He said his roof leaked and the earth on his walls was crumbling. I looked inside. It did look a little drab. It depressed me to think of the choices. I dropped architectural considerations and directed my attention to the person. He was speaking to me clearly and had a kind smile on his face.

He asked me if I liked Japan and I said I did. He said that my Japanese was very good and I replied, "Not yet." We went on with the formulas for a while. I thanked him and he apologized for helping me so little. We bowed, tilting our bodies, said goodbye, and I walked on to the coffee shop he had suggested. It did look inviting, with shuttered windows and flowers in front—I went in.

It was a small cluttered joint with just two booths, the tables inlaid with electronic poker games. There was a swarthy fortyish man in a business suit playing at one of these tables. In the corner in front of him, a TV set was on. I sat at the counter and bid good day to the proprietress, who seemed pleased to see me. She was friendly and inquisitive, in her forties I guessed, short and energetic. She looked right at me, smiled and welcomed me in the customary way, "Irasshaimase!" Her hand guided a towel over the counter in front of me making sure everything was clean. I ordered black tea. "Miruku ti onegai shimasu," I said, meaning "Milk tea, please." It's either *miruku ti* or *rimon ti* and I don't like lemon in my tea. At least they don't say *chi*. Like us, they say *ti*, which is a sound not included in their language. When I say miruku ti I always think of miracle tea, which it sounds like, and expect marvelous things to happen.

The lady was easy to speak with and drew me immediately into a conversation, asking the old standbys like where am I from and what am I there for. She was fascinated that I had come to this area to live in a temple. She was also excited that I came from the Bay Area. She had always wanted to go to San Francisco. While the TV continued broadcasting a quiz show wherein contestants tried to guess the cost of unusual products and services, she played a CD with Tony Bennett singing "I Left My Heart in San Francisco." I had only been in Japan one day over a fortnight and already I had heard this song about ten times. It's a sad song with an unhappy ending. The man who wrote it took his own life. As I listened and sang along with the parts I remembered, I thought of him hanging limply from a rope in a nondescript San Francisco hotel room.

I snapped out of it as a small pot was set on the counter before me with a sense of style and a kind word from the lady in charge. I noted the care that went into everything she made or wiped or put away. I picked up the cup I was to pour my tea into. It wasn't very typical—usually they give you very proper little tea cups and fill them halfway for a couple of bucks or more. The cup I got was more like a coffee mug. It had a cute white bear in a log cabin and a tiny, happy, bouncing boy with a pointy red cap dancing outside by a snow-laden evergreen tree. The picture was framed on the white cup with a painted ribbon and wreath. There was an inscription in English written amidst happy young faces. It read:

> *Silent and pure night*
> *Night flying*
> > *Innocent*
> *His gift*
> *It's your   Snow Kids*

I drank my tea, which was fresh brewed from loose leaves; strong and tasty, maybe English Breakfast. The lady was on the phone now. I got out my Japanese-language book. Time passed.

Two young women came in after a while and sat at the other end of the counter, only a few stools away. They ordered rice omelets. I peeked over at them. They had short hair and overalls, and looked tough, bordering on butch. I continued studying what might be called negative potential forms of respectful requests to those of a higher station. I could see out of the corner of my eye one of the women sizing me up. She called over to me in a husky voice and I put down my book.

I started talking to them and we exchanged the basics. They were electrical workers at a nearby power plant, and were maybe thirty. One was stocky and the one behind her was wiry. They had a mischievous air about them, not that demure modesty that so many women have here. I wondered if they were lesbians. They were different from what I'd encountered up to that point.

As we talked, the lady behind the counter was stirring their coffee, which was brewing in an open-topped glass container above a glass beaker over a thin flame that had heated the water to boiling and sent it up to brew and filter through. It would be strong and rich, unlike what you get at most places in the States.

After they'd finished their omelets she served it to them apologizing in the customary way for making them wait, and they received their coffee with words of polite thanks.

The proprietress chatted with the two women, and as they talked she took a soda can from under the counter, held it under the light and peered into it. She turned it upside down over the counter and shook the can until, much to my surprise, a large, shiny, chocolate-brown beetle fell out. She said good evening to it. The other two women seemed pleased to meet it. I watched as its captor held it and they fussed over it. It was shiny, a few inches long, and had two menacing-looking pincers that protruded from the sides of its jaws. It was similar to a rhinoceros beetle.

While her guests watched in interest, the proprietress brought it over and held it up to me so I could see it better. I cringed slightly. She said it was called a *kabuto mushi*. *Mushi* means bug. A *kabuto* is a helmet, as I confirmed by looking up the word in my pocket dictionary. She got out a magazine and showed me an advertisement for a samurai movie. In the foreground was one of those warriors all decked out in his fighting armor. Sure enough, he looked just like the beetle.

One of the tomboyish women took the beetle and started playing with it, saying stuff to me about it that I couldn't understand, in what seemed like an aggressive tone. Her friend leered over grinning. The stocky one showed me how the beetle could clamp down on her index finger. I watched as this pit bull of the insect realm pinched in on her finger and marveled that she had the nerve to do it. I wondered if it hurt.

I've always been hesitant to get physical with insects. I remember how my childhood friend Jim would grab bees and wasps out of the air and let them go as if he were impervious to their stingers. I was certain at the time that if I were he, they surely would have injected me with painful venom. I regarded this adventurous woman with admiration. She seemed to me to be braving the perils of amputation.

She looked at me, eyebrows arched and lips sliding up to her gums, revealing more holes than teeth. I swallowed and smiled, trying to hide my nervousness. Then she pointed to the zipper of my pants and suggested something that I didn't quite understand, but which she made fairly clear through gestures. She was suggesting that I take something out from behind my zipper and let her sic this minimonster on it. She put the beetle on the counter and acted it out. Her left hand played the part of the beetle, with thumb and forefinger for pincers. The index finger of her right hand played the other role.

She tilted her head and looked my way. "Want to try it?"

I quickly reviewed the data to make sure I'd gotten it right. No mistake. This was really happening. I thanked her very much but declined the offer. It was not at all the sort of conversation that I had expected to get into so early in the evening.

My hotel was in the center of the buzzing night life of Kikuoka. This night life seemed to consist mainly of Japanese businessmen in the streets and young Asian women in the clubs. By Asian, I mean not only Japanese but also Philippine, Thai and maybe young women from other countries. I saw them going in and out of the clubs, restaurants and lodging establishments. They didn't look like wives—I didn't see many wives. Some couples and a few kids could be seen here and there, but not many. My hotel was only for men, salesmen, businessmen and also some earthy guys who I supposed were truck drivers. I said hello to them and they laughed at me, not even trying to respond.

I had the cheapest room in town—it cost three thousand yen for the night, about twenty-four dollars. It was a "capsule," the lower bunk at the end of a room with about forty of them, each behind a curtain. Open the curtain and crawl into a rectangular beige plastic container. It looked like a traveling case for Marmaduke. I put my shoes and bag in a compartment outside, locked it as I'd been instructed, crawled into my tube and closed the curtain. It was warm and snug inside, about seven feet long and three and a half feet wide—barely high enough to sit up in. It had rounded, plastic walls that shone and reflected my feet. There was a shelf for personal possessions and I put my notebook, Japanese-language book, pen, wallet and change on it. I would have put my watch there like most men but I didn't wear one or even own one at the time. A radio and a mirror and a clock were built into the capsule. At the end was a TV, which could be watched for free except for a special channel that I supposed had movies. Beneath me were sheets, at my feet a blanket, and I stuck a bean bag pillow about the size of a loaf of bread under my head.

I'd been traveling and walking around all day, so I took a nap. It was about seven-thirty. I woke up at nine in the evening and put on the black-and-white-patterned thin cotton bathrobe that was provided, slipped my toes into the green slippers waiting on the Astroturf-like carpet outside my capsule, grabbed a towel that said in cursive letters, "Elite Style—Happy Days Glowing," and went downstairs to the baths.

It seemed that every place in Kikuoka had hot spring water piped in. The cheapest hotel in town was no exception. I got a key and a washrag-sized towel at the desk and went to the locker area, where I left my stuff. A couple of old men were coming out of the bath area holding their small towels over their genitals as they walked, the way Suzuki and Katagiri used to do at the Tassajara baths.

Inside, the bath was about ten feet square, with a big phony clam shell behind it, a chubby cupid with bow and arrow standing inside it. The hot water flowed out of the clam into the bath. I washed off properly beforehand at one of the low faucets that lined the wall, using soap and rinsing by pouring hot water over my head from a wooden bucket. I entered and soaked in the white-tiled plunge. It was as hot as I could take it. About a hundred and twelve, I thought, judging from my years of bathing in the Tassajara hot springs. There was an adjoining smaller cold plunge next to the hot one so I went back and forth a few times, enjoying the wet extremes and gasping with the changes.

As I lolled about in the hot water, an old bent and wrinkled woman came in, cleaned a bit here and there, and straightened the soap, shampoo, loofa, buckets and stools. There was a middle-aged man generously soaping himself down and scrubbing excessively. She paid him no mind but gave me a few quick glances. I got the definite feeling that she was checking me out for size. I guess not many of us jumbo outsiders had stayed in this hotel. I wondered if all women in Japan would be as interested in my private parts as they seemed to be on this last day before I entered an all-male monastic practice.

I went out to walk about, eat dinner and take in the slightly sulfurous Kikuoka evening air. I ate at a crowded *yakitori*, a Japanese shish kebab restaurant. Next to me was a strong elderly man with rough hands who turned out to be the owner of a local sawmill. He was draped with two rather large and loose-looking women he'd come with from the bar across the street. They looked straight out of a Fellini movie. The bar was called "Heban," written in *katakana*, the syllabary that's used for foreign words. Outside I had mouthed it, my eyes going into the top of my head till I knew what it meant. Ah, it's how they pronounce the Good Place! For heaven's sake. This friendly, loud old geezer had swept me up as he made his way across the street from Heban. He plied me with a glass of *shōchū*, clear crude booze. At about 25 percent it was strong but not too strong, and it had a smooth woody taste that delighted me as it slid down. Just my type of drink. I knew some about carpentry and wood so the sawyer and I had a good time talking. He said he'd been to Hōgoji a few times and heard that there were foreigners there now. He was impressed that I was going there and said that a monk's life would be too hard for him. He invited me to come stay with him when I came out of Hōgoji. I said that it would be an imposition on him and his wife, but he said no not at all and made me promise that I'd come. I finally agreed. We talked some more but soon he wished to return to the attentions of the two damsels at his side and since I'd had enough to eat and drink, I was ready for a walk.

I strolled around in the night, finding a narrow winding path with a *ryokan* at the end nestled in a bamboo grove. The Japanese translate "ryokan" as "traditional Japanese inn," and that's just what it was. There was a garden lit by a swinging yellow paper lantern in a cherry tree. The lantern reflected in a pond with large stones set at the perimeter. Through the bamboo I could see light coming through the shoji windows of the ryokan. I knew it was a ryokan because the kanji were on a sign in front. In English it would be called "Crane Inn," an old standby. I liked my capsule, but I wanted to be here. It was a little battered but all the better. I thought of *Wind in the Willows* and went in to inquire about prices. The lady there didn't seem to want foreigners. Maybe she thought her establishment, with tatami mats, no chairs and Japanese breakfast, would be incompatible with my tastes.

I visited a few *sunakku*, "snacks," which is what they call nightclubs. Pretending to ask directions to an imaginary spot gave me the opportunity to check out the scene without having to spend any money. Those places charge far more than they'd be worth to me. The first sunakku I entered seemed to be decorated for Christmas. Teenybopper Japanese rock was in the air, and lots of young hostesses were standing around waiting, or sitting next to businessmen and fawning over them. There were several women for every man. These ladies were acting as if they were having the time of their lives pouring and stirring the men's drinks and putting their hands on the men's knees. Some of the men would go "Heh heh heh," and see how close they could get their hands to a woman's breast or her panties. The women would giggle and scold the men and maybe even slap them playfully. What a way to spend a lot of money.

As I stood by the door a hostess took notice and suddenly half a dozen young ladies were enthusiastically welcoming me. I very quickly made it clear that I was merely asking directions. No one seemed to care. If it had been on Broadway in San Francisco a bouncer would have booted me out in nothing flat. The ensuing conversation took a while. I greeted the *mama-san*, the lady who ran it. They didn't know the name of the place I was seeking, but they were friendly and accommodating, and when we parted they thanked me profusely for coming and stood on the street bowing goodbye.

In the third sunakku I went in, one of the hostesses was sent out with me to make sure I found what I was looking for. We walked around for an hour, looking for a little *jinja* (shrine) I'd made up the name of. There were so many little *jinja* that no one doubted its existence. So we'd ask and be sent this way or that in search of it.

She was a rather homely and plump eighteen year old with braces. She came from the nearby countryside and stared at me with her mouth open and her hand covering it. She didn't know how she was supposed to act with me but she was put more at ease when I asked her about her family. She was out of high school and lived with her mother on their farm where they grew rice. I didn't ask about her father. She helped out at home and worked in town at nights. I wondered if her mother thought she was a waitress. She wanted to get married and have just one child. After a while I said I was giving up, wished her good luck, thanked her for helping me, and watched a little sadly as she turned the corner on her way back to work.

In the middle of the night I sat studying Japanese on a couch in the lounge area outside the capsule hive. I heard feminine laughter coming up the stairs and soon found myself surrounded by a number of attractive young women. They were Filipino dancers at the club downstairs and they stood giggling as they asked me questions. It was three in the morning and they had just gotten off work. They had a row of capsules to themselves, with a separate entrance off the small lounge where I was reading and writing by the light of the emergency exit sign. They crowded around me and were excited to meet a Westerner and said very sincerely that I was quite handsome—a real stretch of the imagination. They asked if I was married. Some seemed naive and others had a kind of professional vibe about them—one made flirtatious suggestions. I talked to them without returning any mating signals and the feeling gradually shifted from flirtatious to friendly.

English is the official second language of the Philippines so they were easy and fun to talk with. I learned they had almost no time off and were watched by the management. One who was small, shy and very sweet said she hated the Japanese men who paid to watch them dance and who apparently didn't treat them with respect. The others chimed in yes yes yes in agreement. I told them that I'd met many fine Japanese men and that I was sorry that their circumstances selected for such unpleasant encounters. The oldest one, who was probably in her late twenties and who seemed to be their leader, said that I treated them with respect. The others nodded.

We talked more. It seemed they were all dying to get back home, where they sent the good money they made—either as a gift to their families or as savings for their education. They really wanted to get back home and get married. Each had her story but they all boiled down to "make money and get out."

Some of them went off to bed, but a few stayed to talk. I felt like an honored guest at a Philippine slumber party. Eventually only the small sweet one and the older more experienced one remained. The little one ran off for a minute and came back with a photo of herself. It was a darling picture of her in front of the Kikuoka bus station. She seemed so innocent. On the back she had written in meticulous script: "Embrace this keepsake from your cherished friend and treasure always in fond remembrance." She gave it to me shyly and looked down when I smiled and thanked her. The older one, big sis, went out and came back with her own picture, in which she was all dolled up in lots of thick makeup, scantily clad and sexy on the stage. She turned the photo over. On the back she had written carefully, "Embrace this keepsake from your cherished friend and treasure always in fond remembrance."

"Well, thank you very much," I said, wondering where that line came from. I put up a finger and said, "Wait a sec." Then I ran to my capsule, leaving them puzzled. A half minute later I was back. "This is someone very special to me," I said, and showed them a picture of a young brunette American woman near their age standing on a cliff by the ocean in the wind, wearing blue jeans and a green sweater, beautiful and smiling. They were very interested and went "Oooooh." We looked at the picture together. "Is this your fiancee?" asked the younger one.

"Oh, I don't know," I said.

"She looks like she loves you," said the older one, looking at me for confirmation.

"Maybe," I said and put the picture away.

Oh, these sweet young ladies, I thought. I could feel their yearning and it was not for me. They didn't want any brief pleasure. They wanted to take care of their families. They wanted to get married—if possible, to someone from the States or a European. I could have saved one of them from this indentured service and paid for her grandmother's hernia operation. But I was going off the next day to a temple in the mountains. I told them so.

"Are you a priest?" said the older one, pulling her hand from my head, which she had been stroking.

"Uh, sort of," I answered.

"Will you bless me?" she said.

"Oh, I'm not a Catholic priest," I said, embarrassed. "I'm just a Buddhist . . . uh . . . I mean I don't do any priestly things."

She held her hands together and looked at me entreatingly. "Please bless me," she said.

Oh gosh, I thought. I'm watching the kind of urges that get priests in trouble and she wants me to bless her.

"How would you like me to bless you?" I said, looking at my feet.

"Put your hands on my head," she said, placing them up on her long silky hair. I felt the hands of a woman who has pulled men down on her many times. I held my hands on her head a minute and hoped for the best for her and said in my mind, Oh, please help her and her friends, anyone out there who can. May they all find what they want.

We said good night smiling and backing into our respective areas. Earlier that day I had noticed one or another of these ladies going into or out of the regular-sized rooms with men or getting keys at the desk or returning them. I thought there ought to be a better social security system in the Philippines. I also couldn't help but envy the men on the other end of those room keys.

I went into the capsule room and walked down to mine. The night life was over and everyone was in his comfy container. As late as it was, the TVs were still on in a number of the capsules, so I turned mine on too. I checked around for something interesting and didn't find anything so I put a hundred-yen coin in the box attached to the TV. The hotel clerk had shown me how earlier when he had oriented me on capsule use. The sound came on first and immediately I noticed that it was synched with that of the other capsules. There was certainly no ordinary movie on. A young, naked, attractive Japanese couple was having sex before my very eyes. I felt stupid for not having realized that was what the pay TV channel was. It wasn't bad either. I lay back and watched. It didn't have the degrading, disgusting quality that a lot of American porno has. It was more polite, which didn't surprise me at all, considering it was Japanese. It was mechanical in a way, but nice to watch. The genitals were fuzzed out. I'd heard about this. No genitals are allowed in magazines or in movies. You can actually see a bunch of women in panties bouncing around sets bare-breasted on prime-time TV, but at three in the morning grown people in private rooms are not allowed to witness pubic hair, much less genitalia.

I looked at the fuzz closely to see what I could make out. It was composed of tiny bouncing squares. I gazed at the squares all surrounded by heaving thighs and undulating faces and was even getting aroused. Pleasant experiences from my past came to mind. Then my attention was drawn to the shiny plastic wall to my right, where a reflection of the TV screen revealed the same exciting activity. The young couple was now doing the two-backed beast. My eyes looked hard at the reflected show and I was impressed at the quality of the image on the wall.

"My, these people sure do clean things well," I thought. Not a smudge or ripple in that picture. Wait! Not a smudge? No! And hardly any fuzz! I turned back to the original screen and it was the same old tantalizing blur in the places where there should be what the Monty Python folks call "naughty bits." I turned back to the wall and sure enough, saw the real stuff. The wall, by some strange random quirk of plastic fate, had decoded the scramble of the censors. I savored a backroom thrill at the illicit transmissions and wondered how the appropriate government agency would deal with this. I watched it with forbidden glee.

Suddenly the set clicked off and left me in the dark as if the wrath of a cosmic antiporn crusader had fallen. My time had run out. I was tired and lay back, and in the utter darkness I could hear, on other TV sets, the moans of the same program that I had been watching. There was a slight vibration in the room. I rolled over on my side and realized, as consciousness faded, that I was going to sleep in a room full of masturbating men.

RIDES TO HŌGOJI

KIKUOKA–HŌGOJI, APRIL 29, 1988

The bus from Kikuoka had to stop while going around a blind curve. The driver could see a truck coming the other way thanks to the round, convex, tire-sized mirror mounted on an orange pole on the creek side of the bend. Blessedly, the mirror also worked from the other vehicle's direction and I was relieved to see it stopped too in plenty of time. While the truck backed up I looked above us at the steep verdant embankment, all covered in a heavy metal mesh that looked like giant cyclone fencing. With his white-gloved hands firmly on the wheel, the driver slowly, carefully maneuvered the bus around the turn, managing to neither scrape the truck nor slip a wheel over the gravel edge on the left. Then we were back motoring up the left side of the road, mysteriously passing oncoming vehicles without collision even though there clearly wasn't enough room to get by.

It was the twenty-ninth of April, the emperor Shōwa's birthday and a national holiday. I'd heard the emperor's brief address to the nation that morning on the TV in the bus station coffee shop where I had breakfast in Kikuoka. He was a dignified old fellow. The lady who runs the place and I listened to him respectfully. One guy just glanced up from his *manga* (comic book) and then went back to reading. There was a lonely-looking gal in blue jeans preoccupied with her split ends who never stopped to pay him mind. He's come a long way since the living-god days.

Putting a microphone to his thin lips, the bus driver called out over the tinny speaker system the name of the next stop. His voice had a forced, high nasal quality that mesmerized me with its strangeness. After thirty minutes of going up the wild rocky river from Kikuoka, past occasional bridges and old farmhouses

22

stuck back in valleys in the lovely low mountains, exceedingly green and spotted with tall bamboo groves, we came to a stop where the road butted into another. I recognized the name the driver called out, even in his brand of schnozzle-ese. Ryūmon. He assumed that was where I was going and turned around to see if I was aware we'd arrived. A few of the handful of other passengers smiled and looked at me with interest. An old lady asked if I was going to Hōgoji and, when I answered affirmatively, she put her palms together and said, "Gambatte kudasai," a polite encouragement to throw myself into it.

I thanked her as well as the driver, who thanked me too, and I was left standing on the roadside with two brown stuffed L.L. Bean bags, a big one and a small. I had been lugging those monsters plus a duffel bag across Japan. Thank goodness I'd sent the latter ahead. The two I gripped felt like they were indeed full of beans and my lower back hurt, as it had for days. I was afraid of throwing it out in a painful spasm, which could leave me temporarily paralyzed at the edge of the asphalt. "I should have taken a taxi," I said out loud to a passing crow. I thought the turnoff to Hōgoji wasn't far down the road but I wasn't going to tempt the devil and tote the bags more than I had to. I also didn't want to stand there all day.

A car approached and impulsively I stuck out my thumb. It went on by. Ah, heck. Then I remembered what my friend Bop in Kyoto had told me about hitchhiking in Japan. He said it was easy, but that they didn't use the extended thumb method. What was it now, oh yeah—you just put your hand up and sort of half wave and half signal them to stop. A white minipickup truck came from the bend the bus had disappeared around and I attempted the proper technique, stepping out almost in front of the oncoming vehicle, raising my hand and, lo and behold, it stopped.

The taciturn old farmer who picked me up wouldn't say if he was going my way, but he took a left up the mountain after a kilometer or so. The turn was right in the middle of a small village with tile-roofed wooden buildings both new and old, surrounded by walls of clay and walls of cinder block. There was a small sign that said something was one point six kilometers away, the something being written in kanji, the last of which I recognized to be the character for temple. One point six kilometers adds up to a mile—not far. The road climbed up alongside a mountain creek that cascaded into the stone-filled river we'd skirted to that point. Up-creek not a hundred feet there was a thirty-foot waterfall, glimpsed through the trees as we drove by. The small trees coming up from the creek bed looked like poplars, and some of the large ones were definitely sycamore, which grow along creeks all over California. We continued the steep winding climb past rice paddies and groves of *sugi*, a type of cedar that is planted to harvest all over these mountains. Everything was so wet and green. It was getting lovelier and lovelier, but I was becoming tense. Looking down into the valley I reflected on freedom in nature and remembered the nature of monasteries is to restrict one's physical freedom—in order to assist in the pursuit of mental freedom, true liberation, I told myself unconvincingly. My old teacher used to call it putting a snake into a bamboo tube. The truck went around a switchback as I held on tightly. The old guy stopped his pickup on a wide bend in the road at a ten-foot-high black stone that had those same Chinese characters on it that I'd seen at the bottom of the hill. Must be Hōgoji, I thought. I got out, retrieved my bags from the back and thanked him several times as politely as I could. He just nodded, pulled into a turnout and drove back down the hill.

I looked up a long expanse of steps shaded by *sugi*. These steps were made of rough hewn beams the size of railroad ties. The landing of each step was a yard deep, two wide and filled with reddish brown cedar bark. Cautiously carrying my bags, and for the sake of my lower back not making any quick moves, I climbed up toward the sunlight. When I reached the top of the steps, I walked out on a gravel path to a well-tended lawn surrounded by short pruned hedges. I stood in the breeze and admired a round cement monument on an elevated area. Above and below were terraced fields in countless shades of green.

Accompanied by a quadraphonic chorus of swallows, acrobatically catching insects on the wing, and the high buzz of an unseen weed eater from the rice paddies below, I slowly crossed this open area to a narrow asphalt road with mountain runoff gushing down wood troughs on both sides. I entered the shade of a pine grove guarded by oaks, put the bags down for a moment and groaned in relief. Beyond a clump of large rocks surrounded by swirls of gravel, there was an old house. It was shadowy and mysterious and I looked at it uncomfortably as I trudged up a long flight of stone steps in stages with my load of beans.

Stepping onto a stone path in a sunny, flat, raked gravel area, I sighed and set the bags down, lifted my head and saw those old temple buildings for the first time. The air smelled wet and fresh—of vegetation, of spring—but with a touch of . . . of something musty, ah, of course, incense. What a wonderful, hidden spot, I thought, and shuddered in mixed anticipation and dread of the time that lay ahead.

GANGBUSTER ZEN

MARUYAMA, MAY 16, 1989

I close the front door and enter the cool darkness of our garden in the wee hours. A maple branch brushes my head as I manage the brief path of stepping stones. It's still too early for spider webs. A step to the asphalt drive and a hop over the foot-wide *mizo* (drainage ditch) bring me to the edge of the bamboo grove in Daianji's grounds. To my

25

right, by the stone wall which bounds the deeper, wider mizo, once a creek, a night heron stands still in the sludge. Skirting the bamboo, I cross the sandy soil past knee-high stones and stone shadows cast by a distant flickering fluorescent light. On the central walk by a stone bridge in the dark I hear the deep honking of an *ushigaeru*, a sumo-sized bullfrog that calls from beneath the flat lotus leaves in the water of the pond below. It splashes abruptly in the blackness, fleeing to the bottom.

I walk in the shadows under the massive *sanmon*, the interior "mountain gate," with its dusty old life-sized wooden carvings of human and semihuman saints slowly decaying in the sealed upper chamber where the monks visit and chant to them on New Year's Day. Straight ahead, I see the lights of the *hondō*, the main hall. An *uguisu*, a nightingale, calls from the surrounding pine trees. The morning bell reverberates through the temple grounds and out to the sleeping homes.

The sputter and put-puts of a motor scooter can be heard approaching from the street outside. It might seem an unwelcome intrusion into the natural sounds, but it's just another regular visitor of the dewy dim morning. It enters the quiet temple compound following its headlight along dirt paths to deliver the morning paper. The scooter putters out and away, down a narrow side street.

The hondo at Daianji is even bigger than the sanmon, with a two-tiered tile roof that sits on it like an oversized hat. All the buildings of Hōgoji in Kyūshū would fit inside this one hall of Daianji. The light from the hondo shines through six large bell-shaped windows with thick lattice work. Two stone lanterns, as tall as I am, are positioned on either side of the walk. While I'm waiting I like to stand before the lanterns and line up their silhouettes within the glow from two of the bell-shaped windows. When I get them centered just right, the entire form of the building sits in my head in a way that I quite like. Sometimes I pretend that I have discovered a secret position that can unlock the mysteries of the mind. One morning when I stood so, the right half of me fell off into deep space. The left side didn't follow for some reason. Maybe it wasn't lined up right.

A cloud passes between the moon and me, over the hondo and down the connected buildings and walled-in gardens. Large wooden doors in the hall leading to the hondo swing open, releasing light. Footsteps come from the corner between the bell tower and the entrance to the kitchen. It is the women coming from their rooms.

On the other side a hand bell rings and a procession of men comes from the *zendō* (zazen hall) area behind me, their hands together at the solar plexus in the position called *shashu*. They follow a path through the pines and swing around in front of the hondo. Their heads are all bent down watching the uneven stones in the path and I join the end of the line. We leave our sandals on the floor inside the entranceway by the wall, and quickly step onto the walkway and up the stairs into the hondo to chant the morning sutras.

Three and a half centuries back, Lord Imeda supported the construction of Daianji. According to Taizen, a monk from San Antonio, the temple was built to be stately and expansive, not only because Imeda was a benefactor of his faith but also to show off his wealth and power, though apparently the venture crippled him financially. Taizen said it was built quickly, utilizing every available worker in Imeda's territory for several years. Daianji still dedicates services to Imeda's ancestors. Sometimes on our way up into the woods Elin and I walk behind Daianji through the Imeda family graveyard. It's not a usual *ohaka* where ashes are interred, but a true graveyard where corpses are buried. That is still the imperial thing to do. In Japan they didn't lay them down though, but sat them in the *seiza* position, resting on their knees. The grass grows high around the many prestigious tombs. Unlike the regular ohaka, which can be found on other parts of the hillside, the Imeda graves are untended. There is no bouquet of flowers nor glass of sake, no burned matches, candles or incense butts. Often from that hill, Elin and I have surveyed our level neighborhood below, the suburbs of Lord Imeda. Since his lifetime, buildings have spread over the rice fields below and there are far fewer birds. Only the temple buildings remain the same.

At Daianji morning service, the gang lines up in robes on both sides of the altar—about thirty feet apart. It's an interesting and diligent crowd of about twenty, five of whom are women. At one minute to four A.M., they will be found standing on tatami overlooking a central wooden floor that shines like a pool. There are six from the U.S., three French, a couple of Germans, a Canadian, a Spaniard and a monk from India. The Japanese population now stands at about eight, among them two strong-willed nuns. This sort of collection of foreign and domestic monks and lay men and women is rare. Elin and I treasure living next door to these people. They're busy running after the schedule, sitting zazen till late at night and taking naps in the afternoon, but we meet each of them now and then—in the temple kitchen, on a path, at the kiln, at our house. Some we see more often. But during service, as in all formal practice, one doesn't relate, one listens.

The small brass bell is hit—we quickly bow and sit. I pull the sutra book out of my sleeve and place it in front of me parallel and adjacent to the edge ribbon of the tatami. The bell, hanging from a beam outside the back door, is still being rung—we're waiting for the abbot. A young German visitor sitting next to me is told by a French student to sit in line with the rest of us, with knees about six inches from the tatami edge. The sutra book he's been loaned is positioned for him. He straightens himself up and looks around anxiously to see if there's anything else that he's doing wrong. The others look relaxed and comfortable, sitting with straight backs.

Watanabe Roshi, the abbot of Daianji, comes in as the mid-range hanging bell concludes its rolldown. He moves down the wide wooden aisle that skirts the edge of the spacious hall, wood that flows toward the altar, going between square pillars of *hinoki* (Japanese cypress valued for its longevity and beauty) and under long beams. There he is. The master of this place for sure. He is always there with his incense and presence doing his job day in and day out. It is because of him that each of us is here. He is a rock—short, solid and fifty. I watch him walk up to the altar. Everything he does has punch, style and attention.

As usual, the opening chant is the Heart Sutra, the Prajñā Pāramitā Hrdaya Sūtra, the core of the perfection of wisdom, one of the principle scriptures of Northern (Mahāyāna) Buddhism. It articulates the central philosophy of emptiness. Remarkably, it is recited first in English. An hour later, the last chant is the Four Vows, in Japanese and then in English. It goes something like this:

> *Beings are numberless, I vow to save them.*
> *Delusions are limitless, I vow to cut them off.*
> *Dharma gates are boundless, I vow to enter them.*
> *The Buddha's Way is unsurpassable, I vow to become it.*

It's a tall order. I was taught by Soto Zen teachers just to chant it and not get hung up on the impossibility of it. Watanabe's Rinzai Zen way is more like a fist hitting a palm saying it's possible—try to do it as hard as you can every instant. Taizen says Soto is soft, Rinzai is hard. It doesn't bother me to move from one to the other. In this business you get used to contradictions—even if you stick to one sect or one teacher. If contradictions are in the way, then the Four Vows will be impossible.

I'd never had anything to do with Rinzai before, outside of reading. The first time I visited Daianji and ate lunch with the monks, I was struck by the difference in style between Daianji and Hōgoji. It was rough here, compared to the proper Soto eating style. They chanted loudly and energetically, passing the aluminum pots and wooden bowls of food down with thumps and serving themselves quickly. It was the Wild West to Hōgoji's Boston.

Watanabe sits at morning service on a long thick purple cushion while beneath him, under the floor, in the center of the room, rests a rowboat-sized earthen bowl that resonates the voices, drum and bells like the body of a guitar. Rich tones and overtones are created by the chanting in the wide high-ceilinged wood room. It's the Daianji dharma train blowing its whistle in the tunnel of night and steaming on through forests of sound. It's not beautiful in the way that Gregorian chants are, but it wears well, calls profoundly to our deep intentions and is a dynamite way to start the day. Soto Zen temples begin the morning quietly with zazen and get to the chanting later, but in Rinzai it's gangbusters from the word go. Rouse that *ki* energy in your belly and give it all you've got.

There are times when the energy in my spine gets activated and I feel like there's an earthquake happening. One morning I felt that way and then I noticed the room rippling, the people bobbing up and down and the pillars shaking. That *was* an earthquake, a 7.1 a few hundred miles away.

After about an hour in the hondo we file out to the kitchen altar, where we chant some more, and then silently cross the grounds to the zendo where the morning service concludes with the Heart Sutra. Watanabe leaves and the monks take off their kesa and hang their rakusu around their necks. At one whack of the clackers everyone assumes the zazen position and I walk out of the room through a large opening at the rear and sit on a raised tatami platform, in the guest area. A monk picks up a mallet and hits the *han*, the wooden board that hangs inside. Then silence. From far away a new ringing is heard—it's Watanabe striking the small *sanzen* bell. Time to meet the roshi one on one. The head monk in the zendo hits a hand-held bell three times, there is electricity in the air—he hits it a fourth.

The first time I was there, I was just hunkering in for an hour and a half of zazen with no idea of what was going to happen next. Suddenly everyone leapt up, jumped down to the floor into their *zōri* (sandals) with a kaboom! and tore out of there as fast as they could like the building was going to explode. They weren't trying to get away from something, they were rushing pell mell to sanzen with Watanabe, hustling as an expression of their enthusiasm for their practice, for breaking through to an understanding of what life and death are.

Now I run with them. Some of us are working on *kōan*, the translogical questions of Rinzai Zen. Some are developing breathing through the practice of *susoku-kan*, breath counting. But all of us are haulin' ass to get back to that building we just came from.

Once people get to the door, their position in line to see Watanabe is determined, and they stop running and act like ladies and gentlemen again. But until they get there, it's full steam ahead. They cut through the woods and cross the stone walks and they leave behind a few sandals here and there. If it's dry they raise dust, if it's wet someone may slip. The head monk leaves the zendo last and gathers up stray footwear on his way over. He doesn't run—he pulls up the rear. It's his job. A friendly French monk named Dai-san takes his time getting there too. He likes to be last in line. He even comes in behind Den-san, the blind nun. I always go fast enough to be ahead of her. She's getting faster by the day. She knows every stone and bush. Sometimes while I'm chugging ahead I turn back and see her moving steadily forward, her red-tipped white cane snappily probing the ground in front of her. If I see she's gaining on me, I give a little extra push and make sure to get in before her. I have some standards.

TITLES OF RESPECT

MARUYAMA, MAY 17, 1989

I call Watanabe "Hōjō-san" because people at Daianji call him that. Hōjō-san is what chief priests are called in their own temples. It has a nice everyday affectionate sound. I looked up *hojo* in the dictionary and found it meant "assistant, helper" and thought, oh how interesting and humble. I remember proudly explaining it to a foreign visitor I showed around the temple. But he knew Japanese better than I and explained that it was a different *hojo*, meaning "temple." I looked in his dictionary and sure enough, there it was amid a dozen different homonyms. (I had stopped at the first one.) The fourth entry for *hojo* was made up of the kanji for "dharma" and "castle." Neat, dharma + castle = temple. So I started telling people that Hōjō-san meant "Mr. Temple," though I assured them that the literal translation doesn't really convey the correct nuance. I mentioned this learning experience to my Monday morning adult English class and Morikawa-san, a slightly plump lady in her sixties, said that I was wrong again. I objected but she insisted that the kanji for *hojo* used as a title for the abbot of a temple meant a space of about four and a half tatami—about ten square feet—and the others agreed with her. I asked how that could be. Her classmate, Mr. Shimizu, the proprietor of a liquor store, said that was once the size of the space allotted to the abbot. Okay. It's Mr. Ten Square Feet.

We got to talking about titles. *San*, of course, is Mr., Mrs., Miss and Ms. all wrapped up into one, but more than that because it's used after given names as well, though they're rarely used. Unless you're going for crude, rude, or tattooed, you've always got to add some word. And not only after people's names, but sometimes their professions or places of work as well. A carpenter is a *daiku*, often *daiku-san* in conversation. There's *chan* for little kids or for informal affectionate use for an adult. There's *kun*, mainly used informally by boys in school for each other. *Sama* is a high-class "san." I know of two priests who are called "Hōjō-sama" in their temples. I asked the class why those priests use "sama." Mrs. Morikawa, who does not like religion, said it was because they thought they were so important, but I think maybe it's just the custom of those temples.

These titles carry a lot of weight and are always used for others, but *never* for oneself. *Sama*, for instance, is generally used after a person's family name in the address of a letter. Don't forget it.

One time our friend Ann in Kyoto was staying in a home with a Japanese family. She asked the man of the house if he would write his name and address for her. She explained she was going to photocopy it on mailing labels and send it with her letters so that there would be no mixups in receiving responses. He thought that was a good idea and told her that Americans must be very smart. A couple of weeks later she got home one evening and he was furious. He screamed at her how rude Americans are, while holding up and shaking a letter for her from the States sent in care of him. He pointed to the kanji written in his own hand on the address of the letter. "There's no *sama* after my name!" he fumed. "No *sama*!" Ann tried to explain that it was just a copy of what he himself had written as his address, but he wouldn't hear of it. She immediately mailed out corrected labels to her friends, but for the next few weeks, until the post was clear, she always made it home before him and wrote *sama* after his name on the letters she received so he could see them and be pleased before he passed them on to her.

As with any cranny of Japanese culture, people who have studied Zen almost always use some specialized vocabulary at their centers or temples (which can vary from place to place): *samu* for work, *tōsu* for toilet, *tanden* for belly. Then they try these words out on non-temple Japanese, who look at them blankly. The title *rōshi* is used extensively in America for Zen masters, but in Japan I've only heard it used by monks and Westerners. I referred to Watanabe when speaking to my calligraphy teacher, calling him "Watanabe Roshi," and she tilted her head as if she didn't understand. So I said "Watanabe sensei" and she nodded. Most people in the neighborhood call him Watanabe-san, but I've heard Daianji-san, and if I say Hōjō-san, they'll understand. I couldn't even find the word *rōshi* in most dictionaries.

Sensei, to the contrary, is used everywhere. It means "born before" and thus signifies someone more experienced. It is a term of respect used for doctors, lawyers, teachers, scout masters and such. People who are called *sensei* are respected.

Until just before I came to Zen Center in '66, Shunryū Suzuki was called Suzuki Sensei. One day Alan Watts wrote a letter saying that *sensei* wasn't an appropriate title for Suzuki and that he should be called *rōshi*, which was a much more traditional and appropriate term of respect for Zen masters. It was said that when Suzuki was told about this that he laughed quite hard for a long time. But some started calling him Suzuki Roshi, a moniker that stuck. Before he died, Suzuki told us to call his successor, Dick Baker, "Baker Roshi." Horrors. We only wanted to use it for the Japanese.

At the Monday Morning Class, Shimizu scratched his head, repositioned himself in the rattan chair and said that it's in bad taste to use such a prestigious term for your own teacher when talking to someone from outside your temple. He said Japan is a country where you play down what's associated with yourself.

In the West the word *rōshi* has taken on new meaning. It no longer follows the Japanese rules. This year I got two letters from Zen teachers in the States (one of them Japanese) signed simply "Roshi." It has become an English word.

Having been called *sensei* myself, I can feel the respect the Japanese hold for their teachers. I was talking to a boy in one of my classes who goes to the best high school in Maruyama and makes good grades and I asked him, "What do you want to do for a living?"

He replied with decisiveness, "I want to be a teacher."

"What kind of teacher?"

"A high school history teacher," he said with pride. It surprised me—I'm not used to hearing that where I come from.

One day I was walking down an old covered shopping street going to classes at a culture center and, as I passed his store, a shopkeeper called out, "Thank you for teaching the children, Sensei!" It was encouraging. In his voice I heard the whole country taking care of itself, holding together.

Sometimes families will pay big bucks for the sensei title, especially when it means "M.D." One day our neighbor Ishitaki-san was working in her garden and I hopped off my bike to help her put a new tree into a hole and afterwards she gave me some apple pie and coffee.

With her apron, glasses and hair pulled back conservatively, Ishitaki might appear your typical Japanese housewife, but she is anything but. She went to college in the States, speaks excellent English, and has remarkable insight into both of our societies. She is one of Elin's and my prime advisers.

Her husband is a doctor and we got to talking about medical schools. She told me about a local doctor who has four sons. Three of them got into the prestigious medical school here and paid reasonable tuition. One, however, had bad grades and did poorly on his entrance exams, so he had to go to a private medical school to which "donations" are expected in addition to tuition. These donations can even run into the neighborhood of a half million dollars. Pop doctor was so impressed with the amount his son's education cost that he ended up starting his own medical school for bad students of good families and became very, very wealthy. His school doesn't have a good reputation though, so doctors who graduate from there often go far away from this area to practice medicine.

SOUNDS OF THE NEIGHBORHOOD

MARUYAMA, MAY 18, 1989

The ritual sounds of Daianji, the calls of the birds and the noises of the neighbors rise before the sun and set after twilight. In the sweltering summer the accompanying locust volume is like the undulating roar of jets from an airport. Often at night we can hear the screaming engines of the *bōsōzoku*, the motorcycle gang members, usually far off and unchecked by the police. Periodically trucks come by with loud-speakers announcing their business: selling drying poles for clothes and bedding, delivering groceries from the co-op, or trad-ing toilet paper for old newspapers, magazines, books, cardboard and rags. Right now in late afternoon, it is quiet except for a dog occasionally barking in the distance. All dogs are locked up—a lot of them in cages or held by ropes or chains. There's one mutt on the other side of the temple grounds that yaps at everyone who goes in the temple's back door. At times that yap is sharp and unrelenting and I think uncharitable thoughts about the canine and its owners.

The bellows of the bullfrogs begin in the spring. Shimizu-san, a student of mine who owns a liquor store, says the ushigaeru were sent over from America after the war—to be eaten. There was a shortage of food. Some got loose and their descendants are now spread around Japan, or at least in this area. Until he told me that, I translated their name as "cowfrogs," and thought they were indigenous. During the late spring and summer, they produce deep foghornlike sounds that can be heard all over the countryside. It's surely a mating call. Elin and I are attracted to it. Just yesterday morning the birds were singing the treble, the bullfrogs were the bass and Elin was tapping rhythm. I was in the *ofuro*, the tub, seeking the midrange. It seemed as if the trees were full of joyous bells and whistles and the pond and mizo were scattered with cellos. I walked out of the ofuro dripping, opened our standup organ and checked the register of these musical amphibians. The lowest was the C below C below middle C. There were two going F and three F# in that range, one mooed G and one slid from A to G. Sometimes the ushigaeru do sound just like cows. One day Elin was taking a walk with her mother, who was visiting, and convinced her that they were on their way to a dairy.

This morning there was an advertising plane buzzing our neighborhood. I got out the video camera to capture it for posterity. I was expecting to hear the usual ad for a clothing store that's down the busy road toward town, forgetting that they only advertise by plane on Sunday. Sound trucks blow foreigner's minds, but these squawking invasive ad planes elicit the *most* intense response from our Western house guests who frequently, when they get over the initial shock, express a strong desire to be in possession of a surface-to-air missile. I can never quite believe it's real and am always perversely delighted when they circle our neighborhood.

As I videoed the plane approaching, Seki-san came out of her house across the street and called to me. She's in her forties and is a sweet lady, though a bit scatterbrained at times. I tried to shush her and get her to wait but she stood in front of me in her white apron and insisted I come over and video something at her place. I gave up and did what she asked.

There was a swallow's nest over her doorway with baby birds

in it—a propitious sign, and it *was* charming with the parents flying in right over our heads and feeding the kids. I got a minute of it and ran back out on the street in time to get the last swoop of the airplane booming out its message over our area. It wasn't till then that I noticed what it was saying.

"Forgive me! Forgive me! I am so very sorry!" the aerial loudspeaker blared over and over. As it flew off I asked Seki what that was about and she explained it was a local politician apologizing for accepting a bribe in the Recruit scandal. He was subsequently reelected.

The wind in the trees and through the bamboo grove is a mellow background for the garbage truck's "beep, beep, beep, beep, beep" while backing up. Yesterday was burnable trash day. I heard the housewives trotting out to deposit their trash at the proper spot beside the tree-lined street and in front of the temple's small outer gatehouse. After dropping a box and a bag, I looked at the pile and wished people wouldn't put so much plastic out on burnable day.

Trotting seems to be the official step of the housewife. It shows us she's busy and doing her duty. It does look like she's desperately trying to keep up with something. At first it threw me off—I would think there was an emergency and wanted to offer assistance. But now I am accustomed to it and when I see a woman trotting, or acting anxious, or saying how busy she is, I know she is merely following good form.

Elderly Okamura-san next door (who does not trot) says that *she* isn't busy. "I just putter around in the garden sometimes." She says Tokyo has such a fast pace that it puts Maruyama's trotters to shame. "There you'll see *men* racing about as well." This is a phenomenon, she claims, caused by the effect of ancestors rushing for thousands of years to escape the wrath of volcanoes, earthquakes and tidal waves.

MEETING OLD FRIENDS

Y ou must be the ugliest thing standing."

"The only exception is before me," Norman rebutted in his deep soft voice.

It was good to see Norman, Katagiri's American disciple. He'd been at Hōgoji for a year and a half already with Shuko-san, a Japanese monk who had practiced at several Zen Centers in the States. It had been about five years since Norman and I had last met. He approached the deck outside Katagiri's room where Shuko had just cut and shaved my unruly head of hair and was now drawing a straight razor over Katagiri's five days of growth. Norman stepped up and around my clumps of hair fallen on spread newspaper, grabbed me and gave me a bear hug. I'm pretty big but he easily lifted me up and squeezed the air out of me. I could see Katagiri over Norman's shoulder as I turned blue and he was grinning widely, obviously enjoying the good ol' boy greeting from back home. Norman is six-four. He put me down. I groaned and felt my lower back.

"Did I hurt you?" he said.

"No, quite the opposite. I think it's better now."

We stood there for a moment smiling, and I wondered, am I really uglier than he is? Heaven forbid. His bald head is lumpy and makes him look like he'd come to the monastery because he fled an angry wife who beat him continually with a rolling pin. A blood-stained bandage covered a place where he'd nicked himself shaving. His face was white, with large, slightly misshapen features, as if his head was a partially completed clay bust.

He's not called Norman at the temple. He goes by Ganko, a Japanese Buddhist name. Everyone calls him Ganko-san, but I first knew him as Norman and still call him that most of the time. I have a Buddhist name too that was given to me by Suzuki when I was ordained twenty years ago. I don't use it. In fact, Suzuki never used it and neither did Katagiri, Baker, or anyone else. It didn't take. With Norman it's the opposite. I'm the only person who calls him by his Christian name. Most people don't even know his name is Norman, or was. If he asks me to call him Ganko I will, but until then he's Norman to me.

So there he was in his *samue*, monks' work clothes: loose grey pants and *hippari*, which are short kimonolike jackets tied with strings. His was half open, revealing a white V-neck tee shirt. Big feet. I'm a size eleven. He must be a thirteen. He looked over fifty, though he wasn't out of his forties yet. Too much studying and sitting and not enough exercise or fun, I thought. He should get out in the sun more. I didn't let on what I was thinking though. I never like to hassle people about their appearance—especially after I've told them they're the ugliest thing standing.

"You've put on weight," he said, looking me over. "We'll take care of that here. Just stick to the food that we eat and that ugly fat will melt away."

I tried to act nonchalant and unaffected by the blow. I plastered a smile on my face as best I could. "Good. I just came here because it's cheaper than a fat farm," I answered, already regretting my discretion.

He showed me my nook, a corner of his side of a room he shared with Jakushin, whom I had not yet met. Norman had cleaned the area out for me and thoughtfully put a low table against the wall. I was quite used to sitting on the floor, having hung out in the midst of Nippophiles for over twenty years in the States. Norman had fixed up a rack that I could drape my robes on and had put a board across the wall with hooks in it to hang my work clothes. He'd also set aside some room in the closet where I could put the rest of my paraphernalia. I could slide the paper door open from where I sat at the desk and reach in. I felt welcome.

We spent a couple of hours catching up with each other, sitting in a relaxed cross-legged position on the *zabuton*, the thick black square cotton cushions that are softer than the tatami. His shoji door was partially open to the outside deck so that the warm spring breeze could join us.

"You came on a good day. I'm glad we have time to talk."

"Yeah, I did it on purpose. It's the twenty-ninth, and I assumed four-and-nine days would be days off."

"How long you gonna be here?" he asked.

"About six weeks."

"Just here for a tune up, eh?" He smiled, but not in envy.

"Something like that."

"Good. That'll give us plenty of time to get tired of each other. What brings you here now?"

"I knew Katagiri was here, and of course you and Shuko. I figured it would be good to practice with friends for a while at the beginning of my stay in Japan. I just arrived two weeks ago."

"So where are you gonna go then?" he asked me, lighting a stick of incense.

"I want to look around and find a place to live and a teacher if I can. I don't know yet. I'll poke around for a while. I know I don't want to live in a temple."

"Live outside the gate?" he asked. "Layman's practice?"

"Yeah." I looked around at his possessions. Not many. Mainly robes and books. His entire fortune was all within a few feet of us.

"So how's it feel being in Japan?" he asked.

"A little scary," I answered, "Starting from zero—again. But exciting, full of juicy possibilities. We'll see. I've been more nervous about being cooped up inside here than anything. Seeing old friends right off the bat helps."

"You won't have any trouble here."

"I just have a thing about institutions—monasteries, classrooms, jobs, jails. But give me three days, I'll adjust."

"Yeah, you'll get in the groove—once we break your spirit."

He grinned and snapped a seaweed-covered tea cracker in two and handed me half.

I studied Norman's imposing figure. Elin says that when she first saw him at Zen Center, the sight of him intimidated her. She says he lumbers about like Chewbacca from *Star Wars*. I wondered what impression he makes on Japanese people.

All Norman had been doing for the prior two years was living at Hōgoji and the head temple of Suienji, and he was fairly out of touch with everything else. He said he was there because Katagiri wanted him to train in a Japanese temple for a few years under the guidance of Nishiki Roshi. Katagiri and Nishiki had studied under the same teacher after World War II and were thus dharma brothers. Nishiki is the abbot of Suienji and of Hōgoji, one of its subtemples. He visits at least every six months when there is a memorial ceremony called *hōyō*.

Norman had been studying with Katagiri since the ripe age of thirty-six. He's got a little age on most folks in the American Zen scene. Lots of us were born at the end of World War II. The Japanese surrendered about the time he entered kindergarten. He was out of college before the war in Vietnam was going strong and the draft missed him. He was post–Korean War too, so his schooling was of the fifties and early, preradical sixties. He was teaching English in a junior college when the antiwar and hippie movements got going. He caught up quickly and before the school administration could say "counterculture" he was demonstrating with his students and then dropped out.

Norman got up and slid the shoji open more to allow additional sunlight in. He continued. "Anyway, I got tired of teaching kids who couldn't read and write, and with the war and all, things started losing their meaning."

So he left the academic environment and became a welder. "Better money and not without human interest," as he put it. He made a bundle welding in nuclear power plants. He used to work at one site till his exposure to radiation had gone over the limit and then he'd go to another till he was over the limit there and by the time he'd used them all up he could go back to the first one. He said that was standard practice. I feigned backing off. He told me how they'd cut corners on the job. For instance, he said they were always having to attach pipes to the walls for one reason or another and the pipes would be mounted on steel plates that had to be connected with four deeply set bolts each. The trouble was that they were always hitting rebar, which meant that the plate would have to be reset. But the rebar was all over because the structures are so overbuilt. "What we'd do in a case like that," he said, "is cut the head off the bolt and just weld the head to the plate. Then the inspectors would come along and check everything, which included pulling out some of the bolts to make sure we were putting them in right. Well, we'd sit there praying and having conniption fits, especially the foreman. I never saw them hit a bad one but I dreamed of it."

Norman's a city boy from Milwaukee. He said that his parents were racists and this was an embarrassment to him. In the 1970s he was living in Minneapolis and got involved with the Weathermen, not in violent acts, but in harboring refugees who were running from the law. As a result of this he would, years later, be denied a security clearance to teach Zen at the nearby federal prison.

For a while he was making money by playing lead guitar in a rock band. He spent a lot of time hanging out with black friends from the music scene, which led to meeting politicized blacks. He was getting angrier and angrier about racism and the plight of the poor. The Weathermen in the basement added to the paranoia of the situation. One day he was reading *Zen Mind Beginner's Mind* and decided he needed a change and would give Zen a try.

"So, you know how I found the Zen center in Minneapolis?" he said.

"No, how?"

"I looked it up in the phone book. I just opened the phone book and turned to Z and there was 'Zen Center.' I went there, met Katagiri Roshi and here I am."

"That's funny," I said. "That's just what happened to me, except it was a different part of the country and a different decade. Found it in the phone book and met Katagiri. Suzuki was visiting Japan at the time. And here we are."

"And you were into civil rights and SDS in the sixties too."

"Yeah, we're practically twins. Are you still committed to racial and economic justice?" I asked him.

"Absolutely," he answered.

"Me too," I said. "What are you doing about it?"

"Nothing."

"Me either."

"Well, let me think," he said in a voice of reason. "I'm poor and I'm a priest. Buddhism has been a gentle but powerful revolutionary force for the poor, not always, not much in Japan, recently at least, but it can be. I'm doing what I can. It's not enough but it's hard to help anyone."

"Like they say: you can spend your whole life trying to do just one kind act."

"Ah, well, I guess we're just a couple of frustrated guilty liberals," Norman added. "But keep in mind that most of us ended up in these ridiculous robes as a result of frustration from desperately wanting to help others and failing miserably. Remember?"

"Yeah," I nodded. "I guess so."

"Katagiri never gives his blessing easily to people wanting to run around helping everyone. But he takes it seriously. Just look at the number of students of his who are nurses or therapists or in one helping field or another. Japanese don't respect dabbling. But if you throw yourself into something and stick with it, then they respect it. Katagiri just wants people to know who they are first."

"Yeah," I said, "That's his job. I remember during the Vietnam war when Katagiri told some of us to stop demonstrating and not to interfere with the government. We jumped all over him and he backed off when he saw we meant it. Later he was more supportive. I asked him if we should be like Zen monks were in Japan during the war, just going along with it. He kept quiet then."

"Usually no one here challenges the contradictions like that," Norman said. "Especially they don't challenge authority. But there were some Japanese monks who went to jail because they wouldn't go into the army."

"Yeah, and Katagiri was just a kid being swept along—he didn't like it. He admired a friend of his in the army who shot into the air because he didn't want to hurt anyone. Katagiri never saw any action, right?"

"Right."

"The whole country was on one fanatic trip. I asked Katagiri what did the Zen world do during Japan's recent militaristic period and he said, 'Rinzai went crazy and Soto went to sleep.'"

Norman seemed well and I was glad to have him there to advise me and keep me out of trouble. We went on like this—going in circles and philosophizing, talking about one thing and forgetting the other, mentioning this side and ignoring that, trying to understand the conflicting passions inside us. Eventually we were all talked out and sat there silently basking in the afternoon sun coming through the open shoji.

INTRODUCTIONS

It was almost four-thirty in the afternoon of that first day when Jakushin returned from a shopping trip to town. Norman introduced me and Jakushin nodded. His face reminded me of Bela Lugosi, morose, yet handsome but for the pockmarks. He didn't give off a friendly vibe. He looked at my corner and how it was set up—especially eyeing the robe rack that separated my desk from where his bedding was folded up against the wall. He pushed it more over to my side without saying anything. "Gomen," I said, excuse me, and moved it even a little further in my direction. I offered him some tea and chocolate that I'd brought in, but he shook his head no. Then he left without a word.

"Gaaah!" I feigned trembling terror. "Is he mad that I'm here?"

Norman wasn't pleased. "Why does he have to act like such a tyrant? That was completely unnecessary. I was very careful to make sure that rack didn't use up any of his space. There're three of us here and he still has half the room. He's pissed 'cause he wants a room of his own." Norman got up and started to move the robe rack back, but I insisted he not do so. I didn't want to get on my new roommate's bad side.

"Okay, but don't let him push you around," Norman said.

"Well, let's not worry about it. I don't mind being bossed around a little."

"You'll be sorry. If you don't play along with them, their power trips won't work. When I was first at the head temple, Suienji, the monks tried to haze me—to get me to do things like hand them a pen that they were sitting right next to or make them tea and I just said, 'Do it yourself.' "

"How could you get away with that? Isn't that the tradition —newcomers don't say no?"

"I'd been a monk longer than any of them. I'm too old to play nursemaid to spoiled boys away from their mommies for the first time. You come in this place, it's like going to prison. You establish what your relationships are going to be like real quick. But after that we got along fine and I made a number of close friends."

"Well then, do you think I should go for breakfast in bed?"

"Good luck."

Just then Shuko stuck his head in. "Your turn for the bath," he said to Norman and then to me, "You're last. Maku's next to last. Can he find you here?"

"Sure. But I don't know who he is."

"He'll know who you are," Shuko said. "Is everything all right?"

"Yes, Norman has provided for me well. But there is one thing."

"Yes?" Shuko was listening.

"I want breakfast in bed tomorrow morning at nine."

"Service will be at four-thirty, soon after your bath," he said.

The *bonshō*, the big black-green brass outdoor bell, was ringing for service. Norman was sprawled out snoring and I had to step over him to get to the robe rack. His eyes opened immediately after the first round ended and pretty soon we were both flowing in black and off to chant the Dai Hi Shin Dharani, a fairly untranslatable incantation designed to evoke compassion from Avalokiteshvara, the bodhisattva who listens to the cries of all beings.

We stood facing each other to either side of the altar with our hands folded at the chest in shashu. I was standing back a ways where Norman told me to—in the guest zone. Maku, a cherubic, shy monk, was a yard in front of me. Facing him and next to Norman was a slight but sturdy, serious looking fellow whom I hadn't seen before. At the end of the third round of the bell, Katagiri came in, followed by Shuko, who carried a stick of incense pinched between the thumb and first two fingers of each hand and held at eye level. Shuko walked around and thrust the incense in front of Katagiri as he stood before the altar. Katagiri took the stick, planted it in the ashes and we were off and running on my first service at Hōgoji.

It was a short *banka*, evening service. The monk I hadn't met hit the large and small bowl-shaped brass bells and the *mokugyo*, the wood fish, a hollowed-out drum that is carved to resemble a fish. It's hit with a wooden striker bound with a rounded leather pad at the end, making a soft, rich thump thump thump. Norman led the chanting in his baritone voice. I'd chanted the Dai Hi Shin Dharani countless times in the States, usually with at least twenty people. With just six of us there, we each had to chant with force and yet pay close attention to unison.

After service we all moved to the dining room. Jakushin brought the dinner out and set it on the long low table. Everyone else helped by bringing bowls, *hashi* (chopsticks), a tea pot and wooden clackers. Flat zabuton cushions were placed on the tatami around the table. We kneeled on them in seiza, a distinctly Japanese position wherein one's body weight rests on the shins with the buttocks on the heels. Norman sat on a *zafu* (a round zazen cushion) in lotus position (with his legs crossed). Like many Westerners, his legs couldn't take seiza for long. Barely moving my head, I examined my new *sangha* (Buddhist community). We were a sight—seven shiny-headed men in robes. Only one wore glasses, Jakushin. I was tingling with openness—like a first date—and I was beginning to remember that being together with others in this intimate way is a type of love-making.

Jakushin hit the clackers and we recited the last verse of the Soto Zen meal chant, which I half remembered. Dinner was *soba*, buckwheat noodles, which we dipped in a *shōyu* (soy sauce) broth. There were scallions and dried seaweed to add to the broth and white *daikon* (radish) pickles on the side. We didn't talk while we ate but everybody slurped the bejeezus out of the noodles. I didn't mean to be rude but I just can't do it. I silently put my noodles in my mouth and chewed them, hoping it didn't gross anybody out.

Dinner isn't called dinner—it's *yakuseki*, the medicinal meal. It's an old Zen name for the evening meal, which originated in China. One of the original Buddhist rules is that monks not eat after the sun reaches its zenith. But the Chinese population didn't like begging, which had been well accepted in India, so the monks couldn't depend on offerings in order to eat. Baizhang, a revolutionary Chinese master, initiated the policy, "A day without work is a day without food," and the monks started growing their own rice and veggies. Then, because they were working, they got hungrier. First they tried hot stones on the stomach. After a while they instituted an evening meal. But to pay lip service to the rule, they didn't call it a meal—they called it *yakuseki*, which literally means "medicine stone."

Yakuseki was over quickly and was just as quickly cleaned up. Everything was washed, dried and put away, the table wiped and the floor swept. I stood around looking for something to do, but it was over before I could make myself useful. Then we all sat down again at a low square table with a kerosene lamp on it in an adjoining room that was between the dining room and the kitchen.

Katagiri introduced me. I didn't understand everything, but I knew he'd said that I was a disciple of Suzuki and that we'd known each other a long time. He asked them to help me out. With prompting from Katagiri I said that I was a very poor monk and to please be good to me and they responded in unison that they appreciated my efforts and to please try to do my best. It was a formality that I hadn't been told of but I thought I'd gotten through it decently for a very poor monk. Katagiri bowed in *gasshō*, palms together. We gasshoed with him and he retired to his room.

The remaining five monks went quickly over the next day's

schedule and activities, each according to his position, which rotated every five days. The guy who had hit the bells at evening service informed us what sutras would be chanted the next morning. Norman jotted them down in a small notebook and stuck it in his sleeve. Jakushin read what the meals would consist of from a list. Shuko said we'd be cutting firewood during work. A few other matters were agreed on. Every evening we would go through this traditional procedure and every evening the information would be almost identical—and the longer I was there, the more eagerly I awaited the slight variations.

We gasshoed again and everyone relaxed a notch. Shuko smiled and welcomed me again, but this time informally. I was introduced to Koji, the one who had hit the bells at service and the only monk I hadn't met yet. He bowed his head. He was the shortest guy there and the most intense. Almost as short was Maku, a curious guy with an air of lightness.

Walking out of the dining room onto the deck, I could see lengthwise across the courtyard the last streaks of the setting sun striking the roof of the bell tower. I slipped into my zori and went out to the steep, narrow asphalt road and walked up till it met the road from Ryūmon curving back up behind the temple. I stood there and gazed down at Hōgoji's tile roofs nestled in the trees. A soft warm breeze stroked me over and over. The air was clean, full of the twilight callings of birds and frogs, and carrying the thick sweet aroma of wet spring blooming. I could hear a creek flowing down below these wild-flowered fields and see a nearby low mountain covered with a crop of sugi and a swath of old-growth oak and tall pines rising up on the other side. In the direction the water was flowing, there were ever-descending rice paddies and a marvelous expansive view of mountains rising and valleys beyond. And the whole view was crisscrossed by power lines and punctuated by the impressive towers that supported them. There I stood in the spell of the valley and watched the day glow to an end. It was the most beautiful sight and I was overwhelmed with emotion. I had arrived and met the few comrades I would be living with. I'd had a taste of the place and it was good. I realized I'd been drunk with needless anticipation and worry. The sunset burned that cloud away. I stood there feeling raw and grateful and walked back down wiping the corners of my eyes with the sleeves of my robe.

Shuko got out his sewing kit and coached me while I repaired my robes in a few places. He was methodical in the way he opened the sewing box, found the right needle and materials and watched over me, making sure I did everything correctly. While I stitched he made green tea and brought out another kerosene lamp from his room to make sure I had enough light.

Shuko was in his late thirties, about five-five with a handsome olive complexion and a round face. He was lightweight, but didn't look at all skinny. A shaved head looked good on him. His pate was smooth and well formed, unlike bumpy Norman or pointy me. Norman and I are, I suspect, the result of the foolish American obstetric practice of using forceps to bring forth soft little babies.

"Zazen is free tonight," he said.

"Free? I don't have to pay?"

"Optional, since today is a four-and-nine day. And it starts later than usual." He has a kind manner but his sense of humor isn't as good as his English.

As I sewed and we sipped our tea he asked about Zen Center and I brought him regards from several stateside Zennies he'd known well. I told him the gossip—a lot of repeats from the talk with Norman: who had married, who was living together and who had broken up, comings and goings. There was some sad news about a gay monk who had AIDS.

Shuko shook his head and said that you could only have this sort of talk about the American Zen world.

"Our lives are pretty boring—it's mainly men and none of them are dying of AIDS because there are no homosexuals."

"No homosexual monks in Japan?" I asked.

"I don't think so."

"Baloney."

"Oh," he responded, surprised. "You think there are?"

"Wherever there are people there are homosexuals, Shuko. I've known many Japanese priests and I've got some interesting stories I'll tell you someday if you've got the time."

He looked off balance and shifted his position.

The sunset bell was struck and Shuko excused himself to get ready for zazen. I got up, hoping I hadn't said anything that bothered him. I can never control what I say anyway, things just come out.

It would've been better if I'd followed the admonition of Dō-gen Zenji, founder of Soto Zen: think three times before speaking and then choose to speak in only one out of ten of those instances. I reflected on how distant I was from that ideal.

Free or not, everybody showed up for zazen. Katagiri offered the incense. He sat cross-legged in front of the altar facing out toward us and we all sat facing the wall.

Sitting cross-legged like this is certainly not necessary in order to do zazen but it's the most solid of positions, rendering the body stable, compact, yet open—parked on its own tripod, the knees and butt as the three points of contact with terra firma. Most folks place their behind on an additional cushion. The natural position of the spine isn't straight but curves in at the lower back, and we sit accordingly. The top back of the head pushes up, pulling the chin in. Sometimes I imagine there's an insert there at my apex with female threads. I screw an eyebolt into it and let a crane hook it and hoist me up. Zen teachers often advise us to keep focused on the *hara*, the lower belly as the center of gravity. We try to keep our eyes half open but sometimes they close and sometimes we fall asleep.

I sure didn't fall asleep in zazen that night. I sat with a mind whirling about with the passions of the day, and as I sat I watched it all spin into butter. I reflected on the basis of our practice, the bodhisattva's vow, which extends our desire to help ourselves and our loved ones, through the power of the vow, to all beings for all time, which means we include all beings completely and turn into butter together.

OWL AND DREAMS

HŌGOJI, APRIL 29, 1988

Jakushin told me to shush and I put my hands to my mouth apologetically. He quietly pointed out that we're supposed to be silent from the beginning of the sunset bell that precedes evening zazen till the formal morning tea is over. I gave a let's-go-outside sign to Norman, but he whispered he wanted to go to sleep. He handed me a couple of thin books with folding pages. One had *Soto Zen Sutras* on the cover, the other was blank.

"They've got a lot of mistakes and are tough to read in the candlelight but they're all we've got."

"Looks like they've had some use," I whispered, looking at the frayed corners and cellophane patches.

"Here's the order of the sutras tomorrow." He handed me a piece of note paper with page numbers opposite the sutra names.

"Okay. Thanks."

"Take your bedding out by the altar—anywhere out there. We're all supposed to, but only Maku will be there too. If you hear noises don't let it spook you. It's just rats. They never bother Maku, but then nothing wakes him up. He slept right through an earthquake last year that brought everyone else scrambling out to the courtyard."

Jakushin eyed us.

"See you tomorrow morning." Norman gasshoed.

"Night." I gasshoed back to him and to Jakushin, who nodded.

I picked up my futon from a shelf in the closet and walked out to the dark room. A spasm reminded me that my back was weak and I made sure to bend only my knees in putting the futon down. Then I went back and got a flashlight and the rest of my bedding, which included a big fluffy quilt, a very small pillow stuffed with beans that had what seemed like a towel around it for a pillow case, and sheets that were too small and also made from terry cloth. I had a feeling that I'd been getting since I arrived in Japan: like I was in a parallel reality where everything was just a little bit different in each aspect from the way it was back home.

After doing some exercises for my back I got under the covers, exhausted. What a relief to be in bed and to be alone in the dark. I rolled over and looked at the altar in shadows behind a large column that was between us. A sound came from the pitch blackness behind the curtains and gave me a start. Scampering—a mouse, a big mouse or a rat. I rolled back over on my other side. Dim light glowed through the shoji of Maku's corner room. I lay on my back and looked toward the ceiling.

A blanket of calm and sadness fell over me. I had been in Japan for two weeks and in Hōgoji for one day. "I am here," I whispered. I thought of Kelly, my fourteen-year-old son in Spokane. We'd never been apart for long till recently. I missed him. I didn't want to be away from him, but it just had to be for now. It made my heart hurt to think about it. And Elin, my bright young brown-eyed love, far away in Atlanta writing her thesis. What would become of us? Would I ever see her again? I groaned. And I thought about my mother, whose boyfriend and mother had just died. She was all alone in Texas. And my sister and her family and my friends in California and elsewhere. I kept sinking deeper into homesickness and self-pity till I was afraid I'd start crying and be heard. I started thinking about the month-plus of slavery to temple life that lay ahead and was afraid I couldn't do it, and didn't want to do it, and I thought about running away. I felt like I had committed myself to a mental institution, or found myself in jail. But there was no way out—I had to do my time. I lay there getting sad and paranoid, until I started noticing the sounds of the night, the frogs and the creek outside, and they were my lullaby and my comfort and finally I fell asleep.

I slept deeply for hours, but at some time in the middle of the night, I rose from that peaceful depth to dream, and the dreams were intense, vivid and disturbing. I sat up in bed confused as bright colorful spinning objects that I thought of as "astral toys" rolled onto the futon. I looked at them without wondering and fell back down to sleep. Again I awoke, unsettled, and found my bed full of live disembodied heads. I noticed ghouls lurking on the edge of the futon as I picked up one of the heads, misshapen and alive in my hands. It looked at me. I spoke to the god of bad dreams and asked him to please explain what was happening but he wouldn't say. I sank into sleep. Next I found myself in the midst of shining blue light so overpowering that I just lay there saying, "buddha" over and over. As the light dimmed and I fell back into unconsciousness, I could hear an owl hooting and scratching incessantly and I felt it was trying to tell me something.

At three-thirty when one of the monks ran around with a small hand bell, I awoke refreshed and elated though slightly trembling from the night's frightening journey. I stared in the darkness for a second getting my bearings, threw the covers off, leapt up onto the tatami for my first full day at Hōgoji and found myself standing nose to nose with someone. A lamp was lit outside and from its slight light I could see that it was Maku, who stood there smiling sweetly with his bedding in his arms.

PART TWO

SETTLING

ON A SLOW TRAIN HOME

MARUYAMA, DECEMBER 13, 1988

Elin and I were on the train going back home at night from a long day's English teaching. We were reading, nestled into the cushion seats in the clean and almost empty car, sitting across from each other with our sock-feet stretched out onto the opposing seats. Even though I'm taller than she is, her legs are longer than mine, and not so thick.

Buses can make me queasy, but on trains I feel secure and content, especially if there's room to lounge. Heat blew out from the grate beneath the seat. The car gently rocked and clicked its reassuring rhythm, which put me in a meditative mood like a ballad around a campfire. I wouldn't have traded it for the Bullet Train.

How cold it had been waiting at the countryside station for the 8:32 to come. While we stood under the shelter, we read the advertisements tacked onto the wall behind a row of benches where an old man sat waiting and drinking a glass of hot sake he'd gotten from a vending machine out front. I said, "Sumimasen (excuse me)," as we were standing close to him looking at the wall. It was, I think, an appropriate thing to say, but he nervously waved a hand in front of his face, muttered "English no!" and quickly scooted down to the end of the bench holding tight to his sake glass. We continued studying the advertisements.

One poster in particular caught our attention. In it, an intense, tall, young Japanese man in Western clothing was kneeling on a tatami mat in a tea room just like the one in our house. He held a teacup in both hands. His back was self-consciously straight and he stared seriously out from the picture as if something extraordinarily significant or profound was happening. It seemed to

59

us such an arrogant ad. His face was thoroughly splattered with the stains of somebody's soft drink.

As always the train pulled up exactly on time. We opened the doors, as they're not automatic during the coldest months, and we stepped in. The car was warm, but not too warm as they sometimes are. We put our coats and bags above the seats and settled in for the half-hour ride.

Elin pushed her shoulder-length brown hair away from her eyes and took *The Japan Times* out of her purse. I read a magazine for "dedicated students of the Japanese language." The train pulled out and rattled softly along. We talked a minute, rubbing each other's feet, and then went to our reading.

My eyes turned to the chilly night outside. A couple of large bright pachinko parlors, Japanese pinball palaces, dominated the view. Their lights were so many and so bright. It reminded me of driving into Las Vegas. The size and audacity of the buildings, framed by large parking lots, the shining, blinking facades and glowing interiors dazzled me—what a light show. Kelly calls it the single most prominent sight in Japan. I wondered what the thrill was.

The train stopped at another small station. A lone woman waited in the cold. She had a striking face, high cheekbones, and was thin, like a magazine model. I thought about my compatriot in Japanese class, Rod, and his ill-fated Number Ten—surely what he would have called this lady. The adultery finally got to him and he'd told her they couldn't go on seeing each other. I pictured him in Kyūshū holding his beautiful housewife lover and mother of three back as she struggled to get out of his grasp and leap from the fourth-story balcony of his tiny apartment. The lady outside my window entered the car in front and I stared at the empty platform as though in a petit mal until the train moved on down the line.

Moonlit bamboo groves and shadows shuttled by as Elin began to read aloud from *The Japan Times*. There was a letter to the editor from a burned-out English teacher commenting on four other foreign English teachers who'd been fired from the Nagoya school system for having had the nerve to recommend changes in the curriculum. The author of the letter was foaming at the mouth, saying, "Well what did they expect? Hadn't they learned yet that there's no way to teach English in Japan and have any self-respect?" We got a kick out of it. The letters to the editor in the English-language newspapers here are terrific—and they help relieve some of the pressure.

The conductor came by and Elin stopped him to purchase our tickets. He was middle-aged and skinny, with a nicely trimmed mustache and a friendly politeness. It was obviously a professional challenge to him to be able to negotiate this transaction smoothly. Elin zipped through the necessary dialogue with graciousness and ease. The exchange went by without a hitch and after the closing formalities he went briskly on his way. I was proud of her. A couple of months ago it was such a struggle. Now she's having long conversations with friends and neighbors. American couples are notorious for not learning much Japanese.

"Very good, darling," I said. We looked around and stole a kiss.

Then she read some Tokyo apartment listings. They were unbelievably high. It's always good for a laugh. We, fortunately, don't pay much rent. A couple can live here on a thousand dollars a month if they try—we don't. You get used to spending money here. And as a matter of fact, as the train pulled into Maruyama station, we were so tired we talked ourselves into foregoing the bus and taking a nice fifteen-minute, thirteen-dollar cab ride to our house by the temple. We love the trains, sometimes we like the cabs too, and we especially dearly appreciate going back to our peaceful home at night where we can cuddle up with each other and disappear into sleep.

KOBASHI TO THE RESCUE

When Elin and I first moved into Maruyama we were running out of money, which is sort of the way we'd planned it, me enthusiastically and her reluctantly. If we were going to be fiscally responsible, then she wouldn't have been able to spend her first three weeks in Japan traveling around, seeing things and meeting people. I had assured her that work opportunities would be plentiful and not to worry. I'd already been in Japan for half a year when she arrived, and I had watched with a keen eye those *gaijin* (foreigners) who prosper and enjoy themselves, as opposed to those who just get by. The former have faith in Japan. I had faith. After all, when Kelly and I had returned from Thailand, we had flown into Narita with less than one hundred dollars. We had friends to stay with and knew how to get by on very little, but when he left two days later, I was down to zilch. I couldn't even afford to go to the airport with him. I survived for the following five weeks on a few days of sheetrocking for an American friend in Tokyo (who made me spend my last coins of yen so I'd be down to zero before he paid me), eight hours of writing advertising copy in Osaka, and twelve hours of English conversation-class substitute teaching in Yaizu.

Since that time I had also traveled twice back and forth to Maruyama from Tokyo, a sizable distance, and still had five hundred dollars worth of yen on me when I met Elin at Narita. All it had taken to remain solvent was some hitchhiking, staying with friends and eating cheaply, which is surprisingly easy to do.

Even though our helpful and industrious English-speaking neighbor Ishitaki-san said she'd have some kids' classes for us in

December, there was no bird in hand and Elin was getting more and more nervous and eager to secure a regular income. I had no interest in working for one of those slimy language schools that don't pay well and make you hang around between classes. I don't like to work for other people unless they're very understanding and don't take a big cut. So I was looking for substitute work or private classes and had to convince Elin to be patient. It was frustrating that we couldn't advertise and had to be discreet—we were still on tourist visas and it is illegal to work on a tourist visa.

So I was pleased when Jessica, our best friend at the temple, a forty-five-year-old lay practitioner and Hōjō-san's translator, told me that one of the lay members of Daianji had asked her if she knew someone who could substitute for a few English classes at a local shipbuilding yard. He was a regular at the Sunday *zazenkai* (a zazen group for the lay community). Elin and I had started attending this Sunday zazen meeting in the hondo, the large hall at Daianji where services are held.

His name was Kobashi-san. I knew his son, the only lay Japanese who lived at the temple. The son was the gardener, a very sweet and painfully shy fellow who never said a word, and either couldn't or didn't want to make it in society's rat race. Pop Kobashi is short, stout, grey-haired and wears thick glasses. We had seen each other on the previous Sunday but we hadn't formally met. Jessica introduced us during the tea following *zazenkai*. The two of them standing together were such a comic combo. He was all pinched tight and proper in his Western suit and tie, and she in her baggy, faded and patched grey samue, looked out of some oriental hobo tradition, like chubby Hotei, the so-called Laughing Buddha.

Kobashi started off as a lot of people would if there was some prior relationship with one of their family members: "Itsumo osewa ni narimasu (you're always doing us favors)."

"I never did anything for him," I told Jessica. "Does he have me confused with someone?"

"Just say 'kochira koso.' It means 'no, no, it's the other way around,' " she explained.

"Kochira koso," I said.

He gave me his business card and said my Japanese was very good and I said oh no, it's very bad. He was polite and nervous (really nervous—as if he were naked on stage). He asked me a lot of questions, like where did I come from in America and was Japanese harder than English. He said we could talk again the next week and asked me if I would prepare a resume for him. When the tea was over, we bowed and said thanks a few times. He apologized for having rudely bothered me and I said please be good to me in the future, as I was supposed to. Then we parted. I was very pleased and I think he was too—after he calmed down.

I talked to our neighbor and adviser, savvy Ishitaki, about the resume and then called up Bop, our generous host in Kyoto. They are our mentors in threading the natives' sociopolitical needles. He gave me further advice on how to write the resume. I appreciated his suggestions, many of which I followed. I did not, however, say that I had a Ph.D. from Harvard in teaching English as a second language. This disappointed Bop, but I have some scruples. He agreed with Ishitaki that it should be written in English. "Otherwise you may insult them," she'd said. "They have all studied English many years."

The next week, at the get-together after zazen, Kobashi was pleased to get the resume, which he glanced at quickly and tucked away. Bop had assured me that I could have written nothing but profanities on it—no one was going to read it, only look at the piece of paper and file it.

After we'd drunk our tea, Kobashi showed me the schedule of the English classes. There were only three of them to be taught, three times each. He asked if it was alright as is, or if I would prefer to make some changes in the schedule. Either way would be fine, he said.

"Oh," I said. "Well, let me see."

"Do you want it as is," he repeated, "or, would you like to make some change? Which would be the most convenient for you?"

"Alright," I said, looking at the schedule to make sure I understood it. "How about having the Tuesday class on Monday instead? That would be better for me."

He paused seriously and breathed in and said, "Sō desu nē." (Yes, that's so.)

Oh good, I thought, it's okay with him.

"Oh," he said. Long pause. "Hm," he moaned, looking deeply into the schedule he had brought.

I soon sensed that maybe that wasn't such a perfect day for him so I said, "How about Saturday?"

He breathed deeply and said, "Sō desu nē."

After a while I thought to myself, I don't understand this. I was just learning that "Sō desu nē" frequently means "Oh, isn't that too bad."

"Let's just leave it like it is," I said.

He beamed. "Okay," he said. "If that's what you want."

"Yes," I said. "That's fine."

"Well," he said, "if that's fine with you then that's fine with me too."

It was a little weird, but I enjoyed talking to him because it was all in Japanese.

He also brought train and bus schedules, neatly underlined in the appropriate spots. It would take me about an hour and a half to get there by bus, transferring once, or about two hours if I went by train.

"Either way," he said. "It makes no difference to me."

"I'll take the train," I said instantly.

"The bus is more direct and faster," he said.

"I don't like buses. I love trains." I was adamant.

"Very well," he said. "Then take the train."

Oh good, I thought. He had me worried there.

Then he lowered his voice and said that my fee would be 15,000 yen a class. That's 120 dollars, I thought. Less transportation costs it was about 98 dollars for teaching an hour and a half class. He asked me if it was enough and I replied carefully that it was adequate. Adequate? I was desperate for work and I'd never made that much money in my life. And *he* seemed so grateful.

I looked beyond him to the pond and temple garden. A fish leaped into the air and splashed down into the cold water. I knew then that we would pay the rent, I would catch up on child support and that eventually my debts would be taken care of. All my anxiety fell away and Kobashi appeared as if bathed in a subtle light.

OLD SCROLLS, NEW MATCHES

HŌGOJI, MAY 19, 1988

I sit in the shade on the wooden deck outside the room I share with Norman and Jakushin, who continues to be sad and dark. It is sunny today, the temperature is perfect and there's just the slightest breeze, which is a friendly touch to this tee-shirt weather. I am the only one wearing a tee shirt, however. The other guys are in baggy samue. What a tranquil setting—Hōgoji is indeed far from the sights and sounds of the normally noisy and fascinating fast-paced life of Japan.

Norman and Jakushin are both inside reading and writing letters in their respective languages. We stay in a corner of the main temple building in what was once the monk's study, an eight-tatami room. Traditionally, this is how you say how big a room is. Tatami are about three feet by six feet, so an eight-tatami area is about twelve square feet.

Across the tatami and about thirty feet away from our room is an even smaller room where Maku-san sleeps and reads. He's quiet but not morose—he's the pixie of the place. It's a day off and everyone's enjoying the free time on this fine May afternoon. Bees are buzzing and birds are singing and tonight there will be frogs and crickets to join with the creek's rushing flow below.

In front of me, two large, blue-black butterflies with green markings and fat fuzzy bodies flutter about some terribly beautiful very red flowers, which engulf a row of shrubbery. Maku says they are *tsutsuji*, which my dictionary says is azalea. Behind these shrubs there is moss on the ground, a short variety of palm tree, bamboo and pines rising above the shade. Often from the heights of those branches comes the soothing voice of the *yamabato*, the "mountain dove," really a turtledove: "Hoo hoo hoo, hoo hoo hoo hoo." I think of it as "the Laurie Anderson bird" because the cadence and coo of its call reminds me of one of her sequenced rhythm patterns.

To my right where the azaleas end there are two shrines, one about the size of a Coke machine and one the size of a birdhouse. Maku says they are the homes of local spirits called *kami*, which protect us. I graciously accept any help that's offered. Beyond all that is a hedge bordering the narrow and ridiculously steep asphalt road. Sometimes farm vehicles and even taxis coming to the temple use it. I sure wouldn't.

Earlier in my stay here I swept the leaves off that road with a bamboo broom and I looked at the blooming thistles in the fallow rice fields and admired their beauty and toughness. Later I would cut them down with a *kama*, a short-handled Japanese sickle, and burn them with the weeds. Thistles remind me of Katagiri's supportive and strong-spirited wife, Tomoe-san. Back in the States she'd place these thorny stems and their strong flowers on the altar. When I tried to do the same at Hōgoji, I was gently chastised. No thorns for Buddha here.

Further over to the right of the deck where I sit is a great bell hanging in an old wood-beam tower, moss on its four-foot-high stone base and moss on its faded orange tile roof. Sometimes I gaze at the moss and sometimes I gaze at the joinery. Next to the bell tower, on a corner of this leveled area, is the verging-on-dilapidated tea ceremony cottage, now used by Koji-san, the head monk, as a residence. It has become important to me, a sanctuary within a sanctuary.

Next to Koji's tea shack, growing around the stone wall from below, is a huge oak tree, the granddaddy of the place. It's climbable—massive low branches providing a large tangled room within. Continuing clockwise around the perimeter of the open courtyard are stone steps that go down to the level of the caretaker's house that had seemed so mysterious to me when I first walked in. In this forbidding structure, beneath the shade of the pines and oaks, lives elderly Yoshiko-san, formerly the caretaker of Hōgoji and the good witch of the woods. Beyond the top of these steps is the long roof-covered sink for hand and face washing, tooth brushing, laundry and vegetable cleaning.

The temple has two main tile-roofed, heavy, wood-beamed buildings perpendicular to each other and connected by a covered walkway. The principal one we call the *hattō*. Hatto means "dharma hall," the hall of Buddhist teaching or law.

The other main structure houses the kitchen, dining area, abbot's quarters and bath. We call it the *kuin*, though the name actually just means kitchen. The steps and entryway there are the social center of Hōgoji. That's where the mailman leaves the mail and picks it up. We serve tea informally to guests and chat with them there in front of the dining room. We sit on those steps and on the deck during fifteen-minute breaks in the morning or afternoon work periods. Norman and I drink green tea and the Japanese monks have instant coffee.

At that time Norman might say, "I'm American—therefore I drink green tea."

And Koji might respond with, "I'm Japanese—therefore I drink coffee."

Inside the wide thick hatto doors is an expansive tatami room with big round posts and a high ceiling of boards two feet wide. The wood there and everywhere in the temple is rich, exuding age and nobility. Straight ahead is a deep, somewhat cluttered altar, made from hand-planed *hinoki*. Almost all the wood in Hō-goji is hand planed because that's how temple wood is prepared, but the altars are especially smooth, smoother than if sandpapered.

This main altar has multiple tiers and rises behind a parted maroon curtain. In front center is a massive three-legged incense bowl two-thirds full of ashes that have been carefully prepared with a cute doll-house-sized leveling tool into a smooth surface. Next to it is a black lacquer box with thin green sticks of incense. To the sides are thick white candles and two brass vases containing shining brass flowers. There are various other ornaments and offering trays leading back to a small golden Buddha figure surrounded by foot-high guardian deities who are partially obscured by brocade curtains. I know every inch of the altar. I know every joint of the railing on the top level. I know where the dust collects unnoticed. I know the glassy smoothness of the surfaces as I wipe them with wet rags. I know the look in the eyes of the Buddha up there and I know all the stuff that's stored below—blackboards, notebooks, sutra books, brooms and stacks of ashtrays for guests to use.

The area directly in front of the altar has twelve tatami. It's here, by candlelight, that we do most of our chanting. I'm not allowed to participate in services in this central area because I'm a guest and haven't gone through the entering ceremony. So I stand and sit, as appropriate, a few steps back in an adjoining tatami area outside the posts. It's not considered the same room although there are no separating walls. It's also right by the room where I live—I can hop out there for service at the last second.

When visitors come for service, they sit out here with me while their kids squirm and run around. Shuko says that listening to the service for merit is a valid way to participate. They're here to catch the vibes. Fine with me. The children's playful voices add a delightful soprano to the drone of the chanting and I like to sit near the visitors and catch *their* vibes.

The single item on the altar that I can see most clearly in my mind's eye as I write is the matchbox. It is no ordinary matchbox. The matches are regular old strike-anywhere wood matches, but the container is striking. It's an A-frame box about six inches high. The matches are in a drawer on the bottom of the *A*, with a rough striking zone on the front of the drawer. On each side of this matchbox there's a photo of a middle-aged Japanese man giving the "thumbs up" sign. He's winking, sticking his chin out and tightening his lips in a beaming smile—all in a way that immediately conveys a gung ho, agreeable attitude. In big bold letters across the side of the box are written the words THANK YOU AND OK! For a time, every altar in the temple had one of these boxes on it, and they were also scattered all over the kuin —in the kitchen, study and Katagiri's room. Everywhere I looked that man was giving the thumbs-up sign and saying THANK YOU AND OK!

When we first saw one of these matchboxes, Norman and I had a long laughing spell. We didn't know what the purpose was, but it was surely some sort of advertisement. As an isolated event, it was goofy and humorous, but then we saw them everywhere and were at a loss to understand what on earth they were doing there. The Japanese monks, unlike Norman and me, didn't seem to notice them at all.

It was thanks to these matchboxes that I first became aware of the brotherly nature of the relationship between Norman and Shuko. One day after work, Norman and I were just outside our room talking. Maku was nearby getting the altar ready for evening service. Shuko came in with some flowers. Norman saw his chance. He walked over to the altar, held up one of the aforementioned boxes and asked Shuko, "Where did this come from?"

"What?" said Shuko.

"This," he said pushing it closer to Shuko's face.

"From Akagi-san. He gave us a case of them." Akagi-san owns a liquor store in Kikuoka and was one of the best friends of the temple.

Norman looked concerned, "He gave us a case? What for?"

"To light things. We don't have electricity here. We need a lot of matches," Shuko said.

"Thanks for the information," Norman said sarcastically. "What's wrong with the plain brown matchboxes we've been using?"

"We can use them too," Shuko answered.

I kept quiet and out of the way, watching developments with Maku. I'm sure he didn't understand much of their English, but he was listening intently.

"You're not really going to leave these up on the altars are you?" Norman continued.

"Yes," said Shuko, "of course."

"They look stupid, Shuko."

Shuko spoke in a monotone. "You know, our way is not to complain so much."

"And who is this 'we' who don't complain?" said Norman, perturbed. "Do you mean 'we Japanese'?"

"No," said Shuko.

"Then just who do you mean?"

"That's the tradition of Buddhism," Shuko answered.

"Listen, I'm forty-eight years old and have been studying with Katagiri Roshi for twelve years. Don't talk to me like I'm a child."

"Why don't you like them?" Shuko answered with a question.

"Shuko, come on. They don't fit. Look. Look around. Everything is hundreds of years old. These matches stand out like . . . like . . . well, there's nothing as absurd as they are to compare them with." Norman glared at him.

"This was a gift to the temple," said Shuko.

"Good, I'm going to give the temple a neon sign that says BUDDHA SAVES."

"It's not the same," said Shuko.

Maku and I looked at each other, opening our eyes wide and making a silly what's-going-to-happen look.

"Shuko, you're always saying that you want to follow Dōgen's original way of eight hundred years ago. Right? Ha, ha, ha. Thank you and OK!"

"Some things would be too impractical," said Shuko.

"Oh, now we're getting practical? Then why don't we run some electricity in here?"

"All temples use matches," Shuko pointed out.

"It's not the matches, it's the design," Norman said exasperated.

"What's wrong with the design?"

"Look at this." Norman held it up again. "See that guy? 'Thank you and OK!' "

"What's wrong with that?" Shuko asked.

"We don't say that," said Norman with exasperation.

"Japanese people don't read the words."

"I do—David does," said Norman. "And not everyone is Japanese. Isn't this an international temple?"

"You shouldn't discriminate so much," Shuko came back, using an old standby Zen admonition.

Norman was incensed and the smoke was rising in circles. "What do you mean I shouldn't discriminate! Do you think you never discriminate? We could use them up in the kitchen, but your discriminating consciousness decided to put them on the altars next to five-hundred-year-old scrolls."

Shuko was quiet.

"Ah! Why do I waste my time!" Norman threw up his hands.

I stepped up. "How about let's be especially devout—lighting incense and candles at every opportunity, holding extra services, toasting marshmallows around a bonfire, whatever we can think of, and those matches will all be gone in no time," I said, standing between the two of them, grinning and shrugging my shoulders.

Maku tilted his head. Norman and Shuko both looked at me blankly.

JENGLISH AND ENGLESE

MARUYAMA, APRIL 19, 1989

It's raining!" Okamura-san called out to me in the kitchen where I was sitting studying Japanese at a deep brown wooden table.

"Thank you!" I responded, opening the sliding screen door. She was outside taking the clothes off our line and putting them in the basket that was under the overhang.

I walked out apologizing and started helping her help me. "I'll get this. You'll get wet."

She picked up an umbrella that was leaning in the corner and held it over me as I got the last of the laundry out of wet's way.

We stood under the overhang talking. Grey-haired Okamura-san was in a small-patterned white floral dress protected by a light blue apron with a ruffled edge. Like most Japanese she is not a bit overweight. She comes up to my shoulder and is about the same age and build as my mother. She lives with her husband behind our house in a large two-story home with a walled-in flower garden. Their driveway passes by the side of our house. Across that driveway and through the bamboo grove we could see the Daianji monks weeding with the help of a crowd of young laypeople who were at the temple for a three-day training.

"There are many trainees," she said. "It's a lot of work for the monks to keep up with them all."

"They're the new employees from the Sobi Bus Company. There are seventy-five of them."

"Taihen desu nē (Lots of trouble, isn't it)?" she said, shaking her head.

"Hōjō-san is going to give them a special lecture when he gets back this afternoon."

"Where did he go?"

"To the leper colony out on the Inland Sea. He visits there every couple of months."

"What a good priest he is," she said. "Always working hard for people's benefit. Not your usual priest."

"He's very diligent."

"I've been bothering you," she said, taking her leave.

"Here, take this river (kawa)," I said, handing her the umbrella.

"Kasa," she responded softly, with a twinkle in her eye.

"Oh, of course," I said. "Take this umbrella (kasa)."

"No, thank you. I only have to walk to the door and it's not raining so hard."

But I insisted so she took it, thanking me and apologizing for being rude.

I went back inside thinking what an idiot I am—always getting even the simplest words confused. I had the morning to myself and was using the time to study Japanese. I loved our house—especially after we'd replaced all of the dreary fluorescent lights with incandescent bulbs, and switched the tacky plastic hanging fixtures with handmade paper lanterns I'd picked up from an old papermaker in Gifu.

Neighbors, including those at the temple, had helped us furnish the house by contributing not only art, but furniture, utensils and bedding. We filled in the rest with *sodai gomi* and stuff from secondhand stores. *Sodai gomi* is "big trash." On an appointed day every few months it is deposited at collection sites and picked up and crushed like regular trash. We borrowed a white pickup truck from the temple and rode around at night to the various drop-off spots in our part of town. We went through mountains of discarded furniture, appliances and household goods and had picked out everything we thought would like a home in our home. We'd gotten a chopping-block table as well as sundry pots, pans and dishes for the kitchen. We chose our favorite among various refrigerators. There was a good bicycle with big front and rear baskets in one pile. Elin had selected two much newer ones, but another trash-picking lady, also going through the pile with her husband, meekly mentioned that those bikes were theirs. It was there I found a long red plastic shoehorn, not worth much, but it was in perfect working order and is a must for all entranceways. As Bop said: "There may be more lawyers in San Francisco than Japan, but there are more shoe horns in Kyoto than America." The organ in the front hall also came from *sodai gomi*. No pianos though. I read in the paper that twenty pianos are put out on the street in Tokyo every day. The rest of our furnishings we'd filled in by going to secondhand stores. There are just a few of them and they aren't very popular, so the prices are good. That's where we got our bed, the living room set and a rice cooker that says "neuro-fuzzy" on the front.

We like the rice cooker because it has a setting for brown rice. Every time we mention to Japanese that we eat brown rice they look at us with bewilderment and say, "Brown rice is very healthy—not tasty, but very healthy."

Next to the rice cooker we keep a wide-mouth glass jar filled with *waribashi*, throw-away wooden chopsticks that we couldn't bring ourselves to throw away. Whenever we eat out, we have to use them. You snap them apart, eat and dispose. We have our own nice permanent lacquer hashi to take with us so we won't have to be part of the *tsukai-sute* (use and throw away) society as they call it. These traveling hashi are in tasteful cloth cases with drawstrings at the top. But if we happen to remember to bring them along when we go out, we invariably forget to use them. It's frustrating. So we've got this jar with a growing collection of plain pine chopsticks that I'll have to throw out when they get moldy.

One day Hashimoto-san, a high school English teacher and friend, dropped by unexpectedly with crustless, white bread, triangle-shaped sandwiches from the local bakery. During her visit Elin made a disparaging remark about the wastefulness of wari-bashi. Hashimoto defended them, saying it would be considered rude and unsanitary to give used hashi to guests. And she pointed out that America's use of paper towels seemed wasteful to her. I'd never thought of it that way. It wasn't as cut and dried as I had supposed. It was more . . . neuro-fuzzy.

Words like that—Japanese-English—attract our attention as much as the Japanese we are always studying and trying to figure out. A lot of it is quite creative. We have a tall white plastic wastebasket in the kitchen that we bought new at a local *hōmu sutōru* (home store) that says:

> *This expresses our life vision*
> *LET'S*
> *Supreme Can*
>
> > ("Let's" is the brand name)

While riding the bus to town Elin and I have made a mental list of interesting names of commercial establishments along the way. Some of the names are cool, like Niagara Moon, a coffee shop. Some are uncool, like Infect, a lady's dress shop, and a bicycle rental store at the train station called Shity Cycle (that's "city"). There's a coffee shop named Guns and Coffee, a barber shop named Cut and Bro, a beauty parlor called Haircutter Freak and, at the busiest intersection downtown, a men's clothing store called Brains Organic Matter. I copied a message written in large letters on the wall of the video rental store nearby. It says:

*This is the space where we can be willing to coming so it gives
a lot of good amenity and rental A&V for you.*

Sometimes I surprise my teen-age English students when I
ask if I can write down the messages on their tee shirts. Here is
a sampling:

Pay close attention to various objects and be calm

*Doc Holiday stokes his chin and regards you through hooded,
hostile eyes, You stare at your head or hand
SENSATIONAL*

*HAIL TO THE QUEEN He spokes as if to say in that low
cautious tone of voice, "you Bastards." INFORMATION*

*ADVANCED PROGRAM POISON GAS SPECIALIST
SPATS*

I copied that one off the back of a motorcyclist's jacket.

*New Basic & Trendy Fashion,
Good Feeling Life for Young Mind*

Sleep With Me Tonight

*for the player who demands the ultimate best sensitive comfortable
fat fashion good things exist throughout time*

*Princess Cat
There is something graceful about cat. Cats represent cute, cooing,
sweet, everything is oh, so nice love.*

Dick Baker told me that when he and his wife were living in
Japan they saw a sweatshirt with PEPPY CASUAL written on it and

thereafter spent a good deal of time trying to find one to buy, but had no luck. He also saw one that had the round Harvard University seal with "Charlotte, North Carolina" printed below.

A college-age English student of mine wore a totally shocking sweatshirt to class one day and I told her that it referred to oral sex in the crudest way, stating in no uncertain terms a commitment on her part that she might not be interested in fulfilling. She was shocked. A month later she had it on again and I made a subtle comment. She just shrugged and said that no one understood it and she liked the design.

I looked down at my notebooks, full of idiomatic Japanese phrases and useful words. The cover of one notebook says, "White Superior Note—always be along with you." Another reads, "NOTEBOOK —please use this note book politely, and use up the last sheet. And then please use your brains everyday." A third that I use for random thoughts in English is more apropos. It pictures three kittens with bat and ball and says, "SHOWING OFF," then on each page at the top, two cats dressed like the Bowery Boys walk along arm in arm and it says, "a couple of crooked priests that you just can't seem to dislike."

Okamura-san was calling my name again. I was staring at the table at the time—the one that she and her husband had loaned us for the duration of our stay. At first her voice seemed to come from beneath the table's surface, but then I caught her in the corner of my eye standing out on the driveway. The rain had never really gotten going and the sun was out. She had a clipboard with a message on it that was being passed from neighbor to neighbor. She explained that there would be a neighborhood cleanup day on a Sunday three weeks away and that if I couldn't attend I should give three thousand yen to the housewife Seki-san across the street. I initialed it and took the clipboard to pass on to the botanist,

Numoto Sensei, who lives on the other side of the parking lot in front of the temple gate. I always wait till he's home to take it over because I think I scare his wife.

Okamura-san started putting the clothes back up on the line. I told her to stop but she wouldn't, so we did it together.

I looked for something timely to say. Of course—her cherry tree. It's a late-bloomer with double flowers. A lot of the cherry blooms in this area were all rained out and blown away by mid-April, but hers still looked pretty full. As I pinned a shirt to the line a breeze came up and a flurry of petals took to the air and wafted gently, circuitously to the ground. Mmm—they use the word "snowing" for that.

"The fish (sakana) are snowing," I said.

She looked at me, smiling. "Sakura (cherry blossoms)?" she asked.

"Yes, yes, how stupid of me—the cherry blossoms are snowing." I pulled a clothespin from my teeth and grimaced.

LAUNCH AND LUNCH

UZU, NOVEMBER 23, 1988

Kobashi asked me to make a preliminary expense-paid trip to the shipbuilding firm at Uzu, where I was to teach. He had a consulting firm inside the gates of the same company, which it turned out he was retired from. A man in uniform at a guardhouse had my name on a list and directed me to Kobashi's office. It was in a three-story slatted white wooden building that looked about fifty years old. The whole place reminded me of the Presidio, the old army base in San Francisco. I got there just after nine in the morning and sat at a metal table waiting for Kobashi to get off the phone. His friendly partner kept me company while their OL (pronounced "o eru"), office lady, trotted off nervously to get me coffee. It was a perfect business meeting. We went over the contract in three minutes and then left for a tour of the facilities.

A company limo, black and complete with chauffeur, was waiting for us outside. I guess it was a Japanese car, but you don't see many that big. He drove us past partially finished ships with giant hulls spotted with fearless welders. I gasped at humongous equipment and rolls of monstrous cables and shops the size of low mountains. I was gaga. Nothing makes me happier than big equipment except bigger equipment. I wanted to teach English there forever. Kobashi did most of the talking. I was thumbing through my twenty-year-old trusty green pocket dictionary as fast as I could and asking him for clarifications. Some people know how to speak to foreigners. He's good at it. He speaks clearly, not too fast, and he instinctively knew what vocabulary I'd understand. I was probably understanding a good 60 percent.

The high point of the tour was when we parked the limo and walked over to a jumbo dry dock to see what I thought must be the largest can on earth. It was a rust-colored skyscraping container with proportions that made me wonder if maybe it was being built for giant peaches. Maruyama is famous for normal-sized ones. The cranes next to this towering vessel were so big and wonderful that I thought it must be a dream. We were standing on the tracks of one that was moving very slowly toward us. We must have looked like ants to the driver up there. I felt relieved when we stepped to the side.

It turned out the canlike structure in between these magnificent Bunyonesque cranes was going to be floated across the Inland Sea to Kōbe, where a suspension bridge to Shikoku was being built. There the container will be filled with cement and sunk. It has to hit the sea bottom at the exact right spot or they can't use it. There were a bunch of these tubs being built. This one wasn't even the biggest. And they were all going to be filled with cement. The round metal wall reached to within a foot of the edge of the dry dock on both sides. Standing in the massive shadow of that cylindrical cement form—big enough that a baseball game could be played in it—I could see that the world was going to be used up, and in a very impressive way.

Next on the schedule was *ranchi* (lunch). But first Kobashi had to go to a meeting—if it was alright with me, that is. That was fine, I assured him. "Just give me a place to sit and read and I'll be content as can be."

He took me upstairs and showed me a room with pea green walls, folding metal tables and chairs, and standing ashtrays stationed every three feet. Then he took me to a nearby carpeted room with overstuffed leather chairs and footrests. "You can have this room or that room. It doesn't make any difference. Which one would you like?" he said.

"Oh, I'll take this room." I said, of course selecting the one with the easy chairs. "It looks so comfortable."

"Sō desu nē," he said, drawing the "ne" out. He sighed and pointed to the left of the door at a sign-up sheet that indicated the room was reserved in ten minutes. "I guess I'll have to talk to these people about rescheduling their meeting."

"On the other hand," I said, "I might fall asleep in there. Would the other room be alright instead?"

"Yes indeed, if it's alright with you," he said more positively. "Either one is fine."

"In that case, I'll take this one," I said smiling and entering the big, ugly, uninviting room. I bid him farewell till lunch.

Kobashi came back sooner than I imagined. I mentioned that it seemed a little early for lunch. He said we had to go quickly or we'd miss it. After we got the English words "lunch" and "launch" straightened out, everything was just fine. Launch is also *ranchi*. And indeed, it turned out he was taking me to a boat launch. Terrific. The ceremony was surprisingly quick and the champagne bottle broke on the first try. The ship slid gracefully out into the Inland Sea. I watched it, mesmerized, as it got smaller and smaller. It was a navy ship and there was a row of Japanese naval officers bowing and smiling like in World War II movies. Everywhere I looked there were military people and more navy ships, some with guns. I envisioned warships being launched and tanks being produced on a massive scale, and American Congressmen demanding that they spend more and more money on more and more weapons when they're now only second to the U.S. in military spending. This tiny island, these nice polite people don't need so many weapons, I thought. It might have a bad influence on them. Suddenly I felt like an American, like a foreigner. I turned to the left—eyes were on me. I turned to the right—people were looking my way. I wondered if they were going to arrest me as a spy and stick bamboo slivers up my fingernails. I looked around for an escape route. Kobashi turned to me ominously. Kobashi! Of course, that's why he's been so friendly. "Ready for lunch?" he said, using the foreign loan word *ranchi* again. This time I got it.

We stood in a mall while businessmen, factory workers, old bent-over ladies in kimono and teenagers in leather walked by.

"Where would you like to eat?" he asked. He gestured to the left toward a spacious attractive establishment. "We could eat sashimi," he said. (Expensive, I thought.) "Or"—he gestured to the right where a street vendor stood by his cart smoking a cigarette—"we could eat noodles." (Cheap, I thought.) On the other side of the street vendor was a little noodle shop. "Either one," he said. "It makes no difference to me."

I pondered. Sashimi makes me drool as much as heavy equipment and I eat noodles all the time. I paused for a thoughtful moment. "How about . . . noodles?"

"Okay," he said. "If that's what you prefer, let's have noodles."

TEA TIME

HŌGOJI, APRIL 30, 1988

What did he say?" I turned to Shuko, who wouldn't answer. Katagiri had said something to me and everyone was laughing. Finally Katagiri obliged me with the English.

"I see you've still got diarrhea of the mouth, David." It was morning tea break on my second day at Hōgoji. I'd been telling about every single thing I'd done so far in Japan, using my Japanese to the limit and getting excited in the fresh energy of making new friends.

"I'm sorry," I said. I could feel myself blushing. It has been said that the all-important editing function of my brain is damaged. It seems as if every day of my life since I started going to school, someone has told me in one way or another to be quiet. I looked at an adolescent cherry tree in the courtyard.

"Tell me about yourselves," I said, trying to make up for my insensitivity. This just made them laugh more. Katagiri pulled me out of the hole I was digging for myself.

"They want to hear more. Your diarrhea is still new and interesting to them."

"More, more, I beg you," said Koji.

"What were you doing in Fukuoka?" asked Jakushin, who was in a much better mood than the day before.

"How did you know I was in Fukuoka?" I asked.

"The bag that you sent ahead came from Fukuoka."

"I was visiting a former monk," I said. "Do any of you know him? His name is Gyūhō Ōtsuji."

Katagiri nodded and raised his eyebrows. The others went "ahhhh" and opened their eyes wider.

No one could forget Gyūhō, who had been a visiting monk

at Zen Center years before. He came when Suzuki was starting to get ill. For a while he practiced at Tassajara. He was the camp nerd, bright-eyed and bushy-tailed and oh-so-naive. Soon he started picking up on American culture. He was curious about everything. His English improved. In Big Sur someone turned him on to pot and his transformation accelerated. He moved to the Zen Center building in the city so that he could do *shiatsu*, Japanese pressure-point massage, on Suzuki who was by that time clearly dying. In his spare time, Gyūhō was learning more and more about the San Francisco of the early seventies. After Suzuki died, Gyūhō left Zen Center, no longer able to bear the restrictions. For a while I lost track of him, but a year later I saw him at a hippie commune led by a Japanese artist. I used to go there to visit and play music when I was in town from Tassajara. Gyūhō had long hair, smelled of patchouli oil and wore blue jeans and a Guatemalan shirt. The nerd was no more.

He had started his own temple in San Francisco and he gave me a card for it, asking me to look him up there. He said that he had an American girlfriend and asked if I'd like to see her picture. I of course said yes and he pulled out a half dozen photos of him and a buxom beauty naked in suggestive poses. And what a temple he had. It was called the Columbus Nichiren-Zen Total Liberation Temple. I asked him why Columbus? and he told me because Columbus discovered America and that he and his students are discovering a new world too. I noticed when I looked at the card that the address was on Columbus Street. That was probably also a contributing factor. I dropped by the place and found Gyūhō surrounded by a band of followers, which included some young women. He invited me to stay there and fast with them for the afternoon and evening in preparation for taking LSD at midnight. The plan was to chant homage to the name of the Lotus Sutra, a practice of Nichiren Buddhism. It would be "Namu myōhō renge kyō," for the first three hours while the effects were peaking, and then when we had come back down into the Realm of Being again we could explore the wonders of our bodies and minds in union. I paused to think. Then I said thanks a lot, but I was in the middle of a good book.

The next I'd heard, Gyūhō had returned to Japan. His brother had died unexpectedly and he had had to go back home to run the family temple, a large prestigious one in Shikoku. A book on places for Westerners to practice Zen in Japan said that it was a good temple to go to if you wanted to stay up all night involved in lively discussion. He shaved his head and performed his duties well, but didn't let Japan hold him back one bit.

"He's the one who was arrested for having LSD in Tokyo, isn't he?" asked Jakushin.

"Yes," I said. All heads moved closer. They seemed to have heard about him. "How do you know about that?" I asked.

"It was on the front page of every newspaper in Japan," said Koji.

"Yeah, I have a friend who was there. He said that he went to a party and all of a sudden the whole house was full of police and that the most interesting thing was that the cops all took their shoes off before entering the house. Gyūhō said that someone who was mad at him tipped off the cops. He only ended up getting a suspended sentence, a minor miracle I understand."

"Gyūhō didn't go to jail?" asked Jakushin.

"No."

"Why not?"

"He wore his robes to court, which established him as a pillar of society. Other monks came in robes to lend him support. So there were he and his friends and the judge all in robes and the judge asked him if he had anything to say before sentencing and Gyūhō said that whereas it was wrong for the average person to experiment with dangerous drugs such as LSD, that it might be okay for an esteemed person like the judge, who must be better informed than the general public, or a meditator who plummets the depths of the mind. Gyūhō said that he had done it as a monk, a pioneer on the fringes of consciousness. He said that being a monk and sitting zazen drove some people crazy too and that it was just an extension of an already dangerous quest."

"He got away with that?" asked Norman.

"Yes, but he also said that he now knew that he was wrong to try artificial methods and that he would never touch drugs again. The judge said that he would have sent him to jail if he hadn't explained himself so well." I didn't mention that Gyūhō had told me that getting busted had helped turn his life around for the better. He said that he'd run the whole course from grass to acid to PCP, and at the time of the arrest he was considering smuggling heroin to Japan from Thailand, not exactly what Buddhists would call "right livelihood." He'd gotten about as far off the Eightfold Path as a monk could. Then he got busted and from that point, he said, everything happened perfectly to assist him in charting a new course for his life. He went back to his temple and his wife and led a calmer life. I asked him how on earth could he stay as the head of the temple, after having received a suspended sentence for drugs. Why didn't his congregation throw him out? He said, "Oh, you know Japanese. They pretended it never happened. They don't like to bust big shots here. The judge even pretended the whole thing was over LSD when I'd been arrested with marijuana and cocaine as well. There was a lot of overlooking going on."

"You can't get much luckier," said Norman. "Japan has a merciless criminal justice system."

"But he left his temple, didn't he?" asked Shuko.

"Yep. He said that he stayed there for a couple of years more and then one day he just walked out. He decided to reject the glory and the duty and become a regular person. His wife, an American woman, the same one from the pictures, had to run the temple for a year by herself, which makes her one of the only non-Japanese ever to be in charge of a temple in Japan—certainly, the only lay woman foreigner to do so. I ran into her in America just before I left the Bay Area and she gave me Gyūhō's address. He does shiatsu in Fukuoka now and he has a lot of interesting friends whom he sits up with late at night talking."

"Did you take LSD with him in Fukuoka?" Jakushin asked.

"No no no, of course not," I said to the curious monks. "He doesn't do that anymore. But he and his girlfriend took me to a Shingon priest, a lady, who led us to a waterfall where we put on white robes and stood in gassho beneath a hammering cold waterfall for an hour."

"Takishugyō (waterfall practice)!" said Maku.

I paused, thinking for a second. "You know, I learned something important from Gyūhō."

"What?" asked Koji and Jakushin in unison.

"I learned about takkyūbin."

They looked puzzled. "Takkyūbin?" It's the Japanese package-delivery system.

"Yes, when he saw me off at the train station he said that I should send all of my bags ahead like everyone else. I said it was too expensive and he said, 'This is Japan. Japanese people are not afraid to spend money. The money will come. Do it.' I just sent the heaviest one. If I'd listened to him my back wouldn't be hurting. That's what I learned from Gyūhō." They looked disappointed.

The story about Gyūhō had blown everyone's mind. To me it had just been dropping in on an old friend who now leads a simple life. But to them it was a dangerous and exciting adventure. They asked what I planned to do when I left and I told them that first I would go stay for a few days with the logger I'd met in the *yakitori* restaurant in Kikuoka. I was interested in seeing what his lifestyle and business were like.

"Do you want to meet Japanese women?" asked Koji, "Have a Japanese wife?"

"Oh . . . I don't have any ideas."

"Don't you have a girlfriend?" asked Shuko.

"Yes, well, no, not now. Maybe," I said, wavering. "She's far away and we don't know . . ."

"Are you engaged?" said Maku.

"No no."

"And what next?" asked Koji. "What after the logger?"

"I don't know in particular," I said. "Just whatever happens."

"Don't you have a plan?"

"To look around and visit some people. Friends and friends of friends, priests, artists. Maybe look for a teacher. And I gotta find a place to live."

"You must have a lot of money," said Maku.

"Oh no, not at all."

"But it's so expensive in Japan," he said almost with alarm.

"I have many friends to look up. I'll hitchhike if I have to."

They all said, oh no, don't do that, it's dangerous.

"Are you serious? Japan isn't dangerous at all. The foreigners I've talked to say it's one of the easiest countries in the world to hitchhike in." They continued, though, insisting that I shouldn't hitchhike.

"Where will you live? What will you do?" Jakushin asked as if I hadn't just said.

"I'll find out," I said. "It will come. The universe will provide."

This was met with a mix of incredulity and interest from Koji, Jakushin and Maku, the three monks who hadn't been to the States. Shuko and Katagiri had been following along with interest, not surprise, but these others acted as if I was jumping off the edge of the earth into the great unknown.

"Ashita wa asu no kaze ga fuku," said Koji, nodding. This was met with grunts and more nods.

"What?" I asked, and he repeated it. I thought about it. "The wind blows tomorrow?" I asked, looking at Katagiri.

"Tomorrow's wind blows tomorrow," he said. "It means tomorrow will take care of itself. He means it's the way you live."

"That's right," and I tried out the phrase in Japanese. "Ashita wa asu no kaze ga fuku." My attempt was met with laughter, but Katagiri assured me it was right.

It was time to go back to raking. A breeze was taking some leaves from a pile I'd gathered together and was tugging them off. I looked at one of the errant leaves and said it again: "Tomorrow's wind blows tomorrow."

JAKUSHIN ON THE BOTTOM

HŌGOJI, MAY 7, 1988

Being in a fresh setting, I basked in the rays of the all-important harmony of temple life. At times when I spoke to Norman though, I was reminded that cultural conflict would be swinging its aggravating tail, and each additional day I was there, comparison, that lowly beast that prowls around the edges of pure experience, would be waiting to barge in and smell up the place. If I were not on guard, I could see that, inevitably, dissatisfaction would take root and grow.

Before long I was forced to find refuge in the practice of nondiscrimination as best I could. This calls for not paying so much attention to the editorials between the ears. To me it meant following the breath, opening to body-mind with the center of attention being in the belly, as Suzuki and Katagiri had told us over and over. "Just sit. Just work," they both had said so many times. It's the Soto mantra. When the bell rings, go where it beckons. Don't take your thoughts so seriously. Nothing to it but to do it. That sort of thing. And what a perfect place to use such nondevices to express original shining mind, which is what Koji reminded me Dōgen said we were all doing. I would just have to take their word for it. Sometimes it didn't seem so. Disturbing things would come up.

One day during the afternoon tea break on the steps Norman handed me an English-language newspaper that he'd bought in town. There was a story in it about some kids in one of the public elementary schools whose paintings had been accepted at a national exhibition until a mistake was discovered. The mistake was that their school was a "Korean" school and they were therefore not eligible to enter the contest, which was for "Japanese" children.

"These are kids who were born in Japan—some of their grandparents were born in Japan," Norman spoke softly so that the others wouldn't hear. "But because they are of Korean ancestry their art was rejected. Can you imagine how those little kids felt? They were probably all excited about the fact that something they had made was in an important national show. Brutal."

"But wait," I said. "Progress is being made. A public hospital in Tokyo hired a 'Korean' nurse. Can you believe it? She was born and educated in Tokyo and that made front-page news."

"A quantum leap."

"You think discrimination here is worse than in America?" I asked him.

"Different, not worse for sure. But we can't ignore it here just because it exists there. It's ugly no matter where it happens. Especially against kids."

Jakushin is half-Korean and on top of that an orphan, a parentless child without a country. One day he went to Beppu to the alien registration office. They've got his fingerprints on record. He's got to carry an alien identification card—like me. Koji says he can become a citizen through effort if he changes his family name to a Japanese one. Norman says even if he did so he couldn't erase the stigma, only obscure it a little. The situation didn't seem to bother Koji much. He thought it was only natural.

"Why are they called Koreans," I asked him, "if they're permanent residents here? Most of them were even born in Japan. That's not Korean. That's Japanese."

"No, they're Korean. There's more to being Japanese than just being born here," he said.

"But he looks and talks exactly like any other Japanese. How could you possibly tell the difference if someone hadn't told you?"

Koji just looked at me askance.

With a thoroughly decent fellow like Koji having opinions like that, I got a sense of the depth of the problem.

"It's hard for us to get a handle on discrimination in Japan," said Norman. "They just don't have the assumptions that we have about race, equality and people's rights. It's a totally different mind set, different history. Not saying I don't think they're dead wrong. They just don't see what we do when we look at the situation. They think of the U.S. and, especially, South Africa as racist countries and of themselves as blameless. For a South African to enter Japan, they have to sign an affidavit that pledges that they aren't racist. Ha! To each his own—denial that is."

All that would be enough to give a Korean-Japanese a chip on the shoulder, which is exactly what Jakushin has. He struts around with paper-thin pride that hardly masks his sense of inferiority.

Koji said Jakushin's parents died in an automobile accident when he was a baby. He had a hard childhood being raised by poor friends of the family and, by all appearances, a miserable time of it in adulthood too. He had to go to a segregated school for kids of Korean ancestry and wear a uniform that identified him as such. Koreans as well as *burakumin*, also called *eta*, the Japanese "yellow trash" who likewise suffer terrible discrimination, can always go into the *yakuza*, the Japanese mob, if they want a better chance for advancement. Jakushin chose the priesthood instead. Buddhism also offers a system at least intending not to discriminate. But he's on the bottom of the heap at Hōgoji. Norman and I are off the scale.

And Jakushin blows it by being a creep. It's hard to blame his problems on discrimination because his attitude and behavior toward others is so bad—it's a vicious cycle. When he's not acting pathetically arrogant he's complaining about being left out or short changed. He has been annoyed that he was thrown in with Norman and now with me, when everyone else had his own room. Koji said he's in there with us because he arrived last and that's all there was for him. Jakushin kept insisting it was his turn for a private room, so it looks as though Maku is going to trade with him soon. Norman says that maybe then he'll stop going into other people's rooms, eating their cookies and reading their mail.

I went in during a break and asked Jakushin if I could help him in the kitchen. I was curious about him and the thickness of his shell. He accepted my offer and had me measure out the rice for dinner and wash the white powder off it. We didn't have any exchange, but there was no problem. He was quiet and serious and seemed as dark as the room to me. The only way I could extend myself to him was to wash the rice. I told myself that that should be good enough, there was no need for anything added. This is what we're here to do—to be quiet and practice together. So I gave up my idea of being friendly, let him be himself, and washed the rice. It took me a moment to adjust.

Koji told me that Jakushin's been told that this is his last chance. If he doesn't do well here he'll be asked to go off to the temple he came from, which is too poor to support him. That puts him in a desperate position, because if he has to start all over at another training temple then he'll lose his seniority and that's all he's got. At most training temples the new monks get kicked around terribly by their seniors. It's not something anyone would want to go through twice. Sometimes Norman and I decide we should put the poor guy out of his misery and have devised various "arsenic and old lace" schemes. Poor Jakushin. It hurts me to think about him.

MARITAL BOWS

There's a famous train here, the Shinkansen, often called the "Bullet Train" in English though it literally means "New Trunk Line" (I see elephants for cars). I much prefer the names of Hikari (light ray), for the super express that doesn't make so many stops, and Kodama (echo), which stops at every Shinkansen station. To me, riding the Shinkansen is like being in a plane that's taking off, only a little bit cheaper. It's often crowded and I like to pay a few hundred extra yen to get a reserved seat by a window so I can gaze at the tile roofs and rice paddies flying by or catch a row of old farmhouses, their weathered wood and mud walls in a blur. Sometimes I study the minutiae and sometimes I just groove. Other times I read a book or doze off. Mr. Shimizu from the Monday Morning Class complains that the Shinkansen rolls a little from side to side, but it seems pretty smooth to me as it shoots along on elevated tracks safely above all kids, animals and cars. Its massive two-story reinforced cement structure starts in the south in Fukuoka (in the northern extremity of Kyūshū) and runs to Morioka (in northern Honshū), with some significant branch tracks out of Tokyo. All in all, there are over 1600 miles of track in the sky for the Echoes and Light Rays. It is Japan's Great Wall. A pamphlet from the station proudly states that since it was built in 1964 there hasn't been a single fatal accident, and indeed, I feel close to immortal when I'm lucky enough to be a Shinkansen passenger hurtling somewhere through the day or night.

One cold December morning that somewhere was Osaka. Elin quickly fed a ten-thousand-yen bill into a vending machine in the wall and got two regular tickets. The unreserved cars were full. We walked up through the reserved cars and could have applied our tickets to a couple of empty seats in any of them, but we were a little hung up on money at the time. We had only recently arrived and were just starting to collect some spending money from our first few English classes. We went on, past the expensive and almost empty Green Car to the dining car, where we got a nice window table for two. There we would remain for the hour of our travel and spend over twenty dollars on orange juice, sweet rolls and coffee, leisurely consumed.

"Oh, to heck with it, why not splurge?" said Elin. "It's a special day."

It was indeed a day to celebrate: the fifty-fifth birthday of Akihito, the next-and-soon-to-be emperor, two days before our first Christmas in Japan, but most notable, it was to be our wedding day. We were on our way to the U.S. consulate to procure the proper papers and to follow their instructions.

While the last kilometers streaked by at almost two hundred an hour, we sipped and nibbled, she read the paper and I caught up on the scenery, which was starting to consist more and more of concrete housing projects and stark grey office buildings with an occasional minipark, walled-in temple, or shrine huddling in the midst of the drabness. I kept an eye out for these redeeming details amidst the consequences of a total lack of zoning laws or city planning.

On the evening of Elin's second day in Japan we had gone to a section of Tokyo that was overflowing with jewelry stores. We were going to be traveling around for a few weeks and staying in homes and temples and didn't want to make people uncomfortable—they do look at ring fingers. The aesthetics of our choice of ring were strongly balanced by economic considerations. We bought the cheapest one we could find, a platinum and gold band so thin that it first reminded her of a prize out of a cereal box.

We tried to get married on that trip, but didn't because I couldn't produce my divorce papers for the authorities. So for a while longer we had to fake it. We were gaijin and thus not so subject to the horrendous social pressures of the Japanese. Still it seemed we would be stretching things too far to let it be known in Maruyama that we were an undocumented couple. It would have been especially unfair to the temple, or, more correctly, to Watanabe, who had gone so far out of his way to help us move into the house next door and get set up. He was personally guaranteeing us to the authorities and, in a sense, to the neighborhood. He understood foreigners well and seemed open-minded, but Jessica, who has been translating for him since they were fellow students, assured us he was still quite traditional—as were the neighbors. It all reminds me of Texas in the fifties.

It was easy to fake it. Secrecy and privacy are built into the language and culture. Japanese leave you an out in any discussion and it's easy to be vague. Just use the right words in introductions and greetings and you're home free. Be discreet and you can do anything you want inside your house. I think that if one followed the correct forms on the outside, that one could practice devil worship and animal sacrifice behind closed curtains, and the neighbors wouldn't pay any attention, even if there were occasional muffled cries emanating from the house.

We received my divorce papers three days before Christmas. And that is how our wedding date was determined.

As we detrained at Osaka on that morning of the twenty-third, we were greeted by a pop version of "Rudolph the Red-nosed Reindeer." We'd heard that a lot recently. There had been Christmas music in the shopping streets and public areas since mid-November. There were also colored lights in the trees in downtown Maruyama to go with the purple and cream-colored decorative cabbages that lined the sidewalks and medians. At home, presents from the States and a few friends in Japan awaited opening under our decorated pine branch, which we had cut from a tree on the ridge above the temple. We were about the only ones exchanging presents though. The only Japanese I knew who thought of Christmas as a time to exchange presents were those who had lived in the States. Everyone else I ever talked to thinks it's a holiday to eat cake. Really. Christmas cakes abound in the bakeries and department stores at this time. Elin and I have both had discussions about this in our classes.

Most common example:

"What does Christmas mean to you?"

"Cake."

"What does it mean to Americans?"

"I don't know. Cake?"

Apparently there's so much cake left over after Christmas that lots of it gets stale. I was at a year-end office party (a big deal in Japan) and one of the secretaries was thirty and unmarried and the guys were teasing her that she was "really stale Christmas cake." Prime marriageable age for women is about twenty-five. After the twenty-fifth of December, Christmas cakes are drastically discounted. They chided her for being on the shelf so long. She got hitched a year later—to a friend, she said. "It was time for both of us to get married and we couldn't find anyone else, so we married each other."

Waiting for a subway to take us from the Shinkansen station in Osaka, we were jolted from our Christmas carol trance and reminded of the day's true purpose. There was a massive billboard on the wall opposite the tracks, a wedding dress advertisement. In the ad a young Japanese lady was decked out in a fancy white gown with veil and train. Her smile told the story: get an expensive dress like this for the most important day of your life and be happy like me. But if any tourist gets the idea by looking at the wedding gown ads (and they are fairly common) that Japanese weddings are like our traditional weddings back home, forget it.

. . .

Yasushi and Kaori Namba live in the countryside of Gifu prefecture. One night they showed me their wedding pictures and talked to me at length about the event. I was amazed at how involved it all was. Kaori changed attire five times. On the morning of her wedding she walked from her house to his with her eyes cast down. She wore a blazing red kimono, heavy white pancake makeup, and traditional zori, thongs of woven silk and gold thread. At the groom's house she changed into a long silk kimono with an *obi* and a hood, all pure white. The hood is called a *tsunokakushi*, which literally means "horn hider." She was ready not only to marry her husband but his family. Thus she must drape her body in pure white and be prepared to be "dyed in the family way." The hood covers her "horns" of independence. Yasushi wore a blue *hakama* and *haori*, the pleated skirt and coat seen in samurai films.

About twenty members of the two families attended the wedding. They could have walked a couple of hundred yards from his home up a wide gravel path, beneath large cedars, some wrapped wonderfully with ritual rope around their trunks, up by the mountain creek, to the old rough wood neighborhood *jinja*. But instead they went to another town to a newer, larger concrete shrine to have their ancient animist wedding presided over by a Shinto priest.

Afterwards they went to the shrine's adjoining meeting and party hall, where their families joined with a hundred friends and coworkers to celebrate the tryst with music, food and drink. Esteemed citizens gave praise and blessings. Kaori appeared in a fancy multicolor kimono and *obi*, with wig, fan and heavy makeup. To cut the cake, she came out in a Western wedding dress. Yasushi wore a tuxedo. Their friends applauded. This gown, indeed her entire wardrobe, was rented and came with attendants who knew the proper way to put everything on.

When they departed for their ten-day honeymoon, she wore a stylish dress with corsage and he a new suit and tie. Before long they were across the ocean posing for photos at the Golden Gate Bridge and Disneyland.

Yasushi was a used car salesman at the time and Kaori had a job in a bank. He said that there's no rule for how weddings are paid for but that families frequently split the cost. They spent about fifteen thousand dollars on the wedding and a little less for the honeymoon, quite frugal, according to him. A major expense of that trip was *omiyage*, obligatory souvenirs to be distributed to friends and family.

I asked him how many Japanese have weddings like his and he said most everyone does, though the extravagance will vary. Some brides will model three different fancy kimonos.

The Nambas love to talk about the high points of their lives and show me the photo trail. Now they have a cordial, peaceful relationship and haven't slept together in five years—since their third child was born.

In front of the Hanshin Department Store Elin and I stood on a walkway overlooking a busy Osaka intersection and watched an amazing concentration of people going rapidly but peacefully to work. Almost all of them were slim and well dressed.

"Everyone looks like they're wearing new clothes," she said.

She had on a nice, long green dress and a practical full-length overcoat, and I wore my best pants and shoes, camel hair coat and brown striped tie. It was the most dressed up we ever got, but as I surveyed the competition and compared, my grandmother's words came to mind: "Honey, you look like a ragamuffin!"

Elin and I were just starting to get friendly that day. We had been in a matter-of-fact mood, even a little irritated at each other—well, her at me. Nothing bad, but not our best for sure. Our conversations had been stilted and collided clumsily. I found myself babbling nervously and facing responses like, "Well, what do you mean by that?" and a mildly disgusted "Why are we getting married anyway? We're not even getting along on our wedding day." At that point we stopped the small talk so as not to give vent to our prenuptial jitters.

One of these well-dressed people we were surrounded by, a dignified man who seemed to be in his fifties, came up to us and asked in English if we needed any assistance. We got to talking and it turned out he was a judge. When he found out what day it was he insisted on taking us to *mōningu setto* ("morning set," Western breakfast) at a comfortable nearby coffee shop. Aside from the diminutive porcelain cup of coffee in a saucer, what that establishment served was one scrambled egg, an almost raw piece of bacon, a tiny salad with mayo on it and a slice of thick white bread toasted, buttered and cut into three rectangular crustless strips. While I poured imitation milk from an inch-high stainless steel pitcher (drop by drop, watching the fluid designs), the judge told others in the coffee shop our good news. All were encouraging and wished us well. One old man laughed and exclaimed, "Jinsei no hakaba!" The judge explained in his halting English that the old fellow was calling marriage "life's graveyard."

He said that the Japanese view toward the alternative is even gloomier, especially for women. A widow is a "not-yet-dead-person" and a spinster is "unsold goods" or "a widow who never went to a husband's house." He said that the incidence of young people living together before marriage is on the rise in Osaka and that it was a common practice in ancient times. It was called "inserting the foot," he said winking. As he explained these terms, he drew the kanji quickly with his right index finger on his left palm.

Later Elin and I entered the taxi that would bring us to the consulate and the judge's phrase "inserting the foot" came to mind. We had indeed enjoyed a leisurely courtship.

Most of the Japanese married couples I know came together much more quickly than I'm used to seeing. In my experience almost all young Japanese are dying to get married; otherwise it seems they feel their lives will be empty and meaningless. When introducing themselves in a classroom setting all my unmarried women students say, "I am not yet married," or, "I want to get married and have children," or, "I am marrying age. Marrying age in Maruyama is twenty-four or twenty-five." It's totally pre-dictable. And they don't court long. It seems like some take the first guy who asks them or whom they ask (as was the case with one lady student of mine). One week a student will say, "I am not married," and I'll ask, "Do you have a boyfriend?" and she'll say "Oh no," and giggle, and the next week she'll say she's engaged. "When did this happen?" I'll ask, and I'll get an answer back like, "Oh, we met last week." It's a whole different concept.

I began to wonder how these couples come together so quickly. Etsuko, the school teacher from the MMC (Monday Morning Class) said in class one day that she was twenty-nine and ready to marry. She's bright, positive, and cute in a quirky way. And she's so informal—she's one of the few Japanese I know who asks to be called (at least in English class) by her given name (I can't say "first" because with them it's second as they use family names first). She said she would wait one more year before going the formal route in seeking a husband.

"Formal route?" I asked.

"Arranged marriage," she answered from the chair where she sat next to the couch that held three other women students.

"Arranged marriage? Your parents tell you who to marry?"

"No. That was the old way. But Japanese are still shy with each other. Many of us, even today, need encouragement to meet a prospective husband or wife." She smiled and tilted her head. She was the shortest and perkiest of the group and always wore bright red lipstick that seemed to announce readiness for the ar-rangement. She said that the decision is that of the couple after they've met through introductions from family or friends. "It's called *omiai*. Sometimes we do it ourselves through professional matchmakers. Many people exchange questionnaires and photos before deciding who to meet. The families usually check up on each other too."

Our dear friends in Maruyama, the Hashimotos, met through omiai. It was his first try, she had done it many times. She said when she met him the omiai turned into *ren'ai*, a word for love. He was twenty-eight and she was twenty-four.

She said, "If I'd been a beauty he wouldn't have married me. He doesn't like the so-called *bijin*, the beautiful woman."

"That's just your modesty," I said.

"No no," she said laughing, "That's true."

I didn't argue. I guess she's right from the point of view of the mass media. She's too short to be a model and pays little attention to her appearance. At the time she was wearing some baggy wool pants. Her hair is always somewhat uneven, since her husband cuts it. She is wise and accepts herself and doesn't seem to fret much about what other people think of her. Elin and I find her refreshingly honest and uninhibited and Elin is always happy to have her to talk to when they get together.

"He was a high school English teacher then and I was working for a company."

Their *nakodo*, the middle-person who brought them together, was Mr. Hashimoto's neighbor, a man of good position. The nakodo has a role in the ceremony and continues to be like a godfather to the couple throughout their lives.

"I was getting discouraged about omiai and asked my neighbor, who had cooked up this scheme with the nakodo, why I should meet this man she wanted to introduce me to. She said because we had graduated from the same university in the same department."

"Oh, really?" I said perplexed.

"First we exchanged *tsurigaki*, fishing-writing. If we didn't like what we read then there would be no meeting."

"So, what interested you?" I asked her.

"That we graduated from the same university in the same department."

"Hmmm."

"I expected we'd have a lot in common to talk about. I saw his picture and remembered him. He had been a senior when I was a freshman. I thought he was studious, hard working, modest, and truthful. I decided to meet him and he was as nice as I expected and we talked a lot. We left the neighbor's house after an hour or so."

"Yes, we went to a coffee shop," he threw in.

"No. We took a streetcar to the hill where the tracks end."

"That's the woods," I said. "You went to the woods? That's quick." And then looking at the Mr., "And you forgot?"

"Not in that way," she said, laughing. "At the street car stop he asked me which way I wanted to go, downtown or to the hill, and I said the hill. There was a special reason. His professor whom he respected so much had committed suicide there. He had been my professor too. We went to that spot and talked about him and got to know each other. No one knows why the professor did it but it was during the nationwide student protests, perhaps it was related to that. We talked about our experiences, what we'd studied with the professor and what we learned at his summer seminars. Then we went back to town and ate soba in a noodle shop."

"No, we had sandwiches in a coffee shop," he corrected her.

"No, it was noodles. Then he took me home. I asked him if I could see him again and he said yes. He proposed after one month and we married eight months after that."

"I was going to propose on her birthday," said Mr. Hashimoto, "but my mother urged me to do it quicker because women are more worried about getting married or about the man's intentions. We went to a coffee shop."

"Yes, that time was a coffee shop. Maybe I should have asked my parents," said the Mrs., "but I said yes on the spot. Then we did *kikiawase*, asking around. Our parents knew nothing of each other. His family relied on their neighbor, the nakodo. But my father had a car and he and my mother thought it would be a good idea to bring my aunt and go to my prospective husband's village. They drove there and asked an old man the way to the Hashimoto house and inquired into the family's reputation. Later we found out the old man was my father-in-law to be. I don't know what they did once they found the house. Maybe they asked questions of some neighbors. I guess they already knew it wasn't a Korean or eta neighborhood, which is the main thing parents worry about. So they just went through the motions."

"That was it?" I asked. "You passed the test, got your parents' permission, and made wedding plans?"

The Mr. spoke up. "I had to give her yuinō first. That's bride-groom's money. He gives it to the bride to help prepare the wedding and if she backs out she has to give double back and if he backs out she keeps it."

"How much was it?"

"Thirty man," she said. That's three hundred thousand yen —twenty-four hundred dollars today but half that back then.

"It was forty man!" he said. "My father went with the nakodo and delivered it to your father. It's a formality. The decoration alone cost ten man. It was wrapped in fine silk and placed on a tray."

"The tray and the wrapping cost a hundred thousand yen?"

"Yes."

"How can that be?"

"Well, it is highly decorative. A doll comes with it and the wrapping cloth is made of fine silk. It's like a culture tax, the price of keeping tradition," he said. When I continued looking unconvinced, he added, "They always stick it to the consumer on obligatory expenses."

"It's put on the *tokonoma* (a traditional alcove with flower arrangement and scroll)," added Mrs. Hashimoto. "But my house had no tokonoma so we put it on the altar. The bride used to have to give a dowry, but not now. I don't know of anyone doing that these days.

"I got up early and dressed up in a wig and a special long wedding kimono and went to greet his neighbors and his family for the first time. Because it was in the country it was far to walk between places in fine ladies' zori. When I passed the junior high everyone looked out because my husband's big brother taught there. I waved, which surprised them because I wasn't supposed to do that.

"The nakodo was the manager of a big hotel near my husband's village so that's where we had the wedding and the party."

"How many times did you change clothes?"

"I would have felt like a doll modeling all those different fancy kimono and dresses. The wedding kimono was enough. So I didn't change clothes during the wedding party. I could do that because we invited only our relatives."

As Elin and I entered the consulate, handed our bags to the uniformed guard (who didn't speak English) and went through the metal detector, I thought of the Hashimotos and their easy way with each other.

The first time I was married was in '73. It was a big wedding at the Zen Center in San Francisco complete with a reception and many guests. Baker Roshi, decked in his finest robes, performed the ceremony. Bells rang, people bowed and chanted amidst incense, flowers and candles. We exchanged rings and drank from a black Navaho wedding pitcher. I wore my black robes, and my bride, a white cotton two-piece outfit with flowing ankle-length culottes. (I always like to say for shock value that I wore a dress and she pants.) We took the same thirteen vows we had taken at our priest and lay ordinations. Zen weddings *are* ordinations, and so are the funerals. In Japan, Buddhist temples cover the funerals and memorial services. Shinto covers the happy stuff: weddings, blessing babies, New Year's. To my Japanese friends, a Buddhist wedding would be like getting married in a funeral home. There are exceptions. I know one mixed-nationality couple who were married in a Buddhist temple and I had a Japanese student who was married in a church. I asked if she was Christian. "No," she said, "but church weddings are becoming fashionable."

Elin and I had a small, discreet—uh—ceremony? It was quite lacking in form. A lot of people have the mistaken idea that Zen is free and formless. Anyone who's been around Zen institutions knows that it's also full of form. This wedding wasn't Zen at all and it was heavy on formlessness.

At the consulate Mrs. Ōishi went over our papers. She's got a great name. It means "big stone" but sounds like the word for tasty. When Mrs. Ōishi saw my divorce papers she smiled and provided us with a certificate that said it was okay with the U.S. government for us to get married. Then we had to round up a couple of witnesses. I asked a businessman from Utah who was sitting on a couch if he'd mind witnessing our wedding. He apologized and said that he was too busy. Mrs. Ōishi told him all he had to do was to sign. He and she did so and wished us good luck. We stepped into the elevator to make our final descent from the legal realm of "lone bodies" (*dokushin*, usually translated as "being single" in English).

Holding hands, we proceeded to the nearby North Ward Office. It was a plain cement building with no endearing aesthetic quality within or without. We walked in through the swinging glass door. There were sturdy metal desks on the other side of a waist-high wooden-slat partition, and at these desks sat mainly young women, quietly doing their jobs. One of them stood up and pleasantly asked us what our business was.

"Life's grave," I responded.

She looked at me blankly.

"We'd like to get married," Elin said, kicking me gently.

Several women at their desks and the one attending to us started laughing with their hands over their mouths.

The lady asked us to please wait. Soon a distinguished elderly public servant, a tall and handsome man, came out, introduced himself and sincerely congratulated us.

"Not yet," Elin said. "You have to marry us first."

He had us each fill out a form that was in Japanese and though he didn't really speak English, he helped us out by pointing to the questions and uttering key explanatory words in English. It was obvious that he did this a lot.

There was a hitch when he got to transcribing the male witness's name. He couldn't read the signature. Neither could we. It was a slightly awkward moment when we explained that we didn't know the witness personally. This elicited raised eyebrows from the gentleman but he focused on the problem at hand. He needed to write a name in katakana. We fudged.

The most dramatic moment was when I had to run back to the consulate around the corner, over a pedestrian bridge and another half block away, in order to retrieve a document that we'd forgotten to get from the lady who helped us. It was like forgetting the ring. Exciting! I didn't have to worry about the ring because we still had the cereal-box one from Tokyo. As I ran back I clutched it in my pocket. Elin had taken it off earlier on the way up the elevator. Planning. I went back as fast as I could because my poor bride was standing alone at the altar waiting for me—sort of. Actually she was sitting on a wooden bench, reading the morning paper. To me my errand was heroic and urgent. I returned panting with the certificate. The kindly civil servant apologized for having made me get it, took the document in hand, asked us to please wait and disappeared into the maze of desks and partitions. The young secretaries looked at us, smiling shyly and with romantic innocence in their eyes.

After about thirty minutes, the man returned with the wedding certificate. It was written in attractive kanji and had a square red seal stamped on it. The paper was beige with a design of light brown leaves and grasses around the border. It was the large size as we had requested, about the same as legal paper, only wider. We admired it with him. After paying a fee of three thousand yen, we thanked him for his kind help and departed to smiles and calls of congratulations, "Omedetō gozaimasu!"

We returned to the consulate, where Elin had her name changed in her passport and we received a document in English translating the Japanese marriage license and certifying the legal union of us truly. That's where the paper chase ended.

"Yiperoo!" said Elin.

There was an Arby's across the street from the consulate. We had a wedding feast there of barbecue sandwiches with french fries and milk shakes. We were in high spirits. And the ring, oh yes, we had forgotten the ring after all. I pulled it out of my pocket.

Elin put her hands in mine. "Which finger does it go on?"

"You don't know what finger it goes on?"

"Well it's the fourth finger of either the right or left hand, but I'm not sure which," she said. Reading my expression she added, "Well you know, I've never been the sort to study *Bride Magazine*."

I started to say something unnecessary but she cut me off. "Shut up and put it on the right finger, the, uh, correct finger," she said sweetly. We kissed as the french fries cooled beneath our noses.

UNDER THE BEAMS

HŌGOJI, MAY 9, 1988

At Hōgoji we rise at three-thirty, put our bedding away and go wash our faces—except on *shiku-nichi*, the "four-and-nine day," when we get up an hour later. Washing the face is not an optional part of the schedule. On my second morning I didn't do it and Jakushin asked me after breakfast why I had skipped face-washing. I said there was no good reason and that's when I learned it's part of the collective morning regimen. That part of temple practice had never been passed on to us quite as strictly at Zen Center, possibly because of the less centralized layout of the modern plumbing. After that admonition I always went right out to the lantern-lit long sink, splashed my face and brushed my teeth with the guys. On the next day Jakushin pulled me aside and told me not to go to the sink only in my kimono, that since it was a morning practice, I should wear my *koromo*, the more formal robe, as well. I had thought it was a rule *not* to wear the koromo to the sink, but then I realized that the difference was that in the States the sinks are next to a toilet and in Japan they're separate. Two rules had collided and I'd never known it: wear koromo to wash the face and take it off in the toilet area. When Jakushin instructs me like that I say, "Hai!" like a good boy. Now and then he continued to point out slight infractions to me and that was how we knew each other.

We spend about an hour and a half sitting in the zendo in the morning and from one to three hours at night. At no other *dōjō*, or practice place, that I've been in could the word "about" be used in that way. Everywhere else it's definite. But at Hōgoji the times aren't exact because the timing is based on the rising and setting of the sun. Morning zazen ends when the sky starts to get light and the bonsho announces the sunrise. Some Catholic monasteries expand and contract their times of practice in accordance with the length of the days. The monks get more sleep in the winter that way. At Hōgoji the zazen periods are longer than the forty minutes I'm used to, but one may get up at will to go to the toilet or to do *kinhin*, walking zazen, outside the zendo. I'm not sure how the wake-up time was traditionally determined, but I imagine incense was used. These days we throw away tradition cavalierly and use alarm clocks.

The zendo is a narrow room at one end of the hatto, separated from the main room by removable *fusuma*. There's no action in there except walking in, sitting down, swaying from side to side, putting one's hands together palms up, sitting up straight with the eyes half open, breathing, and then, after a long while, the preceding actions in reverse. The zendo is deeper than it is wide and we sit facing the wall on either side. There's an altar at the end with a three-foot-high seated wooden statue of Daigyo Zenji, the founder of Hōgoji. The names of many deceased monks and lay people are written on small plaques that are placed all around this altar.

The zendo is the heart of the temple. It means Zen room. I was showing a couple of high school girls the zendo at Tassajara once and one of them asked what's so Zen about it and I said, "Well, it's where we sit zazen, and Zen means zazen." It comes from the Sanskrit, *dhyāna*, which is "right meditation." The word originally meant "trance." Zen is the sect that emphasizes dhyana, especially cross-legged sitting. When the Buddha is reputed to have attained enlightenment sitting under the bodhi tree, he was practicing dhyana. According to Zen he was practicing the "new" dhyana: nonobjectifying, nongrasping awakeness in all postures.

So she asked is it more Zen than any other place and I had to agree that it was no more "Zen" than any other room or anything else. So, as we are striving to bring our zazen into every aspect of our daily lives, each room at Hōgoji is the heart of the temple when one is there.

Sitting zazen for hours a day may seem like a lot of nothing when there's so much to do, but it's the Buddhist treasure hunt and the reason we keep still in this search is that the treasure is supposedly always right here just waiting for us to find it. Suzuki, my old teacher, once said we find our treasure by watching and waiting. Gary Snyder, a teacher of Buddhist hunters who prowls the Sierra Nevadas in California, has suggested that hunting is one of the experiential origins of meditation. Indeed, throughout human history hunters have had to sit and wait motionless, even for days at a time. And Dutchananda, another sportsman on the track of this timeless snark, once pointed out that *marga* ("the Way," "path" in Sanskrit) is not a regular old trail or street, but is a word that originally meant the hunter's path. The course is unknown ahead of time to the hunter, who must sniff and look for signs and watch and wait.

We move silently through the morning schedule together. I have been surprised at the lack of authoritarianism and bravado in these structured and peaceful hours, or at any time. I'm pleased that there's no *kyōsaku*, the stick for striking sleepy sitters on the shoulder with a loud whack. I've heard of very few other zendo in Japan without it. If the stick is used it's counterproductive to fight it—you sure won't get any support from teachers, who'll just say don't discriminate! just sit! Zen is famous for the stick. It's the first thing most Japanese people refer to if the subject of practicing Zen comes up, the stick and the pain of sitting so much in the lotus position. Most of the locals I talk to seem to respect Zen practitioners only because of the pain and hardship they endure, not because they find anything wonderful or help others to find it. There doesn't seem to be an idea of Buddhism helping anyone or offering anything accessible to the average person in terms of daily practice. Buddha must be rolling over in his stupas.

Further down from the zendo there is another altar in a small room that is used for special services. The focal point of that room is a bigger than life, standing Medicine Buddha with a wonderful soft countenance.

Next to this statue is the *taiko*, a large drum on a stand. It's a big hollowed-out round piece of wood over two and a half feet wide and three feet long, with tight leather heads at each end, one of the few animal products in the temple. There are large brass rings hanging down from the side. The taiko is hit with two broom-handle-sized foot-long strikers with rounded ends. It's used in ceremonies, to call us to work and at the beginning and end of the morning zazen and at the end of evening zazen in contrapuntal conjunction with the big bell and the thick, resonant block of wood, the *han*, which also hangs outside. The end product of these sounds is to tell us how many quarters past what hour it is. We don't really need to know the time but it's a pleasing tradition—and my favorite song.

I remember at Tassajara once talking to a classical composer and musicologist named Lou Harrison. I apologized to him for the lack of music there and for the fact that there was even a rule against having musical instruments. "Nonsense!" he said. "This place is full of music. You have all the musical instruments and music you need. I hear your bells, that thick hanging board and the drum going from morning to night. There's a lot of space in your music but it's all you need."

After zazen there are various services, the main one being in the hatto and lasting about an hour. It would take a long time to get all these tongue twisters down, but Norman has done it admirably. I know the basic material, the Heart Sutra, the Dai Hi Shin Dharani, the Sandōkai and others. But there are also some long unfamiliar humdingers. I can't even follow them with my romanized sutra books. I do the best I can, mumbling similar deep syllables till it's over, and every day I learn a little more.

As much as I enjoy the consonance of group practice in these halls, I relish tiptoeing around alone in the dark after everyone's asleep—especially if moonlight is coming in through the windows. It's like being in an old shadowy, magic museum. Sometimes I stand by the drum looking at the Medicine Buddha, enchanted in his shadow, and listening to the long empty space between the last evening and first morning drum beats.

The *tōsu*, toilet area, is off the covered walkway from the hatto and past the hanging han. *Tōsu* means "east room" because that is the position where it was originally located, in a rigidly structured temple layout. However, the *tōsu* have been located on the west side for about the last thousand years or so. They just haven't gotten around to changing the name yet. We may have lots of specialized terminology, but the toilets are just regular squatters —outhouses just off the deck. But they are clean and don't smell, because they have vent pipes. Between them is an exposed urinal. So far, about half the time when I use it, I turn around, start to walk out and bang my head on a low beam. I may curse, standing throbbing in front of the toilet altar as I bow out.

That is not the only place I bang my head, either. There are a lot of low beams around here. After a year in these environs Norman still has periodic nasty run-ins with beams. When that happens, his very worst thoughts about cultural differences surface, sometimes augmented with particularly colorful language.

As a painful-looking lump on his head appeared to visibly swell, I overheard him telling Shuko through clenched teeth that he was of a mind to go get a chain saw and take some of those beams out. Shuko suggested that if he were more mindful, he wouldn't hit his head, adding that those beams were his teachers.

I could hear Norman's blood pressure rise. "Maybe they should be lowered then to *your* head level so they can be *your* teachers." He asked Shuko if the new buildings that were being planned for Hōgoji were going to have more clearance.

Shuko said they would be traditional, like the practice.

"But this is supposed to be an international monastery," Norman countered. "How can it be international if the height of foreigners isn't considered?"

"The practice will be for foreigners as well as Japanese." said Shuko.

"But this is going to be your temple someday," continued Norman, "Don't you even want to try?"

Shuko didn't say anything.

Norman went on, his voice was rising. "You won't say anything because you'd rather that generations of gaijin—outsiders, went around banging their heads rather than your having to disagree in any way or make any waves with . . . with whoever's deciding these things."

"Japanese are getting taller too," said Shuko. "They will also have to be mindful."

"Do you want a temple or an obstacle course?"

"I don't know what that is," Shuko said softly.

Norman opened his mouth and lifted a finger. But before a word came out, he must have thought better of it for he paused with a quizzical look on his face. "Oh, of course, I see. How stupid of me," he said and walked off.

At the afternoon tea I presented a sketch to all. Although it revealed a decided lack of artistic talent, it was nevertheless well received. It was a rough draft of what I predicted would become the first official addition to Soto Zen monks' garb since the wristwatch. It showed a tall monk walking toward a low beam. Protruding forward from a headband were two antennae that perceived the approaching beam and sent an unobtrusive vibration to a wire in the headband, thus alerting the monk. After evening zazen I ended up with Koji in his tea house intently discussing the appropriate name for this revolutionary apparatus. The English name would be "Beam Alert." Koji, I think, had never encountered anything so bizarre in his life. He participated in that silliness though, with the same gung-ho energy that he brought to every temple activity, and there was even an added enthusiasm as one might find in a child playing a new game. This was the beginning of our friendship.

Japanese Buddhism must be the most togetherness-oriented religious practice in the world. Soaking in the bath is about the only part of the schedule that one does alone at Hōgoji and I was surely not alone in treasuring that private pleasure in the company of candlelight and the smoke of incense. It is only during bath time at the end of the day that Hōgoji is truly a "monastery"—a place for monks to be *monos*, solitary.

The ofuro is a small room with blackened board walls. There are stretched plastic windows by the tub through which one can see the cast of trees on the hillside and hear a choir of birds that sings in those trees. There's a big light blue plastic garbage can full of cold water next to the tub that's there to help cool it down if it gets too hot or if one wishes to douse and invigorate oneself. There are brushes, a loofah, soap and little wooden buckets to pour rinse water with before entering the bath. There is a small round wooden platform thoughtfully placed on the bottom of the iron tub so you don't burn the bottoms of your feet. The fire is right below, stoked with wood from the outside. The tub itself is an old iron pot that is set on an elevated cement surface and is just barely big enough to squat in. No one can ever quite believe that I fit into it.

I remember that first bath at Hōgoji. I was watching an ant crawl out of a crack in a huge old stump in the courtyard when a monk came up to me and said "bath" in English. I asked if he was Maku and he said "Hai," and stood there as if waiting for another question. I couldn't think of any other questions so I thanked him and started off for the . . . I turned around. He hadn't moved.

"Could you tell me where the bath is please?" I said in English. Since he'd spoken to me in English first I thought it only polite. It seemed he wasn't sure what I'd said to him so I repeated it in Japanese. He started walking toward the kuin steps. We walked around on the deck to the right, past the *tōsu* and through the back door of the building. In the bathroom he gave me an orientation by pointing at objects, handing me a tiny towel, showing me where to hang it when I'm through, where to light incense, and he indicated where and how I should bow, doing a pantomime of the steps I should go through. I felt like I'd received instruction in bath procedures from Harpo Marx.

After I'd cleaned myself, I entered the minuscule tub and scalding water—as hot as I could take it. The iron was so hot I had to squirm into the most compact and precise still position so as not to touch the menacing side. Precarious, yes, but I savored that solitary period, my thoughts drifting to the large plunges of the hot tubs of Tassajara, in contrast to this pot. The bath is a place for zazen, "second only to the zendo," said Suzuki. While cooking there in the Hōgoji water I dutifully returned my attention to the flickering room and my breath in the cauldron. I soaked till I forgot where I was and thus was I baptized at Hōgoji, distinct from any immersion I'd had before.

All the burnable trash plus twigs and branches gathered from the temple grounds are used to make the bath water hot. The first time it was my turn to make the fire and keep it going, I noticed that there was a lot of plastic in with the paper, cardboard and wood. Norman and Shuko were nearby raking leaves up behind the kitchen and I called them over for a consultation. "Do you burn plastic here?" I asked.

Shuko immediately responded, "No, it goes in with the unburnable trash."

"Oh good," I responded with relief. "I'll separate out this stuff."

He looked down. "No, you can burn that."

I stopped to think and in the pause, Norman broke in. "Why do you say we don't burn plastic here?" he asked pointedly.

"We don't," said Shuko.

"What do you call that?" he said, pointing to the plastic bags and wrappers in the cardboard box.

"Well that's not much," said Shuko.

"What do you mean it's not much? It's plastic."

"Yeah, but it's not big—it's not thick plastic. It's burnable."

Norman countered, "You said we don't burn plastic. We do. Here it is. Admit it."

"We don't burn hard plastic containers that make that thick, strong-smelling smoke," Shuko said.

"Admit it," said Norman, raising his voice.

Shuko looked down in the box. "Well, that's like cellophane."

"It's plastic."

"Don't worry about it, that's how it's done here. Everybody burns some of this paper-thin stuff."

"Yeah, but you should stop. It poisons the air," Norman answered.

"Oh, is that so?"

"I've told you a million times."

Shuko was unmoved. "Industry here doesn't pollute as much as in America and there aren't so many cars so maybe it's more important that you don't burn plastic in America."

"This is a global problem," Norman said grinding his teeth on the word global and dragging out the *o*.

"You have a lot of acid rain there," Shuko continued. "You're destroying all those lakes and everything, it's terrible."

"Shuko, it doesn't matter where you are. I agree it's terrible —acid rain in America—but two wrongs don't . . ."

"You should clean up your smokestacks," Shuko added.

"And Japanese factories are polluting the air all over Southeast Asia," Norman countered, quickly adding, "but that's not the point. We should just do our best here—now."

"The air here is very fresh, burning this won't make it dirty," Shuko observed.

"You are being stubborn," said Norman. "And you are being passive aggressive as usual."

"I don't mean to be," said Shuko, disappointed by Norman's inability to understand his point of view.

Afterwards, when we were alone together, Norman said he'd given up on this solid waste management issue a year or so before and should have known better than to have butted into the conversation. He said that in the past he'd talked to everyone about it and that they'd all nodded and seemed to agree. He'd thought the matter was taken care of, but the very next day there was the aroma of burning plastic in the air. Norman was surprised to find that nothing had changed. He said it was a very slippery situation with the monks continuing to agree and act concerned while never changing their routine in the slightest.

The addition of yours truly had reawakened his environmentalist zeal. He and I decided to take matters into our own hands. Every day we dutifully sorted out the plastic from the paper and saw that it was included with the other, bigger unburnable stuff that got buried. It worked pretty well, but sometimes someone else would notice a plastic wrapping or bag in the unburnable trash and pull it out and burn it with the paper and cardboard like it was "supposed to be."

ŌRYŌKI THE TRUE WAY

HŌGOJI, APRIL 30, 1988

Breakfast at Hōgoji is formal, and calls for the use of *ōryōki*, the cloth-wrapped nested set of black lacquered monks' bowls and utensils. This daily meal ceremony was the precursor of the Japanese tea ceremony. Every motion is prescribed.

It's the last thing that my friends back in Texas would have imagined me doing with large chunks of my life. It's nothing I would have volunteered for. But it's part of the Japanese Zen package, a very important part to the Soto Zen teachers I've known. They would feel naked without it in monastic life. The largest Tibetan Buddhist group in the States took up the practice. I must admit that I look back warmly on many years of oryoki use.

It's not your chow-down approach to dining. I think John

Madden would not appreciate it if he caught us eating in formal oryoki style at a tailgate party outside Candlestick stadium. Neither is it the austere eating style used in some Catholic monasteries where scripture is read during meals because, it seems, the monks aren't supposed to enjoy the food—the meal shouldn't distract them from their prayers. A Catholic monastic told me Saint Francis had a weight problem and felt he was too greedy, so he threw ashes on his food. The use of oryoki, on the contrary, intensifies the experience of eating. It zooms one in on the victuals. In keeping with the teaching of just sitting, just working and all, the oryoki encourages us neither to jump at the meal nor to deny it. Just eat it and just enjoy it.

During meals, chants are the only vocalizing and we don't chant with food in our mouths. Eating silently is a pleasure. Suzuki used to say we could talk or we could eat but that we couldn't do both at the same time, and indeed I have noticed that conversation covers a meal so that the act of eating becomes automatic and the taste of the food is lost. When Suzuki and his students ate together informally on a shopping trip or a picnic, there would sometimes be a tense silence with each of us trying *so hard* to "just eat." He would often ask someone a question and get a little talk going and thus nudge us to relax and be natural. Ah, this path of just doing things naturally can be so full of unnaturalness, overdoing and inappropriate application of methods. What humorous dolts we are. It seems upon close scrutiny that our way, all of us, teachers and students alike, is to just bungle along together.

Oryoki, on the other hand, is the ultimate in grace and economy. The outer piece of fabric that wraps around the set of bowls functions as a tablecloth and there is a folded napkin that goes on the lap. The bowls are set out carefully on the first cloth. Oryoki achieves the pinnacle in water conservation as the bowls are washed at the end of the meal, with part of the wash water being drunk and the rest ceremoniously collected in buckets. And the water from those buckets is collected and poured on the garden. There are a wooden spoon and hashi that come in a cotton envelope with an implement called a *setsu* that looks like a tongue depressor with a swab at the end, with which the bowls are cleaned after the meal. All the implements are lacquered wood. There's even a cute little bowl-drying cloth. Everything has a special name. It's sort of like a toy tea set.

Nishiki is considered to be the world's leading authority on oryoki and various other details of Soto Zen monastic life. There seems to be a certain amount of pride around Nishiki's temples in being a part of a monastic system that continues that original true way of doing these things. I have heard Koji openly scoff at the prestigious Soto Zen training temples of Eiheiji and Sōjiji, which have strayed from the "correct" oryoki path. Norman looks down on such petty distinctions: "Like they tie their knot a little different and stuff like that."

Dōgen, the founder of Japanese Soto Zen, wrote a treatise on just exactly how to do it. He left a lot of tracts on how to do this or that just right in the monastic life. How to get up, wash, clean the teeth, dress, walk, study, wear your robes, make meals, greet senior or junior monks, you name it, he told exactly how to do it. It was all part of his way of *menmitsu-no-kafū*, or extremely careful attention to the minute details of daily life.

There was a visiting roshi at Tassajara a long time ago while Suzuki was still alive who gave two-hour talks every night on all that minutiae. Some of us called him Bulldog Roshi. He was a complete menmitsu-no-kafū freak. He had been the *ino* of Eiheiji for thirteen years. That means he was in charge of discipline and ceremony. We all just wanted to sit zazen with a reasonable mix of ceremony, lectures and work, but this guy OD'd us on Dōgen's details till they were running out of our ears. It was like being trapped in the Amy Vanderbilt school of etiquette by an anal retentive who had a messiah complex and it caused a great deal of resentment.

At Tassajara when someone got too finicky about following Dōgen's way, someone else might roll their eyes and say, "Nine clay balls." That referred to Dōgen's instructions as to how the monks should wipe their asses. Katagiri said that when he was at Eiheiji he tried to do everything just right and even practiced "nine clay balls." He said he was the only one to do it, perhaps for centuries. He never did explain to me exactly what that practice entails. But he did tell me that the only essential practice of Zen is zazen. Dōgen said the same thing.

To be fair to Dōgen, he probably did develop a communal monastic way that was as aesthetic and refined as anything ever could be and it certainly has given lots of monks a harmonious, simple, graceful form to follow that was so involving that there was less room for petty thoughts and almost no time to get into trouble. It extended the *samādhi* of zazen into every aspect of their lives. In that sort of practice, there is nothing personal left and not much room for choice. It's the Dōgen dance and he indicated that the only way to do it is to do it completely. I'm certain that it has helped many people to find their treasure and it has surely produced many fine temple priests. But to those who can't just take it and leave it, sometimes it seems that what Dōgen is saying is that if you don't do this particular practice just like this, then you will likely be born in ghostly realms for a virtual eternity with the same chance of running into the One True Path as Voyager has of hitting a dime floating out past Neptune.

I was eating with oryoki for the first time in years, and after a breakfast of bungling and holding the group up (there's a teamwork aspect), Katagiri suggested that I take a refresher course from Shuko. Shuko went over the whole procedure with me in the study while Maku and Norman were washing the dishes. Koji stayed and watched.

Shuko reminded me that the first bite should be from the big bowl, Buddha's bowl, which usually contained rice. And then every second bite should be from that bowl.

"Oh Shuko, I was taught that at Tassajara long ago," I said,

"I wouldn't do it any other way." He didn't look impressed. Oops, I'm just supposed to listen.

Shuko was showing me the proper way to put the offering to the spirits on the tip of the setsu and I said, "Oh wow, that's new to me. At Tassajara we do it like this," and I showed him.

He smiled and gently reproved me, saying that Dōgen originally taught this particular method and it's the way he intended for his monks to do it. Koji agreed, nodding and grunting seriously.

Just then Norman stuck his head out from the dishwashing area and said, "Yeah, Shuko, but that was a long time ago. Anyway, haven't you heard? Dōgen's dead."

Shuko forced a slight smile that didn't hide his irritation. Maku was looking on bewildered and Koji glanced at me for translation so I obliged him, but that didn't increase mutual understanding. Koji looked back at Norman, and Maku dried a soup pot.

Shuko continued the lesson until he heard my stifled laughter. Norman came out saying, "What's so funny, David?"

Shuko sighed, for he couldn't control us. Ever since Bodhidharma, the first patriarch of China, said that nothing's holy, there's been an opening for an occasional pie in Buddha's face.

"I'm sorry. I remembered something from when I was ten years old and couldn't help but laugh."

"What?" said Koji.

"We should continue with the oryoki instruction," said Shuko.

"Hey, Shuko," Norman broke in, "Koji's the head monk. Don't impose your will on him. And I want to hear too."

Shuko froze and looked down. Koji looked on with interest.

"Well, friends used to spend the night with me a lot. If they were new to my house and didn't know my mother, they wouldn't be at ease and would try to act proper and make a good impression. My mother is unjudgmental and doesn't mind a little zany cutting up. But they wouldn't know it, especially since she's quiet and dignified. It was a perfect setup. On the first occasion that my friend Jim was over, we were eating breakfast cereal with milk out of big bowls as kids in the States frequently do. Asking if we wanted anything else, Mother hovered over the table where Jim sat self-consciously watching his p's and q's. Catching his attention with a 'Hey Jim!' I plunged my face into the milk and cereal."

Norman laughed loudly. Shuko was pale.

"It completely blew the kid's mind." I looked at Shuko. "I guess it was a little sophomoric, wasn't it?" He didn't understand.

"What did your mother do?" asked Norman.

"She just laughed and said 'Oh David!' As long as I didn't leave her a mess, she didn't care."

My Japanese dharma brothers were mute, their worst fears of American barbarian character having been attested to. "My question is," I looked at them sincerely and placed my hands around the large oryoki bowl, "how would Dōgen have me do that?" Koji was wide-eyed, on system overload. Shuko was trying to maintain dignity. I looked Koji in the eye with a sincerity that I reached to find and he put his head down on the table in his arms. Shuko kept a neutral glazed look.

Norman came over and nudged Shuko. "And food fights, Shuko, how did Dōgen lay that one out?"

The lesson was over with, the holy sacraments shattered. Shuko went back to his room, Norman and Maku to the kitchen cleanup. I picked up Koji and helped him back to his cabin. As we passed Katagiri's room, he was looking through an opening in his shoji and smiling like he was wondering what just happened. In this and many ways, trying to follow Dōgen's supreme and detailed path has guided and informed us.

REMEDIAL BREATHING

MARUYAMA, FEBRUARY 2, 1989

It's a little warmer today than usual. There was no ice in the mizo or on the pond. I knew as soon as I got up that there was a thick cloud-cover way up in the sky. But even on a bitter cold day when being still inside the temple buildings is like being stuck in a walk-in freezer, a toasty glow generates inside me. I sit zazen in the back of the room where we wait our turn to see Hōjō-san. It's a comfortable place to sit, darker and more anonymous than the zendo and there's no one walking softly and carrying a big stick. The silence is periodically broken by the ringing of bells, feet on the tatami, the squeaking of the shoji opening and closing, a spoon hitting the side of a pot in the kitchen and shouts of zealous monks coming from the sanzen room.

Hōjō-san's little handbell rings with its distinctive tinniness. The sound triggers the next in line to twice strike the here-I-come-bell, which is an eight-inch miniature of the big bells that hang outside temples in their own towers. It's suspended from a foot-high scaffolding and is struck with a wooden mallet like a tiny tack hammer that will soon be replaced because it'll break from constant and emphatic use. People hit this bell in quite different ways, some very hard and some softly, some nervous, others bright. I wait till the tone of Watanabe's bell has ended. Jessica is Miss Gung Ho. This woman has been over here for twenty years and she's still an exemplary eager beaver. She's what every teacher must dream of. She's leaning over waiting with a hair trigger on the mallet. I'm sitting thirty feet away and I can almost see her hand move before the sound of Watanabe's bell reaches me. The light's hardly turned green and she's off down the corridor to get the big E.

When it's my turn to walk down the covered walkway to see Watanabe, I hold my hands in gassho, my feet bare on the wooden deck that leads to the building where he waits. I take a look at the small mossy garden to the left and note the increase in light as spring approaches. I stand and wait for Jessica to come out. When she does we bow to each other without eye contact, then I step inside the building and prostrate myself outside the sanzen room.

When I get in front of Hōjō-san, he is sitting like a pyramid, waiting and breathing in a low rumble. It's not asthma, this is his breathing yoga. Sometimes when I come in he'll be chanting softly. Other times he nods off between interviews—alertly sleeping, maybe like a soldier, still ready to respond instantly. I make a standing bow and walk forward a few steps in the semidarkness illuminated only by the candle on the altar behind him in the corner. There's a string with a bead at the bottom hanging down from a round paper lantern and I always consider it part of the ritual to barely brush it past the side of my head just above my right ear on the way down to a prostration. I come up from this bow on my knees, pull myself forward a few inches, and sit in seiza a couple of feet in front of Watanabe's knees. A thin trail of incense often floats between us. He sits firmly, at home with himself, a foot-long carved teacher's stick held at each end in fists that vibrate on the thighs under his light grey robes. This stick is the *nyoi* (not to be confused with *nyōi*, which means "urge to urinate"). It's slightly curved in as the lower back should be in zazen and on the end is a carved mushroom representing wisdom. His black eyebrows and eyelashes are the only hair I can see and the lids leave a sliver for the window of his eyes. It's no-nonsense time.

At first he observes my breathing, my *susoku-kan*. After a few breaths he lets out a guttural "Hai!" which means "yes," "okay," "got you," "roger." When he says it he grips his teacher's stick and the energy he puts into it causes him to launch off his cushion a tad. Today he says nothing and just demonstrates his long, steady, rumbling breathing. Sometimes he will ask me a question or tell me something and I will struggle to understand and respond. There's a lot happening between the words, that's the heart of these meetings.

He rings his bell, black metal and shaped like a donut. It's over. I stand, bow deeply, and back up with my hands in gassho past that dangling cord, feeling it graze my right temple.

On the deck I pass young, thin Den-san on her way in without her red-tipped cane. As I go through the waiting room I can barely see in the dim light the photos of past abbots of Daianji hanging on the wall, a bunch of tough-looking cookies.

This morning when I step outdoors, it is still dark and cloudy. Walking on the stone path amidst the temple buildings after sanzen, I feel a sense of place, as though I could die in this spot with the old tile roofs I love.

I reflect on the sanzen and get a pleasant rush, a sense of immediacy. "That's why I'm here," I say out loud and walk on down the stone path. An old man chanting in front of the hondo turns and looks at me.

BEANING THE SPIRITS

MARUYAMA, FEBRUARY 3, 1989

Oni wa soto (Devils out)!" we shouted resolutely as we tossed small handfuls of roasted soybeans into the garden in front of our house. "Fuku wa uchi (Good fortune inside)!" we cried as we scattered the beans around the house. We took turns. I did the living room and Elin did the kitchen. I threw them over our bed and she splattered the closet room. I got the entranceway and our study and she did her classroom. Then, to make sure, we covered the storeroom, toilet, bathroom, laundry area and hall. Previously we had counted out and placed in teacups roasted soybeans equal in number to our ages. These we ate in a ceremonial more than a gustatorial manner. They were dry and crunchy. Thus we completed our Setsubun (season-dividing) ceremony. For tomorrow is Risshun (spring stands), February 4, the first day of spring according to the Japanese lunar calendar. It's also the first day of the lunar year. Convenience stores stock clear plastic bags filled with soy beans and cardboard devil masks that parents give to kids.

We did the ceremony at home after having been instructed in detail by Okamura-san, the kind old housewife next door. Earlier in the day I had called up my student Kubo-san and grilled her about it. I like to call her because she's talkative and it's challenging Japanese practice. But her husband was coming home that night as he does once or twice a week and so she was frantically cleaning the house and getting ready to go pick him up at the train station. We agreed to pursue the topic at the MMC, the Monday Morning Class.

Having expunged the undesirable spirits and invited all that brings favor, Elin and I made some black tea with milk, tidied up the kitchen and moved into the study with our new computerized kerosene fan heater. Soon it was blowing warm air into the cold room. As soon as the heater turned off the heat would disappear through the uninsulated floor, ceiling and walls and the heater would turn right back on again. There I studied Japanese and Elin sewed a few buttons for me before she went off to team teach with her friend Hashimoto-san. Periodically we stopped to kiss and say a few sweet things and already I could feel the benefit of our unusual morning ceremony. A little time spent encouraging goodness and light is always worth the try. It's not totally distinct from budgeting or exercise. Later I will dance with the devils— until I do they will hide at the edge of our garden, waiting for moments of weakness and confusion.

I asked a couple of high school kids who came to study English with me about Setsubun but they didn't know anything and were even less interested. "Louise" (we give them English names for class use) did say she was pretty sure we were supposed to have waited until nighttime for our ceremony. They thought we were weird for having anything to do with it. It was hard to tell because they were inexpressive like almost all the kids get after they enter junior high. Except when "George" came in, he stepped on a soybean, and, looking down, he said, "Ah, mamemaki (scattered bean)."

The next Monday morning the MMC met as always in our living room, which was never intended to be a guest room because you have to walk through the kitchen to get there, a shocking tradition-breaker. On the far end are shoji doors, and a few feet beyond are sliding glass doors that lead to our garden. The curtains were closed on the glass doors and the shoji were shut tight because it was a cold winter day—a cold winter day in which we discussed the earliest beginnings of spring. Six of us sat on cushioned rattan furniture around a matching glass-topped table, all the legs set in rubber casters so as not to harm the tatami. The cushions are of a leaf-vein design and the rattan is dark brown. I always sit in the high-backed rocker and Mr. Shimizu in the non-rocking chair. Three ladies sat on the couch and the fourth, Etsuko-san, on a chair from the kitchen. The gas heater was going strong and burning clean. I asked them about Setsubun.

I was surprised that Shimizu didn't know much about it since he's my age and seems to know so much about everything. He was dressed in his pressed and spotless brown work jumpsuit with the name of his liquor store on his breast pocket: SUPIRITSU MARUTO (Spirits Mart). His face is smooth and expressive, his eyes always bright. "Yes, tell me about scattering roasted soy beans," he said to the others in careful and correct English. "We don't do such a thing at our home."

Kubo said that it's fun for little kids, but ever since hers were ten years old she's forgotten about Setsubun entirely. When I phoned her earlier, it had reminded her that her son was trying to get into a good private school and she had better do all she could to help him out.

"So I went out and bought roasted soy beans and we scattered them and wished for good fortune and ate some. I had better not to take . . . er uh . . . any chance because my son likes to play at sports and he's not so sure like my daughter to be successful in his studies." I watched her intently while she spoke. She is so animated, always smiling to some degree, her large mouth opening wide, exposing her tongue and big white teeth. And when she's saying something that might be embarrassing, she laughs nervously and talks faster.

She caused some discussion among the class members when she said that the number of beans one eats should be equivalent to one's age plus one. The others said that they didn't know about this extra bean. Finally it was agreed that both ways were okay. The reason for the extra bean was that ages were computed differently prior to World War II. Before then a person was considered one year old at birth.

Bespectacled Morikawa-san, the intellectual, slightly plump and outspoken professor's wife in her late fifties, said there's a woman who lives in one of the university houses who skewers a sardine head on a holly branch in front of her place on the first day of the lunar spring and changes it exactly a year later. The other ladies went "Ehhhhhh?" together in rising pitch.

"I never heard so," said Mr. Shimizu.

I wondered how the sardine could still be there after a year.

"I do not know why she does it. Maybe it's tradition," said Mrs. Morikawa.

"The smell is to get away the devils," said Kubo and they ehed and ahed some more and we exchanged other details about the lunar spring, seasonal words for use in letters and poems and other fascinating tidbits.

To get my classes talking, I simply ask them about Japan—it's what they know and what they like to talk about. It's an endless subject, a complex sport and a lifetime hobby. But they were getting too excited and were beginning to lapse into the natural tongue for such discussions when I curtailed them with "English! Speak English!" They started giggling and slowed down enough for me to insert a question. "Why does the traditional spring start in the middle of winter?"

"It is sakidori," Shimizu said. "It is very important word to Japanese. It means to feel the season early before the real season. It is also used in haiku and tanka poetry." He then drew a circle representing the year and showed how the traditional seasons all started six weeks earlier than the modern ones.

Bright young Etsuko-san, the only unmarried MMC member, mentioned how, as an elementary school teacher, she keeps up with seasonal events, making costumes with the kids and acting out myths.

Middle-aged Tanahashi-san, always so delicate and gentle, told about her two girls of eight and ten who eagerly look forward to throwing the roasted soy beans on the night of Setsubun. She said they wore masks they made in school and that they ran around the garden being little devils while their parents threw beans at them and shouted: "Devils out!" And then the parents took their turn with the masks and the kids threw beans at them. As she talked I watched her and listened to the soft tremble in her high, feminine voice.

"These ceremonies are for children," she said, "and teach them about seasons and are because we treasure children." I loved the thought of her passing on her tenderness and the mysteries of the seasons to her daughters. And, as much as Japanese people complain to me about how their culture is dying, I sensed this transmission extending in all directions.

CREEPIN' *MUKADE*!

MARUYAMA, FEBRUARY 9, 1989

There are eight plastic containers sitting on the flat stones where our gate would be if we had one. We don't because the bamboo gate that was there when we arrived was so dilapidated that I tore it out on our first day and took it over to the temple to be burned. Soon the nearby *gasu sutāndo*, gas station, will send someone here to fill those containers with kerosene. Each one is about twenty liters, like a five-gallon gas can. Four of them are new blue. We bought those at the local *hōmu sutōru*. Four of them are dirty red. They're old and we got them on *sodai gomi* day. I had to tape up some of their screw-on lids because they were busted and I didn't want water to get in.

I remember the morning I brought the old containers over. Ishitaki-san was standing out front on the road talking to Seki-san, the giddy lady across the street. The two housewives watched me as I carried the four plastic containers into our garden. They were laughing at me half admiringly for getting something out of the trash.

"I don't think I would be seen doing such a thing as that," said Ishitaki in English. "People might say I was a beggar. I would have to sneak out to take them in the middle of the night when no one could see me." She translated it for Seki, who laughed in a high giggle.

"We're shameless," I answered in Japanese. "We love to rescue perfectly usable things out of the trash. And now we'll have eight of them."

"Why do you need eight?" asked Seki. "Four is enough. You can order more kerosene when you need it."

"That's more trouble for me and for the gas station," I answered. "Isn't it more convenient to get twice as much half as often?"

"But eight cans will cost twice as much as four," Seki countered. I looked at her puzzled.

"We Japanese prefer to buy things in smaller amounts more often," said Ishitaki in explanation, now speaking in Japanese. She turned to her friend. "In America they buy everything in large quantities. They buy one whole side of beef at a time." Seki laughed and laughed. The housewives around here tend to go shopping, do their laundry and clean house every day. I was perturbed at being laughed at for wanting to buy six weeks' worth of kerosene at a time and felt falsely accused of hoarding slabs of beef, but I knew I wasn't going to be able to set things straight with them. Whatever I said, Ishitaki would look at me smugly and Seki would just laugh at me more and say something to the effect of "Oh, you silly Americans!"

The delivery man arrived with a tank of kerosene in the back of a pickup and I heard him as he began filling the containers. I went out and greeted him and he greeted me and said thanks for our many kindnesses and I said why it's the other way around and we agreed on what a nice day it was. He was young, strong, thin, and eager to do the best job he could. Best of all, he wore white gloves. I picked up two containers, took them around to the back side of the house and returned for more. He got the fourth round before I could get to it and positioned them carefully. He handed me the bill, apologizing. Just under six thousand yen, about forty-five dollars. Not bad for six weeks' heating. I paid him, thanking him, and he thanked me energetically and I thanked him and we kept thanking each other until he'd driven off.

I stood in the sun on the driveway with my change and receipt in hand and watched an egret, wide wings closing and opening, zoom into and out of the moatlike mizo, running alongside the street in front of our house and the temple. The water in it was low—only an inch above the sludge. I looked for signs of life— only the algae. I peered into the bamboo grove. Nothing obvious. Keichitsu, which Mr. Shimizu from the MMC called "bug coming-out day," is in early March—not yet. But there was a stink bug on the cold floor the other day in the sanzen waiting room. I remember flicking it away with my third finger and putting it right side up later in the empty room as I walked by on my way out. There was a cockroach in our place. It was dying due to the carpets of boric acid spread in those dark, hidden areas under cabinets and the refrigerator. I bowed to it and apologized, squashed it in a paper towel and put it in the trash, saying, "Become a buddha."

Ah, approaching spring and birds and bugs. The ground will abound with the crawlers and the air will be alive again with flying insects. Up will go the screens. We will walk in the hills and stand in our garden and sit looking out from our tatami-floored living room. We'll look out through the open shoji on the new season, feeling its generous warmth and greeting its active little beings. I wish they were all as benign and beautiful as butterflies and dragonflies or as fascinating and admirable as the wasps and bees we defer to with respect, or as venerable as the spiders.

Oh, but I shudder to think of the *mukade*, the poisonous centipedes that appear on the walls and in the tub. Hōitsu Suzuki (the son of my original teacher) got bitten on the lip by one while he slept in Yaizu. He said it was extremely painful and his lip was badly swollen for four days. Morikawa from the MMC says that one morning when she woke up there was a giant mukade on the pillow next to her sleeping husband's face. One day when a tiny one crawled out from under our refrigerator, Ishitaki said smiling that where there's one baby there're ten.

I remember with a shiver of horror the last mukade of fall. Elin and I were sitting at the kitchen table studying. There was a little plop sound from the direction of a plastic bag a foot to my left. Upon investigation I discovered much to my dismay a mukade crawling on the bag. It must have fallen from the ceiling—it could have fallen on one of us.

The first few we encountered I caught and put outside. Elin noticed their tendency to come aggressively back toward us after being emptied from jars onto the ground. I can't stand to think about it. I hate to kill them but it's expected of you and I also don't want them to multiply in the immediate vicinity. So I put them in the tub and wash them down with scalding water and pity them and apologize and say, "Become a buddha!" just like they were cockroaches.

Glen, a student at Daianji, was sitting in the zendo one day with the regular group of twenty or so assorted men, women, monks and lay people. A mukade came down the board on the front edge of the tan, the raised platform that runs the length of each side of the room. These people are supposed to be sitting alertly with their eyes open. No one moved. I would have been on the ceiling. Glen saw it approach from the left and then he watched it turn right when it got to him. He let it crawl inside his robes. Is this the product of Zen training: a person who allows a poisonous centipede to get lost in his clothes? At the end of the period he went outside and shook it out but not before it had crawled up over his head and back down inside his robes. My life would have been over and he just shrugged.

Norman saw his first one while sitting zazen at Suienji. He didn't know what it was but he had time to study it. It was a light brown critter about four inches long with many little segments, a pair of legs for each segment and two black pincers in front. After the bell rang to end the period, he leaned over and in a whisper asked the monk next to him about it. The monk pulled him back so violently that they both fell off the raised tan. Then the monk got up and smashed it to a pulp with his sandal.

It seems almost everyone has a story. "George," the eleven-year-old student of mine who lives down the street, got bitten next to his eye while he slept. In the summer I look under our covers and all over the walls in our bedroom before I go to sleep. To me it is the black cloud within the silver lining of living by the peaceful woods on crime-free streets with thoughtful neighbors.

Taizen, the Texan monk at Daianji, had said, "Oh, mukade aren't so bad, but they don't let go. Once they've clamped down on you, it's hard to get them off." It reminded me of *The Treasure of the Sierra Madre*, in which Humphrey Bogart claimed that if a gila monster bites, you can cut off its body but the head stays clamped on till sunrise.

I see mukade out of the corner of my eye as I sit alone and read. I fear them on the floor and ceiling as I type. The other day I opened the door to the study and pictured the floor crawling with them and I wondered, am I going crazy? and I reached down and picked up a handful and held them up to take a good look and said no they are real. But then when I tried to shake them off I found no hand beneath but only squirming centipedes in the form of a hand becoming a body of centipedes becoming a mind of centipedes and I sat down on the spot and followed my breath and asked my psyche to protect me and all beings from the mukade, our least welcome neighbors.

KOJI, BOUND BY DUTY

It was break time and Koji and I found ourselves at it again. "Well come on man, come with me. Let's go. What's keeping you? I used to leave home with a nickel and come back two weeks later with a dime. Ready?" I leaned over and looked into Koji's eyes. He was so excited. He knew it was possible. He loved the idea but he couldn't do it. "Why not?" I pushed him. "Okay, forget being a wanderer. You could be a priest in America. That would be different. That would be an education. Where's your spirit of adventure? You'd learn a lot from them and they'd learn a lot from you. They'd learn more about working together and you'd learn more about being free. Come on." But his story was already written and he wouldn't even proofread it, much less attempt a rewrite.

"I am tied by duty," he said. And what a dutiful life he has led. At his father's poor country temple he'd get up early, sit zazen (unusual outside of training temples) and clean the place. After breakfast he'd work in the fields, do cabinet work in the afternoon and go to school at night, followed by judo class. Frequently he would give his father long massages before going to sleep. He attended the Soto Zen university for four years. Again he had a full schedule, sitting zazen in the morning and practicing karate at night. Then he went straight to Suienji and Hōgoji, where he has been practicing for four years.

"Diligent life, Koji," I said, "What a work ethic. You seem to enjoy it though. You're going to be a great priest."

"No, I won't, but it feels good to me," he said. "I envy you and I do not see a way to have freedom of movement like that. So I feel I must be as good a priest as I can, help others and find freedom of the heart."

"I want the same thing except I don't want to be a priest."

"Do you want to get married again?" he asked.

"I think so."

"To the lady in Georgia?"

"Uh, well, let's see if she writes first."

"Do you miss her?"

"Well, sort of, but it's so much fun being in Japan I haven't had time to miss her much. I might have to forget her. I don't know yet."

"I think you will have a love marriage," he sighed.

Years ago he'd promised a woman he'd marry her, and she was now thirty. If he didn't then she might very well never get married and he was afraid she might even kill herself. He just *had* to marry her and live with her and his parents in his father's temple and help his father out and do what was expected of him till it became his own temple. There was no way out—no honorable way out. I got a strong sense from him about what duty is and what they mean here when they say "tied by duty."

The more we talked the better my Japanese got. Koji said he wanted to learn English, so we agreed to do something about it. What this meant was that I studied Japanese and that sometimes we talked in Japanese about how he wanted to study English. We were in Japan—it was natural. Anyway, saying that you want to study English is one of the important set phrases of the Japanese.

One day after lunch I told Koji that I insisted that he study English for ten minutes a day and that his first lesson began now. Keep in mind that almost all Japanese people have studied English in junior and senior high and in college and so they've got a good foundation for it. But the method of study goes back to the Meiji era, when the objective was to read scientific and engineering manuals in order to catch up with the rest of the industrial world. To actually speak a word of it verged on the unpatriotic. The ancient and infamous translation method, abandoned in most of the known universe, tragically still has a stranglehold in Japan. The cruelty of this system is evident when they are called upon to speak English and can't. Reading is a different matter. Koji read *Of Human Bondage* in English while in college. Word by word. He said that his brother was an English teacher who couldn't speak any English although he read an English-language newspaper every day. He said that once some Westerners came to his brother's school and his brother sneaked out the back door and ran away terrified.

I started Koji off with a rather advanced lesson.

"Are you ready?" I asked.

"What?" he said in Japanese.

"Are you ready?" I repeated.

He sat up at attention.

"I want you to learn this sentence," I said, still in Japanese.

"Hai!" he said like a good boy ready to follow the master's instructions.

I recited the sentence to him. "Robert's lover, the rare rabbit robber, lowered Luther's Luger through the louver."

Silence. Ten seconds passed. Koji averted his eyes. "What was that?"

"Pay attention!" I said sternly in Japanese. "Now once more." He prepared himself, opening his mind as if for the very dharma of Buddha. I repeated the lesson. "Robert's lover, the rare rabbit robber, lowered Luther's Luger through the louver."

Another moment of silence. "They all sound the same," he said shaking his head.

"They are all different words."

"No. It can't be. I can't hear any difference."

"I think it's going to take some time for you to master the subtleties of speaking and hearing English."

"Say it again," he said intrigued.

We spent half an hour on that sentence and though he found it fascinating he never got it down. He said that I should open up a School of Torture English in Tokyo near the temple where he will be helping out when he goes home. I told him I'd consider it but that his fellow countrymen seem to be doing fine without my help.

Koji looked at his watch. There was a little time left before afternoon work. He made us some instant coffee, put sugar in his and we both added Creap, the popular nondairy creamer. After we'd half finished our coffees he opened a small wooden box. There was a cigarette in it, which we shared.

"So how do you like Hōgoji?" he asked.

"It's good but I'm surprised that no one's been pushing me around. I thought that's what happened when you came to a new temple."

"But didn't you hear what Katagiri said when he introduced you?"

"Uh, some of it. Why?"

"He said to treat you like an equal."

"That's very nice of him. But Koji, there's one problem."

"Yes?"

"There's no such thing as equal here is there? Isn't everybody higher or lower?"

"Everybody but you," he said. "You're equal."

PART THREE

WALKING

TAKUHATSU, "TO ENTRUST THE BOWL"

I had been at Hōgoji for a mere four days when we left for an outing of *takuhatsu*, formal monks' begging. I'd read about it and seen pictures of it in books and magazines, and on TV. I'd been told about it for decades by Japanese and American monks who had done it and tourists who had seen the begging monks on the streets in Japan. Norman regaled me with takuhatsu stories the night before and I was really looking forward to it. I even dreamed about it, but in my dream it wasn't orthodox takuhatsu. I was outside Elin's grandparents' home in Atlanta chanting with a guitar. She was supposed to come put money in it. When she got close I was going to grab her and take her back to the monastery. But she only came to the window and looked down.

Koji alone was staying behind to take care of the temple and he begged me to remain there with him and help out. I already was taking a shine to this diligent good-vibe head monk and was flattered that he was so eager to spend time with me, but I wouldn't have passed up the opportunity to do takuhatsu for anything. He argued that he not only needed my help but wanted to get to know me better and that we'd have such a good time. The schedule would be practically all free. Koji's offer was tempting but I told him I was looking forward to the experience. Then he suggested I could go the next time with him and admitted he was concerned about my back. I said that my back was getting better after the beating it had taken lugging all my bags across Japan and that walking would be therapeutic for it. So he gave up.

Sunday after lunch, Katagiri, Shuko, Norman, Maku, Jakushin and I gathered on the deck to the kuin and put on the
traditional gear of takuhatsu. It was a sunny day and we all wore
thin black koromo over our kimono. Katagiri pulled the linen
mesh koromo up under my waist cord to shorten it a few inches.
He said it would make it easier to walk. We put on rough straw
sandals that tied around our ankles, secured curious white cotton
covers on our forearms and shins, and hung an extra pair of sandals
at our sides. Around our necks we put our rakusu, the biblike
cloth of ordination, and over them slung black, heavy cotton bags
holding our begging bowls and wooden-handled bells. Then Katagiri tied a white cloth called a *hachimaki* around my forehead.
It would stop the sweat from going into my eyes, he said. I appreciated all the attention he was giving me. I felt like I was
being dressed for the prom. Last we donned straw hats the shape
of wide cones. They came down to eye level, as good as sun glasses.
Katagiri pointed out to me that they had the name of the temple
in large kanji across the front and solemnly admonished me to be
on good behavior. I assumed a fiercely serious pose and he laughed
in spite of himself. I looked around at my almsmates, now all
bedecked like me. We were dashing.

Koji, Norman and Shuko had been whispering to each other
on the edge of the deck and periodically looking at me. Strange.
What were they up to? After a moment, Norman came over and
said they were concerned that I wasn't in good enough shape and
wouldn't be able to make it. It's a rigorous practice that takes
stamina and I'm a tad overweight. Katagiri patted my stomach
and said it would be good for me. But they also thought my big
feet would be too tender to withstand the constant abrasion of the
undersized, rough footgear. Norman said they'd get covered with
blisters and blood. I said not to worry but Shuko got permission
from Katagiri for me to wear traditional white Japanese socks
called *tabi* and he brought some along for me just in case. They
have a separate pocket for the big toe so they can be worn with
sandals, but they are not part of orthodox takuhatsu gear.

After reciting the Heart Sutra at the entrance to Hōgoji, we bowed toward the temple and to Koji. Then we were off down the mountain on the temple path to the narrow paved road past the rice fields and terraces with wild flowers growing all around, thatch-roofed farm houses, *kunugi* oak for harvesting, wild woods and rows of shaded logs sprouting shiitake mushrooms. The sound of water running down the mountainside came from all around. The smell of spring was uplifting and delightful. At the bottom of the mountain we entered the village of Ryūmon, Dragon Gate. Children came out laughing and ran around us calling Koji and Norman by name and remarking at Norman's and my size and strong features. Katagiri led the way and carried a staff that jingled when he brought it down at each step.

We got to a bus stop after an hour of walking and rode through Kikuoka on our way to the big city—Beppu. The bus let us off in the Beppu suburbs and we walked single file to the weekend home of a wealthy lay patron of Hōgoji, Ogawa Sensei.

Arriving at the front door of his semimodern large house, we belted out our theme song, the Heart Sutra, and were greeted by the sensei, his wife and their twenty-six-year-old son. We stripped off our begging gear in the entranceway and were treated to the use of his large hot tub, bordered with volcanic stones and full of hot spring water, abundant in this region.

We were fed a fancy meal of curried rice with meat and many side dishes. After dinner we did the dishes and cleaned up while Mrs. Ogawa joined her husband in conversation with Katagiri. I was surprised. This is just not done in Japan. Women typically work till they drop. No one else is even supposed to enter their kitchens. Norman said he had been there to witness the transition. Ogawa-*okusan*, the wife, had at first strenuously resisted the monks' attempts to help, but had finally succumbed and learned to appreciate it. Ogawa-okusan says we are helping her learn to be a modern woman and calls us "feminists." Shuko explained to me that in Japanese English it means a man who helps out at home.

Ogawa Sensei, who looks to be about sixty-five, manufactures *kendō* (Japanese fencing) equipment and is a master of that martial art. His son, who works and studies with his father, showed me their antique sword collection displayed in the entranceway. As we stood there admiring steel and bamboo, people started to arrive for an evening sitting downstairs in the spacious, wood-floored *dōjō*, normally used for kendo practice. The Ogawas and the kendo students sat in their loose kendo clothes. Some of the other men wore suits and ties and the women were in casual slacks and blouses. This zazenkai meets once a month, coinciding with the monks' monthly takuhatsu in Beppu.

That night's meeting was especially well attended because of the presence of Katagiri, who gave a lecture after zazen. He introduced Norman as his disciple and me as his guest. I hardly understood any of what he said as it got pretty technical, but I hadn't heard Katagiri lecture in a while so I enjoyed it strictly for the vibes. It was the only talk that I heard him give in Japan and it was to be my last. He never did like to say much anyway —outside of lectures that is. As a matter of fact, the whole time I was there in Kyūshū with Katagiri, he didn't even have *dokusan*, the Soto word for formal private interview. We talked some, but I can't remember what about. So my last recollections of being with this dear friend and teacher are like quiet, simple cartoons with empty bubbles above the characters' heads.

The next day after a pleasantly late six A.M. zazen with the whole family, we recited the Heart Sutra outside the house and walked off briskly single file again to the bus stop. We rode quietly for thirty minutes. Everyone seemed calm, but inside I was tingling with excitement.

Finally the six of us arrived in bustling downtown Beppu and prepared to begin our ritualistic begging. We strode amid modern buildings of glass, metal and concrete and the hubbub of traffic. We walked past an elegant old wooden, tile-roofed home with a mud wall and garden. Somebody who won't sell, I thought, look-ing back at it. We were surrounded by throngs of busily moving Japanese men and women in perfectly fitting, stylish Western clothes. One thing we had in common with the crowd, especially the women, was the color black. I looked over the sea of people and black was everywhere. In their hurry the crowd didn't seem to notice us, despite our garb. Moving intently on the sidewalk single file in costumes that date back a millennium, we were a time warp, a museum without walls, a pageant to the past.

We stopped at a crosswalk. I watched the compact cars go by, clean and shiny every one. In contrast to the people's black clothes, the autos were almost entirely white. Austere color scheme, I thought.

I remember listening to the corny electric tune that accom-panied our crossing. It was "Comin' Through the Rye" and it came through a speaker above the flashing strutting figure that announced "walk" to the sighted.

"These Irish tunes, where do they come from?" I whispered to Norman.

"Ireland," he said helpfully, looking straight ahead.

When the moment was right, Shuko stopped and got out his bowl. Then, using the thumb and first two fingers of our left hands to form a tripod, we raised our bowls to eye level and, holding the bells down with our right hands, we set out calling, "Hō!" and ringing the bells vigorously. (All day long I thought it was the *hō* that meant "the teaching," Japanese for the Sanskrit word dharma. That evening Norman told me he'd heard it was actually an abbreviation for *hatsu*, which means bowl, in this case the begging bowl.) We passed old funky markets and modern convenience stores, traditional shops selling kimono, sweets, altars, incense, pottery and scrolls and into crowded covered modern shopping streets lined with boutiques, coffee shops and drug stores. The people were quiet but the air was filled with loud, irritating advertisements and overlapping music broadcast through loudspeakers. "A Whiter Shade of Pale" faded into a pop version of Pachelbel's canon as we worked our way down the mall.

In this commercial maelstrom, one by one we'd pull out of the group at a door or open storefront and, standing erect, alone and, hopefully, more noble than ridiculous, would each chant the Enmei Jukku Kannon Gyō loudly three times. "Kanzeon namu butsu . . ." and so on. Almost nobody understands this antiquated Buddhist Japanese any more than I understand Chaucer, but they surely know the name of Kanzeon and when they hear it, that's enough. She, or sometimes he, is Avalokiteshvara, Kuanyin in Chinese, the bodhisattva, or enlightening being, of great compassion—the Virgin Mary of Buddhism.

More often than not someone would come running out and place a coin or two in the bowl. In that case the first chant would not be repeated and there would be a second recitation in which gratitude was expressed and boundless merit promised. "Zai hō ni sei . . ." Then that monk would bow, empty the money from the bowl into the black bag around his neck, turn and walk toward the direction of the others while calling, "Hō!" With all of us outfitted thus and going "Hō!" in those shopping areas, I felt like we were related in a peculiar way to the Santas collecting money for charity on the street corners downtown in December in the States.

After one of us was done at an entryway, he would continue on past his stationary chanting comrades until arriving at the next unsolicited doorway. Every once in a while a person would come out and angrily shoo one of us away. An old guy did this to me. I wondered if he was from one of the fanatic sects or maybe a person who regarded Buddhist priests as lazy, decadent leeches of society.

I didn't know the chants by heart, but Norman had written them both out for me and I tucked them inside my bowl as crib sheets. After an hour I didn't need them anymore but I left them in the whole first day in case I got stage fright.

It was great to see lanky Norman in his monk garb bellowing out those lines from the distant past in front of a Kentucky Fried Chicken joint, or to witness Katagiri chanting and shaking the staff that he'd brought, rattling its brass rings in front of a pachinko parlor. He had such integrity and stood so resolutely. He brought the butt of his staff to the ground, accentuating his request for support for the priests' practice. His chanting blended with the cacophony emanating from the pachinko gambling den, the whirl and clatter of thousands of silver balls dropping through hundreds of machines accompanied by raucous marching music.

I stared and absorbed the sound, transfixed, and, suddenly unaware of my role in this rite, time melted enough to transpose onto this scene my last memory of an even shorter Japanese priest, my original teacher Suzuki Roshi, powerfully bringing his similar staff down, the staff Alan Watts gave him, bringing it down at Dick Baker's Mountain Seat ceremony, bringing it down and saying goodbye in that chilling moment. That was the last time I saw him, so brown-skinned with metastasized gall bladder cancer. The ringing of his jangling staff was there at the pachinko parlor for a bent moment and then it was Dainin (Katagiri's Buddhist name) again, his Great Patience waiting for this Japanese pinball Vegas-colored pleasure dream to spit out a sycophantic employee who quickly dropped a coin in Katagiri's slot and darted back into the mirrors and screaming machines.

That night we returned worn out to the Ogawas', to a hot bath and a feast with beer and sake, talking and laughing. Some friends of the family came over to greet us and especially to meet Katagiri. We sat around in easy chairs and kitchen chairs, the TV on and no one paying attention to it. After more talk and laughter, the guests, who were in their fifties and older, started asking Katagiri, Norman and me questions about America and Zen in America.

At one point Jakushin, displaying surprising nerve, came out of his depressed silence and said he understood that marijuana and

psychedelics had played a significant role in America in the de-
velopment of interest in Buddhism and zazen and what did I think
about that and how had these drugs affected my religious path.
Everyone turned and looked at me, waiting for an answer. I froze
with fear. In Japan, legal drugs like booze and cigarettes, or anything a doctor prescribes, are regarded as perfectly all right and
the more the merrier—but illegal drugs are all thrown together
into the same heinous category and are considered to be an instant
cause of insanity, death and societal decay used only by deranged
scum. I really didn't want to answer that question. I said something about learning from many different types of experiences in
our lives and added that we should avoid either seeking particular
experience or trying to duplicate past ones. It was just your boil-
erplate American Zen antidrug rap. This didn't satisfy Jakushin
and he pursued the topic with more insistence, asking me if such
experiences had encouraged me.

I turned to Katagiri who was eyeing me eagerly and I said in
English, "I'm not going to answer that question honestly. Look
at these people. They wouldn't understand—they're much too
conservative and narrow-minded."

Much to my dismay, Katagiri took my plea for help and translated it word-for-word to the interested group.

They said, "No no no, please tell us." I was nervous. I didn't
want to tell them anything challenging or upsetting. I'm not even
sure about it myself. It's far too complicated. I admitted I'd been
encouraged to pursue zazen because of some experiences I'd had,
but said that many people and events had led me along the path
and that I wasn't sure what caused what.

Katagiri then surprised me greatly by saying that many people
had been encouraged to practice because of experiences they'd had
early on with LSD and other mind expanders. He seemed completely unconcerned about saying something unacceptable. These
old conservative Japanese folks who would doubtlessly support a
life-without-possibility-of-parole sentence for anyone caught with
a joint, nodded seriously and made is-that-so? types of responses

to Katagiri's libertarian comments. Katagiri, incidently, like Suzuki, back when it was an issue, asked people not to come to
zazen high. In '66 when he heard that another fellow and I had
given the profits from the sale of thirteen kilos of Acapulco Gold
to the fund to buy Tassajara, he was furious and chastised us in
a lecture. Jakushin was quite pleased with the answer his question
elicited. He listened thoughtfully, but wisely said nothing.

That night there was no zazen and everyone went to sleep
early except for Norman and me. He said that it was nice having
me along and that he was impressed with my stamina. I said it
was great to be there and I was glad I hadn't let Koji talk me
into staying behind.

"It was nice of him to be concerned about my back and to
want me to stay at Hōgoji so he and I could get to know each
other better," I told Norman with a touch of pride.

"Well, I'll tell you a little secret," he said. "The reason Koji
didn't want you to go was that he was worried about the impression your appearance would make. He thought you'd frighten
people and give the temple a bad name."

"He did?"

"Don't tell him I told you," said Norman, laughing. He then
said good night and went to bed.

I stayed up alone till midnight studying Japanese on the concrete steps that led to the Lexus in the garage. Once I went down
and looked at myself in the side mirror. I almost never look at
myself in mirrors. No wonder, I thought, sympathizing with Koji.

The next morning after zazen and service we had a fantastic Japanese breakfast of hot rice with raw egg, a crumbled dried sheet
of seaweed and scallions, all to be mixed together. Each of us got
a whole four-inch baked fish, miso soup with tofu, a tiny potato
salad, homemade daikon pickles, strawberries, melon and green
tea or coffee. While we ate, I sat on a stool at the Western-style
counter and watched Ogawa-okusan whip up a sort of omelet

batter and cook it in thin layers, which were then overlapped into a loaf that she wrapped in foil and added to the *obentō*, the boxed meal she made for us. She suggested we eat it as a late afternoon snack before returning to Hōgoji.

After cleanup over coffee and the morning news on TV, Shuko, Katagiri and Norman inquired into the condition of my feet and body in general. I felt invigorated and ready for more. Katagiri looked my feet over approvingly. "Very tough," he said laughing. I did have one problem, I told them. My thighs were getting raw from sweating and rubbing together unprotected under the robes. Katagiri called Mrs. Ogawa over and asked her if she had anything for my condition adding that there was no time for me to diet. After they were through making fun of my weight and laughing at me, she went out and came back with a jar of salve for dry hands. I went into the bathroom and applied it. I thanked her and gave the container back. She kindly wrapped it up in a handkerchief-sized cloth and gave it to me saying that she had no need for it.

And so we were off for our second day of takuhatsu. During the morning session we invaded a residential area near the commercial district we'd been at the day before. After a couple of hours we went to the home of a lay family, did a service for their ancestors at their altar and then had a sumptuous repast that included about thirty-five little dishes and morsels of various sorts. After lunch and a brief rest in which we all fell asleep on the living room floor, we went out for the afternoon session.

The mendicant six walked swiftly toward the target area chanting the deep and extended *hō* that were the roar of our motors, and then we peeled off like fighter planes at one door after another, each monk quickly standing at attention in his place and immediately beginning to chant so that the lines rang out like a sextet round. First Katagiri, then Shuko, Norman, Jakushin, Maku and me, in the order of seniority of course, together throwing our body-mind units into the dance and song of the home-leavers, buddha's kids, but we sweated like his pigs on the hottest day so far in the year. The longer we'd go without a break, the deeper we'd get into the rhythm of it and the less we cared about our trivial concerns: pecking order, perspiration, thighs, refreshment, coins, reactions. We did it till we could hardly stand up and it seemed that it was the chanting itself holding up our heads and bowls.

An old rule of Buddhist begging is not to hit up the rich over the poor or discriminate in any way while on the job. You're supposed to keep your eyes down and covered by the rim of your hat so you won't know who the donors are and they won't know you in a personal way. Of course I was always peeking, being half amateur sociologist, but it *was* breaking form. Takuhatsu is strictly monks' practice and it's the lay people's practice to contribute to the monks in this way. In old-time Indian Buddhism, which is still observed in Thailand and some other Southeast Asian countries, the monks weren't allowed to touch money and begging was their grocery shopping. Since they had to eat before noon, they only went out to beg in the morning. Takuhatsu is not the sole support of these Japanese monks, who touch money and eat dinner. Norman says that in the rare instances where takuhatsu is still done in Japan, it is largely vestigial and ceremonial. But he proudly added that it covered most of Hōgoji's food costs.

A few people did give food. Maku, the pixie, got a small bag of uncooked rice and Norman got some *onigiri*, cooked rice rolled in dried seaweed. One guy that afternoon stepped out of a liquor store and gave me a glass of sake, which I drank in a gulp in accordance with the established practice of nondiscrimination while begging. There's an old Indian story about a leper whose thumb fell in a monk's begging bowl. The monk ate it without hesitation. Buddha's death is generally attributed to eating some bad meat or, in other versions, mushrooms, that had been offered while he was doing his rounds. It was in that spirit that I drank the sake. Cross my heart.

People would come up to us on the street and give money—not a lot, the equivalent of a dime up to a few dollars. A Catholic priest gave five hundred yen. That was neat. School kids in black uniforms gave ten yen or even a hundred, which surprised me. One old lady who was permanently bent over at a ninety-degree angle saw us on a break at some vending machines drinking hot coffee, cold cola, oolong tea and a sports drink named Pocari Sweat (the most popular soft drink in Japan) out of cans. She hobbled slowly and pitifully over to us, opened up her cloth coin purse and gave six yen to Katagiri. We collectively responded with the thanks chant, which I hope eased her obvious discomfort.

One of the principal lessons that Norman says he has learned here concerns the relationship between priests and lay people and the distinctive roles of each. Here lay are lay and monks are monks, at least when they're on duty. He says that the lay people support the priests to live this kind of life and that the priests practice Buddhism for everyone and in this way the teaching goes both ways.

My lower back pain had all but disappeared, my greased thighs and my feet were fine. I was ready for more. The monks were surprised I held up so well but this old barefoot boy from Texas who's worn beach sandals since the sixties wasn't about to cop out with protocol-breaking *tabi* on the day of the hunt.

This was a treat for Katagiri too. He'd been living in the U.S. for twenty-five years and you just can't have the takuhatsu experience there. Well, you could, but it might tend to make one feel like one of those religious enthusiasts in airports. But toward the end of the day, Katagiri, the bastion of endless quiet effort, got exhausted. He didn't feel well and Norman took him to a park where they waited for us. He looked so disappointed as he walked off. I felt bad for him, knowing he wanted to stay with us.

The rhythm of takuhatsu, the vocalizing and the exercise, definitely gave us a group high and the interchange with the people of Beppu, though impersonal, was impressive and moving. Materialistic and modern as it is, this is obviously still a country with deep religious roots.

While we were waiting for the bus to Kikuoka, we took our *obentō* to the sunny second-floor balcony of a department store and spread them out with some additional goodies and drinks on a table that overlooked a city park. Sitting in that bare cement area in aluminum chairs with plastic straps, we chanted before our picnic, tired and hungry. I glanced around at my fellow beggars and was filled with warmth. We ate eagerly in silence. Katagiri's eyes were downcast as he chewed. Behind his head I saw storm clouds approaching. Maku served us each green tea in porcelain cups that he'd borrowed from a ramen shop inside. A wind started to blow in gusts and it quickly became violent and noisy. Robes were blown up above knees and sleeves flapped in the air. Suddenly the sky had become dark and drops of rain were hitting the food. Staggering in the gale, we tried to move the table inside, but before we could get a grip on it, the wind seized and overturned it. Food and containers were going every which way. Maku grabbed the cups that hadn't broken. The drops came thicker and faster. As we rushed to clean up our mess, sheets of rain pelted us. Norman took Katagiri inside while the rest of us threw our soggy half-eaten lunch remains into a trash bin that then blew over, rescattering our leftovers plus a great deal more. Circumstances being out of control, we retreated into the department store. We had barely gotten downstairs to the entrance when the storm passed. We stepped out to clean air and washed pavement. Norman took Katagiri to the Beppu bus station in a taxi. The rest of us walked in the sunshine and at least weren't dripping by the time we got on the bus to Kikuoka.

At Hōgoji that night, blistered and bushed, but exhilarated by the experience, we spread out our booty on tatami and counted it in the kerosene lamp light while drinking tea. The grand tally was 62,851 yen, one small bag of unpolished white rice, and an unshakable confidence in interdependence.

LEARNING THE BUREAUCRACY

If I've learned anything in my stay in Japan, it is how to deal with bureaucracy. It's not the hardest thing in the world to get the knack of, it just takes time, experience and patience—maybe some courage too. Friends at the temple and savvy Ishitaki around the corner guided and advised Elin and me while Hōjō-san made our stay possible by protecting us under the wings of the temple. But no matter how much help we got, there came those inevitable times when we were on our own, face to face with The Man.

Often if Elin and I didn't pick up on the right way to turn at a fork in the maze, a kind official would give a hint. Sometimes the hints were very clear. A case in point:

Elin and I used the temple address for official business because it emphasized that hallowed relationship and made it obvious to an official looking at our identification that we were good, upstanding noncitizens. We had put some savings in an investment company and learned they were required by law to send all our mail to the address on our registration cards. We didn't think it tactful for the penniless monks at the temple to see that we were receiving mail from the largest mutual fund in the world, so we rode our bikes over to city hall and said hello to the familiar people behind the desks at the Alien Registration office located next to the section for handicapped city hall workers. I have read letters to the editor complaining about our designation as "aliens," but I like the concept. As I walk up toward the sign, I imagine that I am an interplanetary visitor registering at city hall.

A short man in his thirties with horn-rimmed glasses and medium-length black hair walked immediately up to the counter, apologizing for keeping us waiting. He recognized us from previous visits and seemed happy to see us. Elin explained that we needed different addresses on our Alien Registration cards. He went and got a form for us to fill out. One line of the form was for the moving date to the new residence.

"What should we put here?" Elin asked him.

"Have you already moved?"

"No," she answered. "I mean, yes."

He looked at her quizzically.

"That's where we live," she explained.

"The moving date has to be within the last two weeks," he said.

"But you see, we've always lived there," she said. "It's just next door to Daianji. We used the Daianji address at first but now we want to use this one."

"Within two weeks."

"You don't understand, sir," I broke in. "We haven't moved. We just want to change our mailing address from Daianji, to our home."

He leaned over and in a low, firm voice said very clearly and slowly in English, "PRETEND."

Then there's the blank stare. When you ask a question and people stare down blankly it's a sure sign that they can't give you something you've just asked for and they feel bad about it.

Once in Kamakura, Elin and I asked if we could change the destination of our train tickets. It turned out nothing could be done about it because we'd bought our tickets in Tokyo and they'd already been punched for the first leg of the trip. The station employees we dealt with could have just told us, "Sorry, there's nothing we can do. No substitutes on already-punched tickets." But it was too painful for them to tell us so. Together they looked our tickets over carefully.

"So," I said, clapping my hands and speaking in a positive, cheerful tone, "what's the difference in cost? We don't mind paying more."

The two blue-uniformed men in the railroad office didn't answer me. They just stared at the tickets, occasionally turning them over to look at the other side. They said, "Sō desu nē," and other sorts of noncommittal phrases. One of them sighed and the other said it was a difficult problem. Then they went back to staring at the tickets. Finally we caught on and said it was fine, really, and thanks so much—and they were begging for forgiveness and bowing as we left. We were not so much disappointed that we couldn't get what we wanted as puzzled by their behavior. In time we learned that when one meets the blank stare it is best to say thanks and go on one's way.

Occasionally special favors may be granted if there are extenuating social circumstances, if it's not just for little you who should grin and bear it, but for your obligations to others. It was my first tourist visa extension. An Immigration clerk told me indignantly in the very busy Tokyo Immigration Office when I was begging him to take care of me so I could get out of there, "I am *not* a mindless, uncaring bureaucrat. I am doing my best. Look at what we are dealing with!" and he gestured toward a room full of hundreds of foreign students, people from every possible country, dancers and bar girls from Thailand and the Philippines, lots of Anglos, most of them probably English teachers, and other assorted business people, laborers and tourists. He looked at me intensely. "These people have been waiting up to four or five hours and you've only been here for thirty minutes!"

I apologized to him and told him not to worry about it. I said that I could tell that he was working very hard and that I'd come back on another day when he wasn't so busy. I said I'd be happy to stay and wait, but my Japanese hosts had invited guests over to meet me and I'd rather be late in extending my visa than embarrass them.

He looked down for a minute, then leaned over and whispered to me, "I'll have you out of here in ten minutes."

Sometimes I'd get the brick wall. No hints, no stare, no mercy. The first time I met that was in the Department of Immigration in Shizuoka. Elin wasn't even in Japan yet. Hōitsu Suzuki drove me to the office. Since he was my original teacher's son, it seemed it would be appropriate for him to be my sponsor in Japan. I thought Hōitsu could just go to Immigration and say this guy wants to study Zen and Japanese culture and a cultural visa would be granted—I needed it for an extended stay in Japan. He didn't know what the rules were either and, looking back on it, I realize how I asked him to do the impossible, imposed on him and put him in an awkward position—a repeated theme of my stay in Japan.

The Immigration man we talked to was not friendly. His eyes were hard and his lips thin. He looked at me with contempt and spoke sternly to Hōitsu. He said "no way," in a number of ways. It was a bummer and a shock. All three of us were getting out of sorts. He said there's no such thing as a "cultural visa," and you can't get it for studying Zen anyway. But maybe I could get the "4-1-16-3 visa" if I wanted to study one of the martial arts, like maybe judo. That pissed Hōitsu off.

"So judo is more important than Zen?" he said, with his voice tensely raised.

"Maybe he should go to Eiheiji," the public servant suggested.

Hōitsu stared at him in disbelief. "You're telling me where he should go to study Zen? I am responsible for him and I say

THANK YOU AND OK!

that he should go to Maruyama." In spite of how poorly my future was faring in the course of this conversation, I couldn't help but enjoy hearing Hōitsu assertively stand up for me. But after a while I just wanted to get out of there and let him off the hook.

Before we parted, the Immigration official explained that they were under pressure because of all the Southeast Asian bar hostesses and dancers that were in Japan on these so-called "cultural" visas. They'd been getting a lot of press for "selling spring," which is the literal meaning of the kanji for prostitution.

"Do I look like a Thai prostitute?" I asked him.

Hōitsu nudged me sternly.

The bureaucrat went on and made it clear that, regardless, I would have to get my visa in Maruyama, where I was going to live. Hōitsu could not be my sponsor. Period.

And then there were kind, helpful people like Miyake-san. Elin and I had to go to the local Immigration office in Uzu, the same city where I was teaching English at the shipyard. My visa was running out and soon hers would too. Not yet knowing quite what to do about getting "cultural" visas, we went for mere tourist visa extensions. That was in November of 1988. We were new and afraid and there was a real meany there to meet us. He was thin, not too short, and had a severe attitude—looked like he'd never smiled in his life. He asked us what were we doing in Maruyama and I said studying this and that at Daianji and studying the language and calligraphy.

"You shouldn't be studying on a tourist visa," he said coldly.

Oh no, I thought, we're going to be deported. There I go mouthing off again. He wanted to know all sorts of things before he'd even talk about extending our tourist visas.

After we'd failed that he asked sharply just why we were interested in Daianji and when I told him we'd studied Zen in America he just said, "Documents, please." I feared the brick wall, but just then another employee walked over and said hello to us and smoothly took over for mister prison-camp-guard on the pretext that he (the new guy) spoke a little English, although we just continued speaking in Japanese. The friendly fellow's name was Miyake-san. He spoke softly and had a pleasant smile. Is this going to be the nice guy/bad guy routine? I wondered. He'll get us to confess everything and then the other guy will deport us. But I'd soon forgotten such fears in the warmth of his good will. The tourist visa extensions were duly granted.

Some months later we went back to Uzu, disappointed and dejected. In the intervening months we had meticulously gathered the many documents, testimonials and certificates needed to get our visa status transferred from tourist to cultural. Miyake had met with us and advised us several times along the way. I applied for the cultural visa and Elin for a spouse visa.

"He's the pro," Miyake had said to Elin while gesturing at me. "You won't have to prove anything on a spouse visa. It's easiest that way."

We felt sure that our efforts would be rewarded, but when the answer came back from the regional office, it came back negative.

"It's those Philippine and Thai dancers again," I told Elin in the train on the way to Uzu. The heat was coming down on Immigration and it put a squeeze on the whole cultural visa thing. It was ridiculous to begin with. Southeast Asian women are an integral part of the nightlife of Japanese men, especially the guys that run the show. No one had any intention of keeping those women out. The visa screw-tightening was just the twitches of the bureaucracy running interference for the hypocrites talking out of both sides of their lust. There's a saying here: "Edo no kataki Nagasaki de utsu." It means to avenge Edo (old Tokyo) by attacking far-away Nagasaki. Taking it out on us, in other words.

Miyake explained it like this: "You got tourist visas—that means you wanted to be tourists. So be tourists. That's how they look at it." (He said *they*—I loved him.) "If you had wanted to study, you would have gotten 'student' or 'cultural' visas in America. Maybe they think you're trying to pull one over on them."

I replied, "How the heck are we supposed to get all these papers together and find sponsors and teachers and schools and do all that from America? I had to come here and look around. I wanted to visit people and check things out. You don't pick Zen teachers out of catalogues. Our calligraphy teacher and our language school are local and there would be no way we could . . ."

"Japanese just don't do things that way," he said. "They save, they plan, they lay it all out. They just wouldn't do it like you have. To them it looks irresponsible. But listen, don't fight it. We tried that route and it failed." He spoke with the kind voice of experience.

"So we just have to go back to America and apply from there?" Elin asked despondently.

"We can't afford that." I said.

Miyake is a calm and deliberate man. He told us not to worry—everything was okay. "Just go to Korea and get your cultural and spouse visas there."

"What?" Elin said. "Korea? But won't Japanese Immigration have the same reservations there that they had here?"

"No," he answered. "You can get it in a few days. There will be no problem."

"It won't look bad?" I asked.

"No. That's doing it the correct way. They'd see you decided to come to Japan to study these things and that you prepared properly and that all of your papers are in order." Then he pointedly advised us not to bother to apply for permission to work. He thought maybe that had hurt our case and said they would expect us to bring enough money to support ourselves for some time. We nodded in nervous agreement.

We were flabbergasted. Korea was very close and there was a cheap ferry. We wanted to see it anyway. We looked at each other with renewed hope.

Miyake knew we'd need some time to prepare the proper papers all over again and was making out new tourist visa extensions. I was trying to figure out an advantageous time for us to go. We wouldn't have to miss classes or lose income if we went when everyone else was on holiday. I looked at a calendar on the wall. There were some free days at the end of April and, ah! there's Golden Week, the first week in May, which has three national holidays in it. I quickly calculated we could take a two-week vacation if . . . but that was two months away.

"Uh," I said.

"Yes," he replied, halting his pen.

"Maybe we could leave a little later, like in, oh say, late April?" I threw out. He looked at me. Was it with suspicion? No. I don't know. Oh god, what am I going to say? Why do I want to stay till then? My mind raced around. I remembered the chant we said in high school.

> *When in trouble, when in doubt,*
> *Run in circles, scream and shout!*

Let's see, I thought, dental appointment, Mother's visit, responsibilities at the temple. My mother has a dental appointment at the temple? No . . . but before I could tell a lie, Miyake had already given us extensions till June. That was nice of him.

"Don't want to rush things," he said.

I got the distinct feeling that he knew everything: our schedules of classes and the number of students in them and their names. Like the good Nazis in the movies, he's trying to help us, I thought. I appreciated it. We had spent so much time being nervous about teaching illegally and working on getting the right visas. It was important to us. Very important. We wanted to keep living in Maruyama. I was just paying some pressing debts and we were developing friends and teachers and we didn't want to be thrown out of the country. We wanted to stay and our friends and the folks at the temple wanted us to stay. But it was up to the serious public servants at the Department of Immigration as to whether we would be able to stay or not.

When we got home in the early evening from the Immigration event, I called Bop in Kyoto. He said not to worry, it was all just a matter of time.

"English teachers are part of national security," he said. "They need you as much as the Thai hostesses and the illegal laborers from Bangladesh and the Ag students from Nairobi. It's just their habit to keep foreigners out. They don't want to lose control and have riots and muggers in every alley. So at least you have to be initiated."

"Initiated?" I asked.

"Of course, they don't let you do anything in this country without being initiated. For us it's a snap—they make it much harder on each other.

"Look at it this way," he said, and he told me a story about a society in the South Pacific where young people are forbidden to show an interest in each other. It's a serious taboo and two people in love have to escape to another island. Their fellow islanders will indignantly chase them and furiously try to kill them on their exit—but they won't be followed in boats. After the elopers have been gone for a year, they come back and everyone joyously greets them with open arms.

"All you have to do is go to Korea and when you come back, Immigration will greet you with smiles and the appropriate stamps on your visas."

We had stood in the Immigration office earlier that day and smiled and bowed goodbye with Miyake. Behind him, the stern and scowling bureaucrat whom Miyake had saved us from back in November stared icily just over our heads. I hoped he wasn't thinking, "I'll get you yet." I hoped that he was just showing a strict facade as a coverup for weakness. I hoped he would go to a ramen shop after work and drink himself into a stupor with his chums and forget about us permanently.

MOTHER'S DAY CARD

HŌGOJI, MAY 5, 1988

Two of the last things I did before I came to Japan were to help arrange the funerals of my maternal grandmother and my mother's boyfriend. Her whole life had been centered around them and now she was adjusting to the loss. Mother's Day was coming up and I especially wanted to get a card to her. During the takuhatsu excursion I'd seen signs and displays about Mother's Day on the buses and in the shopping areas. I was surprised to find that even in the bus station in Kikuoka there was a selection of Mother's Day cards. I have since learned that the Japanese business world takes advantage of every possible opportunity to herd the masses to the stores to participate in obligatory gift-giving frenzies. I got a cute card with a picture of a nice smiling Japanese mother on it. There was a poem inside praising her for working to the bone night and day for her children. The Japanese was simple, Shuko helped me translate it and I added a brief note.

I had tried to mail it from the station, but the bus for Ryūmon was ready to leave, it was getting late, and everyone wanted to move on. Shuko assured me that the card would get there just as fast mailed from the temple. But the next day when I put the card in the temple mail box, Shuko told me it was a holiday (Children's Day) and the mailman wouldn't come till the following afternoon.

"But you told me to mail it today," I said.

"Today's a holiday. You'll have to wait."

We weren't getting anywhere. "Well, I'm going to town then to mail it," I said.

"It won't help you," he said. "You should just wait till tomorrow."

I retreated to Norman's room. "This is what happens to you when you live here. He's mind-torquing you," he said, twisting his fists in opposite directions as if he were ringing out a rag.

"Are you sure?" I said. "You don't think it's just absent-mindedness?"

He thought about it. "Maybe I'm prejudiced. I don't know. Maybe it was a mistake. Naaaa, it's the old torque-the-individual routine. He might be doing it unconsciously, but it adds up the same. It's one of the things that they think is essential about training. It's not Buddhist—it's Japanese."

"You mean stepping on the individual?"

"Exactly."

"But why me?"

"Because you were there," Norman answered perceptively.

"And why today?" I said, sitting down dejectedly on the tatami.

"No time like the present," he came back. "No time like the present to subject the individual to the group. The group is all that matters. 'Enlightenment' is just the substitution of the group ego for the individual one."

"Hmm," I said. "In Mexico this sort of thing happened all the time with directions and information. Everyone tells you the wrong time or place and nothing works out. But it wasn't to mold you to the group. There was no purpose. They just didn't care. I came to be quite fond of the lifestyle. I learned to relax there and to let go."

Norman leaned over. "Well, here you're going to learn to be uptight and to hold on . . . to the group . . . or whatever the group wants, as told to you by any senior. The purpose of the training in Japanese Zen temples isn't to help you along the path to enlightenment—it is to cultivate you into a refined and obedient Japanese priest for Japanese temples."

"Great, but I'm not in the market for a Japanese temple right now, so in my case I guess most of the rules don't apply."

"Sorry, this steamroller is blind. You are here and it is rolling over you."

"Well, come on now, Norman. I think you just got out of your futon on the wrong side this morning. It can't be that bad."

We went outside and sat on the edge of the deck by Norman's room. Koji came out of his cabin holding a cardboard box full of dirty laundry. I called him to come over. He stood before us smiling enthusiastically. Just the sight of his short, strong frame and friendly chiseled face filled me with warmth.

"Look at him, Norman," I said. "A fine example of this Buddhist system. Alert, kind, ready to serve, he is not only a transcendent boy scout, he is a truly good and wise person. The system has worked for him."

"Indeed," said Norman.

"Nani?" said Koji, meaning, "What's that?"

"I was just praising you."

He just shook his head, smiled and held his laundry.

"The question, Koji, is this: Is the main purpose of Japanese training temples just to produce good Japanese priests to run Japanese temples? Are Norman and I in the wrong place?"

His voice is lower and stronger than his body suggests. "That is especially true," he said, "of bigger training temples like Suienji and Eiheiji, but it is still true to a lesser extent of any Japanese temple where there is training. And yes, it is somewhat true that the practice here is most appropriate for Japanese monks who will have their own temples. After all, we are in Japan. But it is still an opportunity to follow Buddha's way under the guidance of Nishiki Roshi and for a while with Katagiri Roshi. Don't waste your time wishing the conditions were perfect. The important thing is to do your best while you are here to practice in harmony with everyone."

Norman and I simultaneously put our hands together in gassho, bowed to him and didn't bring our heads up till he had gone over to the long sink.

I told Norman and then Koji that I was going down the hill to mail the card. Koji gave me an umbrella to take along since it was drizzling. On the way down, the air had a distinct spring rain smell and little mountain crabs scurried across the road. Incredibly big, fat, blue and purple worms were all over. Big as my little finger. I touched one and it started squirming and hopping about like it was trying to get out of its skin. "Hey, fellow, sorry," I whispered. I walked on past rice paddies overflowing with water and jumped over rivulets on the asphalt.

Rounding a corner, I came to a curious item, an empty beer bottle that had a snake in it. Upon observation I determined that it was the famed *mamushi*. It's the deadly poisonous viper of Japan and has distinctive brown, round marks on the side that resemble the ten-yen coin in size and color. It's said that if one bites you, you've only got an hour or so to get to a hospital. Coincidentally Koji had just informed me about the existence of this venomous serpent that very morning. Many years ago while working in his rice field cutting weeds with a *kama*, Koji's father was bitten on a finger by a *mamushi*. He promptly cut the end of the finger off. Ouch. Some farmer had apparently put this snake in the bottle and was planning to come back and get it later, possibly to consume its flesh or drink its blood and gland juices in hopes of enhancing virility. Or they might be planning to turn the snake in to the local government for a cash reward. I thought about letting the poor critter go, but decided it wasn't my business, especially since it was lethal.

After visiting the waterfall near the bottom of the road, I

crossed the highway and stood in a sprinkling rain before a small store. Alas, it was closed. Assuming that the proprietors lived in back, I knocked on the door and after a moment a lady came out. I had trouble understanding the country dialect but I thought she said there was no post office in the tiny village of Ryūmon. All I understood for sure was that if I wanted to mail a letter I'd have to go all the way into Kikuoka. Double alas.

I wanted to buy a can of hot oolong tea out of one of the vending machines in front, but discovered I had no change and the machine kept rejecting my thousand-yen notes. There was a truck slowly coming down the road on the tight curve. I hailed it to a stop and asked the driver for change. Leaving the truck in the middle of the road, he came over and bought the tea, refusing to take my money. He got himself a hot canned coffee, asked me where I was from and said my Japanese was good. This I denied. Then he asked me if Japan was better than America. I said they were both good and that Japanese people had been so kind to me that in my heart they would always be tied for number one. He laughed approvingly.

Since they couldn't get around the truck, three workers from a van came over and bought some hot canned drinks. We got to talking and they insisted on buying me another can of oolong and gave me a cigarette and we all stood there and smoked and talked about simple things until there was a third vehicle waiting. The rain was also picking up.

The truck driver gave me a ride up the road to the bus stop and went on in another direction after apologizing for not driving me out of his way into Kikuoka. I assured him that he'd done all that was necessary. As soon as I got out of his cab and was standing there alone, it started raining in earnest.

Out in the open I waited for the bus. It rained hard. I waited longer. It rained harder. That sort of progression continued until the wind and the torrential downpour drenched me completely despite Koji's fold-up umbrella, which was about as helpful as it would have been underwater, for even though I held it tightly down on my head and backpack, the rain blew right up inside that flimsy ribbed shelter-on-a-pole until water was dripping down from the top of my head. Then it folded back on itself and was whipped about by the strong wind as I tried to return it to its proper form. I was out there looking surely like a man being jerked around by his umbrella when a bus finally came. A few seconds later I was traveling down the road within the protective shell of public transit. There was only one other person inside, a young lady who kept her eyes down as I walked by. I was completely drenched and stood shivering in the aisle. The driver told me to go on and sit down and held up a towel indicating that he'd wipe it up.

In Kikuoka I left a pool of water in and around my seat on the bus. Inside the station I checked my belongings. Everything inside my pack was wet except for the card in its envelope. It was still in the plastic bag from the store and the opening at the top had been folded over and taped. My passport looks to this day as if it were done in watercolor.

I saw a young man with a tall backpack going down the street and asked him if he knew where the post office was. He didn't say anything at first and I thought, oh how silly of me, of course he's traveling and doesn't know where the post office is.

So I apologized for bothering him and before I could walk off, he shocked me by saying, "I'm sorry, I didn't understand a word you said. I'm not Japanese—I'm Canadian."

Turns out he did know where the post office was. It was rather obvious. We were standing in front of it and it was closed. It wasn't raining anymore and so we stood on the sidewalk and talked for a moment. Seems the Canadian was having a difficult time of it traveling around Japan. Because he was of Japanese ancestry, people were always speaking to him in Japanese and unlike me, he wasn't experiencing them as being so kind, generous and understanding. He said that many people, especially old people, couldn't accept the fact that he didn't understand their language and he was getting scolded and yelled at a lot. One older man told him in English that he was a traitor to his race. Some people would keep on talking to him in Japanese even after he told them he couldn't understand. They just didn't get it. He'd been trying to get a job in an English conversation school, but so far no one was interested because they wanted to hire standard white teachers who had the right look. In one place a French woman with a heavy accent got a job instead of him. So he'd given up and was just hiking around till his visa and money ran out. I suggested he go to Kyoto and look up a friend of mine I thought could help him, an American who owned his own language school. I wrote him a note of introduction. He thanked me and we parted.

After a short search, I found a stationery store that sold stamps. The proprietor was a cheerful middle-aged man who wore a sport shirt he proudly told me he'd bought on his honeymoon in Hawaii. He helped me figure out how much postage to put on the envelope.

I went to a handmade noodle place next to the bus station. The fellow there remembered me from before and we got to talking. I ordered some noodles. He offered to mail the letter special delivery first thing in the morning. I insisted he accept money to pay for the additional postage. I was having a good time talking to him while his toddler son ran up to me and then back behind his father's legs. The kid also followed me out to the john and climbed up on a box outside so he could look through the window and watch me pee.

The bus was pulling out and I flagged it down in the middle of the street. There was just the driver and me. As we rode back to Ryūmon, he asked me if I liked Japan, Japanese food, Japanese women and Japanese weather. He said, "In Japan we have four seasons. Do you have four seasons in America?" When I said yes, he then asked me if it's hot or cold in America and if there are rainstorms. He was interested to hear that we had these phenomena too. That was one for the record. I could place it right next to an exchange I had before I left the States for Japan. A waitress

I was chatting with in a café in a little town in Texas asked me if they could see the moon from Japan.

The bus driver surprised me when he turned right at the stop and drove a mile off his route to drop me off at the base of the obscure mountain road to Hōgoji—at no extra cost.

Walking quickly back up the hill in the late afternoon, I was soothed by the quiet of the countryside. All of a sudden myriad crickets simultaneously launched into a chorus that buzzed intensely in my ears. The sawing of their legs accompanied the pounding of mine. Exhilarated by this ringing invertebrate recital I flew to the black, vertical, inscribed stone and the horizontal hewn steps and soon found myself breathing hard and standing amidst the combed pebbles of the courtyard.

There was still a tray of food on the long low meal table and I felt a bit awkward when Shuko, who was cooking, told me it was my lunch. I brought it into the kitchen and put the food away and cleaned up the bowls. Back at the room I asked Norman why it was there. Didn't he or Koji tell Shuko that I went to town? Norman told me that of course Shuko knew I went to town, but that he'd served my food up and made a point that it should stay there and be waiting for me when I returned. Norman suggested it was just a shame trip he was pulling.

It turned out that Shuko had freaked out when he heard I'd left. He was especially piqued that I had missed lunch without getting clear permission and he had gone to Katagiri and complained. Koji hadn't wanted to get involved and so he hadn't said anything. At first that bothered me but then I remembered what he'd said about harmony and decided not to question his judgment. It was clear to me that I hadn't psyched out the situation well enough. I'd have to take the hit for it.

The next morning at the formal tea after morning cleaning, Katagiri broke the uncomfortable silence. "David, while you are here, you must follow the schedule and the rules of the monastery.

Do you understand?" He looked at me but he didn't have to wait because I immediately answered a loud and clear "Hai!" I was sorry to have put him on the spot and I didn't really hold it against Shuko because that's the way things are in temples. If you want to do something different, you'd better plan it well and cover your bases or they'll get you. I've lived in Zen monasteries and centers much of my adult life and I've always had that type of trouble. You should expect to be treated like a child, and if you complain about it you'll just be told to stop acting like one. It's just one of the occupational hazards. I encouraged my grumbling mind to quiet down by admonishing myself over and over, "Don't complain—don't explain."

At the tea break during afternoon work, Shuko asked me if I had gotten the bus before it started raining hard.

"I was worried you were out there getting soaked," he said.

"Your worries were justified," I responded.

"Did you mail the card?" he asked.

"Well, no, I couldn't. The post office was closed. But the guy who runs the noodle shop by the bus station is going to mail it this morning. It'll probably get there a day late."

"Too bad you didn't stay," he said, "The mailman came right after you left. There's a letter from your girlfriend in the box. Didn't you see it?"

"Well no," I said, flustered. "The post office was closed. And you told me he wouldn't . . ."

"Yes, he came. And he said there were pickups and the mail would go out. Your Mother's Day card might have made it on time."

"Thank you, Shuko. Thank you for telling me that," I said, and turned to the others. "Gentlemen, with your permission," and I started banging my head on a post while they looked on in disbelief.

KOBASHI BLOWS IT

When Elin and I were attempting to get cultural visas with permission to work, I was looking for some business that would give me a letter saying they would like me to work for them part-time. The classes at the shipyard had gone well so I asked Kobashi, who had set them up for me, if he could help. I caught him one Sunday after zazenkai at Daianji. I just wanted the permission, I explained to him. I didn't really need any work. I could get my own work. As a matter of fact, after being in Maruyama for almost four months, Elin and I had about twenty hours a week of classes between us and were doing just fine. Our studies and field trips kept us plenty busy—we weren't looking for real jobs. I said I just needed a letter from a prospective employer in order to get permission from Immigration to work.

Kobashi was not self-employed as I had thought. He worked for a company out of Tokyo and the president was afraid I would hold them to it and demand a job using their letter as a weapon. I could tell over the phone that it stressed out Kobashi no end that he couldn't help me. He kept asking what else he could do. I said not to worry about it, that I had other options.

I called up Bop in Kyoto, and told him that the Tokyo company wouldn't play ball. He said, "What are they talking about? Written agreements are no good in Japan anyway—not as far as you're concerned. They're just formalities that express intentions and are to be forgotten if they don't benefit the employer. They just don't want to bother with you 'cause they don't owe you anything."

A few days after I talked to Kobashi, our cultural visa requests had been turned down by the regional Immigration office in Hiroshima, and Miyake in Uzu had told us not to try to get permission to work for the time being, so we forgot about all that. But someone didn't.

Maybe his company didn't owe me anything, but Kobashi sure seemed to think *he* did. The next Sunday he was speaking very rapidly and nervously after zazenkai. I couldn't understand him as well as usual and he was throwing in all sorts of superpolite Japanese jargon. I knew something was wrong so I took him to see savvy Ishitaki. She's at her best when Elin and I are in trouble and she focused right in on Kobashi, starting off by thanking him profusely for all he'd done for us as if she were our mother. They went at it a thousand miles an hour, and the short of it was that what he'd done was to call his neighbors in Uzu, the good folks at Immigration, and he'd said something like: "Do you know David Chadwick? Good. Well I'm trying to help get him some work. He needs to get a letter for you people. Now he's worked for me and I happen to know that he's an excellent English teacher and . . ."

At that point the Immigration official whom he was talking to (was it Miyake?) said something like, "No, he has not worked for you. He can't. He's on a tourist visa and if he worked for you he could be deported."

And I could just imagine Kobashi backing out of that one with the Japanese equivalent of: "Did I say work? Silly me. What I meant to say was . . ."

The poor oaf had blown it righteously and was acting terribly upset and contrite. He did have the foresight to make out new receipts that said all the money I got was for expenses and gave me the old incriminating ones to dispose of. I tried to smile and be gracious but I couldn't hide the fact that my mind was by then a swarming mass of paranoid delirium.

Desperate, I called up Bop. He just laughed and said not to worry and reminded me that Immigration really likes English teachers and tends to overlook minor infractions. "Just don't open a school with a large neon sign across from the train station and you'll be okay. A guy in Osaka on a tourist visa did that and he got kicked out."

Elin and I wanted to believe Bop, but we sank into a low state of despair, worse than when we were yenless. But we did not attack one other. That cold night we fell asleep exhausted, clinging to each other, staring hollow-eyed into the dark, fearing the future and awaiting what we expected would be the threatening sound of an authoritarian knock on our beloved home's front door. Except they wouldn't knock. They'd call out an apology for bothering us and being rude and then they'd take their shoes off in the entryway before stepping up into the house.

TAIZEN SMOOTHES IT OUT

MARUYAMA, FEBRUARY 27, 1989

Taizen is another good old boy from Texas just like Elin and me. He'd look great in blue jeans and a bolo tie, but wears robes pretty handsomely too. Elin calls him our cowboy monk, but Ishitaki says he has wonderful Japanese manners. He is one of our best friends at the temple and is working on his second decade in Japan. He's paid his dues. He was in a very tough training temple for years. He told me once he cried himself to sleep every night for six months—something about a senior monk continually threatening to smash him in the head with a brick. He survived all this "rough practice" as it's called (although I guess the brick bit is beyond any acceptable norm) but I think it took its toll.

Taizen can read old Buddhist writings as easily as he can browse through the Japanese-language newspapers. He read *You*

Gotta Have Wa in Japanese—it was written in English for god's sake. If anything, his English was suffering.

He was head monk for six years at Daianji. He'd often sit zazen all night. He was really trying to bust through to enlightenment—and this is a real bust-through-to-enlightenment sort of place—but he seems to have met a bamboo wall in his koan practice with Watanabe. He says they don't have *en*, a heavy word meaning something like affinity or karmic connection. He's dissatisfied but still trying.

Unlike Jessica, who takes everything lightly, Taizen tries to fit in and be accepted on Japanese terms and this makes him a little uptight. He's always telling me things like to fix the holes in our shoji (the ones that can be seen from the garden when approaching the front door) or people will write us off. (I did get to it, but not for his reasons.) Jessica was there when he said that and she just laughed at him and offered that we were all written off to begin with for not being Japanese.

His Japanese is proper and polished and the way Jessica throws plain informal language around, especially when she's talking to Watanabe or people in the neighborhood, gives him the willies, but he says she can get away with it because she's a potter and thus allowed to be eccentric. I told Taizen that it seems to me the main thing is that she doesn't care what anyone thinks except for Watanabe and Watanabe doesn't seem to care at all about pretenses. "So *you* get along better with Ishitaki and *Jessica* gets along better with Hōjō-san," I told Taizen, who made a face and said that maybe I was right and it was time for him to get out of Japan.

I agreed, but Jessica wouldn't have. Taizen's proper monkness and Jessica's hippie-funk lay-woman vibes do not interfere with the fact that they are best friends. They're always giving each other presents—he made her an *inkan* (a personal seal that all Japanese use instead of signatures) with the kanji for her Buddhist name, Jodai, carved into the small round end, and she gave him a pair of warm wool socks and a can of instant chocolate for the coming winter. Like Jessica, Elin and I like Taizen a lot—but we do wish he'd soften up a little.

I needed Taizen's help. I had no idea what the folks at Immigration were thinking since Kobashi had so generously called them up for me, and I needed to talk to Miyake to make sure everything was okay. I begged Taizen to help me, because his Japanese was so good and Miyake liked him and I thought that this was no time for unintentionally making an unimaginably rude mistake.

"Ask Jo-san (Jessica)," he said.

"She's no good at stuff like that. And she won't do it. She has a policy against it. You're my only hope."

"Ask her again. You think I'm too uptight anyway."

"That's true, but she's more uptight about the truth than you are. It's funny, temple-wise she's a company woman."

"Yeah, I know what you mean. She's in tight with the boss. Well I'm busy, ne," he said.

"You people are supposed to be doing nothing but you never have any time. Mercy! Mercy!"

"Your Japanese is fine, ne." He's always saying ne, which means something like "isn't it?" or "don't you think so?"

"You're a priest, you're supposed to be helping people. Save all sentient beings. Remember? In this case me."

"You're a priest too, ne?" he said. "Help yourself, ne."

"No I'm not. I failed."

"No more than I have—and don't give me that reverse arrogance trip. It's too easy an out."

"Help me please. For all I know they now regard me as an undesirable alien and I want to be represented by a respected alien monk. It might be my only shot. C'mon Taizen, don't be selfish."

"Hmmm. It's tough, ne. I think what you mean by selfish," he said, "is like someone who's not thinking about you first, ne?"

"You wound me deeply, Taizen, and you are absolutely correct," I admitted.

He hemmed and hawed—I offered the ultimate bribe. It worked. We agreed to meet in ten minutes, just enough time for me to get his bribe. "See you then, dharma brother." I bowed deeply in gratitude. "And Taizen," I added, "you know you're gonna need remedial English lessons before you move back to the States."

He and I met at the pay phone in the parking lot in front of the temple. I gave him his bribe straight off. It was more than he'd dreamed of, a sixteen-inch-long chocolate bar—really good chocolate, rich and not too sweet. It cost a thousand yen. He looked around and when he was sure he wasn't being watched, he tore off some of the wrapping and took a furtive bite. I love to corrupt monks. Everybody's got their price.

With a shaky index finger I made the call and said hello to Miyake after I got him on the line. We exchanged a few pleasantries. So far so good. Then, after asking permission, I put Taizen on and they soon were talking around the delicate topic of our visa status. After a while Taizen thanked Miyake a few times and hung up the receiver. The call went quite well. I was incredibly relieved that Miyake didn't mention Kobashi's call. So it looked like they were not going to deport us after all. Terrific.

A great blue heron lifted out of the mizo by the stone bridge and flew up over the power lines. It was a lovely day.

I bowed down, touching my forehead to the asphalt, physically exaggerating a gratitude I truly felt to Taizen and all our benefactors.

"Stop it," he said with embarrassment. "The neighbors, ne."

"I couldn't control myself," I said, standing up as he looked around uncomfortably.

"Maaah . . . look what's coming," he said, squinting to focus on a figure walking down the street lined on both sides by pines. It was a monk. He was pretty far off but I could make out that he was in robes. "That's the head monk from Shimbōji," he said. "He's on a pilgrimage."

We watched the monk approach. He wore the traditional

monk's traveling gear, similar to the takuhatsu outfit. His conical basketlike hat hid his face from his nose up. I could see a samurai movie stiff-lipped scowl. Taizen bowed appropriately.

"Hey there!" I said without thinking, and waved. Taizen elbowed me in the ribs as if that was not the correct thing for me to do.

"Phooey on him," I said as the monk continued walking silently with eyes down. Except for my unappreciative presence it could have been a scene out of a documentary on the preservation of the ancient and serene way of Zen in bustling, modern Japan.

When he had entered the gate, I turned to Taizen, "I hate monks. They think they're so much better than everyone else."

Taizen rubbed his hairless head. "Yeah, I know what you mean, ne—I hate them too, ne."

A LETTER AND
A TABLE

HŌGOJI, MAY 6, 1988

When I stopped banging my head on the beam, I picked up the letter that had arrived the day before when I was out drowning in the rain. I was tingling with excitement, but I tried to act cool and took a sip of tea before casually opening my treasure. I slowly took out the letter and began reading.

Norman saw the return address on my letter. "Ah, a letter from David's sweetheart."

Everyone looked up.

"The letter you've been waiting for?" asked Koji.

"Yes," I said.

Jakushin asked what her name was and I told him.

"Oh, Elin," said Katagiri. "From Zen Center? The one who took care of my room at Green Gulch?"

"Yes."

"I thought she was from Georgia," said Koji.

"That's where her mother lives. She's just there for a while finishing her thesis for college."

Katagiri smiled. "She's a very pretty young woman."

"Yes."

"And she has a pleasant . . ." He was thinking. ". . . an easy way. Zen is natural to her."

The guys were listening intently. I felt a little proud.

"Opposite from you." Katagiri slapped me on the shoulder. "You are the enemy of Zen."

"Elin's a good volleyball player," said Norman.

"Uh-huh." I was still fumbling the letter in my hands.

"Are you going to marry her?" asked Koji.

"Well, I don't know. I don't know when I'll even see her again."

"Is she a Buddhist?" asked Jakushin, who hadn't understood when Katagiri said she was from Zen Center.

"David's being very quiet," said Katagiri, pushing me. "Maybe you're in love."

There I was, surrounded, with everyone laughing at me.

"You're turning red," said Koji.

"Let the poor guy read the letter," said Norman mercifully.

They returned to their newspaper and I dove into the piece of paper I had been dying to receive. What she said wasn't at all what I'd expected. I thought she'd say that it had been nice knowing me and let's be friends, but she said that she missed me and loved me! Yippee. She went on and on conjecturing why I hadn't written her. She'd received nothing at all from me. In fact, I'd sent her several cards with friendly and restrained notes on them.

"What does it say?" asked Koji, unable to let me be any longer.

"She says she didn't get my cards."

"How long ago did you send them?" asked Norman.

"I sent one almost three weeks ago. Hers only took three days to get here."

"She's gotten it by now," Norman said.

"Maybe it got lost by the post office in America," said Shuko.

"Oh sure, and why couldn't it have been lost by the post office in Japan?" Norman snapped back at him.

"The Japanese post office doesn't lose letters like they do in America. Here all the workers take their jobs very seriously."

Before Norman could counterattack, Katagiri returned us to the subject. "Did she say that she loved you?" he asked, teasing.

I was pleased to answer. "Yes, she did, and she said that she loves you too." Katagiri reeled back as everyone laughed at him.

"Good one, David," said Norman.

"She says hi to you, Roshi, and to Norman and Shuko. I told her in the States you guys would all be here."

"What else did she say?" asked Koji.

"Well, she said that she loves me but she has a problem."

"What's that?" he said.

"She says that I'm too fat and too loud and too old and that I'm an alcoholic." I put the letter back in my pocket amidst their laughter, but I reread it several times before dinner.

When *yakuseki* was over I went to my room and took off my robes. After hanging them on the rack I threw on some jeans and a flannel shirt. It would be a couple of hours till evening zazen and I wanted to get a letter of my own written to Elin and off with the next day's mail. I looked at her letter on my desk and felt a tightening in my throat and chest, an aching. I remembered her affectionate manner, her clear eyes and disarming laugh, how appreciative she was of politeness, attention and small gifts. (She comes from a family that, although large and loving, had an overbearing emphasis on self-reliance and a get-the-next-to-the-cheapest-thing-on-the-menu thrift.) I thought of how she'd snap at me for saying something that was philosophically superficial or careless, how she scoffed at mindless adherence to any path like Zen or the political correctness she encountered at school. I envied how fast she could read, how involved she'd get in books, and how easily she'd cry as she turned the pages. "Ahhh," I groaned, and rubbed my eyes. I must write. What to say? I stepped outside. Perhaps a brief commune with nature would clarify things.

I went down to the steps on the corner of our deck and started to slip my feet into my zori when I noticed something moving in one of my tennis shoes. Oh no, I cringed, not a mukade. I carefully picked up my shoe and was preparing to shake it out when I saw a pair of tiny eyes staring at me from the cave below the tongue and laces. Something moved back further in. It wasn't a mukade. I put the tennis shoe down on the ground, tilting it toward the heel and tapping. A small green lump appeared—a tiny frog. Quickly it came bounding out with what was probably the highest leap of its life and went bouncing away into the bushes. "Ahhh!" I exclaimed aloud, and then in a Miss Piggy whine, "Kermit, I might have squashed you!"

I walked over to Koji's, passing in front of the bonsho and thinking about ubiquitous life. I looked at my feet to make sure I wasn't stepping on anything and thought of the Jains in India who traditionally went naked, filtered their water so as to save tiny life and carried sticks with bells to warn little creatures of their coming. I looked at the big bell in its house to my left. In my mind's eye I pictured it with large wheels and me pushing it and ringing it to warn all beings that my big feet would soon arrive over their heads and to please move out of the way. But, of course, the giant wheels of the bell house were grinding veritable civilizations of microscopic creatures into minioblivion. I mounted it on a balloon so that it floated before me ringing its mellow deep knell kilometers in advance. I flew around the bell, circling higher and higher over Kyūshū.

"What was that all about?" came Koji's voice interrupting my flight. "And don't walk on the moss."

I tiptoed off the island of moss and walked up to Koji's door. He sat down at his low table on a zabuton and asked me to please sit down on the zabuton before another similar and heretofore unseen table that was perpendicular to his. There was a vase on it with wild flowers. And there was a clean, well-trimmed and full kerosene lamp.

"Very nice," I said. "Where'd you get this?"

"Yoshiko-san. She said that she didn't need it. Do you like it?"

"Yeah, it looks elegant. The grain is beautiful," I said, stroking it. "What type of wood is it?"

"Keyaki."

I looked it up in his dictionary—zelkova. I'd never heard of it but I'd seen it in Japanese homes in San Francisco.

"It's for you to use anytime you want. Even if I'm sleeping."

"Ahhh, Koji, that's so kind of you."

He pointed to the window directly to the left of the table. "It has good light."

I slid open the shoji and looked down at the round cement stupa and lawn below, illuminated by the setting sun. "Thank you very much, Koji," I said as politely and sincerely as I could in Japanese. "You are truly my good friend."

Then he made us coffee with Creap and pulled out a couple of cigarettes from a box on his table. I decided to put off the letter to Elin until after zazen.

"I'm happy you are here," he said. "I never get to talk to anyone about what I'm thinking."

"Please—talk away."

Koji did talk away and I learned some about recent Hōgoji history. It turns out that he'd been unhappy at Hōgoji for a year, ever since two dharma buddies of his split. He'd been with them for two and a half years at the head temple and then half a year at Hōgoji. They were good monks he said, but most important was that they were all compatible. For a while it was just the three of them and they lived and practiced together harmoniously, following the schedule and getting the old run-down temple back in order. They were the first team that Nishiki sent when he decided to bring Hōgoji out of moth balls and develop it into an international temple.

One day Nishiki arrived with his disciple Shuko and made him the head monk. Shuko hadn't gone to Suienji from another temple, Suienji was now his home temple. He wasn't sent to train under Nishiki by his father whose temple he'd take over someday like most of them. Shuko's years abroad and unusual command of English would obviously be indispensable in dealing with foreigners and it seemed Nishiki planned for Hōgoji to become Shuko's temple.

Another disciple of Nishiki's arrived at the same time. Shuko and this other monk were tight, like Koji was with his buddies. They came speaking of Nishiki's way and Dōgen's way. They were full of ideas of how to structure Hōgoji so that it would be like Dōgen's original temple near Kyoto. Immediately the chemistry was bad. Hōgoji became polarized. Koji said that Shuko and his cohort didn't practice with their bodies but with their heads. They spent all their time together planning the future of Hōgoji and remade the schedule. He said that they got so fanatic about studying the old systems and rules that they stopped joining in on most of the schedule with Koji and the other two monks, including the zazen. Koji said that they were just in Shuko's room planning all the time. Things got more and more uncomfortable.

Nishiki came to Hōgoji to check things out and one of the monks felt compelled to fill him in on what had been going on. Nishiki was furious and immediately made Koji the head monk. Shuko's friend had to go back to Suienji. Nishiki told Shuko in front of the others that he shouldn't go off on a trip on his own like that. His practice should be to follow the entire schedule and not to try to control things. He was just a new monk and he should practice accordingly. Shuko, humiliated, nodded his agreement. He apologized for causing discord, but said that he was only trying to establish Dōgen's way for Nishiki Roshi. He said that it was obvious that his understanding was flawed and that he would practice sincerely with the others and try to purify his mind.

According to Koji, Shuko had said all the right contrite things and was just laying low and waiting for the time he could come out again. Norman, Jakushin and Maku came from Suienji to give the place some new blood. But for Koji's buddies the damage was done and soon they cut their stays short to get back to their home temples. The magic was gone and Koji was alone.

"Only the egotistical monks are left. Even now Shuko puts on airs," Koji said, shaking his head.

"Weird," I said. I hadn't been aware of any of this. "I thought that only Norman was having a problem with Shuko. Shuko's so quiet and seems to get along with everyone."

"He still has a plan," said Koji. "He wears his yellow robe, the transmission robe. It's like bragging. I have one too but it has no meaning in a *sōdō* (monk's hall) like this. I only wear black robes. All that matters is seniority."

"All that matters is seniority?" I asked. "What about heart or understanding?"

"Of course seniority means nothing by itself. But as for who's in charge, seniority is the determining factor and his yellow robe doesn't give him that. I am the most senior monk in training both here and at Suienji. I've been away from home for four years. No one else has trained here for that long except the officers and head priests. I'm sorry to brag. That's not my intention. I don't want any power but I sure don't want Shuko to have it. He forces me to remember my seniority."

"Well, I'm sorry that all happened Koji. I don't care who's senior but I'm glad you're in charge 'cause you've got a light touch."

"One good thing is it is wonderful having Katagiri Roshi here. He is a great priest. I don't have such a strong feeling for

Nishiki as a dharma teacher, just as a form teacher. Katagiri is an emptiness teacher."

"I agree. It's good to be with him here—sitting and working together, eating, doing takuhatsu, having tea. Not much talking, with him anyway."

"He teaches with his posture and his silence," said Koji.

I nodded.

"Things got better when he came," said Koji, "but only since you came have I been happy again. You have inspired me."

"Certainly not with my silence, but my posture's not bad. Anyway, I'm just having fun," I said to him, "Corrupting the head monk."

He waved me off in jest saying that was just a lie.

"No, it's true. Look what's happening to you Koji. I'm tempting you from your duty and pulling you from your faith with everything I've got. Are you sure I don't work for Mara (the legendary king of the lower realms)?"

"I don't think so," he said, laughing.

"Well, be careful. Do you know what Baker Roshi, Suzuki Roshi's successor, said?"

"No. What?"

"He said that my practice was to lead my fellow students on the path to hell."

Koji put his cigarette out. I rubbed my new table and admired the grain.

A WALK WITH
FATHER SAM

HŌGOJI, MAY 7, 1988

A Catholic priest walked into the courtyard during morning work. Shuko suggested we have the tea break early. While he prepared the tea and coffee tray, I hit the clackers calling all monks to the kuin steps. The priest's name was Father Sam. "Just call me Sam," he said. He was originally from New Jersey and had been with the Jesuit order in Tokyo for twenty-two years. He was of medium height with a neat grey beard and wore loose brown trousers and a soft brown shirt with clerical collar. Everyone was impressed with his Japanese and enjoyed talking with him during the tea break. He spoke briefly with each of the Japanese monks, asking where they were from and how long each had practiced. He was surprised to find out that only Koji was the son of a priest and that Katagiri's family had been Jōdo Shin-shū, which he said was faith Buddhism, the closest to Catholicism of the Japanese Buddhist sects. Sam had a good way with the Japanese. He didn't assert himself too much and he made each person feel special. He talked for a while with Katagiri in Japanese and English.

After tea Katagiri suggested that Norman and I show him around. The first thing he did in the hatto was offer incense and bow, obviously an ecumenicalist at heart. It turned out to be a tour for Norman and me, as he was well versed in iconography, Japanese and Buddhist history and temple architecture. He especially appreciated the Medicine Buddha and suggested that it was made in another part of Japan.

The single item that interested him the most at Hōgoji was a *suzumebachi* (sparrow bee) nest that was sitting under the walkway between the hatto and the kuin. He'd never seen one before. It looked like a hornet's nest except it was as big as a beach ball, over two feet in diameter. He touched it.

"It's like a heavy brown paper," he said. "And look at the design, the layers, like overlapping curtains with these circular dips accented in darker brown. Masterful. Fantastic."

"It was retrieved from the rafters of the hatto when the roof tile was replaced last year," Norman informed him.

"And just how big are the suzumebachi here?" Sam asked, unconsciously fingering his crucifix.

"Big enough to be called sparrow bees," replied Norman.

It didn't take long to exhaust the possibilities in our small temple so we went out for a walk.

Norman and I took him up the narrow asphalt road. Sam only had a light shoulder bag with him and he took it along. The three of us walked slowly and quietly, enjoying the mountain beauty. On the way up we surveyed a gully of trash that the farmers had dumped in a ravine. There amidst the cedars and pines and the call of the nightingale were old bicycles and cans, futon, tires, toys, a refrigerator and plastic containers. A tricycle had been thrown too far and was lodged in the crotch of an oak. "Ho ho ke kyo! Ho ho ke kyo!" sang the uguisu from a branch of a plum tree beyond the trash.

At the road's end we climbed down the bank and continued up the creek bed to where there were two short waterfalls. Sam said he didn't often get to a spot that remote, that he envied the Hōgoji monks living in such a magnificent location. Norman said that Daigyo Zenji had known these mountains well, but that only Yoshiko knew them now. Probably none of the Japanese monks had ever seen those falls.

With some difficulty we went over a ridge and down to another road lined with logs draped with cedar branches growing shiitake underneath in the shade. On the road was an empty box that had contained the short dowels of wood with a mushroom spore in each. There was sawdust on the road indicating that not long before a farmer had drilled holes in the lengths of log, pushed in the plugs and discarded the box.

A dirt trough was flowing with runoff water. Boards were blocking openings to branching irrigation troughs awaiting the time to fill the rice paddies. Little green frogs were jumping out of our way as we walked by. We passed an occasional old farmer. Continuing around the edges of the rice fields, shaped by the contours of the hillside, we came to an undisturbed virgin oak grove. Norman explained that for hundreds and hundreds of years the farmers had never cut down this grove to make more room for growing rice because within the grove there is an ohaka for nuns who had practiced at Hōgoji. The three of us walked in under the shade of the oak trees. It was cool and dark and there was lichen on the mottled stones that had long ago fallen and been collected and put in a neat pile in the center as is the custom with toppled and scattered grave markers. Norman said this ohaka was off by itself because the nuns' remains couldn't be with those of the monks.

Sam nodded, "Can women come to practice at Hōgoji now?"

Norman squatted by the stones. "Hōgoji will be undergoing a major transformation in the next few years. There will be full facilities for fifteen monks. Nishiki says the groundwork is being laid for the formal admission of women as students in the near future. Right now they can come as guests like David, but there's only room for one or two guests. So it's happening, slowly as might be expected, but it's definitely happening."

"The only places where women and men practice together in Japanese Zen dōjō are where there are foreigners," Sam commented.

"Nishiki got the idea to make this into an international temple that accepts women when he went to Minnesota to visit Katagiri. Katagiri planted the seed. Until then Nishiki didn't think it was possible. He's a very traditional priest. It's a big move for him."

"The Catholic hierarchy is even more intransigent than the Zen hierarchy is. We've got no motion going in that direction. I wish we did. I'm familiar with some of the coed Zen temples in Japan, in the U.S. and in Europe and I wish we would follow suit. There are, of course, problems that come up when men and women are together but I think that it causes even more trouble when they are apart."

"How so?" I asked.

"People tend to get petty when isolated with only their own sex. Men get immature and women get vicious. At least that's what I've seen in our monasteries."

We left the nuns' ohaka, walked between rice paddies down to the road that led back up to Hōgoji and stopped to sit by a bamboo grove where we drank cold mountain water that was flowing down a rivulet.

"I was just here a couple of hours ago on my way up to the temple," said the priest, waving his hand before his face to chase off a fly. "We've come full circle. I didn't know where I was." He peered into the shadowed recesses of the segmented forest. "This is what a bamboo grove looks like when it's left alone. It always surprises me. In the tended gardens there are only vertical shafts and the feeling is controlled. A wild grove has many fallen stalks and all sorts of angled lines breaking the up and down." Sam pointed into the chaotic thicket.

"It looks like a Kandinsky painting," Norman said.

"Or a giant pickup-sticks game," I added.

Norman drank some more water and dried his hand on his grey samue. "You seem pretty familiar with Zen. Are you with the group of Jesuits that sit zazen in Tokyo?"

"Yes. There are a few Catholic zazenkai in Japan. I sit with a group at Sophia, the Jesuit university where I teach, and I go to Kamakura once a week to sit and have dokusan with Koryū Roshi, whom I also do seven day *sesshin* (concentrated zazen retreat) with twice a year."

"And how long have you been sitting?" Norman asked.

"Eighteen years."

"What do you teach at Sophia?" I asked.

"Buddhism."

"Do you get any heat for all this?"

"The head of the Jesuits has a zafu in his office in the Vatican. We have to be careful, but as long as we don't go preaching heretical doctrines it's no problem. The Catholic church is probably the most diverse religious organization on earth. Buddhism hasn't had a doctrinal influence on it, but Buddhist practices, especially zazen, have influenced the practice of priests and nuns all over the world. Thomas Merton helped to rekindle interest in meditation in Catholic monasteries and he was greatly moved by Buddhist practices. There are a couple of Jesuits teaching Zen in Europe now."

"What's the difference between Catholic meditation and zazen?" asked Norman.

"Zazen has no object. There have been some disputes in the order about the appropriateness of a form of worship that doesn't focus on Christ or Mary or something sacred to the Church. I also had a problem at first with letting go of an object of devotion in meditation."

"What did you do about it?" I asked.

"Some people, like some nuns I know, combine zazen with devotional concentration. I came to believe that true faith needs no form to support it and that a mere mental symbolic representation of a sacred object in one's imagination is not the holy object itself, and so I sit still and wait, which is an invitation for God to enter. It seems to me that's at least as appropriate as carrying a mental picture into the vastness of meditation. In the end, I cannot hold on anyway and am left naked to face God on God's own terms, not on mine."

Sam looked at his watch and said that he'd better get going.

He gave us each a card and asked us to look him up when we were in Tokyo. We shook hands and he walked down the road, around a bend and out of sight, another fellow being on the path.

HUSBANDS AND WIVES

MARUYAMA, FEBRUARY 20, 1989

My husband hardly ever buys me anything. He says I can buy myself whatever I want. So I can't return this purse, or he'll never buy me anything again." Kubo was telling this to her fellow MMC members, laughing and talking at once as is her style. She reminds me of Lucille Ball. She runs on at the mouth a lot—especially when speaking Japanese. Savvy Ishitaki, who can't stand Kubo, told me if she sees Kubo in the supermarket she'll push her cart to the other end of the store and hide. I told Ishitaki that I thought Kubo might have a chemical imbalance that is exacerbated by caffeine, but Ishitaki sees Kubo's garrulousness as a moral problem, and with a "humph," suggested Kubo should go back to Kyoto where she came from.

Kubo had been going on for ten minutes and soon I'd have to step in to give someone else a turn. Before she got onto her husband and the purse, Kubo had told us how she'd gotten hysterical screaming at her son because he failed the entrance exam to a school she wanted him to get into. Shimizu, who says he never pushes his wonderful, friendly teenage daughters (both Elin's students), told Kubo she should trust her son and not fret.

"Let him follow his sports interests—he'll work out okay, don't worry. People are too hard on their children."

I cheered him on. He's a saint—it's just what she needs to

191

hear. She's not a listener though. She just kept going, rattling on about how her son's life was over and how he'd be a burden on the family. I was relieved when the conversation shifted.

"We don't have love marriage. We are *tanshin funin* (single–work-away) couple. He works in Northern Japan and Osaka and only comes home for one or two nights a week. He calls me on the phone. I say, 'moshi-moshi' ('hello' for the phone) and he says, 'boku' (me). Just 'boku' and the time I should pick him up. I say, 'hai' and he says, 'ja' (something like 'well then') and we hang up. I pick him at the station late at night and drive him back early in the morning. Yesterday he gave me this ugly purse for my birthday. And I must keep it."

It was ugly—green plastic and sequins.

"I am so sad for you," said slender Mrs. Tanahashi, who always waited awhile before she softly entered into the conversation.

"It's okay, I will buy myself another purse today."

"No, I am sad because your husband is not close."

"Oh no! Don't be sad. I am happy. Being apart is good. He never get angry. No drinking. When he is gone I am free. Not slave of home. I can study English and teach Japanese to foreigners and shop every day. I am grateful."

Boy, these marriage stories I get. A high percentage of the women I teach talk about their husbands' absence. Some adjust, like Kubo, and others complain. The main problem is that the guys don't come home, many wives say, till three or four—every night. This was the problem of two wealthy women students of mine. One told her husband she was fed up and would take the children and leave if things didn't change. They ended up "compromising": he'd get home by ten o'clock one night a week. The other, a doctor's wife, has a different attitude about her absentee husband. "My husband works late and goes out too. But I'm happy to have for husband an *erai hito* (esteemed person). I respect him. When he comes in around four o'clock he always says, 'tada ima' (I'm back), and I say, 'okaeri' (welcome back), and go back to sleep."

I asked where their husbands went and they said to the JCs —the Junior Chamber of Commerce. That's what they all say. They must be an actual organization in town but "JCs" also seems like a code word for playing around in the night world of the water trade.

Another housewife told me that the deal she made with her husband is that he could go to the JCs every night of the week but one, if he would take care of their kids for an hour and a half, so she could study English on that one night.

These are attractive, charming, educated, expressive women— their husbands should be happy to come home to them. And they have wonderful children—I meet all the kids. They're so sweet. The guys don't know what they're missing. I have men students who joke about having to spend a day with their family once a month. I ask them, "What did you do last weekend?" Over and over I hear, "I went fishing," "I played pachinko all day Sunday" (most people work on Saturday), "I went to Tokyo with my friends," and of course, "I worked." I just don't get it. Elin said that, to her, the biggest and most incomprehensible difference between the States and here is the relationship between the men and the women. They really have separate lives.

A fellow named Rod whom I study Japanese with specializes in having affairs with love-starved married women. He says they're the only ones who don't want to tie him down—or at least that's what he thought till he got involved with what he called his Number Ten. After her suicide attempt he said he was pretty shaken up and didn't date for a while. But as with any habit, time diminishes the negative memories and magnifies the craving. He comes to class looking tired a lot.

What's weird is that most of the families I know outside of classes are different from what I hear about in class or meet downtown. Some of the men work late, but they usually come home at a reasonable hour and are home on Sunday. And none of them smokes or drinks much. They usually eat dinner together with their families. Our good friends, the Hashimotos, clearly enjoy each other's company. Mr. Okamura next door often eats three meals a day at home with his wife. The young couple down the street, the Tanakas, are together a lot. Ishitaki Sensei works late a lot but he doesn't play around—his wife drives him to work and picks him up every day. Shimizu is always home—his liquor store is downstairs. And instead of going out he paints in his spare time and has a *karaoke* club that meets at his home every Saturday night to sing.

I asked the MMC about the seeming discrepancy. Mrs. Kubo said that people who study English have more money so the men can afford to go out at night. Morikawa, the slightly plump professor's wife, said that people around here have plenty of money and that many poorer men just go to cheaper places and that I'm blessed to have so many friends and neighbors who have close families.

"My husband love to be with daughters," Tanahashi said. "He comes home as early as he can and we are together almost every Sunday."

It's funny, I thought. Our discussions of marriage (and there had been many, with a lot of emphasis on the changing roles of women) are typical of much of our talk. At first the generalizations are built up, and then they get torn down. We spend a lot of our time talking about patterns of culture in the States and Japan. America is too diverse to get a handle on, but Japan isn't easy either. This is a culture with a foot in the ancient past, another in the near past, a hand in the West and another reaching for the future—and the head is wearing a series of different masks.

Poor Etsuko, the not-yet-married school teacher, had been left out of the conversation and sat smiling on the couch. I asked her if she had anything to say.

"Oh, I'd be happy to have a husband who stayed out sometimes and gave me ugly purse—but not drink. So maybe better not stay out. I hate the sake when men drink. He could smoke. I don't care smoke." Her head tilted back and forth. "Hmm, I don't know. I am waiting."

LION AND ROCKS

MARUYAMA, FEBRUARY 23, 1989

One morning sitting zazen and waiting my turn for sanzen, I saw Mind, not as obscure or deep and hidden, but as superficial and immediately available. I sat there breathing and before long I was thinking about how to get our new video camera working. Then I moved on to the day's schedule. I caught myself and wondered how much of a hindrance these thoughts were. The pulling power of my thinking was low and an image arose with the phrase "bones in the corner of the cage." Yep, just old meatless bones I'm gnawing on. And then I thought, well what am I then, the cage? I experienced myself as that room with the cement walls and metal bars, the floor with the bones on it, and some water in a trough by the edge. Hm. The cage? Is that it? I sat and watched and then from within I heard breathing and sensed movement and saw a lion's tail sweep around before me in a circular path.

On another day sometime later than the lion tale, Elin and I sat and talked after Sunday morning zazenkai. She had enjoyed the session, as she usually does, in spite of the fact that in the second period the two monks running the show ceremoniously whack everyone four times on each shoulder with their long whacking sticks. Of course, if they didn't do it, people would complain because that's Authentic Zen—getting hit with a stick.

She said that in zazen that morning she had visualized a rope in the sea with depth markers and she had held a big rock that brought her deeper, deeper, deeper down past the depth markers till she sat on the ocean floor quite relaxed and at peace. She's mentioned using rocks to go down deep before.

She easily settles like a clam into calm states, whereas I have to go through a longer process where I am more like a little fish darting about in the water. I told her that her rock method reminded me of what Father Sam had told me: "We fall into heaven." I visualized her sinking with the rock into heaven. "Rock. Oh yes, Rock. Aha!" I said, remembering. "I had a rock too."

For, while Elin had been deeply breathing and sinking I had been having sexual fantasies and then thinking about my English classes and then about how my Japanese studies were progressing and then I remembered my breath and followed it until I was talking to a group of women in a mist who spoke in unison like a Greek chorus. They chastised me for being dependent on this so-called "Zen."

"Well, yes," I told them, "I guess I am dependent, but I like it best. I feel like it frees me and I'm familiar with it. It's easy. Breathe in, breathe out."

"If it's so easy, how come you say you don't understand it?"

"I'm a slow poke at Zen but, no hurry. Look, with all my cares and confusions and complicated involvements and with being pulled toward this and that, I can sit here and forget it all and still be alert and sober." I thought that was convincing, but they persisted.

"You *are* dependent on it. You should depend on yourself."

Then I saw right in front of me a tube about one foot wide in diameter rising from below. My breath went in and out of it and I looked at the opening, which was covered with a thin membrane that held an image like a watermark in its translucent surface.

That's the self, I thought, and they want me to depend on that? "I don't know who you think you are," I told them, "but I don't get your wisdom."

"Not *that* self, stupid," they laughed, "your Big Self."

I pulled the membrane from over the tube. It had the consistency of a balloon. I tied it up in a knot and started to throw it down the hole, but I thought, "Gosh, I don't want to make it choke." Then I just dropped the membrane as I saw that the tube had a new self image spread across its top. I looked at it and then that surface image was sucked in and the tube itself receded with it and I was left floating in space, seated upon a stone, legs around it, and I noticed it was carved into the form of a stone lion. I nodded in agreement to an intention I felt in the lion and it dropped.

As it went down, I thought, "Just like Elin."

KATAGIRI

MARUYAMA, FEBRUARY 25, 1989

Isabel called from her place north of San Francisco, near Zen Center's Green Gulch farm. She's a buddy from way back. We both started studying with Suzuki and Katagiri in the same year. She's my Zen sister—keeps me in touch with what's happening in the States. Isabel was worried about Katagiri. He'd been sick since the past summer, since shortly after he and I were at Hōgoji. She and Tomoe-san, his wife, had ganged up on him and made him go to the doctor. They had to shame him, asking him what sort of example he thought he was being to his students when he didn't take care of his own health. He was coughing a lot. So he went to the doctor, who said he had a cough. He's been coughing since. And now he's so sick he's in the hospital, but it appears he'll be out soon. Almost all the Japanese priests I've known seem to have such weak bodies—they're always getting ill.

Last fall Isabel and Tomoe had also tried to encourage him to stay in the States and rest rather than return to Japan to lead a month-long gathering of Western and Japanese Zen teachers. He did go and was sick the whole time. He's really into the Japan connection these days. Why's he trying so hard to connect us apples and oranges—this paternalistic hierarchical anachronism in Japan and the wild bunch of American Zen loonies back home? I guess he thinks there's some hope for us all. I hope so. And I hope he gets well soon.

I met Katagiri at the San Francisco Zen Center back in '66 when I, an unkempt semihippie with curly long hair all frizzled out, first came to check it out. The fellow who opened the door, a Caucasian like me, introduced me to Katagiri, calling him Sensei. He and I talked in the small funky office on the second floor of Sokoji on Bush Street, an old synagogue that had long ago been converted into a Soto Zen temple for the San Francisco Japanese-American community. I'd looked around for a place to meditate in California and hadn't found anything I liked so I was on my way to the office of Icelandic Airline to buy a ticket to Europe. From there I planned to get to Asia, where I would seek enlightenment. But I had the thought that maybe I should see if there was a Zen temple in San Francisco. Sure enough there was. Like Norman, I'd just looked up "Zen" in the phone book.

There I was in that run-down old place talking to this shaved-headed, smiling and kindly-seeming Zen priest. He was thirty-eight at the time but looked younger. Wow, I thought, I've finally met a Zen priest. So this is what one looks like.

He was sitting on a couch. "What can I do for you?" he said.

"I want to learn to meditate." I wanted to find a group of people I could meditate with until I could do it on my own, I explained.

"You should have a teacher," he said.

"A teacher?" I asked. "Why do I need a teacher?"

While he answered me I looked him over. He's got nice vibes, but he's nervously tapping the pencil in his hand while he talks to me. Hmm. That doesn't seem to be what a Zen master should be like. They shouldn't have any nervous energy. Aren't they perfectly clear with no thoughts in their heads?

"A teacher is beyond your judgment," he said, making me wonder if he was reading my mind.

"Should you be my teacher?" I asked.

"No. Suzuki Sensei should be your teacher. He's in Japan now, but he'll be back in a couple of weeks."

"Why can't you be my teacher?" I went on. "Could you be my teacher?"

"I could be, but Suzuki Sensei should be," he said with finality. It was Suzuki's temple. Katagiri played second fiddle there for years. He gave me a brief instruction in zazen and showed me the schedule.

I stayed for the evening zazen period, which started at five thirty, and sat on a raised platform in an area called the *gaitan*, where Katagiri had given me the instruction. The gaitan was for people who were late or had to leave early. I sat there by mistake, not knowing that there was a zendo, or even what a zendo was.

After the period was over, as I walked out, someone opened the door to the zendo and I saw a room with maybe forty people in it and an altar full of esoteric religious objects. It looked oriental but I didn't notice any Orientals. They were mainly hippies. Then I heard bells and saw that the people inside were bowing down to the floor. What's that, I wondered? I shuddered as a wave of creepy exotica went rippling through me. Maybe I should get out of here and never come back. Oh well, never mind. Who knows what that is. Maybe some yoga or judo exercises or something, I thought, and I forgot about it. I walked out onto the street, my first meditation experience under my belt, and my first meeting with Katagiri on my mind.

It was another two weeks before I saw him again, by accident, under quite different circumstances. I was visiting a fellow whom I had met at a concert the night before (Big Brother and the Holding Company, with Janis Joplin, had played at the Matrix, a small nightclub). I bought some marijuana from him and was on my way back to my apartment, where my friends and I spent most of our time getting stoned, playing music, painting and rapping. I ran into Katagiri on the street.

I said hello and he greeted me cordially and asked how I was doing. I said that I had been sitting on my own to try to get accustomed to zazen because it hurt my back and I didn't feel as if I was ready to sit with a group yet. He put his hand on my back. "Be sure to take good care of your back now." He laughed and walked on. For some reason I was embarrassed.

I decided not to fly off on Icelandic Airline for Europe to tread my way to the Orient in search of the deepest experience of meditation as had been my plan, but to start sitting every day at the Zen Center. I would do so for one year without judging it and at the end of that year, if I didn't like it I would go to Europe and onward. Thus, I found myself leaving my directionless friends and moving ever closer to the Zen Center and its teachers and students.

READING IN THE RAIN

HŌGOJI, MAY 8, 1988

One day when morning work had been canceled due to rain, Norman, Shuko and I were sitting in the study, passing the time reading and sewing. Norman and I had been hoping that it would rain as we both had many things we wanted to do. The willingness to admit that one desired to do one's own thing as opposed to the temple thing was divided along national lines. Norman and I had prayed for rain to all the buddhas and patriarchs, God, Mary, Jesus, Mohammed, the Earth Mother, the Great Spirit and we went out to the two small shrines outside our room and asked help from the local kami. We were so pleased that our prayers had been answered.

Norman was reading *The Japan Times*, which had just arrived in the mail. He got it once a week and we read every word. Shuko was sewing his robes, repairing areas where the stitching had come loose. I was studying Japanese. The temperature was just right, the air had that remarkable moist freshness and clean smell that comes with rain. I sat there with my friends as we silently went about our tasks.

To me the rain was a type of music, falling in different tones and textures with the sounds of all the drips, drops, sheets and sprinkles on the ground and rocks, in trees and on leaves, into other water and onto the roofs. With wind for backup, there came a chorus of these wet sounds, full, round and ringing, deliciously coming from all sides, through the windows and doors and from the roof. It was a rhythmic message of the immediate, beyond human emotions and symbols, washing through our ears and bidding us stay in, relax and enjoy the show.

I knew better than to share my feelings. My gushy reverie probably would have elicited an irritated humoring from Norman and I was sure to get a "does not compute" from Shuko if I said anything at all positive about rain. Japanese have set phrases for many situations and the ones for rain seem to be all negative. "Horrible weather, isn't it?" That sort of thing. Time and again I have heard a Japanese person express dismay at the same few drops that gave me a tingle of anticipatory glee.

The easiest way to descend from a cherished moment is to describe it, so I sat mutely in the dimly lit tatami room in the mountain temple amidst drenched rice paddies and thick woods and stared through the Japanese characters before me, secretly absorbing the wetness of the moment. There was a flash and then a glorious high-decibel thunderclap peeled through the air, blasting us where we sat. My teacup ranneth over.

Eventually the rain subsided and I sank back into my studies. The three of us had been the longest time together forgetting each other's existence. Such pleasurable harmony can scarcely be created through conscious effort, even that of a religious life, which often as not goes astray—which is exactly what was about to happen. Suddenly Norman was guffawing as the newspaper in his hands was thrust down revealing his animated features and shiny lumpy skull.

"What's so funny?" I asked.

After he'd stopped laughing and had caught his breath, he answered me. "I'm reading this article about a landlord in Tokyo who refuses to rent to foreigners."

Shuko kept sewing but was listening closely. I could feel his attention divide. They frequently comment to each other about newspaper articles or letters that they have read or were reading, each naturally selecting items that prove the points he wants to make. Obviously Norman had just run into some printed ammunition that was about to be used in culture combat. Shuko dug in.

"The man gave two reasons why he wouldn't rent to gaijin: first, they won't know when to put out their garbage." At this point we both laughed for a minute. In the cities, garbage is put out on the streets on certain mornings, which differ depending on the neighborhood one lives in. Typically there's one morning pickup of nonburnable trash and two of burnable trash every week. It's easy to figure out.

"That's pretty flimsy," I said.

"And second," Norman continued, "he said he'd had a family from the Philippines who didn't put away their futon during the day." We laughed some more. "So he says he won't rent to foreigners because they don't pick up their futon!"

Then Norman turned to Shuko, who was pretending to be engrossed in stitching, and started talking about how a foreigner is expected to follow the rules of Japan because the Japanese have no respect for other people's ways. "You're always saying that there's no discrimination in Japan, but you can see that these people are being discriminated against and the landlord gave such ridiculous excuses. They don't know when to put out the trash and won't pick up their futon during the day! Can you believe that?"

"Well, if you don't pick up your futon during the day then you walk all over it."

Norman thrust his eyes up in the air. "Oh, come on Shuko, you can't possibly be serious! Admit it. This is racism."

Shuko placed his smooth, olive hands together. "People shouldn't bring their problems here and force them on others. We should live together in peace."

Norman glared. "Now what the heck is that supposed to mean?" He threw me a disgusted look. "*They're* renting the apartment—it's their futon. What business is it of the landlord's if they put up their futon or not?"

"It's important to take care of futon properly," said Shuko. "If you don't, they get dirty, musty and lose their fluffiness. They should be hung out to air or put away for the day."

"That can't be the law, Shuko. It's up to the individual, not the landlord, for god's sake!"

Shuko turned silent and dark.

Norman tried another tack. "Look Shuko, I know you know there's discrimination in Japan. At Suienji you were reading that book on the eta, the *Japanese* untouchables. You just don't want to admit to a foreigner that there's any problems here. That's it, right?"

Shuko was silent.

"I admit that America has all sorts of problems. We have lots and lots and lots of problems. I admit it. Why can't you admit anything negative about Japan?"

Shuko looked straight ahead.

"Your lack of response is what Japanese people do when they want to ignore something. They don't say anything. They shut up, exactly what you're doing now."

"Now, now gentlemen," I interrupted. "Maybe the solution is to require that all incoming foreigners go through a rigorous Japanese etiquette training program upon arrival. When they've passed the course, they would be issued a certificate that could be presented to landlords and other concerned parties. It might read something like: 'This certifies that so-and-so has duly studied and passed an official government training program in Japanese customs and is thoroughly versed in such matters as how to put up futon in the morning, how to find out when to put out the garbage, how to open an umbrella when only one drop of rain has fallen, and so forth.' " Shuko went back to his sewing. Norman buried himself in the paper. The rain picked up again and I got lost in it.

SMOKE IN THE KITCHEN

HŌGOJI, MAY 10, 1988

Hōgoji's kitchen has a dark wood floor with some frighteningly weak places that I carefully avoid, fearing sudden exits into the netherworld. There is a lower section with a dirt floor that is literally on ground level. The soft, firm footing of this area is not the same loose, sandy dirt as outside. These floors are packed and rich in clay. We sweep them in the morning along with the wood and tatami floors. I am content to work on the dirt floors as I do sometimes when I'm on kitchen duty. I like the way they absorb me.

The kitchen is poorly lit by kerosene lamps, like all the interiors—except you need to see in the kitchen more than elsewhere in order to get your mitts on the food and stir it and whatnot. It's even darker here because of all the ages of kerosene and wood smoke that have blackened the walls and beams and wood slats below the roof in this ceilingless room.

They could use a good lighting consultant. There is one Aladdin lamp, the Rolls-Royce of kerosene lighting, but it's only used occasionally for sewing and reading at the round table in the study. There are hurricane lamps, the kind that are intended for exterior use such as lighting paths. The all-glass ones are better, but often have poorly trimmed wicks and blackened chimneys. I pointed out to Shuko that the lamps weren't well trimmed and cleaned. I said I had years of experience living without electricity and suggested some improvements, but he couldn't see what the problem was. I tried to elicit support from Koji, who said he could see just fine. He suggested I get some glasses on the next town trip.

"But it's not just the fact that it's hard to see," I told him. "There are the fumes too. And the heaters are even worse. Sometimes when we get the kerosene heater going in the study the smell of kerosene gets so bad I think I need a gas mask."

He laughed and said I was a great kidder.

I told him I wasn't kidding and that at Tassajara we kept our lamps burning clean and that when we eliminated kerosene heating from the rooms, the general health of the community improved dramatically.

Koji refused to take me seriously. He wanted the mind of Beam Alert, not the Health and Safety Fascist.

We wash the dishes in cold water, which runs continuously from the kitchen tap. By that I mean it runs wide open all day and all night. The first time I walked into the kitchen I saw the water was on and turned the faucet off. Maku ran over and turned it back on immediately. He put his arms together in an X, but didn't explain anything. Later Norman told me that the water supply is a gravity feed from a hose that comes down from a creek. There's no shortage, but if the flow gets interrupted, air can get caught in the line and stop the water. It's weird to come from California, where every drop of water is precious, to a flow-through system like that. I never did get used to that tap always being on. It may have been the single hardest thing I had to adjust to in Japan.

Koji was washing and I was drying. I was asking how do you say this thing and that action and was writing down what he told me on a sheet of paper I kept in my pocket. I had just learned the words to distinguish the hand towel, *tenugui*, from the cloth which we used to wipe the table, whatever-it's-called. The damp dish towels, the *fukin*, had turned grey with use and I said I'd be happy to wash them, but Koji said they were still clean. To me they looked like *zōkin*, rags used to clean the floor.

"How do you define 'clean'?" I asked him. He said that clean is clean and I said that the Japanese and English words obviously didn't match up.

Even though it's not exactly as Dōgen planned it, the kitchen during cleanup is one time we regularly socialize, chatting some as we wash and dry together after meals, me always writing down new words and sometimes making energetic and diligent Koji fall down laughing. It's easy to make him laugh, but only the rare perfectly timed comment can fell him. One must understand that these Japanese monks, although frequently very good natured, don't joke and cut up, or for that matter, act cynical or ironic or silly or sacrilegious or poke fun at things. At least on the surface, everyone takes this monk trip real seriously. I'm not saying that they can't be easy going—there's a lot in terms of lightness that can be learned from the Japanese monks here by foreign Zen practitioners, some of whom at times get very heavy and dark indeed.

It's just a matter of difference of style. I lurked around the corners of these differences, ready to strike.

Koji was inquiring into my personal history, a topic I was more than happy to talk about. It was almost as if he felt that my answers might contain some gem of wisdom. I'm older than Koji is, taller, fatter and uglier. And I've studied Zen a bit longer too—to no avail, but he didn't know that, and so was relating to me with respect. He wanted me to share with him what motivated me to follow in the footsteps of the Buddha all the way up those seemingly interminable wood and stone steps outside.

"Why did you come here to practice at Hōgoji?" he asked.

I turned to him. He had a serious look on his face, open and respectful. I asked him for a clarification of a Japanese word he'd just used.

He explained it. I added it to my list and returned to drying dishes. He looked a little perturbed and was obviously waiting for an answer. He asked again, saying, "Why did you come here? Are you just here to study Japanese? Is Hōgoji just a language school to you?" He's such a sincere guy.

Maku was sweeping the floor and listening with reserved but keen interest.

I looked at Koji and told him pointedly, "That's right. I have absolutely no interest in Zen at all." He gaped at me. "I came here merely to study Japanese for free. In zazen I review vocabulary." I started listing the words he had taught me in the first week and Koji was on the ground clutching his sides. I even got a reaction from Maku, who smiled. I was pleased and dried another dish.

The *tenzo*, or cook, has a big job and is usually exhausted by the end of the day. He must collect wood, keep the fires going just right, and not burn the food. We cook in big crocks called *hibachi* that are down in the dirt area and are heated with fire from twigs and branches, but hurray! no plastic. The ventilation is poor.

There's the big opening that goes unobstructed to the courtyard out front and a large glass window to the other side that opens up, but it's not always enough. It's a situation where being "traditional" just isn't good enough unless there's a strong draft.

Late one afternoon I was raking the gravel in the courtyard out front when I noticed clouds of smoke billowing out from the kuin. I left my zori at the side of the thick stone step and entered the building. Smoke was hanging in the air and my eyes watered. I walked through the dining area and into the study, the air getting thicker with smoke as I progressed. The source was obviously the kitchen. I entered with some concern and readiness to act. The fumes made it hard to see and breathe and I immediately started coughing. As I stood there I heard a tune being hummed and looked through the haze to see Norman sitting down in the lower section between the two hibachi. Smoke was billowing out from underneath them.

"Norman!" I said for lack of anything else to say. As I got closer I could make out that he was in a semisprawled position, his long arms and legs dangling out. Below his shaved bumpy head was a maniacal grin. This face instantly told the story of one whose day had been long—filled with trials and frustration. There was a distinct look of resignation, even submission to forces greater than ourselves. I realized that Hōgoji was in no danger of burning down, but that Norman might be a candidate for the straitjacket pretty soon if something were not done.

"Norman?" I said again, hoping for a reply.

He tilted his head slightly, looked at me piercingly with his smoke-glazed eyes. Slowly he put his right hand out with the thumb up. "THANK YOU and OK!" he said defiantly through the smoke.

PART FOUR   LIVING

AT ISHITAKI'S

One day I was squatting on the floor of the kitchen tying up the ends of a plastic shopping bag that contained our unburnable trash, when I got a phone call. I would have answered it but we didn't have a phone at the time. It rang at our neighbor's house. Ishitaki came over and gave me the message. She said it was someone named Nambasan from Gifu prefecture calling. I knew at once that it was my car dealer buddy Yasushi, the one who had shown me his wedding pictures. He lives deep in the country on the way from Kyoto to the Japan Alps. In a land of generosity, Yasushi's a host among hosts. He has driven me all over that part of Japan, shown me the day life of crafts people and the night life of Gifu City (8,000 sunakku). He wanted me to call him back as soon as possible. I got my wallet and the trash, and Ishitaki and I headed over to her place.

It was a cool sunshiny day and our botanist neighbor Numoto Sensei was in the vegetable garden across from the temple grounds. He was preparing for the spring.

"Tell me a new way to greet him," I said to Ishitaki as we approached him.

"Oh, he will understand you in English," she said.

"I know that," I answered with irritation. (Since she's so Westernized, I tend to be frank with her.) "Can't you understand I want to speak Japanese?"

"Then why don't you speak Japanese to me? From now on let's only speak Japanese."

"Your English is too good."

"Well okay. Mmm. Say, 'Uguisu wa nakihajimemashita,' the

nightingale has begun to sing," she said. "It's a sign that spring is around the corner."

I tried it on him. He stood up from the bed he was tending, his long white hair falling almost to his shoulders, an eccentricity granted a retired professor.

He smiled and answered back in English, "Oh yes, it has, hasn't it?"

"Please speak in Japanese to David, his Japanese is quite good, you know," Ishitaki said to him in a formal high tone that slightly mocked me.

He apologized and repeated the simple reply in clear Japanese, "Sō desu nē," as if I needed to hear the most basic sentence in the whole language.

"Now I feel like an idiot," I said to Ishitaki.

"I wouldn't say such a thing," she said.

We turned in front of the temple gate and I placed the trash bag in a pile with twenty or so others at the edge of the garden just as the garbage truck backed up beeping. The garbage men with their white gloves hopped out and politely waited for us to pass before approaching the heap of bags and assorted rubbish: an old rice cooker, a bunch of cookie tins in a cardboard box, some toys tied together with a frayed electric cord, two kerosene heaters. As we passed, Ishitaki thanked them for their many kindnesses.

We walked toward Ishitaki's large welcoming home hidden behind a nondescript cinder-block wall and exposed doorless garage cluttered with bikes, garden tools, boxes, and stacks of newspapers, magazines and flattened milk cartons to be recycled. Entering her gate, we were surrounded by the flourishing evidence of her green thumb. I brushed by a lemon tree and glanced down at the slow-moving goldfish in a clay pot covered by a sheet of glass.

We stepped into her spacious and clean house, leaving our shoes at the entranceway, but not putting on the customary slippers.

"And by the way, here is something we have received that we don't need." She handed me two tins of black tea.

"Are you sure you don't want them?"

"You know, people are always giving doctors so much," she answered.

"Well okay," I agreed, "but you give us too much."

"Nonsense."

"How much do you get?"

"Oh, you'd be surprised," she answered. "And we are not even so important. In the case of an older or more important doctor or large company's president, they might put a tent outside the house and hire someone to receive the year-end or midyear presents. Then they will select what they want to keep and there is a special business that will buy what they don't want for one third or so of its value. The direction of the giving is always up, to the boss or to those who can bestow favor. In some ways this is still a feudal country," she said, shaking her head.

She gave me the number and said to please use her phone. I declined, saying that I'd make the call from the green public phone in Daianji's parking lot across the street.

I was beating my finger on her dining table. "So, before I go, tell me something, would you?"

"I will do my best."

"I've been teaching English now to Japanese for half a year. You did it for many years. I don't mean any offense by this . . ."

"That would be nothing new."

"Well, maybe just a little offense . . ." I searched for diplomatic phrasing and sighed.

"Maybe they are just sitting there like rocks?"

"Yes, uh . . ." I said, relieved.

"Except for maybe the sixth-grade boys, who are hard to control?"

"Yes—but that's just the one class. Rocks is the rule."

"Most kids . . . they just sit there . . . and don't respond. Or they talk to each other. No one seems to be interested except for the exceptional student. And I hear over and over that it's the same way in the schools too. Kids go to classes so much—school six days a week and *juku* (private cram schools) after that and then English conversation, piano and whatnot on top."

"They get worn smooth, like stones in a river, and they lose interest."

"After what I've experienced teaching here, I don't understand how . . . how Japan could be doing so well economically, in the nitty-gritty test of the world market."

"Yes, the school system here just gets them into cramming for tests and they forget it all when they learn that way. And once they get in college they don't have to study to pass. All that matters is which school you get into. But you want to know the secret—why Japanese business does so well?"

"Yes, please, tell me."

"They don't expect new employees to have learned anything in school, even college—except how to read and write and how to use a calculator. Businesses start from the most simple beginning and educate them in every single thing they will need to know for that job. They treat them like babies and make them into what they want. It works very well."

I was just about to ask her more, when the phone rang. Ishitaki's voice jumped an octave and took on a singsong quality, her words full of apologies, gratitude and praise, all delivered with a syrupy intonation. It's not so different from listening to some women I have known back in Texas. I picked up the tea and, catching Ishitaki's eye, nodded thanks, waved goodbye and departed to the parking lot to make the call to Yasushi in Gifu.

I looked at my phone card. On it was a scene of islands in the Inland Sea. On the side were perforations that indicated it had six hundred yen of phone time remaining. That should be enough. I slipped it in the slot and dialed while watching Numoto Sensei digging in the garden.

THE FOURTH GRAPE

"Four is an unlucky number," said Maku. Four is *shi* and "shi" is also death. I had brought him four grapes. He took three.

"You could still say *yon* for four, couldn't you? It wouldn't be unlucky then, would it?" I asked.

"Superstition is not so logical," he said, peeling the large green muscat.

"Of course," I said, eating the fourth grape. "What do you do about four?"

"We say *yon* or *yotsu* a lot." He sat on a cushion facing an open shoji screen. A kerosene lamp burned on the desk to give him light.

"Anything else?" I asked, pleased to be having an actual conversation with untalkative Maku.

"Hospitals don't have four in their phone number and we don't do things in fours so much. Many items, like table settings, are sold in fives." He put a green ribbon as a marker on the page he was reading in a thick book, closed it and put it to the side. "Nine is also unlucky."

"Why's that?"

"*Ku* also means suffering. That's why we often say *kyū*."

"I was born on the ninth," I said.

"Nine is lucky in China," he added tactfully.

"I don't think I could keep up with all of it. I'll just have to depend on faith and hope I don't step on any cracks."

"Cracks?"

I told Maku about cracks and mothers' backs. He said, "Cover your thumbs when you see a hearse, or you won't be with your parents when they die. Same goes if you cut your fingernails after sunset."

I wanted to hear more, but I had to get going. "The reason I came in is to ask if you want to go to town today."

"I don't like to do things on days with dates that have four or nine in them." He ran his fingers along the spines of books in a bookcase to the right of his desk.

"Then how can you ever do anything on days off?"

"I try to cook on four-and-nine days and get another day off."

"Does the monastic four-and-nine day tradition derive from these beliefs?" I asked.

"Maybe," he said. "Life is full of superstition. And Zen is full of magic. Zen comes from Taoism, not just Buddhism. Taoism is full of magic. So is Buddhism. So, I believe, is Christianity." He was still looking for a book while he talked.

I told him that Edward Conze, a cranky and eccentric Buddhist scholar, said once in a class I was in, "If there's no magic, there's no religion."

"But what is magic?" I asked Maku. "I didn't understand Conze. Suzuki Roshi and Katagiri Roshi never taught us anything but sitting and not getting caught by things—by things like magic."

Maku tilted his head then straightened it again. "Everything is interconnected. Magic is just a result that uses connections you don't see. New technology is magic. The natives in New Guinea during the war when Nishiki Roshi was there thought airplanes were magic. When they first met Europeans, they thought mirrors were magic. To young children, parents are magic. Maybe the ultimate magic is enlightenment."

I'd never thought of it that way. Norman said that in Japan they practiced magical-faith-Buddhism as opposed to America's psychotherapeutic-Protestant brand. I watched as Maku found the book he was looking for and brought it down on his desk. I'd always wanted to see what sort of magic books he was studying. I scooted up to his desk to see. Good, I thought at first glance, there are pictures. I moved in closer and was bewildered to see English. *I See Everything* was the title. He opened it up. It was a large glossy book full of color pictures. The page he opened up to had "backpacking" written in big letters across the top. There was a drawing of a hiker with a backpack and a tent and all across that page were pictures of camping items with the names of everything in English next to them. Maku turned the page. "A department store" was written across the top, and the next two pages were full of pictures and words of that scene. He kept turning the pages and smiling. "I see everything," he said with a twinkle in his eye. "I also study English," he said in English.

A STITCH IN SPACE

HŌGOJI MAY 10, 1988

Norman does many things well. His head is good, his voice is good and his hands are good too. They're strong and intelligent, with long fingers. In his day Norman has used his hands skillfully for finished carpentry, lead guitar, elegant calligraphy, and finicky kesa and rakusu sewing. Even though Norman is always frustrated in one way or another because he feels he's treated as an outsider who can't *really* understand or master any Japanese way of doing anything, no one can deny that he sews a superb kesa. The kesa is covered with lines of stitches that look like closely spaced dots that hold together the small pieces of cloth it is made from. His dots are always perfectly spaced and straight as Bodhidharma's stare.

There are few places where monks or laypeople still sew these robes for themselves. Most of them are machine sewn and store bought these days. Suienji is one of the only places in Japan that I know of where monks and laypeople alike sew their own. Some of the Zen groups in the United States require that ordainees make their own holy vestments, as Father Sam referred to them. Joshin-san (of the missing digit) patiently taught us this specialized sewing at Zen Center. We'd chant "Namu kie butsu" ("I take refuge in the buddha—I plunge into buddha," was her twist on it) with every stitch and would thus sew the vow of taking refuge into the very fabric of the garment. (Taking refuge, or plunging, in the buddha, dharma and sangha is as central to Buddhism as communion is to Catholicism.) Unlike a certain old monk at Suienji, Joshin never brought cultural competition into her teaching or doubted our ability to sew "Buddha's robe."

After lunch one day, while we were resting in our room, Norman told me a Buddhist sewing story. Once, he went to Suienji for a two-week sewing session. In the first ten days he whipped out a new kesa and matching *zagu*, the bowing cloth. He then joined a group of Japanese laypeople, mostly women, who had come to sew their own rakusu. Rakusu aren't just for monks; laypeople sometimes wear them too. An older monk was there to instruct in how to go about this exacting task. He demonstrated how to lay out the cloth, measure it, cut it, fold the pieces, do the stitches, how to make the straps to hang around the neck, every little detail. He didn't pay any attention to Norman, who was working away in the corner.

The next afternoon when he was checking people's work, the monk walked over to where Norman sat sewing. Norman kept on sewing in a concentrated fashion. The old monk looked at his work and did a double take. He asked Norman if that was a rakusu he'd been working on from before and Norman said no, he'd started with everyone else the day before. The old monk examined it carefully, glanced at Norman and looked at the rakusu again. You'd think the guy would be happy. "I mean what's the point of the whole trip?" to quote Norman. But he wasn't happy—he was furious. His face tightened into a scowl and his breathing became audible. He turned around, glared fiercely at the unsuspecting lay sewers and commenced to scold them vigorously for allowing a . . . a . . . a gaijin to sew a better rakusu than they, than Japanese! He fumed and paced the room as he shamed them for this inexcusable insult to national pride. Norman, disgusted, went back to sewing as the outraged monk brought his fellow countryfolk to tears.

LECTURE PREP

MARUYAMA–KYOTO, MAY 11, 1989

When I returned Yasushi's call, he asked me to come to Gifu in mid-May and give a talk to his Junior Chamber of Commerce cronies. He'd mentioned the JCs to me before. He was the president of that chapter. All these guys were buddies of his and I knew I'd have to do a good job. Hmm. It would be great to see Yasushi and it would be challenging Japanese language study. So it was decided. After only one year in Japan, I would give a forty-five-minute talk in what the Jesuits used to call "the devil's language," it being next to impossible for them to learn well enough to convert anyone.

That night at home I sat at the *kotatsu*, a unique Japanese form of heating utilizing a low table. The blanket over my legs held in the warmth generated by the heat lamp under the table-top. In front of me was an empty notebook. My Japanese wasn't that great, I thought, but if I prepared, I could do it. "Heh heh," I laughed to myself—Bop had said that, having an American wife, I'd never learn Japanese. I'll show him. Now let's see. What will I talk about? Yasushi had suggested that I contrast my impressions of Japan with America. How typical—comparisons. Humph.

After I had spent all of my spare time for a few days writing down notes, I met with Kubo from the MMC to begin to put it into Japanese. She was excited that I was going to go through with this. "What are you going to speak on?" she said. "Your first year in Japan? Living in Japanese suburb? Comparing America and Japan?"

"None of that," I said, dismissing the predictable. "Why tell them what they already know? Anyway, I hate comparisons. Comparisons are the lowest, most superficial form of thought. I'll tell them something new, something they don't know about, something stimulating."

Kubo thought for a minute. "But you should tell them a little bit about your Japan impression and what you like about Japan and Japanese people," she said while smiling and nodding and making a motion with her hands like she was grinding something. This is *gomasuri*, grinding sesame, a Japanese symbol for buttering someone up.

"But look, Kubo-san, here's the story. I've got a great story to tell them." And I proceeded to lay out for her what I was sure would be a captivating talk about a socially important topic that would both hold their interest and expand their horizons. The movie *Mississippi Burning* had been in Japan for over a month so they'd be familiar with the background of what I was talking about. I had spent time with the civil rights movement in Mississippi during the same time covered by the movie and had worked with SDS (Students for a Democratic Society). I could mention the movie story and my own experiences together and bring it all up to date.

Kubo listened and nodded and said it sounded like a very difficult subject. She finally gave up trying to advise me and started working on the speech with me. But she was instinctively putting it into extremely difficult oratory Japanese that would take me forever to get down. She seemed to be getting bored and suddenly said she had to go to pick up her son at school. So all I ended up with that I could use was a vocabulary list that I would tie together with my more basic Japanese later.

I worked it out in English at first, writing and remembering and developing a talk that criss-crossed back and forth between Mississippi and San Francisco, with a bit of Texas thrown in.

A few weeks later a letter arrived from Yasushi that briefly reiterated the basic facts of my coming trip. Included was the invitation that went out to the JCs, which had a picture of me with a brief bio. It said I had worked for a government youth program in the States (I had worked for the California Conservation Corps for a couple of years) and that the title of my talk was "The Japan That I Have Seen." I shrugged, thinking that the guy just can't get it straight. I didn't come to Japan to give them a talk on Japan.

On the way to Gifu to give the talk to the JCs I stayed at Bop's in Kyoto, a small old falling-down prewar one-story building nestled amidst newer two-story structures. Bop is a medium-height ex-surfer from Colorado who's blond where he's not bald. Elin says he's cute. He sleeps next door with his ladyfriend Keiks, so his place is available and he always lets me stay there when I am in town. It is Grand Central for a disparate crowd of Japanese and foreigners—monks, bluegrass musicians, an ex-Jesuit, art collectors and English teachers trying to save money and hold on to their sanity.

The night I stayed there on my way to Gifu, Bop and Keiks were entertaining some buyers who were there to look at Bop's kimono collection, other types of traditional garb and beautiful old material. The prospective clients were a sophisticated Japanese couple.

We got a lot of talking in and they said my Japanese was very good—in fact everyone was complimentary about how much

221

I'd learned. I hadn't prepared my talk as well as I'd planned to, in fact not at all, and so was a little nervous about it. I went over the whole story with them and they agreed that it was indeed quite interesting. There was a lot of smiling and nodding and the whole evening was just the boost of confidence I needed.

There was one weird point in that conversation, when I compared the plight of blacks in the United States with that of the eta in Japan. "Ooh, don't say that word," Keiks said, holding her arms and shivering. I noticed everyone was uncomfortable. I asked her why can't I say "eta"? There's a big eta section just down the street about a thirty-minute walk away.

"I *hate* that word," she said. "Don't use it." And it stopped there.

Bop quickly changed the subject back to my impending talk, but his advice made me wonder. "Just look at the audience and say, 'I'm from America, I like ice cream.' " He pointed to his nose the way Japanese do to indicate themselves, smiled and nodded as if in front of an audience of five-year-olds. "That's all you have to do. This'll be a piece o' cake for you. No problem," he said, slapping my thigh.

"Yes, do not worry, David," said Keiks, easily shifting gears. "Just be very simple. Don't try too much." The visiting Japanese couple were nodding and chiming in sounds of agreement.

"You'll knock 'em dead. Say, 'I like sushi, I like Japanese cars and Japanese women,' " said Bop, "and Japanese toilet paper and Japanese forks." They all laughed.

I tried to act amused, but I really didn't get the point. It all seemed sort of rude to me—to the audience. But the important thing was that they all had confidence in me and after a second I adjusted and gave a little chuckle because after all, we don't have to understand everything each other says.

KNOCKIN' 'EM DEAD

Late the next morning when I arrived in Gifu, it was raining lightly. An old lady ran out of a coffee shop and gave me an umbrella. I tried to tell her I was okay, but she insisted. I'd been in Japan a year and I couldn't count the umbrellas I'd been given. It was green and contrasted nicely with the grey buildings and grey sky in Gifu, a city of a million, northeast of Kyoto. I walked on to the bus station, looking forward to arriving in the countryside of Shiragawa where Yasushi lived, an hour's ride away.

The teenage girl behind the window was obviously so embarrassed at having to deal with a foreigner that, after I uttered a simple request for a ticket, all she could do was whisper excitedly to her fellow workers, hold her hand over her mouth and giggle. I didn't see anything funny about it and I repeated myself. She looked at me and burst out laughing.

"Don't you understand me?" I said with irritation. "I want a ticket to Shiragawa."

She waved her hand sideways before her face and said she didn't speak English and I said that I was speaking Japanese and I repeated my simple request as clearly as I could. She just looked puzzled and started giggling again and finally ran away. The confidence I'd gained the night before at Bop's was eroding. A man came over to the window and said that he couldn't speak English and I said the same old stuff all over again in slow, clear Japanese. Granted it surely had a bad American accent but it was pretty close to correct, I knew it was.

He paused for a moment and looked down seriously. "Which Shiragawa?" he said.

What? Oh. There's more than one. Uh. What's the other

name? I thought. "Hachiman," I finally said, and watched. He gave a sign of recognition and told me the price. Contact.

The next bus was three hours later. I'd be late to meet Yasushi, who wanted to leave his house at two P.M. I kept asking, isn't there some way? Some other way? But all the man would do was to keep staring at the schedule and acting very uncomfortable that he wasn't finding the answer I wanted.

"Look," I said, "just find me some cardboard and help me make a sign and I'll hitchhike." This made him doubly anxious and he consulted with his superior, who started staring at the schedule with him. This went on for a while with me occasionally asking them to just help me make a sign.

When I peered into eternity and saw that the lines did not bend, I said, "Okay—I give up." They looked relieved. "I'll go hitchhike without a sign." This finally jolted the head guy's eyes off the piece of paper they were fixed on and dislodged his brain. He, an employee of the Gifu mass transit system, could not allow this foreigner, this guest of Japan, to degrade himself by . . . by . . . hitchhiking. He ran off and looked at another schedule for a bus that went to a nearby village and asked if that would be okay. I asked how far away that village was from Shiragawa Hachiman and he said five minutes by car but there's no taxi.

"No problem." I said. "When does it leave?"

"Let's see," he said. "At . . . mm . . . mm . . . twenty-seven minutes after."

I looked around for a clock. "What time is it now?"

He looked at his watch and paused. "Twenty-seven minutes after," he said matter-of-factly.

They ran ahead of me past a line of buses and stopped mine, the last one, from taking off without me and we had an enjoyable parting with the problem solved, which made us all happy, and they bowed and apologized and I thanked them profusely. I could see them bowing until the bus turned the corner and they were out of sight.

Soon I was riding out of the city and by the big river. The

cormorant fishing boats were tied up for the winter. Picking people up and dropping people off, the bus went past farmlands and villages and onward toward the foothills of the Japan Alps. As we got further away from the big city, there was less and less cement and more and more softness of vegetation and good old dirt. We arrived at the village that the bus driver said was the closest stop to Shiragawa Hachiman. He dropped me off at the bus stop in front of a store. As a gesture of kindness to a foreigner, he refused my money.

The lady who ran the store welcomed me and asked what she could do. Well for starters I'd like to use the phone, I said, and told her who I was going to see. Her family and the Nambas were old friends and she insisted on making the call for me. Then we almost got into a fist fight over whose ten yen to use. I lost. I was thirty minutes late and Yasushi wasn't even home yet. One of his workers would come to pick me up. I got an apple drink and talked to the lady and waited. She said my Japanese was really good and I said no it's still really bad. She asked me some questions like where was I from? Did I like Japan? Why? Did I like Japanese food? What Japanese food did I like? Are the cars small? Are the roads narrow? Was I married? Is America dangerous? Did I carry a gun there? Why was I in Japan? Is Japanese harder than English?

Very soon a car pulled up and nice young slightly-nervous-to-see-me mechanic was opening a door. As he drove I answered his questions. I'm from San Francisco. I like Japan. Because the people are kind. Oh yes, I like the food. Pardon me? Oh yes, all of it. Yes, your car is big enough. Yes, the roads are narrow, aren't they? Yes, I like the ladies here very much, but I'm married. Yes, the streets are a little dangerous in U.S. cities sometimes. Japanese is harder for Americans and English is harder for Japanese. He said my Japanese was really good and I said no it's still really bad. He said that his uncle had been to Hawaii and had eaten an American steak and that it was tough and didn't taste good.

We drove by the *torii*, or gateway, to the local shrine and continued on to Yasushi's home and business. I stood in his driveway breathing the fresh country air and looked out over the rice fields checkered with homes. It was still drizzling. The friendly young mechanic who had picked me up ran into the shop and returned immediately, bringing me an umbrella, apologizing as he handed it to me. I'd left the other one in the bus, darn it. I thanked him and opened it so as not to cause him grief.

There's a big sign on a tall pole at Yasushi's car dealership advertising his business. I wonder if it strikes anyone the way it does me, as a completely unnecessary intrusion of metal and plastic in what is otherwise a fairly decent neighborhood. There are new and old homes and spacious ornamental and vegetable gardens and rice fields next to cedar woods and a mountain creek. There is no need for that sign—absolutely anyone who has the remotest chance of buying a car within many kilometers of there knows exactly who he is and where he is. The sign is there for fun and pride and because that's what car dealers do, I guess. They put up big car dealer signs, even here next to the wilderness. There were about ten new cars and ten used ones all lined up and shiny beneath the sign.

Next door to his house the vacant lot was gone and in its place Yasushi's dream, a large new auto shop with three stalls and three mechanics busily at work. When Kelly and I were there visiting the previous July, we had participated in a morning groundbreaking ceremony with Yasushi's family, workers and friends. It was a Shinto affair. Afterwards we had all drunk beer till we were silly.

I walked around and said hello to the workers in the clean metal building. It had a computerized toilet with heated seat and built-in optional bidet, bottom rinse and blow dry among other features. In the guest meeting room upstairs a couch opened up into a bed and there was a programmable remote control heating and cooling unit.

The large two-story house is typical of suburban houses all over Japan—grey tile roof, cement instead of clay on the exterior walls. Outside, carp streamers flew high on a flagpole. There were four colorful banners in all, three of them in the form of fish, and they rustled in the wind. They announce the existence of boys in the family and are flown for about a month at this time every year.

Kaori, Yasushi's wife, was busy on the phone in the office and suggested I go watch TV and wait for Yasushi. She's used to foreign guests. I snooped around a bit. There's a room with a large black lacquer family altar in it with a Buddha figure in the center and little tablets with Chinese characters on them, the names of departed relatives, in gold script. On the wall above are old photos of parents, grandparents and great-grandparents, the patriarchs of this once papermaking family turned auto entrepreneurs. The only youthful pictures were those of two young men in uniform.

But this altar room is not only for the dead, though death and its ceremonies are the specialty of Buddhism. Included were signs of Shinto as well: the zigzagging twisted white paper and an offering of sake, requesting a good life and protection from harm. Kodomo-no-hi, Children's Day (though it's really for boys), had been a couple of weeks before, so there was still an elaborate display on a stepped platform of samurai warrior dolls and *shogun* lord-of-the-land dolls. There were about twenty of them all authentically dressed up. Fresh irises adorned both sides of the platform. Hinamatsuri, Girl's Day, with its lady dolls, had been a couple of months before. I stood on the tatami and inspected the foot-high guy dolls and wondered about their significance in the psyche of the children. One thing for sure, Japanese children have a lot to identify with—they are told who they are by all that surrounds them.

I peeked in Kaori's kitchen, which is large and well stocked with culinary tools and food from East and West. There was no idle space but it wasn't cluttered. The whole house is unusually neat. I slid open a door off the kitchen. What room is this? I thought. An old lady sitting on the tatami in a kimono barked at me to get out. Oh gosh. Who's she? Oops.

I retreated into the small TV room, which is where I'd been told to go in the first place. I turned on the TV, then turned it off and looked around the room. It has Yasushi's liquor cabinet. It's here that Yasushi and I talk until late, sipping cognac or high-quality cold sake. I always enjoy these talks that go back and forth between his twin loves—the Western world and Japan. He is not only into Hollywood movies and cars from both hemispheres, he also promotes the renewal of Japanese arts and crafts, which he worries are dying. He has gotten his local government to sponsor Kabuki and traditional papermaking workshops for foreigners. Bop said that to the locals these workshops must seem as far-fetched as having a bunch of giraffes coming to study the native ways. I told Yasushi that and he agreed that it challenged the hosts as much as the guests.

Yasushi has proudly shown me bottles of whiskey that cost over a thousand dollars. This is not an uncommon thing to run into and I do not comprehend it. I think it must be some sort of marketing hoax. I can see a cognac being really expensive, but not a whiskey. As far as I can tell, you could get rich in Japan rebottling Southern Comfort, the primary source of vomit in parts of Texas, and selling it as some rare, aged American bourbon masterpiece. These bottles are often never opened, and sit in the case for show.

As I sat in this room alone I remembered first hearing of the moon calendar and the dates of the old seasons. It was in this room that Yasushi taught me about the good days and bad days and the half-and-half ones—a sort of daily biorhythm superimposed on the calendar. I asked him about it because one day he had to get home to sell a car between twelve and one. The rest of the day wasn't propitious—could sour the deal.

"It's an old superstition that goes back to China, like so much of Japanese culture, and I can't do business without honoring it. It seems to work out."

My daydreaming was interrupted by a voice down the hall. It was Yasushi. I came out and said, "Ohisashiburi!" and he, "Long time no see!" which mean the same, and we shook hands and bowed. He's in his mid-thirties, handsome, smiling and always ready for fun. He got ready in a flash. In the meantime I reached into my bag and got a present I'd brought him. When he came back I was waiting with it in my hand. It was a bottle of Martell.

"It's something uninteresting," I said as they say in his language when giving a gift.

"Ah," he said appreciatively, "Maruteru." He was pleased. I was pleased. He looked at me a little quizzically. It costs a bundle in Japan. "You bought this for me?"

"Well, I guess I shouldn't lie. The head priest at the temple next door doesn't drink and he kindly gave it to me to give to Elin's father who was visiting a month ago. I thought you'd appreciate it more though."

He laughed and put it in his liquor cabinet. "Let's go," he said. We went outside, got into his BMW and were off to the JCs meeting, which was being held that evening in another town further into the hinterland.

Yasushi checked into a *minshuku*, a family inn, and we pulled out our futon and he took a thirty-minute nap.

"You made my mother-in-law angry," he said. "Don't go into her room."

I was embarrassed and apologized. "I didn't know she lived there. I've never seen her before."

"She doesn't come out of her room much. And she's afraid of foreigners. No problem. Just leave her alone." He rolled over and went to sleep.

I didn't sleep. I looked over my notes and vocabulary list. It seemed pretty sparse. What was I going to say again? It would come. Trust in the universe. Yasushi and I had no trouble talking so I should be able to talk to them as well. Just be natural. Stage fright bodes well.

We drove to the meeting hall, a barren, echoing, cream-colored cement building with a lot of flags and folding chairs inside. It was cold. In a back room he and I sat in red overstuffed chairs, drank coffee and chatted. Neither of us had brought up the evening lecture.

"So do you feel ready?" he finally asked me.

"I think so. I looked over my notes while you were sleeping and I went over the whole thing with a Japanese couple in Kyoto last night."

"Good. You're going to tell about your Japan experience?"

"I'm going to tell about America."

"These people don't know anything about America, really. Most of them have probably never heard a talk by an American. They just have a few simple ideas. They haven't traveled like me."

"I'll keep it simple."

"What are you going to say about America?"

"I want to talk about the civil rights movement and race relations."

"That sounds very difficult."

Just then a couple of men walked in the room. Yasushi introduced us. They were the other two officers of the JCs, the vice-president and the secretary-treasurer. They were all smiles, nice guys, and I felt at ease. The vice-pres was about as tall as me—five-eleven—and the other was more like Elin's height, five-six. The former asked what I was doing in Japan and I said studying Zen. They showed great surprise and said that it was so hard, so strict.

"Doesn't have to be," I said. "There can be daily life Zen."

"Maybe Zen is getting soft these days like everything else," said the taller one.

"Priests are too much at the bank. The real ones don't leave the temple except to beg," said the other, nodding.

They asked me what I did in America and I said that I was a Buddhist administrator—something I'd worked out with Ishitaki to say in our neighborhood. She said I needed a label, I kept confusing people by mentioning different jobs I'd had and things I'd done.

"There is Buddhism in America?" asked the shorter one. "What sect?"

"Just about everything. Zen, Nichiren, all the Japanese sects that I know of, Tibetan, Korean, all kinds. My teacher was Sōtō-shū."

"Mmm. Sō-dō-shū," he corrected me, pointing out that the second kanji meant *cave* and is pronounced "dō."

"Thank you," I said, not wanting to tell him that Dōgen liked to change everything, including the way that character is pronounced. But since almost everyone in Japan says "Sōdō Zen" I thought my point would not be appreciated.

They were having a hard time digesting what I was saying. The short guy asked if I was Christian. I said I didn't exclude it. They didn't get that.

"Religion has to be from the heart," said the taller one. "You can't just study it like a subject at school."

"The Christians in Japan, they don't understand Christianity," said the other. "They want to be different."

I was a little embarrassed and unsure of what to say. "Both religions are universal—not limited to any culture or country," I said.

"David is teaching English in Maruyama," said Yasushi, nodding. "He is a very good English teacher."

The guys liked that and said they wanted to learn English, but hadn't done so yet. Then they left us, saying we'd get together after the talk and go out to dinner and a nightclub. Great.

"I think it's better you don't mention Buddhism," said Yasushi. "To them it's impossible for you to be a Buddhist. To them Buddhism means Bon"—a festival in August when the spirits of the departed are said to return—"and priests coming to their homes for memorial services. They have no basis upon which to understand your point of view."

"Oh," I said, thinking about the talk I was to give.

Yasushi leaned over to me. "Just tell them you drive on the right side of the street in America and you don't use hashi."

That was freaky. He sounded like Bop from the night before. I didn't know what to say to him, but there was no time. We were ushered into the main hall.

We walked in to a standing ovation from about fifty guys in their thirties or so, all in suits and ties. The treasurer gave a financial report and the reading of the minutes was waived. (Hey! It was Robert's Rules of Order.) After a few introductory comments by the VP, I went to the podium amidst more polite applause.

I put my notes down and said hello in Japanese. This drew more applause. Everyone seemed pleased. I made a few simple introductory remarks as I knew I should: the weather, how nice this part of the country was. The men were settling in. Some started slumping in their seats. I launched into the meat of the talk.

"America . . . blah blah blah," I said. A head or two went down. "We have many people from different countries and of different races . . . blah blah blah." Eyes started to glaze. "We used to say colored, then Negro, then black, now African-American . . . blah blah blah." Most eyes were shut. "Rosa Parks . . . blah blah blah." I wasn't connecting. I took a sip of water. A couple of fellows were looking up. "Mississippi in 1964 . . . blah blah blah." Hmm, I'm not doing too well, I thought. There were so many things I didn't know how to say. "SDS was a student organization, well, more than just students . . . blah blah blah." I kept starting sentences and getting halfway into them before drawing a blank. I shuffled through my notes. I thought of Yasushi's mother-in-law. "When I dropped out of college . . . blah blah blah." Yasushi winced. "Do you understand ghetto?" No response. The room was spinning, wasn't it? No one cared anyway. "San Francisco, I lived in San Francisco . . . blah blah blah." Some of them were sleeping. Yasushi. I started talking to Yasushi. He can get me going. I said some things to Yasushi and he explained it to them. Why hadn't I just written the talk down and read it?

Feeling flushed and breathing short, I asked for questions. A fellow asked about the whaling issue—I couldn't tell exactly what, but it was about whaling. I answered something but I couldn't hear my words. Somehow I kept going for forty minutes in all. I thanked them and stepped down, relieved and embarrassed. They applauded, a speaker thanked me and handed over an envelope with money in it. I smiled and accepted it, feeling like a worthless beggar. There was another five minutes of business and people started walking out. Time for dinner. I didn't feel hungry.

There was a feast at an *izakaya,* a type of restaurant with all sorts of tidbits, lots of it fried, on sticks and plates, with sake and beer. We had our own room. Someone said he'd heard I was studying Zen in Japan and asked which sect. "Sōdō-shū," I said diplomatically, only to be told that the correct pronunciation was "sōtō." Yasushi brought me a guitar and asked me to sing. I began to feel comfortable. They were so kind and forgiving. Even better, it was obvious they didn't care—they were having fun.

Then some of us walked to a sunakku and were served beer and whiskey by pretty women. There were about a dozen of us around a table and spirits were high.

"I can understand you now. I didn't understand a thing you said in your talk though," said a good-natured fellow who was a car dealer like Yasushi.

"Me either," answered a guy at the table, pouring me another drink, "but I liked it. It was the first time I ever heard an American speak in person. You're nice people. I don't understand you, but I like you."

Everyone laughed and agreed and someone else topped my drink off. (There had been an eighth of an inch drunk from it.)

Yasushi looked at me and laughed. "They never heard of Mississippi or Afro or SD . . . whatever. They had nothing to relate it to."

"What is misupisi?" asked a fellow who was getting drunk. "I can't say it."

"Mississippi," I said clearly.

And then he tried to say it and everyone laughed at him.

"Really, everyone enjoyed the talk—especially the question-and-answer part," said Yasushi. "They just didn't know what the words meant!" And they laughed more. Even he didn't seem to care at all.

I stood up and raised my glass. "I didn't understand a thing I said either. Let's drink to not understanding anything! To international love without the burden of comprehension!"

They all stood and enthusiastically toasted with me and we drank and sang till two in the morning.

IT'S THE ENVIRONMENT, STUPA

HŌGOJI, MAY 11, 1988

When the big standup buddha drum in the hatto calls, I throw on my work clothes and go to the courtyard, where the work leader assigns tasks. Except for the tenzo in the kitchen, we usually work together for a couple of hours in the morning as well as in the afternoon. We work at a consistent and enjoyable overall pace, which varies individually from Koji's driven to Maku's spacy. Work in the temple is not called work, or *shigoto,* but *samu,* which is work-practice, another form of zazen. There may be some talking during *samu* but not much. I'm sure there'll be a lot less when I'm gone. On this mountainside, temple toil is a joy as it should be everywhere. The feeling is natural and unforced and it seems that Dōgen's way takes us away like a leaf in a stream or a turtle in a spin dryer.

I've swept and raked paths and grounds, chopped and sawed

firewood and emptied the outhouse. I've cut grass with a kama till my arms were about to drop off. The Japanese at Hōgoji squat as they work, but Norman and I haven't developed those particular muscles since childhood and after a while we fall down on our knees, staining and soiling our trousers. To them it's bad form and Koji warns me I'll get a hole in my jeans. I say that's all the rage these days. I remember kneeling at the edge of a high stone wall whacking at the vegetation and then pausing to look at the lush, green, irrigated terraces overflowing with water that spills down the verdant steps to Ryūmon.

Frequently Katagiri shows up and pitches in, but not as much as he used to at Tassajara or, according to Norman, in Minnesota. He seems to be fighting some bug, but he doesn't say.

One morning Katagiri, Koji and I were barbering the grass while Shuko, Norman and Jakushin were trimming the hedges around the dome-shaped stupa. I had to mow down many bright colorful flowers. Koji told me not to worry, that they would grow back. I saved these wild blooms in a pile that I planned to take back up with me to the top.

Maku brought cups and a pot of green tea down to us for our morning break. We sat in front of the monument on the steps. It certainly stands out by itself in the midst of all this greenery. The base is a circle about thirty feet in diameter. On the top of the smooth cement dome there is a block with large Sanskrit letters on each face, and out of that ascends a golden spire.

A stupa was originally a shrine that housed part of Shakyamuni Buddha's remains, but nowadays it can mean more than that. From India to China the stupas that claim a bone bit or tooth probably exceed the number of molecules there were in Buddha's body. I'm sure it's the thought that counts.

It turns out that the monument whose environs we were sprucing up contains the ashes of Japanese, American and Australian soldiers who died fighting in New Guinea, where Nishiki was stationed during the war. He was an officer in the Japanese army.

Norman leaned over and whispered, "Wonder if the old imperialist believed at the time that the emperor was a god." I thought perhaps Katagiri had overheard us, so I took the opportunity to ask him if *he* had ever believed that the emperor was a god. He grimaced and vehemently shook his head no.

Next to the stupa two black butterflies were having a time, going around together in circles, parting, landing on flowers (there were plenty left), coming back together. Koji says they are *kuro-koge-hachō,* burnt-black butterflies. They do look like charred velvet on the wing. And those lighter blue and green markings are fairly glowing.

I remembered sadly a brief period in my youth when I caught butterflies in a net and mounted them for display. It was fascinating for a while, having them close up and immobile to admire. But more and more I was disturbed by the transfixing experience of watching them painfully writhe and die from the fumes of ammonia in a cotton pad that I would place in a jar with them. After a period of struggling with the horror I was creating, I realized that their beauty was in their living, their lives were their own.

The ebony pair swept around me. I always see two. I'm sure they're not the same, but I think of them that way—mating for life and all.

Then for all beings who had been born and died, in war or not, eastern or western or northern or southern, remembered or forgotten, human or butterfly, I put all the wild flowers I'd cut and collected at the base of the memorial and we went back to work whacking flowers and grass indiscriminately.

.   .   .

For a couple of days we picked leaves from the tea plants that grow down by the stupa. Miki-*obāsan,* old lady or grandmother Miki, and two other old ladies came from the village below. Yoshiko-san was feeling well and joined in. We worked together all day long. Due to their country dialect I couldn't understand much of what the old ladies from the village said. And every time I tried to speak to them in Japanese, they would laugh loudly, Miki-obāsan showing her few darkened teeth and one silver one.

The tea bushes were low with small, dark green leaves. Some were rounded and some were squared and ran along like hedges. We picked the smallest, lightest new baby leaves off the top and dropped them into cloth bags worn around our necks. Green tea is full of caffeine. Sometimes I would take a couple of tiny leaves and chew them thoroughly, until I'd feel a buzz that would keep me going nicely. While the old ladies filled their bags I would futilely try to keep up with them, expending lots more energy and adding little to the bounty. Their nimble hands had the technique down. They worked steadily and without resistance.

Nothing distracted them, not even the bees that made me nervous. There are a number of varieties including your run of the mill honey bee. Larger than any bees I've ever seen in the States are the suzumebachi. One day I was trimming vines and pulling weeds on a stone wall with Norman and Katagiri. The three of us were standing along the wall on stones that jutted out just for that purpose. We were working away in silence when I thought I heard a helicopter. We turned in the direction of this put-put sound and Norman remarked, "Oh my gosh, it's granddaddy." Sure enough, coming down along the same wall we were working on was a bee of mythical proportions. We slowly climbed down and gave a wide berth to this noble beast: yellow, black, fat and chugging along.

As it passed, I heard Norman mutter in awe: "The Hymenoptera, the Hymenoptera."

THE GOOD WITCH

Yoshiko-san had collected the first-growth, baby tea leaves that we had picked and had taken them to town to a tea shop, where they were dried and prepared. It was only a few days since the harvest and we were drinking green tea from our own plants on the kuin steps. I said that it was the best green tea that I'd ever had. That elicited immediate looks of condescension and pity from the Japanese monks, and even Katagiri gave me a sort of "come now, David" look. They said it was not so good. Too bitter. Well, shut my mouth. Koji, the official ambassador to Yoshiko, went to thank her and brought her some pickled eggplant that he had made. He also brought me.

We walked down the stone steps past the giant sprawling oak into Yoshiko's cool, dark territory and I sensed her strict presence. Under the canopy of the virgin pine we took a winding path through the rock garden and stepped up on her deck. Koji called out, "Ojama shimasu," at her door, ostensibly saying we were imposing on her—a standard line. She called back for him to wait a minute.

Yoshiko's been living down here and looking over this place for thirty-five years. She had taken care of Zuido Roshi, the former abbot, for twenty years. He'd rebuilt the buildings a half century before. She made his meals, heated his bath, took care of his robes and when he was ill she tended to him until his death. Then she stayed on—just her. Zuido had no disciples to take over the temple. Yoshiko didn't fit the job description, which called for a male monk. An idiot could pick up the vibes though—she was his dharma heir. The place was hers. A few years previously when

Nishiki decided to continue what Zuido had started, he first came and asked for the blessing of the matriarch of Hōgoji. Her authority continues. Katagiri shows her respect at every opportunity and visited her several times when she was ill. Other than to Katagiri, she doesn't seem to relate positively to anyone but Koji. She's taller than most old Japanese women or even men and stands thin and straight, in contrast to the old stocky ladies from the village who come up to work. Koji said that she's regarded as a sort of witch by the townspeople below. He says that Yoshiko has spent long periods of time in the mountains around here by herself. She'd just leave and be up there and one day return. No one understood how she survived.

Part of the master plan of Hōgoji, the plan that will transform it into an international monastery, deems that Yoshiko's old house will soon be torn down. I wonder what she will do then. She's pretty old, about eighty Koji says. She's been sick a lot this year. Maybe she'll live with relatives. Everyone seems to have people who will take care of them.

Yoshiko came to the door and she and Koji started talking too fast for me to understand. We'd been introduced before, but she didn't acknowledge me. I listened to her as she spoke to Koji. She is lacking the airs that I've heard in so many women's voices in Japan, affectations that emphasize weakness and subservience. Her voice was sharp and direct. It almost sounded like she was scolding him when she spoke. But he didn't seem uncomfortable. His business didn't take long, they wasted no time, said good day and he and I went back up.

Sometimes I look down there and wonder what she's doing. I don't think she gets lonely, but even if she does I doubt I'd try to go cheer her up. I don't go down there and wander around. I don't go that way at all unless I'm working or with Koji. Norman doesn't venture down there either unless he has a reason. I guess that somewhere deep inside, we have a fear that Yoshiko would catch us and take us into her home to cook and eat.

DOUBTING THE
SUN'S SON

MARUYAMA, JUNE 5, 1989

One Monday morning Shimizu arrived first for class. He opened the front door and called out, "Good morning!"

"Come on in!" I said. "You're early as usual. Come watch me wash the dishes."

"I hate that smell," he said. "Why are you burning incense?"

"Oh, we just light it sometimes for the aroma," I answered, surprised.

He pulled up a chair to the kitchen table.

At nine A.M. sharp Morikawa and Tanahashi, the barely old and not quite young professors' wives, and Etsuko, the elementary school teacher, announced their presence from the front hall. They all came in saying "What's that awful smell?"

"I can't believe it. What have you all got against incense?" I said, breaking the burning end off and turning on the vent fan.

"Makes your house smell like temple," said Morikawa, fidgeting with her flowered blouse.

"What's wrong with smelling like a temple?" I asked.

"It's the smell of death," said Shimizu, his nostrils widening slightly on his smooth brown face. "We only smell incense at funerals or memorial services."

As the deadly aroma disappeared, the ladies soon were looking at me in amazement, chattering and oohing that I was washing the dishes. "Your wife must be so happy," said Tanahashi sincerely in her soft, high voice. "Do you always do dishes?"

"Yes, I have to," I told her. "If I don't . . ." And then I made the signs of an angry wife: holding my hands up to my head with my index fingers extended to represent horns. Tanahashi covered her mouth and laughed.

Elin stuck her head out from the den where she was reading. "It's not true," she said, guessing I was slandering her.

Kubo-san had just walked in at that point and she joined in on the laughter without having to be filled in.

Carrying a pot of tea, I led all into the living room where the shoji were open, revealing the garden in its late spring splendor.

Morikawa started off the conversation by saying she'd been to an interesting lecture in which the speaker talked about the differences between European royalty and the Japanese emperor. The main difference, she said, was that European royalty was believed to have derived its authority from God, whereas the emperor was thought to be a god.

The emperor Shōwa had died half a year earlier. He'd had the role longer than any previous emperor and had presided over the greatest swings in Japanese history. On the news they said he'd died without ever having been told he had cancer—as if such ignorance was a blessing. I was expecting major shock waves and public grief upon the announcement of his death. He died early one morning. I'd wondered why the flag was up at the temple gate. We were downtown shopping and ran into a lady, a college student we knew, on the street and she told us. We felt weird. The head of Shinto, the symbol of Japan, had died, and we couldn't read it in anyone's face—there was no change. No one in the neighborhood had told us that morning. Later I had asked kids in class how the emperor's death affected them and they'd just shrugged or said it had no meaning to them.

Mrs. Morikawa continued: "After the war some Japanese people think the emperor should be . . . hanging. . . ."

Me: "They thought the emperor should be hung . . . uh . . . hanged."

Mrs. Morikawa: "Be hanged. But many people respect MacArthur and he think it's very useful to not kill emperor."

Mr. Shimizu: "Australian Labor Party leader said after emperor's death this year he had no message of sorrow. He said after the war the emperor should have been chopped into many pieces with jungle knife."

Mrs. Morikawa: (laughs) "I believe him to be a war criminal. But MacArthur was very wise—very smart not to kill him. Often in European country they killed the royalty. We never killed emperor or reject emperor system."

Mr. Shimizu: "Japanese emperor is the most historical emperor in the world. Going back the longest and continuing in unbroken line."

Mrs. Morikawa: "But since the Meiji Restoration in the latter part of the last century it has been a special period. Before that the emperor ah . . . very often, uh, didn't appear on the political surface."

Mr. Shimizu: "Sometimes emperor had no power because the shogun had it all, or the general. There was much fighting for power. Emperor just figurehead."

Mrs. Morikawa: "So so so."

As one person speaks, the sos, hmms, ehs and ahs of the others are going on all the while. Japanese get uncomfortable if they don't hear constant feedback—*aizuchi.*

Mrs. Morikawa: "In Meiji era there was the first prime minister, but also the emperor gained respect and that idea continues now. But before Meiji the emperor was not so respected."

Mr. Shimizu: "Some emperors had no money. No one even thought of them. It's not so much the respect or power, but most important is the idea of divinity that increased at the time of the Meiji."

Me: "You're saying that the emperor became more important during the Meiji era?"

Mr. Shimizu: "That's right. More divine."

"That's funny—isn't that when Japan opened up?" I asked. "Meiji was the era of westernization."

Mrs. Morikawa: "Yes. It is irony. In the speech I heard yes-

terday, the professor said that the Japanese have fallen into a dilemma about the emperor. The British king or queen make an
effort to connect with the people but the Japanese emperor still
separate. Now the new emperor wants to contact with the people,
but the people around him, his retinue, don't want this connection. They want him to be on an ivory tower."

Kubo lights up. "Ivory?"

I explain. She goes back to listening.

Mrs. Morikawa: "After the war he became only a symbol of
the nation. Before that many people thought him god."

Me: "Did you think the emperor was a god?"

Mrs. Morikawa: "Yes. I was taught in school he was the god
and I believed till I was ten years old and the war over. Then he
says he's not a god and I was so angry. I hate him."

Elin and I knew there were some people who didn't appreciate
the emperor. In the papers such thoughts were usually associated
with left-wingers and older people in Okinawa, where so many
civilians had died in the final fighting of the war. There were
politicians who vehemently opposed the government spending a
cent on the emperor's funeral or anything imperial. They said it
went against the separation-of-church-and-state clause in the con-
stitution. The heavy-duty anti-imperialists have burned shrines
associated with him. The mayor of Nagasaki was shot by a right-
winger for saying that the emperor bore *some* responsibility for
the war.

Mrs. Kubo: "I don't care yes or no for the emperor. There
will be no emperor in twenty years anyway."

Mrs. Morikawa: "When were you born?"

Mrs. Kubo: "Nineteen fifty-five."

Mrs. Morikawa: "You didn't have to suffer for him. Why
didn't he tell us before he was no god? And the lies about white
devils. All the women who jumped off cliffs in Okinawa to escape
white devils. My family was in China for him. So many died.
Many millions. We thought Chinese inferior and whites were devils and only god, our god, could win the war. Then everything

went wrong. We took the boat back with no food. And they wouldn't let us in because of the quarantine. Just out there in the Inland Sea we waited a week in the boat and my sister starved to death. She starved to death for the emperor. And then the white devils came and fed us. They were fair. They saved us. The whole world was exactly opposite of what I was taught. I will always hate the emperor Shōwa and I want his son to quit."

I'd never seen her so worked up. English class can be like group therapy. It gives people permission to talk about things that might not otherwise be considered appropriate topics of conversation. Morikawa was shaking, but still smiling. Mrs. Kubo was looking a little shocked, but was listening intently.

"I don't hate him," said Shimizu. "He was victim of the right wing too. But I think that politicians who still say they believe the emperor is a god are too old-fashion. But I don't hate. And I was born in China. I was just a baby when we had to run so that's why I don't have bad memories. My mother did though. She shaved her head so that if the Russians caught her they'd think she was a man and just kill her and not rape her. They killed my father, uncle, grandparents and brother. They killed everyone they could. Only my mother and me got away. I am very lucky. And Japan was lucky the Russians never came."

That was all the heavy talk for that day. Kubo said she wanted to talk about something nice for a while. She pointed out that she had just bought a set of ivory bracelets.

"Don't they kill the whole elephant to get the horns?" said Tanahashi with a look of concern. It was the first thing she'd said all morning and it made me aware that I'd neglected to bring her into the conversation.

Kubo quickly broke the awkward silence. "I know I'm not supposed to buy them," she said, laughing. "It's illegal and my children love elephants, but I couldn't resist. They were very expensive."

Behind her I could see Elin in the kitchen, fuming. We'd just seen a documentary on TV about the social life of elephants, which included heart-wrenching scenes of their families being rounded up and slaughtered for ivory.

Kubo looked at me. "Americans don't want us to do this," she said.

"I agree with the Americans," said Tanahashi firmly.

"Americans buy almost as much illegal ivory as Japan," I said, a little sickened, and looked for something to say to express my displeasure tactfully, but Tanahashi had taken that role and anyway, Kubo was off talking about her son and how he played tennis all day and would never get into any good schools. Elin and I happened to be grateful to her son. Because of his bad grades Kubo had given us his TV so he wouldn't be able to stay up in his room and play video games all the time.

I stood in the garden and bade farewell to the members of the MMC. It had been another freewheeling day. I was still chewing on bits and pieces of the fragmented conversation. It's an interesting way to get to know people, through a language that they're struggling with. I'm struggling with theirs too. I think the most overused word for those who live abroad or study foreign languages is "fluent."

"We don't really understand each other," Shimizu once surprised me by saying when we were talking on the edge of the street in front of his small neighborhood store, I on my bicycle and he at the rear of his truck. "I can only really express myself in Japanese. I have a lot of deep and complicated feelings I just can't say in my English or your Japanese. But we try and I enjoy trying. What we are doing makes me very happy. We are planting seeds for the future."

MOO IF YOU
LOVE BUDDHA

MARUYAMA, SEPTEMBER 29, 1989

I walked to the *sanmon* and sat in the open air on a beam that runs across the black rough tile under the massive overhang of the mountain-gate roof. Some tourists trip on these obstacles, but their traditional purpose is to keep out little devils that are so short they can't get over them. I sit to the side on the demon stopper with my knees on an old blanket I bring for that purpose. I've stopped going to the zendo. I just come sit here, go to sanzen and then go home. It still takes an hour and a half. Watanabe said I had to get permission to skip the zendo part from the new head monk.

Taizen had to return to Kyoto to help out his original teacher. The new head monk is a stern middle-aged Japanese guy who put off getting his own temple to come to Daianji to study koans with Hōjō-san. He said, of course I could skip zazen in the zendo and so Watanabe also gave me his blessing. They're so understanding. But our reasons are different. To me, an hour or so of zazen is enough, but to them it's because of the press of duty. They say that since I'm a layman with responsibilities and bills to pay, it's a wonder I can come at all.

Straight ahead inside the hondo the morning sutras are playing while the latticed bell-shaped windows act as speakers bringing me the ancient chanting, largely from the mouths of young foreigners. Before long, I watch their silhouettes walk to the zendo and after a while Hōjō-san walks back alone, passes in front of my gaze and disappears into an entrance. Soon I can hear everyone's feet leap onto the floor beginning the stampede to sanzen.

As they charge across the temple grounds, between the trees and by the bushes, I stand up, fold up and leave the blanket and walk over to take my place in the back of the dark room, where I sit on a couple of folded-over square cushions and wait my turn for sanzen. Since I don't come from the zendo, my place is permanently last, behind visually impaired Den-san and the slow Frenchman. The longer to sit.

I'm working on a koan now. The first nine months it was *susoku-kan*, breathing practice. Since then it's been "Does a dog have buddha nature?" I repeat the question, actually the poem that presents the question, and then I give the answer. The answer is always the same, it's given in the poem. Zenwise it's a very famous answer: *mu*. It is a word that ostensibly means "no," but that in Zen has come to mean something more elusive like "neither no nor yes" or "neither yes nor no nor not yes nor not no," and that can go on and on. It's emptiness and it doesn't have a meaning one can codify. You've got to have it in your guts. Although "mu" is the answer, if one doesn't say it right, it doesn't count, the koan isn't passed and it has to be presented again at the next sanzen.

Katagiri and Suzuki in typical Soto style didn't assign these conundrums to students, but they would sometimes discuss them in lectures. Katagiri tolerated the fact that some of his students, rather than be involved with the Suienji system, studied in Japan with teachers that used koans. Suzuki's teacher once sent him to study with a Rinzai teacher. He said he got passed on his koan without having deserved it.

Some teachers pass their students through a series of koans quickly. I have a friend who studied for less than a year with a well-respected Western Zen teacher and he passed eighty koans. Gentsū Roshi in Fukui prefecture is reputed never to have passed anyone on mu, their first koan, and he's been in business for decades.

Some Buddhist friends from the States were visiting Elin and me and the husband asked if I'd been working on koans.

I said I had.

"How many have you passed?"

"None. I'm still working on the first one, mu."

He asked if I knew that so-and-so was studying with so-and-so and had passed thirty koans in the first month. I felt like the football player who was kicked off the team because he couldn't meet the academic requirements. I'd heard the joke at a football banquet when I was in the ninth grade. All he had to do was spell one letter in one word correctly and he'd make the team. The poor guy spelled coffee "k-a-u-p-h-y."

This morning, such competitive considerations far behind, I sat before Watanabe and repeated the poem.

Jōshū Oshō	Jōshū the venerable monk
Chinami ni soto	was asked by Chinami
Kushi ni kaete	as for a dog
Bushō ari ya mata nashi ya	is there buddha nature or not?
Shu iwaku mu	the priest (Jōshū) answered
	mu

Then I gave that moment's rendition of "mu," exhaling it deep and unadorned.

"Not bad, but not *one*," he said after a pause. "You still don't have the *samādhi* of mu." Then he demonstrated a low steady mu. Inspiring—a hard act to follow. "Keep it up," he said. "Let it come of itself." And he rang the bell.

I love mu. I used to repeat the word "buddha" and some variations on that theme when I needed something to center myself, or when I felt lost. (Once when the slippery walls of confusion had thoroughly surrounded me I thought, this is low enough, this will be my bottom. But how to proceed from here? I then decided to say "buddha" and let that be my rope, to climb and be pulled by— and it would be my sky, to be big and bigger in. Sometimes I would say it repeatedly, sometimes I'd forget for weeks.) Now I go "mu." It sounds like "moo" but it doesn't make me feel like a cow, more like the ushigaeru. And thus it seems like the appropriate practice for this place.

Maybe I use it more like a mantra than a koan (which Watanabe pointedly told me not to do). I don't think I'm supposed to like it this much. I get the idea it's supposed to bring all my delusions and angst to a head, to crystallize the mortal dilemma. Compared to the inspiring directions I get in sanzen and the noble examples from the old stories and Hōjō-san's lectures, I'm just humming a tune and going about my business.

And sanzen. What a system, meeting the teacher every time you go to sit. It's so different from the Zen I was raised on in northern California. I was embarrassed one day having tea informally with Hōjō-san when he asked me what Soto practice was with the teacher. When I told him we didn't work on koans, he asked if dokusan (the Soto word for sanzen) was just like advice or therapy. I said that I didn't know. And then when I told him how seldom we met in dokusan at all, he was just puzzled.

I remembered a time when all the senior priests of the San Francisco Zen Center were called together to meet with Katagiri, who was acting as interim abbot and our principal adviser. Priests came from Green Gulch farm, Tassajara, Berkeley and San Francisco and sat in black robes facing Katagiri as he and the rest of us were informed what the topic of the meeting was. Katagiri was told that many of us had to meet with new and younger students to guide them and answer their practice questions. Could he please give us a teaching on dokusan, the private interview? We wanted him to clarify and codify it for us. A tape recorder rolled on at his feet. We all sat seriously awaiting his answer. He looked pretty serious himself. Pregnant silence. But it was a hysterical pregnant silence, for there was no baby for the basket—the answer never came. He said he didn't know, that his teachers didn't give dokusan or even teach him dharma, and he had had to figure it out for himself. We also would have to figure it out for ourselves. The tatami was pulled out from under us.

I didn't want to talk to Watanabe about what Soto Zen was.

I'd never figured it out myself. As Suzuki had said, it was sitting with wandering mind and painful legs. We also didn't talk much about Zen and especially not about enlightenment. We regarded Zen-that-ran-after-enlightenment as goal seeking, or "having some idea," as Suzuki said. I told Watanabe that I treasured every moment I'd had with my Soto teachers and friends, but that it was good to have something definite to chew on for a change.

BURYING GARBAGE

HŌGOJI, MAY 15, 1988

Koji was drying with the same greyed dishtowels we always used. Maku was sweeping and being quiet while I kidded around with Koji and washed the bowls and pots. I occasionally paused to write down the words for different types of trash and cleaning implements like dust pan and garbage can. Organic garbage, *namagomi,* was put into the compost pile by the vegetable garden below Yoshiko's. Koji asked me to please bury it. I picked up the bucket, made a run down to the pile, threw it in and covered it well with dirt and leaves so it would compost and wouldn't attract animals and flies. In the garden the daikon had sprouted a few inches above the ground, but the Chinese cabbage was large and ready to eat. I returned with the bucket, which I had washed out in a runoff trough.

Placing it in its proper spot, I stood and smartly saluted. "I am namagomi, please bury me," I announced.

Maku turned and looked at me.

Saluting in return, Koji said, "I am namagomi, please bury me."

Shuko walked in. We turned in tandem and said, "We are namagomi, please bury us." Shuko smiled vaguely, shook his head, got a teapot and walked out.

Koji leaned over to me and whispered, "He wants to be a roshi."

"I know. But he's just namagomi. We will bury him," I said, quoting Khrushchev.

"He will bury himself," said Koji taking a bowl from me and drying it.

"Can't he be a roshi if he wants to?" I asked. "Isn't that what you're going to be and what all these monks aspire to?"

"I'm just going to be a temple priest. He wants to be a roshi like Nishiki Roshi, a high, respected priest." He looked around the corner to make sure he couldn't be overheard.

"Do you want to be a roshi?" I asked Maku, who was now wiping the floor with a grey damp rag. He shook his head no.

"It's okay for Shuko to be one, of course," Koji said. "It's just wanting to be one that's a problem. Ambition is one of the great obstacles for a monk, more deluding than alcohol and more tantalizing than sex."

"Pride is said to be the disease of the monk. Anyway, I'd rather have sex and alcohol, roshis just have a lot of trouble."

"Especially the ones who dream of it," said Koji.

"What about enlightenment? Do you think that wanting to be enlightened is a big obstacle to enlightenment?"

"The desire to be enlightened must be transformed into enlightenment. If it remains desire it will be in the way," Koji answered.

Whereas Maku exhibited no desire for fame or fortune, he did want psychic power and spiritual accomplishment. He nodded with his lower lip pushed out.

So then we got into discussing the various levels of enlightenment according to an old Indian Buddhist breakdown: stream-winners who are locked into the path, never-returners who won't be reborn again, *arhats* who are the original Buddhist saints, *pratyeka* buddhas who can't teach others and bodhisattvas who have vowed to save all beings. It took a while to get through each term because I knew them best in English and Sanskrit, and they mainly knew the old Japanized Chinese Buddhist terms. I asked if they believed in all that stuff. Maku said he did. Koji felt that they represented different attitudes that a person could have and were more like literary teaching devices.

I asked, "What do you call the being that can't be enlightened, who is totally devoid of buddha nature and has no possibility ever ever to enter nirvana?"

My question was met with immediate denials by Koji and Maku that such a being existed.

I said, "Yes, yes, I know that, but what's it called?" Again I was told that's not Buddhist and I said, "Yeah I *know,* but they gave it a name and debated its existence. Now what is it?"

Koji put up a lacquer bowl and said, "Oh, in Sanskrit that's an icchantika, isn't it? I forget what it is in Japanese."

"Issendai," said Maku, capturing the prize in our trivial pursuit.

"Yeah. Well, it's true that there's no such thing . . ." Koji leaned an ear toward me. "But . . ." I paused dramatically, "there's one exception."

"What do you mean?" Koji asked.

"You see," I went on, "in the whole history of the universe there has been only one being who is in reality an icchantika and can never ever be enlightened. It's just impossible for this one being to get enlightened."

"What being?" Koji's mouth was open with a half smile of anticipation.

Looking at him with knitted eyebrows, I spoke pointing to myself: "Me—I am namagomi, please bury me." Koji was reduced to a writhing puddle at my feet. Maku rinsed out his dirty floor rag, grinning. I went on washing with the satisfying feeling there had been a meaningful and rewarding exchange between Buddhists of different cultures. We always had a good time doing the dishes.

THE NINJA AND
THE CLOCK

HŌGOJI, MAY 16, 1988

After the evening bell, we all bow down together, touching our foreheads to the floor, and say the traditional Japanese good night, *oyasumi nasai,* which means "please rest." We're supposed to take our bedding out and go right to sleep, but some of us at times stay up late writing or reading in defiance of Dōgen's rules—like Dōgen did.

I always stay up as late as possible. Then the next morning I am exhausted and vow never to do it again. This has been a lifelong conflict. I like to stay up late. I like to get up early. At times I sleep in zazen. I slept through a lot of high school. I used to nap while I was driving.

On a quiet afternoon I was gingerly sweeping leaves off the moss in the courtyard, wishing vainly to lie down on it, curl up and go to dreamland. I vowed that I would get enough sleep that night. This vow was soon forgotten—like the one to save all beings from suffering and rebirth. At about one in the morning, after staying up late with Koji studying and talking, when I was crawling under my futon in the dark and mysterious hatto, I remembered my vow to go to bed on time and thought, oh no, I've done it again. Why don't I listen to myself? Who's in charge here? I'll die tomorrow.

I rolled over and stared numbly at the dark lump asleep not far from me. It was Maku, who also had been up late studying.

I started to fade. But what is that sound? An almost imperceptibly faint clicking. Ah yes, it's his clock . . . clock . . . alarm clock. Hmm. At that point an evil idea occurred to me. I reflected on how Maku always goes to sleep immediately and deeply and is never disturbed by anything. Good, good, I thought to myself. I did a few exercises for my back and then lay on the futon tapping my fingers together and meditating menacingly. I decided to move in the direction of the alarm clock, but I noticed after a moment that I had not yet budged. I felt like I had as a child standing on the edge of a high riverbank, afraid to jump in—trying, giving the command to go, friends urging and then . . . I slid out from my fluffy down cover and crawled toward sleeping-like-a-rock Maku. Slowly, slowly and oh so carefully, like a modern ninja in the night setting a hair-trigger explosive device, I picked up the clock and crawled back, pulling it under my futon, reached for and flicked on my flashlight, turned the alarm switch down and returned the clock just as deftly as I had taken it. Then I turned off my flashlight under the covers and put it back by my side. I lay there tingling and soon fell asleep with a profound feeling of warmth and security amidst the sounds of rodents scampering about and a faint unthreatening ticking.

The next day zazen was late and short. Maku was tardy ringing the wakeup bell and kept scratching his head trying to figure out what had gone wrong. I asked him what happened with the most innocent look on my face. He shrugged his shoulders.

I was glad that people thought it was funny that he'd blown it and he wasn't in trouble as he would have been at headquarters where he would have been up doo-doo creek without any prayer beads.

THE BODHISATTVA'S VOW

I'm gonna get a friggin' baseball bat and smash him in the head with it till he's bleeding from his ears," Norman muttered as he sat working at his table on the chanting book he was trying to put together.

"Anybody I know?"

He looked up. "Forget it. The brain weevils made me say it."

Norman was correct about there being a need for new books to chant by. It's one of the most annoying problems here. I have the two he gave me, which are incomplete. One is handwritten. I frantically leaf through them trying to keep up with some of these seemingly interminable chants. He asked Shuko and Koji one day if it wouldn't be all right for him to put some time into getting one legible sutra book together for me and those gaijin that come after, but Shuko said that there was too much to do right now and Koji went along with it. Norman was all turned around about that but is going ahead on his own, and is doing a paste-up that looks like it's going to be adequate for the time being. I wish they'd let him put some time into it and do it right, because, in addition to the practical aspects, I feel it would be beneficial for his mental health.

Norman's interest in making these books isn't just a desire to do busy work, nor is it merely an interest in efficient and harmonious group recitation. He also loves the message. He is wedded to Buddhist sutras and commentaries, with Chinese poetry as a lover on the side. *Sutra* means "discourses of the Buddha," but we use it loosely to mean Buddhist writings or anything we chant. There's been a lot created since Buddha's day (much of which is questionably attributed to him) and Norman's gobbling it up as time permits. In contrast to his sometimes rough and colorful use of language, the man's an egghead. You name it, if it's a Buddhist text and if it's translated into English, he's read it. He knows a great deal about the background and early writings of Buddhism. Sometimes I ask him to tell me stories from the old days, twenty-five hundred years ago, and he always comes up with a good one. After I've heard it, I think I should study this stuff more. Then I forget about it.

He was particularly happy with a Pali text translated into English that he'd just received from a special Buddhist book store in Bangkok. It was cheaply printed and bound with a paper cover and had all sorts of details about the life of Buddha that he'd never found before. Among other things it described a version of Buddha's schedule. There were a couple of hours for sleeping and periods for different types of meditation. There was even time set aside for teaching beings in other realms. They never talk about that sort of thing in the Zen that I'm used to. It's all no-nonsense here-and-now stuff.

I asked Norman if he thought there were truly beings in other realms or if that was just frosting derived from Hinduism and folk tales—much as I'd asked Koji and Maku when we were doing dishes.

He said that over and over in Buddhist texts from India and China there is mention of countless beings in countless world systems, of endless universes, buddha fields and dimensions all overlapping, coexisting and independently cooriginating with each other every instant. "Not your flat earth approach," he added. "Dōgen wrote of *myōka*, mysterious influence, which could be help from higher beings, guardian deities. If this realm is full of beings why would other levels not be? And now, since you have broken my concentration, I'll stop here and make us tea," he said pleasantly. While he did so he went on talking. "All the weirdest stuff you've heard about—psychic phenomena, astral traveling, ghosts, intelligent life from other star systems or dimensions,

channeling, you name it, it doesn't catch Buddhism by surprise."
He opened a package of *sencha,* a high quality green tea, and put
a pinch of leaves in a teapot. "It's all included and it's all one big
family, so to speak." He went on to say that while Buddhism
recognizes different, maybe infinite realities, it doesn't encourage
fascination with them. Buddha and the teachers that followed said
that all we had to do was to make the most of our human life—
that there is no need to look outside of our own body and mind,
which includes the whole cosmos anyway. "Being born on the
physical plane with a body like ours is, according to Buddhism,
the most precious opportunity in the cosmos to see through the
whole shebang, escape the wheel of rebirth, attain enlightenment,
Christ consciousness, or whatever you want to call it. And poly-
theists, animists, people with no religion or who don't use names
like Buddha and God are not excluded in any way from realization. There's a big basket of options. This is not an exclusive trip."
He poured hot water from a thermos into his small porcelain
teapot.

"That's why I like the bodhisattva's vow," I said. "Our practice automatically includes all beings in all realms. It eliminates
racism, sexism, sectarianism, speciesism. . . ."

"At least theoretically."

"I have only one problem with the ideal of the bodhisattva,"
I told Norman. "There's a fatal flaw."

"What's that?" he said.

"Well, in terms of entering nirvana, if we look at it in this
crude historical space-time way, all the beings but the bodhisattvas would have to go first, right? She or he as the case may be
has vowed to be last."

"U-hm."

"Let's imagine then that the wonderful moment has come
when there are only these bodhisattvas left. All nonbodhisattvas
have gone first. What do the bodhisattvas do now?"

"Well, if we pretend that they're really separate beings, we
can say that they enter nirvana then."

"Exactly—that's the problem. They've vowed to let all others go first. They'll probably stand around and congratulate each other for a while and then one of them will inevitably say to the others with a sweeping gesture, 'After you, everyone.' And then all the other bodhisattvas, probably an infinite sea of them, will answer in unison, 'Oh no, after you.' And Norman, this could go on and on forever with no resolution, a countless number of bodhisattvas trapped in a double bind of unconditional love and generosity."

"Ah, but since everything changes, it could not remain static. I see three possible outcomes."

"I knew you'd be able to solve this one for me."

"Well, the first one, which was worked out long ago, is that they'd all go together."

"But what if the door is too narrow to permit more than one at a time?"

"In that case, another possibility is that one by one they'll sacrifice their vow to enable others to be closer to keeping theirs."

"How noble. Of course. And the other?"

"If the door is too narrow and their vows are too strong to give up, things could get ugly. They could get into insisting, name calling and foot stomping, and before they knew it, chaos could once again be created, out of which the multiverses would form with infinite beings on infinite levels and the cycle of birth and death with all it entails would be back in full swing."

"Oh gosh," I shook my head.

"And then," Norman's eyes looked up almost shining, "a Buddha would arise, and an Avalokiteshvara, Moses, Mary, Christ, Mohammed, Lao Tsu and the endless saints, the Earth Mother, shamans and witches. And beings throughout the cosmos would endeavor to find their inner light and share the good news with all others."

"Why, that's inspiring."

He picked up his tea cup and took a sip. I followed suit.

Norman looked down at the sutra book he was working on.

"And I will have another opportunity to pick up a baseball bat and bash Shuko in the head till he starts bleeding from his ears."

SAVING THE SALAMANDER

MARUYAMA, OCTOBER 4, 1989

Yesterday as we rode our bicycles out to the Inland Sea, Elin asked me if I noticed something different.

"Yes," I told her.

"What is it?"

"I don't know."

"It's the humidity—it's gone. We can breathe again. I feel light."

How right she was. It's not sticky anymore. Fall in Maruyama is especially soothing after the oppressive wet heat of summer. The other day my calligraphy teacher called the weather *mushiatsui* (hot and humid). It didn't seem so to me, so I asked if we couldn't just say "a bit warm and humid," and she said, "No, we can't say that. Just mushiatsui." She said mushiatsui when it was a hundred degrees (which they call thirty-seven around here). It's seventy-five right now on the right side of our Celsius-Fahrenheit thermometer. Here people always say something about the weather when they meet and, mark my words, it's going to go directly from "Hot and humid isn't it?" to "Cold isn't it?" I'm never going to get to say it's warm or cool or just right. I must deepen my understanding of it all.

. . .

This morning I was building a bamboo gate when Elin appeared around the corner on our shopping bicycle—the cheap one with big baskets in front and back. It was like the family pickup truck. She wore shorts, a tee shirt and sandals and had a small potted tree in the front basket that she'd gotten from Ishitaki.

She whizzed by me, saying, "Look at this great new ficus, yiperoo!" and I followed her up the driveway and held the bike as she got the pot out. The deep temple bamboo grove was behind her and they looked so nice together, her curves against the straight bamboo, dense with leaves topside and swinging in the breeze.

"I'm going to work in the garden," she said, and then before I could say anything, she sucked in a little gasp.

I followed her eyes and there was charming, elderly Okamura-san, our sweet and dignified neighbor, squatting on the edge of her gently sloping metal garage roof.

"Ohayō gozaimasu," she called down, pleasantly bidding us a good morning, and we responded in kind, looking up at her on her sunny perch. All the weight of her body was on the bottoms of her feet, her knees up and her posterior reaching her heels. She was pulling the yellow leaves off a tree that grew up next to the garage and putting these leaves into a black plastic garbage bag. This lady is in her seventies and usually when we see her she's puttering in the garden or taking a walk with her shopping bag —not sitting on her roof.

"What are you doing up there?" Elin asked.

"I'm picking the leaves before they fall and become troublesome," she answered while pulling a few more off the tree and putting them in the bag.

Just then the mailman came puttering in on his scooter. Elin and I stepped aside as he stuffed a few letters in the Okamuras' mailbox and handed us ours. One of them was for Mr. Okamura, from Rotary International headquarters in America. We get all the romanized mail in the neighborhood and then I often have to translate it all when I give it to the proper party. I pointed it out to the mailman and he put it in the Okamuras' box. As he started to swivel his motor bike around, he caught a glimpse of our neighbor on the roof and did a double take.

"Ii otenki desu ne (Nice weather, isn't it)?" he said, recovering.

"Sō desu nē," she agreed, and he zoomed down the driveway and off to the temple.

I helped Elin carry the ficus into the garden and walked out to the street to look around. The air was full of smoke from neighbors burning leaves. I loved the smell—it reminded me of my boyhood in Texas, before burning outdoors was taboo. A squadron of scarlet dragonflies was swooping around as I was fishing a soft drink can out of the mizo. I noticed Numoto Sensei, who lives on the other side of the Daianji parking lot, about to get into his Volkswagen Bug. He stuck his hand up in the air. I waved goodbye. He hesitated, then drove over to say hello on his way out. I realized that I had unintentionally beckoned him—our wave "goodbye" is their wave "come here." Fine. I was always happy to talk to the professor. Numoto Sensei is a friendly retired botanist who has made our stay in this neighborhood much richer.

"Ohayō gozaimasu, ogenki desu ka (Good morning, how are you)?" I said, and he answered back in English, "Well, and you?" And I said that I was fine and that it's getting cold and he said, yes it is. And then I said in Japanese, "You're going out?" and he answered in English because he likes to use his English as much as I like to use my Japanese.

He got out of his old white Bug looking casual and like the professor he is, with a pipe in his mouth and horn-rimmed glasses. "Yes, I am going far north in the prefecture."

"What takes you there?" I asked, deciding to speak English with him and not get involved in one of our language wars, each insisting on speaking the other's tongue.

"Takes?" he asked.

"Why are you going there?" I reworded it.

"I am seeking an ancient amphibian."

"How do you say 'amphibian' in Japanese?"

"Ryōsei."

"Both life?" I asked the way we often do, giving the basic English for the two Chinese characters that make up the word.

"Yes," he said. "It lives both in water and on land. This one lives in shade of streams on remote mountain. It is very big. One of biggest amphibians."

"Is it a salamander?" I asked. Sensei checked in a large specialized dictionary he had in the back seat and said that it was indeed a type of salamander. He pulled out some dried persimmons and handed me one.

"Just persimmon now, for I am driving. Come over tomorrow evening and try the new wine I have made from the wild berries in the hills."

"I'll be there," I said. I love to hang out with him. We meet in his private study in back. It is packed full of books and papers—shelves and cabinets around the walls, and tables stacked high in the center. There are two easy chairs on the side with a low table in between and we sit there for an hour or so every couple of weeks, drink his home brew and solve the problems of the world. Last week he told me of his failed attempts to stop the government from cementing the sides of local rivers, creeks and the coastline.

I made the mistake of going into the main part of his house with him once. Like many Japanese homes it was utterly cluttered—not dirty, but full of stacks and piles of household items, magazines, newspapers, mail, wooden and cardboard boxes, tins, and such. As soon as I entered, his wife, hearing my voice, ran in from another room, put on a cloth mask over her nose and mouth and walked around with a feather duster whacking like crazy until we left. People don't go into each other's homes much, except maybe into a special guest room that is kept spiffy. Temples are that way too. The private living parts of them are frequently unkempt.

It's just like the old Gahan Wilson cartoon with the Japanese priest sitting in front of the *byōbu,* the folding screen, a flower in a vase and a scroll at his side (that's how I remember it, anyway)—perfect minimal austerity in front of the byōbu for his guest. Behind it the place was a total mess. Numoto's house didn't correspond to the cartoon in the usual way, though, because there was no tidy, proper guest room in his home. The closest thing to it was his study, which he did not organize for public approval.

Once I insisted that I help bus the dishes in a home where Elin and I were eating dinner. I thought the only reason the housewife protested was that she didn't want her guest to work. But when I entered the kitchen I understood—there was just a tiny aisle that wasn't stacked with magazines and junk. I had to walk sideways to the sink, which was piled high with dishes already. I never tried that again.

Numoto's yard was also not the usual pruned showcase. It was large and natural, his own agricultural lab with many varieties of fruit trees and plants for herb teas. And there was grass we could sit on in good weather while chatting about the disappearing fireflies that families continue to catch on summer nights and put in jars. He thought the insecticides had done them in more than anything else.

Back to the salamander. Numoto does this sort of field trip a lot. Twelve students from the university were meeting him up north.

"I bet this isn't pure science," I said, getting a hunch while chewing with relish on the dried persimmon.

"Why do you say so?" he asked curiously, tamping his pipe.

"Mmm, this is good," I said, looking at the dried persimmon. "I see these hanging up all over when I take walks. It's the best way to eat these hard Japanese persimmons."

"They are very tasty when dried," he agreed.

"I bet they came from your tree."

"Yes," he nodded.

"And I bet that you're trying to stop a golf course from being built," I resumed the topic.

He smiled proudly. "That is right. If we find the salamander then we can slow them down because the golf playground, what do you say?" He stopped.

"Course, golf course," I instructed.

"The golf course will destroy the salamander and it is a very old and important animal. Maybe in this way we can stop them."

"But don't limit it to the salamander," I advised. "Don't just say 'salamander.' "

"No," he said, immediately understanding my point. "It is an indicator of general environmental destruction. It is like the canary in the mines, but to me it is also just for the salamander —and each animal and plant."

"Yeah, but you'd better talk more in terms of the other side, of managing resources so they will benefit people for a long, long time."

"And how else should I talk to people to stop the golf course?"

"Hit them in their national pride. Talk about the ruin of the sacred island of kami and the unique, superior people descended from the sun."

"Oh!" he said, taken aback at my patriotic appeal.

"I don't know—what should you say? Talk about maintaining balance and sustaining this island ecosystem. Responsibility to the future? Wouldn't Japanese respond to that better than Americans?"

"You should give talk. You could save the salamander better than me."

"But you are the expert," I said, deferring.

"But you are an American and Japanese people will listen to you, but will not listen to me. That is the character of the people."

"Really?" I said, surprised. "You mean like if I gave a serious talk on the environment, they wouldn't think I was Japan bashing?"

"Not if you're careful," he said with conviction. "They wouldn't listen to me, but you would make them ashamed and they would think, 'We should not do such a thing.' "

I shook my head. "Naaah, I think I'll just watch the world be destroyed. I can't stop it. I'll just pull up a chair and watch. So you'll have to save it."

"It can't be helped," he said with a smile. "But I will try."

"Well, I admire you for trying," I said. "Good luck and I hope you find lots of salamanders."

"Not too many," he responded. "Just a few would be best."

MR. TEN SQUARE FEET

MARUYAMA, OCTOBER 12, 1989

Elin and I went over to Daianji to welcome back Hōjō-san. He'd just returned from a two-week trip to America. It was nine in the morning and we had an hour. I reminded her that I had a class at home at ten so we should keep track of the time.

These are the best days. All traces of summer are gone. The deciduous leaves are melting to yellows and reds and, as we walked up to the big temple gate, we felt comfortable and relieved in the slight fall breeze. Glen and Dai-san smiled and waved as we rounded the stone path toward the entryway by the kitchen. A wasp buzzed by.

A moment later we entered the large tatami room where people sit in the morning waiting their turn for sanzen. Who would guess that behind the fading *sumi* paintings on the fusuma, Watanabe sits alone amidst stacks of paper and books in his two little rooms, Mr. Ten Square Feet indeed. We could hear him back there on the phone so we went through the adjoining area where meals are eaten and stepped out onto the deck overlooking yet another dreamy garden. Within tile-roofed clay walls, there is a tasteful arrangement of shrubs and stones connected by soft moss surrounding a venerable old tree with drooping branches propped up by forked sticks.

There were a couple of wasps buzzing around. These weren't the little black wasps that collect on the panes by the *ōsetsuma*. I move the sliding doors and brush them out with no concern. No, these are more like what we call hornets in the States. They're big, long and brown. They come in sizes, like tee shirts or bees. I'd seen a medium on the way to the kitchen. These were the larges.

We could tell by the change of timing in his words and the tone of his voice that Watanabe's conversation was coming to an end. Goodbyes in Japanese tend to drag out for a while, with each party adding yet another formalized expression to the prior one. We sauntered over just outside his door and waited for the short parting shots to die out and finally heard the sound of the receiver clunking down.

I called out, "Sumimasen."

Immediately he responded with, "Hai!"

Then in English Elin and I both called out, "Welcome back!"

We talked for a second through the closed door and he bade us go wait for him in the *ōsetsuma*. According to my Japanese-English dictionary, an *ōsetsuma* is a parlor or drawing room, but it's awfully plain to be called by such a dignified name. It's Hōjō-san's comfortable everyday meeting room where he receives guests informally. It's small and slightly cluttered with cushions, tea paraphernalia, books and an open cabinet with papers and tapes of his lectures.

Hōjō-san was there right away and seemed happy to see us. At half a century he holds himself well, with confidence, but not the arrogance that can go with being the abbot of a big temple. His face is smooth and friendly, tan. The top of his shaved head reaches to something more than five feet, but it's hard to estimate because his presence makes him seem taller than he is. We all sat down on zabuton on the tatami and he started preparing some *macha* tea for us. When we sit together on the floor we all seem closer to the same size. He definitely likes that equalizing effect. There's not a single chair in the temple. But the main reason he favors the low level runs deeper. Watanabe says that the basis of Japanese culture is sitting on the floor and he believes that as the Japanese people lose that habit, they lose their center of gravity and their keel. He smiled comfortably as he removed the potent green macha powder from a silver can with a narrow, flat bamboo instrument and spooned it into earthy ceramic tea bowls.

Elin asked him how his trip to America had been. He said he'd gone to lead a seven-day sesshin in Oregon, and after it was over he'd flown down to the Bay Area, where he participated in another meditation retreat with a group of people who had cancer. He went straight into talking about the cancer retreat, obviously touched by the experience.

"I had to give a talk and I didn't know what to say. I wondered what I could tell them that would help. I had pictured them as sick and troubled. But when I arrived and saw their faces, the bright eyes—I knew they were not sick. Their minds were healthy." He briskly stirred a bowl of tea with his whisk. "Then I knew that I could speak to them."

He said he was ready to cut it off at any point for fear that they would tire quickly, but people kept asking questions. A lively discussion ensued for two hours.

"This is the way that we must all practice," he said. "This is the way that we must live, as if we might die any minute, with a knowledge of the preciousness of each day and each minute."

In that morning's sanzen Watanabe had radiated this sense of immediacy. He made it seem that realization is right here and available instead of a billion lifetimes of effort away.

He replied to my "mu" with the usual guttural "Hai!," starting low and moving up an octave, ending abruptly as he clenched his teacher's stick. It didn't have the same casual tone as when he said hello to Elin and me from his room. It had more of a sobering effect, like a judge smashing down his gavel in court.

Making a fist and putting his thumb out, the way an artist might do who was eyeballing a subject for the canvas, Hōjō-san rumbled out from his guts a "mu" of his own and pushed his thumb down till his arm extended in front of his navel. "Not in your head," he patted his shining pate. "In your tanden," he said, hitting his belly.

He put his thumb back to forehead height and pushed it down through the air again with the force of a weightlifter pumping iron, encouraging me to thus concentrate on my koan.

He said, "When you're teaching English," and then "mu-u-u-u-u" his voice riding down with the thumb. "When you're on your bicycle, mu-u-u-u-u-u." He concluded in English, "Concentrate, concentrate, concentrate!"

With the sound of his donut-shaped bell, I stood up and bowed.

These memories came to me in flashes, all packaged and wrapped and zipping by in the spaces between the words while Hōjō-san talked about his trip to America.

"To Japanese, cancer is a death sentence. The doctors don't even tell you if you've got it. They just tell your family. And then your family won't tell you—and most people don't want to know anyway. People put their parents in hospitals just because they're old. They aren't with their parents when they die. That used to be thought of as a terrible thing. Now everyone just wants to run from death. These people were finding great life in each moment of dying. I'm very grateful to them.''

Hōjō-san was rinsing out the bowls and making a new batch of tea from dried flowers. Just then a humongous wasp flew into the room through the open window. "Oh my god," I gasped, "I didn't know they came in extra-large." The tug between his words and my thoughts had vanished, for before us was this wasp, a Goliath, a good two-and-a-half-inch forget-everything-else type beastie. I managed to hide a swoon in a readjustment of my sitting position. The giant hovered above the table and neither Elin nor Hōjō-san seemed to care.

"Uh, uh, what's that?" I said as nonchalantly as possible.

Hōjō-san looked up and said, "Oh, that's a kumabachi."

"Kumabachi—that means bear bee," I said mechanically, holding onto a leg of the table with one hand and Elin's ankle with the other.

"Their bite isn't as bad as the suzumebachi. They're big, but not much of a bite."

"Well, I sure don't want to test it," I mumbled in English, wondering how they could possibly live in a screenless temple when monsters like these could fly in at any time.

Watanabe asked Elin about how her work was going on some bowls she was making with Jessica. Betraying me, Elin answered him casually, rather than saying that we had to get back soon. I looked at the clock and saw that it was thirteen till ten. Soon I had class. But this beast would surely attack me before that and I would be taken to the hospital in cardiac arrest while Elin and Hōjō-san discussed the natural glazes in local clay.

Then with a hellish buzzing the wasp flew out into the hall. I had not been able to hide my fear and Elin and Hōjō-san were now laughing at me. I chuckled nervously and smiled like some-one who had just lost on "Wheel of Fortune."

I remembered another sanzen session. He had asked me if I understood the word "gyroscope," and I'd said "Hai." I must be more like that, he said—like a gyroscope, concentrated on one spot and centered in one spot and then I could spin and keep my balance no matter where I am.

The bear bee reentered the room and promptly buzzed right into my gyroscope. "Oh gaah," I muttered. I was sure this was the end, but it flew out the window. Hōjō-san had asked us how our classes were going and Elin was telling him how much she was learning from her students.

I looked at the clock. It was ten till ten. All of a sudden I remembered that my class wasn't at ten. "How could I have for-gotten!" My eyes went up and I caught my breath. "Oh no! It's at nine thirty! It was twenty minutes ago!" I jumped up, scream-ing, "Ahhhhhh!"

Hōjō-san looked at me surprised. "Nani?" he said, glancing about to see if the bear bee was back.

I was already half out the door, explaining in submachine-gun style that I'd blown it because this talk was so fascinating, and I hoped he could hear me as I zoomed away—"Excuse me, I'm being very rude! I cannot be forgiven!"—standard phrases. "I can't be forgiven!" I repeated as I ran on the path past the wall outside his window.

"Hai!" he called out at the dust cloud behind me.

SHUKO TELLS ALL

Every few hours visitors walk up the steps. Whoever is around will greet them. The friendliness of the greeting of course differs with the mood and personality of the monk. Maku tends to just bow and smile. Jakushin seems to force his salutation out of the gloom. Katagiri is always cordial but not inviting—he will quickly return to whatever he's doing. Koji and Norman are the most outgoing and each will go out of his way to accommodate the guests. So will Shuko, though he's more reserved in his approach. But he has a way with guests, taking his time and speaking softly. He's not comfortable with people the way Koji is, but he makes up for it in the quiet and attentive way he takes care of them.

On the afternoon of a *shiku-nichi* three ladies walked into the courtyard. I was doing my laundry and said good day to them and they responded enthusiastically. After they had paid their respects at the entrance to the hatto and thrown a few coins into the donation box, I asked them if they'd like some tea. They would. There were two middle-aged ladies and a younger one of about twenty, all dressed casually in slacks and loose blouses appropriate for walking in the woods. Shuko came out from the kitchen where he was making dinner and joined in. The ladies made a fuss over me being a gaijin. Shuko sat on the steps with them while I went to make tea. I came back out in five minutes with a tray, cups, a brewing pot of green tea and some cookies. Shuko was answering a question about the practice at Hōgoji and the ladies were listening respectfully. I poured the tea. It looked like pea soup. Shuko's eyes bulged.

"It looks a little strong, doesn't it," I said, embarrassed.

"Yes, it does," he said.

The mother of the young lady saved the day by saying that's exactly how she likes it. She picked hers up with a "gochisō sama" (what a treat) and took a sip. The other two followed and they all three said, "Oishii (Delicious)!" They also told me my Japanese was excellent. Nice of them, considering I'd only said a few simple words. I knew that for the rest of their lives they would tell this story, laughing and saying how gaijin can't make tea.

They asked me if I was a monk and before I could say no, Shuko said yes, that I was a very good monk. So I countered by saying that I was a *namagusa-bōzu,* which is a monk who "stinks of being raw," a decadent monk. They got a kick out of that but waved their hands sideways, signifying disbelief.

The young lady was attractive despite a youthful complexion problem. I might have been the first foreigner she or any of them had ever met. She kept staring at me. She said I was very handsome, which made them all giggle and then she asked if I was married, which made them quiet until I said no and then they giggled again. It was taking much the same course as the talk with the Philippine ladies in Kikuoka had. I said that I was engaged, which wasn't quite true, but things were leaning in that direction. This elicited ehs and ahs and in no way diminished their interest in me. The conversation drifted till we all found ourselves saying gosh, it's getting late and we've so much to do, it's been wonderful talking to you, do come back and the like. The young lady looked at me sweetly when they left and stirred my mind and body for the rest of the day where it had been still for a time.

"Well, that was nice, wasn't it?" I said to Shuko back in the kitchen as I washed the cups and he sliced the dinner pickles.

"Yes, you are very good with guests," he answered.

"You're the one who has a way with guests. You snow them."

"Snow?" His English is good but he doesn't know everything.

"Um, charm them. Charm them with the dharma, charma dharma or should that be charming dharming?"

"Oh," said Shuko, unsure whether it was a compliment or a put down.

"But the tea! Oh, I'm sorry, you must have been terribly embarrassed."

"Oh no, it's all right," he said. "You'll remember next time."

"Yeah, listen, I used to know how to make green tea. I'll practice on Norman some so that doesn't happen again. He's expendable."

"Good idea," he said with no hint of sarcasm. When Shuko speaks English, the tone is flat, the way that Japanese is spoken, without the hills and valleys of intonation that we have in English. So it's hard to see where he's coming from. But I don't care. He can be coming from anywhere he wants. I dried the cups individually, walking each one to the cabinet where they were kept.

Once Shuko was out on the deck while I was talking to an old lady visitor at the temple. She said of him, "Odayaka na kao," a peaceful face. Shuko does have a peaceful face and it stays that way almost all the time regardless of how things are going.

Norman says that it's often a superficial peace. "You never know what's going on inside," he said. "But that's generally true in Japan. Appearance is everything—facade is art."

Shuko lived for eight years in the States. Elin says he was considered attractive by the women at Zen Center, where he spent a good deal of time. He makes a good first impression. At Zen Center he was helpful to people when they needed him. Many students, especially the newer ones, prefer Japanese monks to Western ones. They look the part. Funny thing is that Shuko got interested in Zen in America and was ordained by a lovable recluse Japanese priest who lived in the mountains north of San Francisco. Shuko had not studied Zen in Japan up to that point and was less experienced than a lot of the Western priests and even some of the people he was advising. Ironically, it seems he fit in better in the States than in Japan.

That evening after zazen Shuko invited me to have tea with him. We didn't have it in his room. He closed the shoji door quickly and motioned me toward the study area. He made *genmai cha*. Some of the kernels of rice had popped, creating little puffs of white. He put a few pinches in a small reddish brown teapot. Sliding the pot over to the large thermos and pressing the thermos top, he pumped steaming hot water out of the spout and down into the pot. After a minute of silence, he poured the tea.

"This little teapot comes from my home prefecture. There is a special type of clay there. This pottery is important to the people from where I come. A poor family or a rich family, either one will have a teapot like this, or a cup or a vase on the altar or some pieces in the cabinet. It can be the most important object in the house. If there is a guest they will bring it out. If it's considered valuable it won't leave tatami level unless it's being held with both hands and one elbow on the mat."

"Like in tea ceremony."

"Yes, that is the way to care for something so that it won't break in a thousand years."

I leaned down and looked at the aged brown earthy implement and thought how wonderful to come from a place that prizes simple, straightforward, functional objects like that. "Where I grew up we valued oil fields, slaughterhouses and bombers," I said.

Shuko was unusually forthcoming that evening and reminisced about his past. He comes from a poor farming family in northern Japan. He did well in a commercial school and after graduating did accounting work for a company in Nagoya. He was working hard in the day and going to night school. He said he wasn't your typical country boy, or your typical Japanese boy for that matter. He had some bright ideas and he told them to his boss. "Pretty forward behavior in Japan, especially for a new employee. Stack one miracle on another, my boss listened to me." He became the boss's favorite and was quickly promoted.

Things went along rosily for a while, but he got full of himself and created resentment in the organization. "This grew into a lot of resentment," he told me, staring out the window into the darkness. "We've got a saying here that the nail that sticks up gets hammered down."

"Yes," I said, "I've heard that often."

"I thought that being on the good side of the boss would protect me from that sort of thing." He paused. "I could see only a promising future. But I was rising too quickly." He stopped.

I could see the nail rising above the others and a giant hammer pausing before its powerful descent. Something happened. And what that something was, he wouldn't say. Something behind the peaceful face. At times, he has told me about various things that he's sad or discontented about, like his marriage breaking up or his relationship with Norman, but I couldn't get near whatever happened to him in Nagoya. Something bad.

He left Japan right after that and went to college, choosing the American University in Beirut. He said he had to get out, out of this stifling conditioning, out of this constraining and at times humiliating country.

"I wanted to go anywhere. I was sure that anything would be better than Japan. I chose Beirut because I could get into the school there quickly. I took the first plane that I could make."

There he met his wife to be, a small Irish-American from Boston who was defying her parents' wishes by going to school in Beirut. She took a liking to this Oriental stranger and started bringing him fruit and doing his laundry. He didn't know about dating and Western ways and so he responded in the only way that he knew how. He asked her to marry him. She immediately accepted.

He went to America with high hopes of the favors he would

receive as the son-in-law of a lawyer, but found himself living for the first year as a stowaway in a sorority house. There he improved his English and came to be fast friends with many of the sisters. Sadly, he was never accepted into his wife's family and he couldn't get a good job. He and his wife never adjusted to each other and before long he ended up on his own and very unhappy.

Now he has the yellow robe and will maybe have this international training temple as his own someday, way out in the middle of nowhere. It sounds romantic, but I wonder if he can hack it forever here. If he does stay I wouldn't be surprised if he gets married by arrangement and lives in a house down in the village. Just a hunch. Temple priests usually get married.

Shuko was raised strictly. He said that his mother wouldn't let him in the door if he was hurt or had been beaten up—not until he'd stopped crying.

"Beaten up?" I said. "Did you get into fights?" I couldn't imagine this gentle man as a scrappy kid.

"Oh yes, I caused a lot of trouble until I got older and realized that the only way out of that place was to do well in school." His parents worked long hours. He received much of his rearing from his grandparents.

"In my family nothing was supposed to be fun. Every minute was a chance to make an effort or bear up under some difficulty."

His grandparents had the ultimate say in the big farmhouse where they all lived. They decided when he could go out and for how long. "This ended up meaning that I couldn't go out. I had to stay in and study all the time. I read a lot." He sat up a little straighter and bit his lip. "You know what my favorite book was?"

"No, what?"

"*Huckleberry Finn*. I had a Japanese translation that my father gave me. It was the best gift I ever got. It represented to me everything that I wanted that I couldn't have. I lived in beautiful countryside like Huckleberry Finn, but I couldn't get out and run around in it like him. I felt like a prisoner. I wanted to have adventures."

When he was bad his grandparents would hold him down and burn the back of his neck. He said that most kids only got that sort of treatment once and that from then on they would never again do anything to merit such punishment. However, in Shuko's case he received this frightening negative programming a number of times.

When asked what he might have done that was so horrible, he said, "Oh, I'd go fishing at night with friends." I asked what was so bad about that and he reminded me that he wasn't supposed to go out at all at night and that his grandparents considered fishing to be dangerous because, as is the case with most Japanese people until recently, he didn't know how to swim.

"They were really stupid," he said.

Ah, I thought, I can see the anger on his face. Now his bitterness will come out. "Why do you say they were stupid?" I asked.

"Because they would come right up to the light."

I searched for the meaning of this statement. I imagined his sadistic grandparents holding a torch, the torch they were about to burn him with, their faces near the light. "But . . . why did that make them stupid? I don't quite get it."

"Because we could catch them," he said, smiling.

"What would you do with them when you caught them?" I asked.

"We'd eat them of course."

I must have missed something. The kerosene light flickered slightly as a cool evening breeze entered the room through the opened window. The woodwork creaked. He went on. I listened intently.

He laughed again. "They were so stupid. We'd hold a flashlight down to the water and they'd come right up to it and we'd catch them in a net with a long handle and then we'd make a fire and cook and eat them on the spot."

"You would?"

"Yes. That's how I learned to clean fish and that's the first time ever I cooked anything."

"Oh."

"Yes, and it was the smell of the fish on me that would wake up my grandmother when I got home and she'd get angry and scold me. She'd wake up my grandfather and they'd burn me on the back of the neck with incense." He explained that one reason why this punishment had not stopped his erring ways was that, upon first being touched with the hot incense, he would scream in such an anguished way that his grandparents would be convinced that he had reached that ultimate degree of pain necessary to change him forever.

I have since come to realize that what happened to Shuko wasn't as horrible as I had first imagined. I've asked a few Japanese about it and from what I can piece together a lot of older people thought that poor behavior could be "cured" by *okyū*, or moxibustion. It's like acupuncture except it's hot instead of sharp. I've had it for an embarrassing physical ailment—with good results —and it didn't hurt much.

Whenever I think of Shuko, or his name comes up, or his smooth, round face appears in my daydreams, I remember him as the monk who ate his stupid grandparents in a fit of revenge.

OUR DUST RUNNETH OVER

HŌGOJI, MAY 20, 1988

The dramatic part of the morning temple cleaning is when the monks charge over the woodwork and floors with wet rags, moving fast to try to cover every surface before it's time for tea. We hold the wet rag down with both hands and the whole body's weight as we run down the length of the floor. After years of being wiped with water, wood becomes dark and has a deep richness to it. Norman says the secret to keeping the temple clean is to try to get to some new, forgotten area every day. One morning we were all silently shining the place up, working as busily as the termites in the foundation. Koji and Jakushin were sweeping the tatami in the hatto, Shuko was wiping the floor in the kitchen, Norman was dusting the dining room, Maku was out front scrubbing the sink, oblivious to a half-dozen yellow-and-black-striped bees that were drinking on the other end. I was running down the covered walkway on all fours with a rag, and Katagiri was sweeping the back hall. It was a picture of industrious Zen temple harmony.

Koji is the head monk so it's okay if he makes suggestions to others. It's in the job description. On his way to the kitchen to get a bucket, Koji pointed out to Norman that he had missed some dust in a corner. I was ringing my rag out nearby. Norman, who does not like to be told what to do by people who were in diapers when he was playing lead guitar in sleazy bars, said to Koji that everybody was missing something or other and why didn't he get back to his job and make sure that *he* didn't miss anything. Koji stomped off. In the system he's used to, you don't answer back like that, you simply say "hai!" and do what you're told. But he let it go rather than cause a scene. So we were all sweeping and wiping away and then from my vantage point on the deck I saw Norman abruptly stop and walk across the courtyard to the hatto with his broom and dustpan in hand, disappearing inside. I got curious and crept around the covered walkway to the door to that building, slid it open and peeked in. Norman was bustling about where I couldn't see him and Koji had just arrived at the steps with some rags and a bucket and was scrubbing them down. Then Norman stepped out of the shadows from behind the altar, walked over to Koji, thrust the dust pan in front of his face and said, "Here's something you missed."

Norman is used to dealing with Shuko, and even though Japanese do have common denominators, they are as different from each other as they are from us. Koji instantly turned red and screamed unintelligible rapid-fire Japanese in Norman's face, pushing him in the chest. I feared for dear Koji's life, as Norman can get angry too and is twice his size. But Norman took it like a monk at that point, after he hadn't taken it like a monk to begin with. He stood there silently and even backed up a little, surprised at the tempest he had brought on. Thanks to Norman's newfound calm, Koji survived and it was over.

Soon we were in *gyōcha,* the formal morning tea. A heavy silence sat with us. Koji was trembling. Norman kept his eyes down. Katagiri stared ahead, solemn and alert. Koji spoke first. He apologized before all of us for getting so angry. After a moment, Norman turned to him and shook his head. "My fault," he said softly. After another uncomfortable few minutes, Katagiri spoke. He said that what may look like anger at times may be a kind teaching. He added that Hashimoto Roshi, his teacher at Eiheiji, was always disappointed that his attendants, of which Katagiri was one, didn't do a better job of cleaning, especially in the out-of-the-way places.

Koji's outburst was understandable after the way Norman had incited him, but I didn't take it that Katagiri was only saying that Koji was right and Norman wrong. He was also the guest teacher at a temple not his own and was upholding the senior position of the head monk at the expense of his own student, Norman.

Then Katagiri, keeping his chin in and his face held in a serious expression, his mouth rounded downward, lips held tight, eyes still straight ahead, stood and gasshoed. He turned around and walked to his room. Maku opened the sliding shoji. Katagiri went in and Maku slid the door closed behind him. I sat there and wondered, isn't he just teaching rote form?—anger can be kindness, clean thoroughly. Then I thought, how ridiculous of me, still picking apart his every word and gesture, looking for the so-called "emptiness" and not allowing him the room to be unexceptional. The emptiness I was looking for was just something extra. He'd done his job of helping the boys to cool the stew of their own much-ado juices and gone off without adding anything.

Each of us got up quietly and walked out. Koji, however, stayed, and kneeling outside of Katagiri's door, said, "Gomen kudasai," a polite excuse me. At Katagiri's "hai" Koji slid the door open and went in.

Norman stood at the bottom of the steps looking glum. "Brain weevils," he said, hitting his forehead with the butt of his hand and moving off.

I stood in the courtyard facing the massive, passionless oak and grey pines rising from the incline immediately below. Through the branches and trunks I watched the morning sun illuminating the slopes beyond while a few bright rays streaked in from over the temple roof to catch my eyes. The coo of the mountain dove sang through the trees and mingled with Koji's uncontrolled sobbing coming from the abbot's quarters.

That night Norman, Koji and I had a tea of reconciliation. They told me about Daigyo Zenji, the founder of Hōgoji. He was the sixth generation from Dōgen. He stayed on this mountain, mainly alone, for twenty years, practicing zazen and deepening his understanding. When the feudal lord who gave him all the land in a radius of six miles lost an important battle, Daigyo was forced to leave by the victor. He founded another two temples, also on the island of Kyūshū. One is at Takana, where every year for two days they display writings and artifacts of Dōgen Zenji that Daigyo had possessed. On one of these days the monks from Hōgoji had gone to visit that temple and Norman had held Dōgen's kesa in his hands. Maybe it would be something like a Franciscan being able to touch a smock of Saint Francis.

Daigyo Zenji is well known for the poetry he wrote at Hōgoji during the secluded years. Here is one of his poems, which the three of us translated that evening.

sitting on a hillside
with a young oak
a leaf falls
on the sleeve of my robe

incense does not
become the smoke
nor do I turn
into a dragon

surrounded by the
mountain sangha
I walk to the creek

and wash my face
with the stars

PART FIVE

LOOKING

DRIVING ME CRAZY

My first trip to the Maruyama Driver's License Test Building had been spent mainly helping the clerk do an analysis of my passport, enumerating the countries I'd visited, the dates I had gone in and out of the U.S. and other countries. The stopover in Hawaii for an hour on the way to Taiwan three years previously was properly noted. The space of time between the Taiwan trip and my arrival date in Japan was marked down. My month in Thailand and the side trip to Malaysia, as well as the times of visa extensions in Japan, were not neglected. It was a curious procedure. This was local government, not Immigration, and I did not get the point. But mine not to reason why.

I was told by the precise and bespectacled clerk that I had the honor of being eligible to apply for a Japanese driver's license although I would have to come back on another day to do so. I made an appointment and thanked him for his assistance. He expressed gratitude for my cooperation and handed me a form in Japanese that he said I should fill out before my return.

A week later I came went back to the Driver's License Test Building, arriving between 8:30 and 9:00 A.M., as I had been instructed. It took about an hour and a half on two buses to get to the building which was way out of town toward the Inland Sea. I brought everything I was supposed to bring, including copies of my California license and every page of my passport. It was only a quarter till nine and the building was already filled with young people, housewives, a few middle-aged men and some older people who must have come to get their driver's licenses renewed. Hundreds of people. There were endless lines and folks mulling about. No wonder I was told to come so early, I thought, it's

285

gonna take me all day merely to get to the window. But I didn't know which window to go to, so I went to the information counter. There was no line in front of it, which meant to me that I was the only person in the room who didn't know what to do. But I liked the answer that I got there when I asked where to go: I was sent to another deserted window where I was met by no fewer than four nervous Driver's License Test Building employees. I felt very special. I was.

One employee wearing a neat blue uniform and thick glasses sat in front of me as the other employees looked on. He smiled and said good morning in English and I smiled and said good morning in English and then in Japanese to all four of them. The observers all bowed, smiling and relieved that I could say, "Ohayō gozaimasu," and they nodded and laughed among themselves in approval. So far, so good.

I presented my bundle of documents to the man in front of me and he looked through them carefully and seemed pleased. We reviewed the itinerary of past travels without a hitch. The others left us alone, having done their part in assuring me by their presence that I was being well taken care of.

The man who was left with the task of helping me straightened his glasses and went straight to the form that I was supposed to have filled out. I hadn't. I had tried to fill it out with savvy Ishitaki but since nothing applied to me she had decided it was a mistake. It wasn't. At least it was no mistake that it was going to be filled out. Still, I had a lot of trouble understanding it. I had my dictionary out and we were going at it, but we were having problems right away, as much because I couldn't believe what he was asking as because of not understanding the words. He spoke a little English and between that and my Japanese we managed to get through it—but not without a good deal of imagination stretching. What actually happened is still unclear, but it had to be done. (Just doing things that have to be done is a particular talent of the Japanese.) Since this gent was going to so much trouble for me, I was game too, and went to trouble for him. As I recall, it went something like this:

Him: "When was your last written driver's license test?"

Me: "When was my last . . . ?" I said and stopped to think. He was waiting with his pen on the page. He needed to fill in an answer and I should not fail him. Vaguely remembering taking such a test in Marin County, California, at some time or times in the present geological age, I said, "Let's see, five years ago . . . the first Tuesday in May." My tone was definite and authoritative. We were off to a good start.

Him: "Um-hmm. Five years ago. May 1984. Very good."

He continued in a nasal tone of voice that rose in pitch at the end of each question: "And was it a multiple choice or true-false test?" Actually he was speaking a mixture of English and Japanese and throughout this account I am sparing the reader questions like, "Tesuto wa A-B-C choisu make did? Or other rike true?"

Me: Stretching back, I looked for an old driving test memory and sure enough, there it was. I could see the paper and the questions with the blank line on the left. How many feet can you safely drive behind a . . . yes, it must be . . . "Multiple choice," I said, wondering why anyone cared.

Him: "Yes. Hmm. Multiple choice. Okay." His follow-up threw me. "And what was your score?" He kept looking at the paper.

Me: Okay. What the heck. "Ninety-two," I answered proudly.

Him: Writing carefully and drawing his voice out, "Ninety-two." He continued his quest for precise details. "And how many questions were there?"

Me: Unhesitatingly and enunciating clearly. "Twenty." Wouldn't everybody say that? It might be right too (but then the score couldn't have been ninety-two, I realized later).

Him: Relieved and writing it down. "And what make of car were you driving then?"

Me: (Without trying to calculate for sure.) I've gone through a lot of cars but most of them have been, "Toyota." I'm getting into the swing of it.

Him: "Very good." And then spelling it out as he wrote with increased confidence that this was something we could in fact do, "T-O-Y-O-T-A." Now catch this. His next question: "What was the rank of the officer who administered this test?"

Me: I'm reeling in delight. I hadn't hoped for anything so wonderful to happen on this day. "He was an inspector."

We are on a roll. We are one. He puckered his lips ever so slightly and neatly entered the word "inspector" on the form in katakana. The way he wrote it, it would be pronounced *insupek-kutā*.

Him: "What office administered the test?" (At this point he listed some completely inapplicable Japanese government agencies.)

Me: "The DMV," I said truthfully.

Him: "Di-emu-bi?" He repeated it as they do in Japan, using their fifty sounds.

Me: "It stands for Department of Motor Vehicles," I explained. He liked it, I could tell.

Him: "And what section of government is the DMV under?"

Me: "The California State Police," I said, and then thought back to my days of working for state government in California. No, it's probably directly under General Services, but ah, who cares. He liked the state police idea anyway. Now get this.

Him: "And what language was the test administered in, Japanese or English?"

We were brought together soaring in a unique surrealistic world. Time stopped as I cherished the moment. When I heard the question echoing for the third time in my blissful state, I leaned down and, with a slight pause to show that I was considering the matter carefully, answered precisely:

"English."

Him: "English," and he circled it. "And did you take a driving test?"

Me: "Not at that time." I was trying to be honest. I probably should just have said yes.

Him: "When did you take a driving test?"

Me: "In 1978." Total stab.

Him: "Nineteen seventy-eight. And was that your first driving test?"

Me: "No."

Him: "When did you take your first driving test?"

Me: Gee, it had been a long time. My very first one? I had one back in '65 I think, but I was thirteen and a half when I got my beginner's license. Thinking a second. "Nineteen fifty-eight."

Him: A little thrown off. Looking up. "Nineteen fifty-eight?"

Me: "Yes. Back then in Texas . . . farm kids had to drive . . . it's very . . . wide." I stretched my arms out. The word "wide" did it. It's one of the main words they use in Japan to describe the U.S. It accounts for many differences and had just explained why I had a license at an age that must have seemed unthinkable to him. I wouldn't doubt that at that moment he formed the permanent thought that all people in the States, at least in Texas, start driving at thirteen, a fact that he might have connected with our high crime rate, but that was now also likely to be associated with the concept "wide."

Him: Having been thrown off a little, returning to the flow. "And was this examination given on a test course or on the streets?"

Me: "Both." We're climbing again.

Him: "What make of car did you take the test in?"

Me: Never flinching, but with no clear idea. "Chevrolet."

Him: "Would you spell that please?"

Me: "C—abc, H—hello, E—E.T., V—VSOP." I was proud of my clear choices up to that point and went confidently into the next letter. "R—Rambo." (A Japanese word, incidently, pronounced about the same, means "violence or rudeness.") He quickly wrote the "R." I went on to "O—Okay." Now, the big one. "L—Lucky," and just to make sure, I gave it the Japanese pronunciation, "eru." ("R" is "aru.") He wrote it down, seemingly appreciative of the hint. "E—Elvis," he liked that, "T—Truman." He was old enough to know who that was. He looked up. There was a pause. I knew we were near the end. His lips parted.

Him: "How many cc's was the engine of the car?"

Me: I spoke back from timelessness and without thought. I had come to Japan to study the teaching beyond words and letters, and here I had surely found it. "How many cc's does a big car have?" I heard emanating from my throat.

Him: "2000 cc's."

Me: "2000 cc's."

After that, everything went white. I only vaguely remember floating from window 19 (where I'd arrived from no. 17 and prior to that from no. 5), floating, floating to window no. 1, and from there to no. 6. I had my picture taken twice, once in black and white for their files and the second time in color for the license itself. Between windows there were long waits which I spent across the street in a coffee shop. I would come back at the time they had told me and wade through throngs of people milling around or standing in lines that seemed to have nothing to do with me or what I was doing. There was never anyone at the windows that I used except the helpful and nervous public servants on the other side. They seemed to be easing me along as painlessly as possible. Little did they know that they were propelling me into states of ecstasy.

The last thing I did on the main floor of the building was to receive a membership card to an auto club. There were two bubbling young ladies at a booth there who presented it to me with a free velvet and plastic pocket-sized photo album. I was then told to proceed to room 3 on the second floor. I returned pretty soon to ask directions again, because I had opened the door to a room that was full of people sitting in school desk chairs listening to a lecture in Japanese. It turned out I had not opened the wrong door.

"Hurry!" they told me, excited and trying to help by running ahead, "it's already started." A few heads belonging to uniformed employees stuck out of their windows and watched with concern, several fingers pointed to make sure that I was going in the right direction. I ran behind one young blue-uniformed lady, trying to keep up with her quick, short, deliberate steps up the curving staircase that gave me a view of the dwindling throng below and the places I'd been. There were a number of people looking at me the compulsive way people everywhere look at someone different. I looked back up and she was there holding the door open, not the back door but the front door, and I walked into the room to find myself face to face with the speaker, a decorated, uniformed officer. He gestured kindly toward an empty seat and I walked in front of a hundred or so people and sat down to about forty minutes of a driving lecture in Japanese. I tried to understand as much as possible, while a very high percentage of the audience slept. I caught a bit and I think the speaker appreciated my efforts as I appreciated everyone's efforts there that day to guide me through what "cannot be helped," as they say.

Looking back on that event, I cannot remember at what point I received my license. I do have it, but it's hardly used except to show off. "See, I've got one."

We had a motorcycle for a while that was on loan from a friend who lives at the temple. I drove it downtown and back once and it took as long as it does by bicycle and I just got terrified instead of exercised. I always worried too when Elin, who has an international license, drove it. She noticed that people didn't relate to her on the road with as much courtesy as they gave her when she was on a bicycle. People look out for you here when you're on a bicycle, but she came home on the motorbike shook up a few times because she'd practically been run off the road. So we returned it. Cars are expensive to maintain and run. If a foreigner gets in an accident here it's a real hassle and, according to Ishitaki, if a car is in an accident with a bicycle or a pedestrian, the driver of the car is always considered to be at fault. So maybe it's better not to drive a car at all, she had suggested. Bop in Kyoto says that if one does drive, it's better to feign total ignorance of everything, including the Japanese language, than to carry a license. Often the police will just let you go rather than face the hassle. That's an old trick I used in Mexico many years ago. And with the wonderful mass transit system here, why bother?

Nevertheless, I do have my official Japanese driver's license. I'm proud of it and it reminds me of a transcendent experience I had with Japanese bureaucrats one autumn day by the Inland Sea.

READING PALMS

HŌGOJI, MAY 21, 1988

Almost no man-made sounds from the valley make their way up to Hōgoji. There is an occasional car on the road or a piece of farm machinery in the distance. I hear scratchy music from a delivery vehicle down below now and then. At seven in the morning, noon, and six in the evening from a loudspeaker somewhere in Ryūmon, a brief tune is broadcast in toy piano tones. But the greatest treat is when an amplified male voice makes announcements in the dark, booming like a giant come out of a cave. Those humorous smatterings of quirky racket poke out and are gone. Mainly we are blessed with the sounds of birds, crickets, frogs, creek, bells, drum, wind and rain.

The most glorious of people-made sounds at Hōgoji is the bonsho in its antique hut. Its deep reverberations remind us to drop everything, slow down and prepare to awaken dragon mind. The han for zazen begins after the sunset bonsho, which, before the advent of clocks, was hit when you couldn't see the lines on your hand.

I told Koji that it seemed to me that there could be some fairly comical timing differences depending on people's eyesight and the depth of the lines in their hands. And what if the sky was darkly overcast? He assured me it worked out. But I retorted that the regularity with which the bell is hit could only be explained by the fact that the person hitting the bell, whether eagle-eyed or blind-as-a-mole, has a watch on.

One evening after the sun had sunk below the mountains and only a glow remained in the sky, Koji and I sat at our desks together in the light of the kerosene lamps. We read the Sunday funnies from the *San Francisco Chronicle*, which my sister had kindly sent.

"What does 'kipu za feizu' mean?" he asked.

"What are you reading?" I said, looking over. "Oh, Doonesbury. Um, keep the faith—it means 'goodbye,' at least in this case."

"Goodbye?" he said, perplexed.

" 'Shitsurei' doesn't really mean 'I've been rude,' does it? It means 'goodbye' or 'excuse me.' Like that."

"What does 'kipu za feizu' mean before that?"

" 'To believe in your Way—trust in God. To have courage.' "

"Kipu za feizu. Kipu za feizu," he repeated as if trying to set it in memory.

Suddenly he jerked his head and looked at his watch, gasped and asked me if I would be so kind as to go hit the bonsho for him as he had to talk to Yoshiko for a few minutes in her house below us. He had planned to speak with her earlier but he'd been talking to me instead. I said I'd be only too happy to ring the bell. He thanked me, got on his robes so he could go to the zendo straight from Yoshiko's and departed. I left his cabin, blowing out the kerosene lamps, and went to get my robes on.

I hurried out into the courtyard from my room on the way to hit the bell and paused momentarily. The sunset had been over for some minutes but there was a turquoise glow where the mountains met the clear spring sky. I went up the steps of the bell tower and onto the platform. The bronze bell is bigger than me and hangs to my solar plexus. It's a dull green-black through oxidation, an old bell with a deep, rich, low, steady tone that permeates the valley below, sharing the sound of our schedule with the local folk. There are to be nine hits and after the first stroke each begins when the reverberations of the prior ring have died down. There is a *goza*, a thin straw mat to bow down on after each hit, and there are nine small stones (not to be confused with nine clay balls) placed on the railing so that one can keep track by moving a stone after each hit. I was just about ready for the first toll when I remembered tradition and looked at the palm of my hand.

Let me diverge for a moment to tell what happened once when I was waiting in a coastal Marin County, California, clinic for my first wife to get through a prenatal examination. I snooped around the rooms checking things out and tried the ophthalmologist's chair, where he later found me snoozing. We got to talking about the eye biz and before you could say glaucoma I was reading off one of the lower lines on his chart. He said, "That was good. What's the next one?" and I read it and then he said "Very good, what's the next?" and it was quite hard but I got them all. On the last line the letters looked like dots. I stared at them until they flashed. I got them all right but one, saying an "s" was an "h." He said that my eyes were one in a thousand. Must be the Indian blood. I looked at my hands. Fifteen years had passed since that day. My eyes had grown older but they weren't bad.

Since I could still see the lines on my hand, I went out onto the road just beyond the backside of the bell tower to admire the last subtle colors of the evening sky unobstructed by the treetops in the compound. After a few minutes of soaking it up I checked my hands again. The glow of the sun was almost entirely gone but I could see some lines on my palms which I held facing the direction of the sunset. In a few minutes it got down to where I could just barely see the deepest and last line disappearing. Just then a slight glow appeared on the crest of the opposing hills. I looked in that direction. A quarter moon popped over the top and rather quickly rose white and bright in the clean mountain air. The lines on my hands danced before me. I realized I would be able to see them till long past when I would wish to retire to sleep. Maybe this isn't fair, I thought. It was getting cold. Maybe if I turn my back on the moon and hold my hand next to my body with my shoulders hunched and the other hand shading the top and yikes! Koji was standing right behind me.

"Koji, you scared me!"

"David, are you going to hit the bell? You're late."

"I can still see the lines on my hand." I showed him.

He looked at me with his mouth open. "*I* can't," he said, and went running to the bell tower. On the way he turned to me. "Kipu za feizu!" he called, and ran on.

DUELING SUTRAS

HŌGOJI, MAY 22, 1988

Norman's attempt at in-house publishing was not being well received. He was still trying to come up with a user-friendly sutra book for foreigners. The Japanese books are in classical kanji, which almost

no foreign students can read. Kanji aren't phonetic and their pronunciation has to be memorized. There are thousands of them in
the sutra books, many of which aren't even used anymore, and
those that are still used are often not the modern simplified kanji.
Most foreign students of Zen in Japan, unless they come for a
long time, can't even speak Japanese, much less read it. That's
why we need romanized books—legible ones. Norman had a mission and it seemed reasonable to him. He would have been happier
if he'd been less diligent, if he'd been able to drop the subject,
but he couldn't. Enter Shuko.

Shuko came to me and asked if he could see the romanized
sutra books I was using. Innocently I passed them over to him
asking him how long he wanted them, since I couldn't get by in
the complicated morning service without them. He said he only
needed them for the afternoon.

That day Shuko, Norman and I went into town together to
do errands for the temple. There was a French fellow coming to
Suienji in a few days and Norman wanted to make a copy for him
of the romanized sutra book that he had been working on. It was
far from finished, but he'd pasted each chant up in the best version
he could find and it was better than anything else available. We
were sitting at a metal table at the modest local bus station. Our
business was all done, we had just finished eating some *ramen* and
were almost ready to return to the temple.

Norman had cleared the table surface and was doing touch-
ups on the chant book he'd put together. Shuko admired his work
for a moment and then walked over to the copy machine. Norman
didn't pay any attention to what Shuko was up to and I'd forgotten about giving him my books.

After a while Shuku returned and sat down with Norman at
the same table and started cutting paper. Norman asked him what
he was doing and Shuko said that he was making a sutra book
for the new fellow who was coming to Suienji. Norman then asked
him what he was making it from. He said he was making it from
the books he'd borrowed from me. Norman went red, he stam-

mered and bit his lip, he started to talk and stopped. Standing up and sucking in his breath noisily, he picked up his work and took it to the copy machine.

I went out the front door to look at the street scene and ran into Miki-obāsan and her daughter, who were on their way back to Ryūmon. They waited for me while I told Shuko I was going back with them. He objected, but I didn't pay him any mind. What a relief it was to be walking up the hill alone forty minutes later.

Norman was still arguing with Shuko when they returned. He might as well have been talking to the zendo wall. Koji joined Shuko in telling Norman that if he wanted his book to be considered then he should present it to the elders of Suienji. Norman was hurt, disgusted, angry—emotions going every which way.

Shuko gave me the sutra books back. I told him I was going to use the one that Norman made. "I might as well," I told him, "It'll just be gathering dust. No offense intended, but you oughta use these to heat the bath with," I said, handing the official ones back to him.

JUST ME AND MY BROOM

HŌGOJI, MAY 24, 1988

Delighting in the unstructured time of a day off, I read and write, take hikes and just romp around like a doggy. Actually, it's only called a day off by Norman and me. Our hosts have almost no concept of day off or time off. To them it's *shiku-nichi* and the purpose of it is to get your personal effects in order, sew your robes, do your laundry and so on. I do those things in the breaks after meals on other days so I can maximize the individual away-from-others (except Koji) and free-from-structure time on a day off.

We had the same dichotomy in Stateside Zen. There are those who would prefer not to have days off because they don't know what to do with free time, or because they want to give themselves to the structured schedule, to hard core "Zen," as much as possible. No diversions. Maybe such devotees think that being part of an ongoing religious practice is bringing them ever closer to the enlightenment that they seek.

Some are in the opposite camp. Like me. I know of many things I'd like to do with my time off and I enjoy almost every minute of it. I create extra time off by staying up late and getting up early. I'm always interested in something else, something other than sweeping or chanting or whatever it is that I'm supposed to be doing at the time.

The eager beaver's problem is the hindrance of goal orientation. Suzuki and Katagiri both warned us of the futility of "seeking practice." But it seems to me that there is also the pitfall of "avoidance practice." This means to run from the task at hand, the present moment, in order to get somewhere else or do something else. If you saw an avoidance type and a seeking type sweeping leaves, you probably wouldn't notice any difference in their appearance—but their attitudes wouldn't be the same. The seeking type would be thinking, maybe, something like, "Oh boy, I'm deep into Zen now. This was Han Shan's practice—sweep the ground, sweep your mind. Any moment now I might be struck by the Great Enlightenment. Then the master will recognize me and I'll be known by all as a great teacher and thousands will flock to hear my talks and . . ."

The avoidance type might be thinking something more like, "Oh well, I can't get out of this, I guess. Hmm, sure would be nice to walk down that valley, in and out of the oak and bamboo groves, walk by the paddies' edges, watch the birds and the butterflies, maybe go down to the falls. . . ."

In that spirit, one day during work, I raked myself off from the others and, putting a leaf in a runoff trough, followed it as it emptied into a larger trough and then a ditch. The leaf floated across and down the hillside, around bends and over miniature waterfalls all the way to the creek. Before I knew it I'd gotten myself far down the hill and had to hightail it back before they put out an all-points bulletin on me.

Often the seeker and the avoider are at odds with each other. Sometimes they even divide into cliques that roam monastic halls. It could be said that the avoiders are seeking and that the seekers are avoiding. They're merely different expressions of the age-old near-impossibility of just being.

Due to the softening effect of zazen, sweeping, and the peaceful environs, both types of people may enter into less cerebral states and just be sitting or sweeping, aware of the motions of the body, the contours of the ground being appreciated and the borders of consciousness slipping away.

I'm quite used to watching my thoughts jump about when I begin some required group task like evening zazen or morning cleaning. I even feel panic at times, or claustrophobia. Then later I calm down and am content as can be. I'm sure that the eager seeker has a sort of nervous grabbing for glory at times that later melts into something more simple and enjoyable.

Suzuki told me once that I should keep sitting and wait for something wonderful to happen. He didn't mean, I don't think, that I should try to create this "something wonderful" by a meditative technique, but rather that I should practice "just sitting" alertly and continue just walking, just eating and so forth without any intention or striving. Over the course of time, something wonderful would happen of itself, not as a result of my effort. He said that I would definitely have "some experience." He defined it as little as possible, but I thought that he meant the type of experience that is sometimes called "beyond experience" and is indescribable and all that. In other words, I didn't know what he meant. So I was very pleased to hear him say that it would definitely happen because I had been all worked up about it back then. But aside from various temporal, lifestyle and therapeutic effects, I couldn't claim that my first few years at Zen had produced anything close to "dropping away of body and mind."

"Don't fight," he said. "That is the key—don't fight." And don't strive to gain what I've already got. The point isn't to bring on spiritual experience but to cultivate the mind that can receive it, realize it—to "widen the stage" as I remember Dick Baker explaining to a Tassajara guest back in '67. And this effort is not at all tied to huffing and puffing or to a forced slow motion, but to just "do what you're doing" (*age quod agis*—a saying of the Jesuits). My teachers imparted the empowering teaching that we are fine as is. No need for something extra: just us as we are is all we need to stand in the footsteps of the saints and to sit on the zafu of the masters.

Suzuki didn't stop at "something wonderful." He went on to say that not only would it happen to me, but that it would happen to everyone. I liked that even though it definitely reduced my sense of being special, because it increased my odds dramatically. It would happen to us all. Good. There was a catch though. "You should continue sitting," he said. "If you continue sitting, this wonderful experience can continue with you. It can be yours forever. But if you have no practice, it will be passing—like a psychedelic experience."

Oh boy, he sure hit the nail on the head with me. As divine and total as my psychedelic experiences had been, they certainly had no lasting qualities—they were mainly useful as encouragement to use other means. They eliminated any doubt as to the reality of the so-called goals of religious life and cast great doubts on the ultimate reality of hard facts and the American Way as some narrowly perceived them.

I had left behind the quick fix of that chemical spiritual masturbation in order to follow the "gradual path," a controversial epithet for Soto Zen not used much by Soto Zennists. It is said that Rinzai picks the fruit off the tree and that Soto lets it fall, but that practitioners of both ways throw all body and mind into zazen. Even though psychedelic experience might, in comparison, be more like scratch and sniff, at least I'd had the whiff. Suzuki seemed to be telling me not to emphasize the glitter of the Way but to get it in my bones gradually, day by day. I have almost forgotten the carrot and have often lost track of any horse or road, but from time to time, like the drunk who pulls himself from the gutter, I pull my legs into zazen position or watch the breath while waiting for a bus. Suzuki is long gone and can't answer my "what was that?" I have continued haphazardly with his colleagues such as Katagiri and the teachers and fellow students he left behind and they have tried their best and have encouraged me greatly. Shinran, the founder of Jōdo Shin-shū, taught that we're all already saved. Suzuki nudged me to keep practicing in order to express it. So I continue plugging away as if by following this way of suchness one could prepare the infinite room for that which cannot be contained.

ELECTION RESULTS

MARUYAMA, NOVEMBER 6, 1989

I am very angry that Recruit scandal candidates won," said Shimizu in an uncustomary huff.

Across from him, Mrs. Morikawa was shaking and stuttering. It was taking her a long time to find the right English words to express herself. "Nothing change . . . it uh . . . like before . . . okay to . . . uh . . . receiving much money."

Tanahashi's sweet voice trembled, "I am ashamed of the Japanese people. They only want more for themselves."

"This is worse than I hoped for. I am so disappointed," said

Etsuko with her head lowered. "I do not want to see the children's faces this afternoon at school."

Kubo wasn't saying anything. She never seems to care what's going on in the news. She had started this MMC off by mentioning that she was going shopping for shoes after we were through. The election results trampled over her topic, but not before she showed off the fine pair of red leather pumps she was wearing to go shopping in. She said that even though she was going to buy cheap shoes, she wanted to be seen shopping in expensive ones.

I let the class talk a while in Japanese to get their election frustrations out of their systems. While they did so I put some water on in the kitchen and brought in a bowl of expensive purple grapes that we'd received in a box from the mother of a couple of girls in one of Elin's classes. I counted the grapes and figured they cost thirty-five cents each. We see these special fruit gifts on display in the train station. Melons will cost up to eighty bucks. Savvy Ishitaki says, "Don't waste a melon on a Westerner."

When the class saw the grapes they stopped talking for a second and exclaimed over how choice they were and thanked me for the offering.

"We have missed an important opportunity to reform the system," said Etsuko, picking her first purple prize from the twig and peeling off the skin.

Hands reached for the bowl, each hesitant to go before the others but soon everyone was peeling and savoring. Before he'd finished chewing his first, Shimizu spoke. He said the problem is that everyone had hoped that the reform would happen elsewhere and that, all over Japan, people voted for the same old establishment, the certainly-not-liberal Liberal Democratic Party (LDP), whose members have totally dominated Japanese politics since the war. Shimizu said that people voted for the LDP candidates because the LDP would bring the most money and construction projects to their home districts.

"But this is not excuse," he said, licking his lips.

He's actually a staunch LDP supporter, though he was opposed to their "tax reform." On top of the latest round of scandals, people were mad at the LDP for the new taxes. Even though he owns a liquor store he was disturbed that the tax on luxury items was adjusted down so that expensive booze costs less than before. (This had the curious effect of causing some of these items to sell less, because they were no longer appropriately expensive gifts for important people.) And Shimizu thinks it's wrong that, even though the consumption tax hit food and medicine, the old and sick received no compensation in their marginal fixed incomes. They were the ones whom the consumption tax was touted as being for in the first place.

None of the members of the MMC really wanted to rock the boat too much—they just wanted to adjust it. Mrs. Morikawa said that the LDP is in bed with gangsters and that its roots go back to prewar fascists. She voted for the so-called Japan Socialist Party (JSP). I asked her what she hoped for if they won control of the Diet, that strange Latin-based translation for the name of their congress.

"Oh, I don't want them to win," she said. "I just want them to gain some seats and have more influence. Their platform is to not recognize the South Korea but the North, and that would be very bad. And they oppose the mutual protection treaty with America, and that is very important to stop Japan from becoming militaristic nation again."

Tanahashi had announced solemnly the week before that, after much deliberation, she had decided to vote for the Communist party (not to be confused with communism anywhere else). It's a strange party and I was a little embarrassed for Tanahashi that she voted for them. She had decided to because they didn't have any scandal-ridden candidates and also because they had been the first to advocate a democratic society with open elections and the right to assembly earlier in the century. But after all that, it turned out that she had the same ultimate strategy. She just wanted them to influence the LDP a little bit—not to become too powerful.

Etsuko had voted for the candidate from the smallest party, the Shaminden. I can't remember the name in English but in Japanese it sounds like a people's socialist party and they are an offshoot of the JSP. She brought me one of their posters and, lo and behold, written in English was: THINK GLOBALLY, ACT LO-CALLY. I thought they must be a really hip environmental group but Mr. Shimizu popped that bubble. He said they mainly tried to get more federal money spent locally and were fairly isolation-ist. He furthermore said that everyone would be better off if Japan thought globally before acting globally. Anyway, Etsuko had the same idea in voting for the Shaminden as the other women.

"Doesn't anyone but Mr. Shimizu vote for whom they want to win?" I asked.

Etsuko pointed out that even Shimizu didn't want the LDP to win big. "We all think they are the experts who know the best foreign policy and keep the nation economically strong. But they should be more honest and care about little people."

Kubo finally spoke up and said she voted for the LDP.

"Ahah! Why?" I asked.

She said the only candidate that she and her husband paid any attention to was a very nice young man whose family was close to theirs. He was untainted by the scandal and was running for reelection. I asked her what this nice young man thought about the consumer tax which she disliked so much, her favorite pastime being to shop, and she laughed and said, "Oh he does not un-derstanding things like that. His family is very rich and his father and uncle are in politics. They do not know about the problems of usual people."

All week in English classes and on the streets in conversation with neighbors, I heard the words "embarrassed" and "ashamed," mainly from people over twenty-five years old, but this was even true of some of the college students, housewives and *sararīman* (salarymen), who had had very little to say before the election.

There was a general atmosphere of disappointment. I can sym-
pathize. The candidates I vote for in the States hardly ever win.
Sometimes I get superstitious and wonder if things would turn
out better if I voted against my candidate. My Japanese friends
are happy to hear me rant and rave about politics back home—
it helps to even the score. Shimizu said that before he met me he
thought that only Japan had politicians to be ashamed of.

One thing we won't miss is the noisy electioneering. The cam-
paign sound-trucks, representing all the various candidates and
parties, will no longer be wandering around the city beseeching
at such insane decibel levels. I asked when the candidates brought
up issues or debated.

"They don't," said Shimizu. "They just say, 'Onegai shimasu,
onegai shimasu (Please, I beg you, if you would be so kind),' over
and over."

"And when someone wave to show support, they say, 'Thank
you, thank you, thank you,' " said Morikawa.

"And the name of the candidate," added Etsuko, eating the
next to last grape and getting her bright red lipstick on the tip
of one of her fingers.

"But don't they ever mention issues?" I asked, eating the last
grape because I knew that otherwise it would sit there forever.
"Like the consumption tax or the cost of elections or land prices?"

Shimizu said that a candidate might brush over the issues in
a five-minute talk at a supermarket, but everyone agreed that even
there, when the candidates are with voters, they mainly just go
around shaking their hands and saying "please be good to us" and
"thank you very much."

"How can you put up with those sound trucks? I don't understand. To me it's just hard to . . . I can't *believe* it," I mumbled,
failing to find adequate words to express my feelings about this
phenomenon.

"Everyone, every candidate uses them," said Tanahashi. "But

I think they are very noisy and should not be allowed. I have tried to stop them in my neighborhood. I talked to my friend who is a neighbor and to the man who is head of our neighborhood association. I also asked him to stop the chimes in the morning and evening that tell the time. They are located near our house. I said we have clocks and it is very noisy."

"Yes, we can hear them from here. What happened?" I asked.

"He said that they would consider it. But they didn't even bring it up in neighborhood meeting. So my neighbor and I are thinking we will go from the house to the house and ask people to sign petition asking no more loud chimes in our neighborhood so we can have a fine living condition."

I was astounded. "That's fantastic!" I said. "You're an activist. Keep us informed." Gentle, fragile Tanahashi was trying to take on the male powers that be.

"People would not allow all this noise in the States," I said. "They'd be furious. I know we're generally noisier people than you are but we have a stronger sense of a right to privacy." I bit my tongue to stop myself from saying we'd blast 'em off the road. They'd take me literally. Etsuko had just asked me last week if everyone in America carries guns.

I'd already blown it just a few days before. It's probably because Elin wasn't there that day to stop me from making an idiot out of myself. I was with a few English teachers after Japanese class at a youth hostel on a hill. There were two sound trucks down below on different sides, wailing up their eerie echoing messages. They were unbelievably loud—and two at once! And how did we Americans and one Australian react? We started attacking them with imaginary machine guns, going "Da da da da da!"

Kubo, who is one of the Japanese teachers there, walked out and exclaimed to me, "But David, this is not Bukkyō (Buddhism)!" I stopped firing long enough to ask her if she liked what she heard.

"They all do it," she answered.

"Not good enough," I responded, and resumed firing.

CLEANING GENE

HŌGOJI, MAY 27, 1988

In one of our late-night sessions I persuaded Koji to grant me a wish. He would let me clean the kitchen the following day. There were surfaces that had been neglected. The walls were sticky with an oily soot. The windows had lost their transparency. There were untended areas that called for organization.

I had tried to persuade Shuko that I could be spared from the all-important morning path sweeping and weeding.

"We sweep the paths every day," I'd told him.

"Even in the spring the wind blows and leaves fall," he answered.

"Can't you just let me give the kitchen a thorough cleaning once?"

"The kitchen is cleaned three times a day," he said.

But as senior monk, all Koji had to do was say the word and I could finally do the job I had been dying to do. I used the argument with him that there was a big ceremony coming up and lots of guests would be there. Like Shuko, he didn't see the problem, but he welcomed the company, as he was tenzo that day.

I heated water on the stove. Koji couldn't understand why I wanted to do that. He said I could just wipe the surfaces with a rag and cold water, but I told him that hot water and soap would help cut the oils.

I started just below the beams that were about six feet up. I got the windows, inside and out. Koji thought it was interesting that I used newspaper. He said that Norman also used newspaper to clean glass. "It's 'cause it does a better job," I said, but he didn't look as though he believed it.

The cabinets were next, even the tops. When I opened the cupboard I found the eggs sitting in cups, Maku's handiwork I guessed. Carefully I placed these contents on the table and attacked the bare inside. It was exhilarating to transfer the smudge to rags, paper and water.

"Why are you changing the water again?" asked Koji. He was so curious at my methods.

"Because it's getting black."

"You're doing a very good job, David. Why do you want to clean so much?"

"This is a true joy. Joy—usually it's just an empty word, something we strive for and talk about." I stuck my head inside the cabinet, which was illuminated by the flashlight in my hand.

"Looking for something?" It was Norman.

"Grime." My voice echoed from inside.

"David is cleaning fanatically," said Koji. "Was he like this in America?"

"David has a cleaning gene," said Norman. "It helps to balance his generally sloppy appearance." He went around the room checking my work and tsk-tsking. "Centuries of layering of oil and soot gave this room a subtle patina, a finish with character —a finish that you have destroyed in a single morning." He shook his head and walked out.

NORMAN
GETS HIS WAY

HŌGOJI, MAY 29, 1988

anko-san, please come down from there!" Shuko called up to Norman.

Shuko was standing in the courtyard underneath the oak tree and I was coming up the steps to get some gloves because I was getting blisters on my fingers from raking.

"I'm not coming down till I can put the pine nuts in the rice." It was Norman. I didn't see him anywhere. I got to the top.

"Please come down now," said Shuko. He was looking up. I looked up. Norman was way up in the big old oak tree.

"Not till I can use the pine nuts," he said.

"Hi, Norman," I called to him. "How's the view from up there?"

"David, please go away," Shuko said to me.

"Why? What's happening?"

"He won't let me put pine nuts in the rice. Every time I'm cook he finds something I'm doing that's not acceptable. I've snapped. I'm not coming down till I can put pine nuts in the rice."

"Where'd you get the pine nuts?" I called up.

"From Akagi-san. It's an offering to the temple, Shuko! Like the matches! Thank you and OK!"

"The Buddha bowl is only for pure rice," Shuko pleaded.

"Fine, I'm staying."

"Why not make an exception, Shuko?" I suggested.

"There's never been an exception. Please go back to work."

"We've had barley in the rice," I pointed out.

"Barley is like rice."

"No, it's not," came Norman's voice from the tree. "It's not-rice like pine nuts. Barley is like pine nuts."

"Barley is a grain," countered Shuko.

"Come on, Shuko," I said, "Norman's tenzo. Don't you want to eat?"

"Please go away," he said, and then, looking up, "Please come down."

Norman climbed up to a higher branch.

Koji walked up the steps. "Is tea late?"

Shuko looked glad to see him. "Yes, Ganko-san is being stubborn."

"What?" asked Koji.

"He wants to put pine nuts in the rice," said Shuko.

Just then Maku unexpectedly came out of the kuin with the tea and coffee tray, set it on the deck and hit the clackers.

"Pine nuts in the rice?" said Koji. "Sounds good."

Shuko stood still for a moment, looking frustrated. The argument was over.

I looked up. Norman was climbing down.

We chanted before the meal and ate our white rice in silence. We always have white rice for lunch and that's after always having white rice gruel for breakfast, which is made from the leftover white rice from the previous day's lunch. I'd rather have brown rice, but white rice is okay and anyway, if one can't adjust to white rice, it's better to stay away from this part of the world. We also had miso soup with tofu, sauteed carrots and burdock root, and daikon pickles. There's very little protein but I'm not fainting on the job. Norman likes it too and doesn't seem to be suffering from malnutrition, which has been a problem for Westerners in some temples.

Lunch was almost exactly like every lunch I'd ever had there except for the pine nuts. In situations of limitation the smallest treat can bring the greatest joy. To me the pine nuts were appreciated as much as if I'd been taken out to lunch at Greens in San Francisco. I chewed each nut separately and thought of Norman in the tree.

After lunch I went back to the hatto to prepare the altar for evening service. A single stick of incense remained in the large white porcelain bowl that rested on the lacquered table in front of the rising altar that housed the Buddha statue. It had burned out half way down. The thin green offering stood at half mast in the center of the smooth grey plain of ashes. I gazed into the bowl and lifted the stick out. It left a tiny hole where it had been situated and I had the impression that I was a giant caddy lifting a pin from the cup on a putting green, or putting grey, on the moon. I watched to see what sort of golfers would walk onto the moondust playing surface.

"This is the last one."

I quickly flew back to earth to find Norman standing next to me. "What? The last what?" I said, wondering if he meant that was the eighteenth hole.

"Thank you and OK!" he said, leering at me. I realized that he meant the matches on the altar. There that fellow was on the side of the box, giving his thumbs-up sign, beaming and bringing a modern international touch to the hatto day after day.

"The last one? How could we use that many matches?" I puzzled.

"I helped the process along a bit," he said. "Practical pyromania is something I learned from the Weathermen in the basement."

"Norman, I've become fond of these matches. To me they symbolize the core of our practice. Think of it. 'Thank you' is gratitude, the gateway to religious joy, and 'OK,' which comes from 'all correct,' represents the perfection of wisdom. This is our mantra. Thank you and OK," I said reverently.

"You are infected with brain weevils," he responded.

GANGSTERS
IN THE MIDST

What's bothering you?" I asked Elin.

"How could you tell?"

"It's not hard. Your posture gets bad and your forehead wrinkles."

"Oh, it's just Ishitaki. She got me over there to give us her old vacuum cleaner, and I feel indebted 'cause she's so helpful, and then she says something nasty or judgmental."

"You mean like when she said that it's hard for Japanese to see why they should give money to Eastern Europe when the people are so fat?"

"No, I mean like criticizing you."

"Oh, she's just mad at me because I hired another teacher to teach her son and the brat pack. Thank goodness."

"No, she was criticizing you before that. I wish she'd just keep it to herself."

"She's just trying to have power over you, Elin. Don't worry about it."

"But I do. It bothers me."

"What'd she say?"

"I was telling her I was worried I'd been accidentally rude to Tanaka-san down the street and Ishitaki said that no one has any problem with *me*, just *you*."

"I think it's mainly her that I rub wrong."

"You shouldn't be so frank with her and joke with her the way you do."

"She's probably somewhat right, but we can't live our lives worrying about what she thinks."

"Okay. That's enough. Let's forget about the Joneses or the Senzakis or whatever. Give me a hug."

And just as we were embracing, who should walk into the garden but Kubo-san who was so delighted to catch us she almost went into hysterics saying how wonderful it must be to have a love marriage and that her husband has never once hugged her. And before either Elin or I could come up with a response, Kubo was explaining why she couldn't bring her children and join Elin and me in the mountains for our three-day holiday. We had booked an old thatch-roofed farmhouse well in advance.

"We can't accept your invitation because we only have Monday and Wednesday off and one day is not enough time."

"What about coming on Sunday and Monday?" I asked.

"My husband will be at home on Sunday so we must be there."

"*Must?*"

"I have to make his meals."

"Oh god," I said, sighing. That's nothing new. She won't go anywhere if she has to cook for her sixteen-year-old son either. "What's wrong with Tuesday?" I continued probing.

"We must go to school for a parent's and children's day. I will go to my daughter's school. My son would be embarrassed for me to come to his."

"You have to go to school for a special event in the middle of a holiday?" I asked, incredulous.

"It is expected."

"Do you want to go?"

"Oh no. It will be very tedious."

"Skip it. Come to the mountains."

"If we are not there the teachers and parents will be angry with me. They will say I am not a good mother and they will say that I do just what I want to and forsaking the children's education. Our neighbors would disapprove also."

.   .   .

Before long the rest of the MMC had arrived and we were seated in the living room drinking tea.

"Revolt," I said. "All of you—please revolt." I'd taken a poll and found that all of them and Shimuzu's wife as well were in Kubo's slippers as far as mealtime obligations went.

They all just laughed at my call to throw off their chains.

I gave up and turned to Mrs. Tanahashi. "Oh, hey, I just remembered, Tanahashi-san, whatever happened with the petition to stop the city chimes in your neighborhood."

"I hear it this morning at seven very loud," said Morikawa who lives near Tanahashi over the low mountain from our house. Her voice was muffled because she was wearing a cloth mask to protect us from her cold.

"Oh yes," said Shimizu, "please tell us. Could you stop it?"

"Oh, we have done nothing," she said.

I was disappointed. "Why not?"

"We were going to take the petition to each house and we prepared it but on the morning my friend got afraid."

"Why?"

"She said, 'What if someone disagrees?' We did not know what to do in that situation and were afraid to offend."

So that was the end of Tanahashi's neighborhood radicalizing: someone might disagree. I was sorry, but I understood her reluctance. Shimizu said that if Tanahashi circulated the petition that her home might be harassed by right-wingers who don't want any sound ordinances that might interfere with the superloud amplified messages from their propaganda trucks.

I asked Tanahashi if they were worried about right-wingers and she said they hadn't thought of that.

"I'm worried about the right-winger," said Shimizu. "Well, not exactly the right-winger, the gangster."

"Yakuza?" I asked.

Morikawa grunted in surprise from beneath the white cotton mask over her nose and mouth, which in combination with her spectacles suggested to me a soldier in the trenches waiting for mustard gas.

"Oh, how do you know that word?" Shimizu asked.

"What do you mean, how do I know that word? How could I live in Japan and not know that word? Everybody knows what the yakuza is," I answered with slight irritation.

"I thought it was our secret," he said.

"The yakuza have a building down the street," said Etsuko. "And important man live in home nearby."

"Head yakuza of Maruyama was shot waiting in my dentist's office. He sat with wife and man shot him in heart and then waited for police," said Morikawa in muffled excitement.

"Yeah, that guy's daughter studied English in this house with the previous foreigners who lived here. She was brought in a limousine and ran into the house for her private lesson.

"Arnie taught her? My old teacher?" asked Shimizu.

"Yes."

"How did gangster know of Arnie?"

"Because Arnie taught English to the police and the police know all the yakuza and they referred him to Arnie." That elicited the rising "ehhhh?" from the ladies.

"I did not know such a thing," said Shimizu.

"You didn't know the police were on speaking terms with the yakuza?"

"No—I didn't know Arnie taught the gangster daughter."

"Ishitaki-san wouldn't let her kids study here any more because of that and when the gangster got murdered she said, 'I told you so.' " She's really got a thing about yakuza and cops—she sees them as rotten peas in a pod. Yakuza men are known for their perms, double-breasted suits, missing finger joints, arrogant swaggers and big black American cars. Sometimes Ishitaki would seem to take this codification system too far and I couldn't tell where the savvyness ended and the prejudice began. We were standing on the street in front of her house when a lady came

walking through the temple parking lot with a tall off-white Af-
ghan Hound, an unusual sight. "Her husband is yakuza," said
Ishitaki contemptuously. "People with large dogs are yakuza."

"The gangsters are very bad," said Tanahashi. "They scare
many people and take from us in clever ways."

"Movies make them seem like the English man in green who
lives in the forest," said Morikawa.

I finally figured out she meant Robin Hood.

"That is because the movies are made by gangsters," she
added.

"Gangster shot in coffee shop across highway one month ago,"
said Kubo. "Near my home."

"I know that place," I said. "I tried to get coffee there once
and they wouldn't let me in. It was obviously open. The man
behind the counter said, 'We're closed—go away.' There were
tough guys sitting at video poker tables. Anyway, Mr. Shimizu,
tell us why you're scared. And why did you say right-wingers?"

"Right-wing and yakuza are friends," he said, "and I demonstrated with crowd at head gangster's house—different group
than building down the street. I stood in street with many people
asking for them to leave. And right-wingers came and looked at
us and act like they write down names to scare us off, but they
don't know who we are so I was not afraid. Those gangsters left.
Head man stay and get into legal business."

"Oh, I'm sure now he's totally legit," I said unnoticed.

"And now I must meet with the brother of that head gangster
for Maruyama at one in the afternoon."

"What? Why?" the ladies and I asked together.

"One of the teachers scolded this man's son in school and he
came to the school and spoke very loudly and rudely to the teacher
in front of students and other teachers. And now I must speak
with him and suggest that he apologize to the teacher."

"Oh no"—I grabbed his hand—"I'll lose my best student!
When is the funeral?"

"I am very afraid," he said, beaming with responsibility and dedication. "But I must do it and he will maybe say his apology at least to me. That would be a good thing."

"I will pray for your safety and success. But why you?"

"I am president of the PTA. It is my responsibility. And because of that I must leave early today, my only holiday in the month. Please excuse me."

"But you have plenty of time," I protested. "It's only eleven-thirty."

"Yes, but I must make delivery for the store."

"Hey, it's your day off!"

"Just one important delivery. It cannot be helped."

"Well, good luck with the gangster."

"Thank you," he said, standing up. "See you again. And now I am off to deliver spirits."

I envisioned a van full of ghosts. "See you later," I said hopefully, and he was off, enthusiastically fulfilling his function in society.

PART SIX

DANCING

PREPARATION FOR *HŌYŌ*

Hōyō was coming in early June. *Hōyō* was a memorial ceremony for the founder of the temple and all those who had been associated with it. In the busy days of preparation for the *hōyō*, we worked straight through a precious *shiku-nichi*. Nishiki Roshi and a bunch of monks from the head temple of Suienji were coming, as well as many lay supporters of Hōgoji. Everything had to be temple-shape. We worked outside every day it didn't rain and inside when it did. Koji, who was in charge, felt the crushing weight of responsibility on his rake. He's the guy you'd want in command. He didn't say anything much, just set an example. If I'd been in his zori I'd have been giving pep talks and invoking loyalty, but he just blazed on and, as the ceremony approached, started weeding, raking and cleaning during services and meals.

Koji's zeal greatly interfered with our bonding as well as my Japanese study. He missed my company too and so he took the boss's prerogative of selecting an assistant.

"Would you work with me outside of the work period?" he asked me. "Shuko's lazy, Norman's sulking, Maku's on a cloud and Jakushin has a complex. It has to be you."

"Well, let me see." I rubbed my chin. "It presents a practice problem to me, Koji."

"Oh," he said seriously. "I'll understand if you say no."

"It's not so simple. I have to consider it. You see, my practice is avoidance. But which avoidance? Should I avoid following the schedule with the group, or should I avoid working extra hours with you?"

Koji handed me a rake.

For the next couple of days we were a whirlwind of efficiency

321

and accomplishment. We went to morning zazen and skipped service to get dressed for work. We ate late, separately from the others, sitting on the edge of the kitchen's wood floor with our feet in the dirt. We kept going till it got dark, took our baths and went into evening zazen late. During the regular *samu* period we worked with everyone else. I was glad no one held our separateness against us.

Koji said we had to make a good impression on Nishiki and the guests. Well, that's what Koji was doing. I was just being with Koji. To me it was play. Katagiri tried not to smile when he saw me. He knew that I'd sneaked through the system again.

There was something wrong with Katagiri, I thought, or he'd be with us more. I'd always known him to get out and hustle when there was a lot to do. He was coming out some, but not as much as I'd expected.

I remembered helping Katagiri cut firewood in the late sixties at Tassajara. It was just the two of us. I was being as quiet and industrious as I could manage. I was an eager young student and he a brown-robed priest. This meant to me that he was enlightened and therefore that everything that he did expressed his enlightenment. It was an opportunity for me to be with him and gain a flicker of that elusive Oriental wisdom—maybe some of it would rub off. Such was my thinking. He was using a Swedish saw and I was wielding a hatchet, chopping the twigs off branches that I then put up on a saw horse for him to cut. He was trying to saw fast, pushing very hard but with poor results. A fellow student who had been a logger and a carpenter was walking by on the bridge. He stopped Katagiri and told him that he wasn't sawing right.

"When you saw, you don't force it, you just go back and forth, cutting the wood on the push, unlike Japanese saws, which work on the pull. Either method is okay, but the key is not to force it, to let the saw do the cutting. Excuse me, Sensei," he added, "but you've just got to be a little more Zen." Katagiri swallowed, bowed to him and adjusted his sawing style. A few times when I fed him branches he laughed and said, "I have to be more Zen."

He was never arrogant—he never acted superior. He just joined in and was an example of continuous effort. But he'd been a little more reclusive at Hōgoji than I was used to. I went to Katagiri's room and asked him if he was all right. He nodded yes.

"Can I do anything?" I said.

"No."

"A massage?"

"No, I'm fine. Just take care of your practice—and Norman."

"Okay, I will," I said, and left him alone.

On the second day, Koji and I weakened and went to buy a pack of cigarettes after lunch. We agreed to hold it to a few a day until the ceremony was over. He said he couldn't be seen buying them so I had to do it.

"Why can't you be seen buying cigarettes? Japan is cigarette heaven. I never saw so many people smoking—the men anyway. And I've seen a number of priests smoking. Why can't you?"

"Nishiki says priests shouldn't smoke."

"Ohhh, I see. Suzuki felt that way too, and Katagiri. I also agree completely."

"I do too."

We stopped and looked at each other.

"Then we are of one mind?" I asked.

Koji nodded.

"Just three a day till the ceremony's over?"

"Just three," Koji answered, and we continued walking downhill—quickly, because we wanted to get right back to work.

Koji said he wished the boys would quit fighting. He was annoyed with Shuko for being aloof and Norman for being cantankerous. "I understand Norman's point of view," he said. "Shuko doesn't treat him fairly. But Norman should remember

323

that the most important thing is for us to be at peace with each other."

"In other words the group is always right?"

"It's so complicated having gaijin," he said, looking at me. "If it weren't for you we would be more confident in our way."

"But listen, Koji, you're also having trouble with each other —not just with foreigners."

"Funny thing is that because of you gaijin we're learning more about working together, which is what we're supposed to be good at. You'd think we'd be learning about individualism—and we are—but it's the group thing that I notice. We only really know how to cooperate with each other, with other Japanese. It hurts us so much to always have conflict with foreigners. I guess our group mind stops at the shoreline."

"And we Americans aren't just learning about harmony, we're also refining our individuality," I said. "It's never just one side. We've both got to adjust all the way around."

"Balance," said Koji.

I took a deep breath and droned, "WE, WE, WE, WE, WE, WE, WE, WE."

"ME, ME, ME, ME, ME, ME, ME, ME," he responded with perfect timing.

"WE, WE, WE, WE, WE, WE, WE, WE," we sang together followed by "ME, ME, ME, ME, ME, ME, ME, ME." And so down to Ryūmon we marched chanting the Japanese-American cultural balance sutra—past farmhouses, by the waterfall and across the highway to the store, where we discontinued our droning and I bought the foul weed. On our return we stopped at a secluded spot and sat down on some rocks only to find we'd forgotten matches.

"Is this place called Ryūmon, Dragon Gate, because of the temple?" I asked.

"Yes, it's like the first gate to the temple. There's an old saying that a monk enters the temple a mouse and leaves a dragon."

"I wonder if maybe the town should be called Mouse Gate until further notice."

The afternoons were getting hotter, but we didn't slow down. After the second day of practically nonstop raking, cleaning and sweating, as the last evening bell tolled, Koji and I sat exhausted in his room smoking our fourth cigarettes of the day. "Persuasive little fellows," I said, putting mine out.

He got up, came over behind me and without asking gave me a godsend five-minute massage. Then he went to his storage closet. After fishing around for a moment, he came back with a tall box and set it on the table. My eyes bugged out as he opened it. It was a bottle of sake. He opened the top and poured each of us a glass.

"Hannyacha (wisdom tea)," he said. I felt the wisdom of its warmth within me. Our tongues loosened.

I made him promise he wouldn't feel angry toward the others for not being as dedicated as him in preparing for the ceremony.

"Being a silent example isn't enough," I told him. "You should be like a good Christian monk—love them in your heart and bear no grudge."

"I will do my best. And what will you do?" he asked me.

"I will hate them and feel superior. But just till the ceremony. I don't get the chance very often."

"Okay," he said, "I will love them and you will hate them. We'll be a team. And we'll cancel each other out."

"Excellent," I said, happy that our balancing act was still in full function.

Koji lifted his glass. "And then we can be good Buddhists and forget the whole matter."

We drank another rule-busting toast.

ATTRACTING CROWDS
OF DERISION

If time is what keeps everything from happening at once, it was not functioning fully on the day before the ceremony. The Hōgoji monks were futzing around with the tools of ceremony: incense, trays, candles, sutra books and esoteric paraphernalia that doesn't often come out from behind the altar. There were impromptu meetings sprouting here and there between Shuko, Koji and others, and subconferences with Katagiri about how everything should be structured: when the meals would be, where they'd be eaten, how responsibility would be divided, what order the monks would be seated in, who would take care of whom and, generally, what would happen where, when, with whom and with what props from the time Nishiki arrived till the time he left. Koji had to be content with the grounds as they were and they were fine. From the bottom of the steps where cars can park at the bend in the road, to the woods behind the temple buildings, from the stupa to the dark garden area around Yoshiko-san's house, all was swept and in order. Soon Nishiki would arrive with his entourage and at least the first impression was bound to be good.

Akagi-san came in a couple of times in the morning with deliveries of food and supplies as well as sake from his liquor store for the guests. Maku was preparing futon for the visiting monks and making sure everything was ready for them. Jakushin was practicing for the ceremony. Shuko and Koji had asked him to be doan and he was proud and uncharacteristically nervous. He was in the hatto going over the chants and marking clearly where which bells were hit. He wanted to make sure that Nishiki, the other monks and all the guests would not be disappointed in his performance.

Gaunt yet spirited Yoshiko, who had been down due to illness, was in the kitchen helping to prepare some of the special dishes for the feast before the ceremony. Miki-obāsan and a couple of the other stout old ladies from the village were helping out in the kitchen too. They laughed and talked while working hard and fast and their charm was so infectious it even softened Yoshiko's severe features. I was in the kitchen with them till Shuko put me on the task of preparing seventy-five sets of bowls for the guests.

Norman came over to help.

"What's up?" I asked, wiping a bowl with a towel.

He took out a stack of bowls, removed the paper from in between and set them next to me. "I'm still pissed about the sutra books."

"You don't give up easy."

"I know. I wish I could. That's one of the problems of being locked up in this way. Like the song says: 'little things mean a lot.' "

"So what are you gonna do?"

"Nothing, I guess. I'd like to go to Suienji after the practice period and finish the job, but I don't want to bother Katagiri about it and he's the only one who could make it happen. If he put in a word with Nishiki Rōshi . . ."

"What if I talk to Katagiri about it?"

Norman sighed. "I don't know. Oh, that's okay I guess."

I spoke in a hush, indicating that Norman was in the next room. Katagiri was cooling himself with a hand-held Ping Pong–paddle-shaped fan that advertised Akagi's liquor store. He seemed so weary of the matter but I pressed him on it. "If they want to be an international temple, then they should provide for Westerners, unless you agree that there should be this sort of obstacle course.

It seems to me that they need to learn something too, not just Norman."

Katagiri nodded.

"Norman could spend some time on it at Suienji, where there are more monks engaged in varied activities. It wouldn't take him long. If you'd just mention it to Nishiki."

Katagiri said that Nishiki would want it to go through Shuko and I said, "Well great—except Shuko'll never get around to it because he's got an inner directive that goes, 'whatever Norman wants, Norman doesn't get.'" I don't think he'd heard the tune before, but he understood the lyrics.

Poor Katagiri. He cared about the sutra books, but mainly he wanted things to go smoothly. Reluctantly, he said he'd talk to Nishiki. I apologized for bothering him and he thanked me for my concern. We gasshoed. I was glad to get out of his room.

Just as I walked out on the deck I heard Norman screaming bloody murder. Oh no, I thought, he's finally cracked. Cautiously I looked to see what I could do. He was pummeling the tatami with the wooden clackers. They're tied together at the end and were banging into each other as well as the tatami and Norman was making emphatic grunting noises as he smashed them down. Katagiri quickly opened the shoji and looked apprehensively at what Norman was doing. Norman stood up, turned around and saw us. The ladies came in from the kitchen and Shuko from the back where his room is.

"Uh, uh," Norman said, looking at us all. "Mukade."

We looked down where he had been banging and saw the flattened corpse of a four-inch centipede. Silence. He turned around, bowed to it and picked it up in one of the pieces of newspaper that had been used to pack the guest bowls. People dispersed and Norman went back to work, embarrassed at the racket he'd made.

Shuko softly spoke my name. I turned around and he gestured me out into the courtyard. He said that Nishiki and his entourage plus lay members who were coming to help would start arriving soon and couldn't I please wear samue.

"You're the only one here in Western clothes," he said.

"Okay, I give in," I said. "But as soon as Nishiki's gone I'm back in civvies." Although he didn't know what civvies were, he agreed and went off to fetch some samue after Norman said that both his other sets were filthy from working outside and they'd be too long in the legs and sleeves anyway.

Shuko came back with the black cotton outfit and it didn't feel as much like prison clothes in my hands as I had expected.

"Put them on in the ofuro," he said, and then turning to Norman, "Did he bite you?"

"No, I bit him."

I went back to the bathroom but Maku was cleaning it out. I excused myself and backed out. Shuko's room is across from the bath so I opened the door. Wow—what a mess. It was full of boxes, stacks of paper, books and piles of clothing, and strewn with candy wrappers, dirty coffee cups and open newspapers. But the futon was properly folded and on its shelf. Ahah, I sighed, remembering how mysteriously and quickly he always opened and closed his door. I closed the shoji quietly. So I took off my pants in the hall, much to Miki-obāsan's pleasure. She cackled at me from the kitchen, where she was kneeling on the floor slicing vegetables on a cutting board.

Shuko was waiting for me. Miki-obāsan stood up and Norman joined her laughter when he saw me. Samue are supposed to be baggy but these were like tights and stopped at my sweaty elbows and knees. Katagiri came in to join in the ridicule and then Yoshiko, the other ladies, Koji, Jakushin and Maku.

"You should see yourself," said Norman in a fit.

"We're really packing 'em in today, huh, Norman?" I said, surveying the small audience.

"Never mind," said Shuko, looking disappointed.

I left the room before Nishiki et al. showed up as I suspected was about to happen. I was sure if I stayed, soon all of Japan would be surrounding me and laughing at my appearance.

SERGEANT IN ROBES

HŌGOJI, JUNE 4, 1988

Nishiki Roshi arrived late that morning with a dozen monks. Shuko and Koji came out to greet them. I stood inconspicuously on the deck near my room and watched them walk in. They came carrying their gear all the way up the steps, the official entrance. Nishiki was tall with a Roman nose. His robes were light brown, thin, and soft looking. Though his head was held high he had a warm smile that disarmed me. As he approached the hatto I sensed his confidence and authority. How clear it was, even from a distance. Before a word was spoken Hōgoji was his and his alone to foster, to guide and to pass on. And as for us—any of us could walk out at any time we wanted, but while we were here, we too were his. The vibes were overpowering and I submitted. The tough-looking monk who followed behind him must be the notorious Dokujiki, I thought. He wore a grimace and walked with a swagger. The monks who followed were in his charge and by the determined looks on their faces seemed to be intent upon doing no wrong, for whereas Nishiki was said to lead lightly, this monk was reputed to comprehend only the heavy hand.

After Nishiki had offered incense at the main altar and made his bows, he left to greet his colleague and guest, Katagiri. Dokujiki led his bevy of Suienji monks to the back of the hatto behind the altar, where they neatly placed their belongings. At Dokujiki's command they then proceeded to remove the fusuma partitions that separated Norman and Jakushin's area from the rest of the hatto. As our castle crumbled we silently scrambled to cram all our possessions into the corner closet. We stacked our low tables and books in Maku's room. Dokujiki walked by inspecting. He paid us no mind, but barked something to his monks. Wasting no time to rest from their journey, they went to the courtyard. Dokujiki told Shuko to fetch the bamboo brooms and his retinue began sweeping the grounds, which were already immaculately leafless. After that they compounded the insult by cleaning every square inch of the hatto and zendo.

For the next thirty-six hours Hōgoji would undergo a marked change and we would be off balance. Whatever petty gripes were going on amongst us were, at least for a while, forgotten due to the common threat to our collective sub-temple ego. Norman made little attempt to hide his contempt for the pomp. He did seem glad to see a couple of the Suienji monks whom he knew from his days there. The rest he said were novices and they jumped to the orders barked by bushy-eyebrowed Dokujiki. Norman called him the "marine sergeant" and he looked the part, being short and thick, and having a military air.

Koji, trying to take care of everyone and everything at once, was propelled into an even more intense blitz of activity. Shuko seemed uncomfortable because Nishiki, his teacher, wasn't paying any special attention to him. Another monk was acting as Nishiki's *jisha*, attendant. So Shuko appointed himself in charge of Katagiri. I was worried that Norman would blow up over that but he let it go, saying he didn't think Katagiri would appreciate being the rope in a tug of war. Maku and Jakushin made an uncommon alliance and hid together in the kitchen with the women, where they could be useful while not having to be bossed around. Katagiri had vacated his room to make way for his old dharma brother Nishiki, because it was the abbot's quarters. He seemed out of place for the first time, with nowhere to go and nothing to do. He hung out in the dining room looking lost.

Norman and I snuck off in the confusion and stood back on

the road looking through the trees at Dokujiki and his troops putting their signature on our handy work.

"I'm glad to see the bastard," he said. "He forces me to have sympathy for Shuko. Did you see how he pushed Shuko around when he got here?"

"He does have a unique style," I said. "I wouldn't want to be on his bad side."

"He can be brutal."

Norman said that at Suienji, when some of the picky senior monks get going, sternly correcting the younger ones, they sound like samurai or gangsters on TV—roles that you never see Japanese men acting out under normal circumstances. "It's a recessive genetic authority defect," he said. "You'll find a monk roaring down the hall with raised *kyōsaku* in hand like a warrior, shrieking at some offender who scratched himself. All the Suienji senior monks aren't like that—but it happens enough." Norman's favorite old monk and closest confidant at Suienji, Godō Roshi, advises the monks never to scold juniors out of anger. According to Norman though, some of those in authority under him don't listen quite as well as they should.

At Suienji there is a Ryaku Fusatsu ceremony twice a month. It's a Buddhist confessional or repentance ceremony that is finished off by repeating precepts. It goes way back to the beginnings of Buddhism. The way they did it in the old days was the monks would gather and each would find another monk to whom to confess whatever rules he'd broken. Then they'd all have a ceremony and chant the two hundred and some odd precepts—add a hundred more for the women. Nowadays in Zen it's become more streamlined, but it's still a beautiful ceremony, many people's favorite. In English, one part goes, "All my ancient twisted karma, from beginningless greed, hate and delusion, born through body, speech and mind, I now fully avow." At the San Francisco Zen Center it's performed once a month on the night of the full moon.

So we call it the Full Moon Bodhisattva Ceremony. I've had several Japanese tell me that the difference between Buddhism and Christianity is that the former has no confession. Not so.

Norman told me that one time when Nishiki was officiating at Suienji's Ryaku Fusatsu, two young monks nodded off. After the ceremony, Dokujiki followed them back to the *sōdō*, the monks' hall. Screaming in rage, Dokujiki grabbed the *kyōsaku* and went after the young monks. Everyone else quickly left the scene except Norman, who stayed to see what was happening. The others called for him to get out, while Dokujiki repeatedly pounded the two terrified fledglings with the thick winter stick. Norman looked on in horror and started to go in. Some old monks came back and pulled him away, saying, "Don't watch! Come away! This is wrong!" As they held him back these older monks told Norman that they knew this was not the way it should be done, that Dokujiki was way out of line. But no one would do anything to protect the poor young offending monks, who were back there cowering at the blows. Since Dokujiki was in a position of authority, nobody said a word to him about his transgressions.

"Some people would tell you that this is a tough form of Buddhist compassion," said Norman, "but it has nothing to do with Buddhism or compassion. It's a perversity that should be rejected. There are parallels to this in schools, business and sports here in Japan. They're slowly growing out of it like the Marines is in the States and I say it can't happen too quickly.

"Even the stick should be dropped. The stick and this stupid macho attitude. At Bodhgaya in India, where Buddha attained enlightenment, there's a Rinzai temple where they carry the stick and hit people who are dozing or who are suspected of improper sitting. Buddhists from all over the world come there and look at that and they wonder what on earth are they doing? Smashing people with sticks and hollering and screaming. What the hell has that got to do with Buddhism?"

. . .

Standing with the visiting monks where our room had once been, in the corner of the now expanded hatto, Norman, Jakushin and I put our robes on in silence while the bonsho rang for the noon service. We went out together into the hatto and took our places, me standing back a few steps as usual. There were about fifteen monks lined up on either side of the altar facing each other. Shuko was running around adjusting people's positions in their lines according to Dokujiki's instructions. One of the senior Suienji monks was on the bells. On the third round of the bonsho the ring of a small bell came from the abbot's room, signifying that Nishiki was on his way. He came into the room followed by his jisha, who carried the incense, and Katagiri. Shuko moved in behind Katagiri and guided him to a front position and stood next to him. Dokujiki was in the rear on my side. Bells hit, the monks bowed to the floor on their zagu, more bells hit and then Dokujiki introduced the Heart Sutra: "Maka hannyaharamita shingyō," with the last "o" rising, falling and drawn out dramatically. After the introduction we all joined in on the beat and for the first time at Hōgoji I heard a wide range of voices try out the building's acoustic potential. We charged through the national anthem of emptiness with drum and bells to the dramatic ending, which in English is, more or less, "Gone, gone, gone beyond, gone completely beyond, Enlightenment! Yahoo! Wisdom Sutra." We were like one big panting celestial animal. No wonder monks chant.

Towards the end of the sutra a young monk slowly brought an important-looking brocade book out from behind the altar. The book was set on a low lectern, proper for holding something to be read while kneeling. The monk placed the lectern before Dokujiki, took a few steps back and kneeled. He must have been new to all this because he looked pretty nervous. Dokujiki recited from this book an *ekō,* a solo recitation dedicating the merit of the service to all beings and various great patriarchs of the Way and other members and donors who have passed on. I looked at Norman, who was facing me, sitting on his shins in the line across.

Ideally, when the eko is finished, the monk who delivered the book comes back, falls to his knees and picks up the stand an instant after the chant leader puts the book back down on it. Then the monk returns the eko book to the back part of the altar. The book is a foot and a half long and ten inches wide, one of the fancy folding type. The monk arrived at the right place at the right moment at the end of the chanting, kneeled down, picked up the stand and swung it around—but unfortunately he picked it up a second too soon, before Dokujiki had put the eko book down on it. The poor nervous monk didn't even realize it.

Norman watched Dokujiki's scowl and bulging eyes. At that point Dokujiki turned around and smashed the astonished offending novice in the shoulder with the book. A boom resounded in the room. The monk was startled and let out a cry: "Agh!" Norman couldn't contain himself and blurted a "Ha!" Nishiki looked up and made a deep, puzzled "Mmm?" type of sound. I giggled, "Hee!"

The sequence of these peculiar sounds was a striking divergence from the expected single bell's ringing that was to have sung through the air at that moment. Following was a hovering instant of silence and immobility. In each person's head it echoed. "Boom! Agh! Hah! Mmm? Hee!" It was like a clip from *The Three Stooges Go to Church*. The silliness of the sounds and uniqueness of the moment diffused Dokujiki's lust for punishment. He grunted and opened his bowing cloth, for it was time once again to prostrate ourselves to buddha, the perfect essence of our being.

INCIPIENT FRUIT
OF LABOR

I started off the MMC one morning by announcing that Elin was pregnant. This elicited a shower of high-pitched oohs and ahs from the women. Mr. Shimizu reached over grinning broadly and shook my hand. Kubo clapped her hands and Tanahashi said, "Omedetō!" Etsuko asked if we were planning to go back to the States to have the baby. I said, "No way—we can find what we want easier in Japan."

"What do you want that you can't get in the States?" she asked.

"Midwives," I told her.

"Ehhhh," came the rising tone of interest from the ladies.

"Are there no midwives in the States?" asked Shimizu.

"There are, but not like here. The situation is improving in the States, but Japan has not lost its wisdom in this area as we have." Whereas midwives in most places in the States are hard to find, hounded, or illegal, they're common and respected in Japan. It turned out that of those present, only Kubo's baby had been delivered by a doctor.

They were curious that we liked the old-fashioned way and wanted to hear all about it. I was eager to oblige. I said that the clinic we chose is owned by a doctor named Kuroda who lived for five years in L.A. He's a busy, cordial fellow whom we trust and he employs a few midwives who exude competence. I guess we trust him mostly because one of *them* will deliver the baby. After we chose Kuroda's, we learned that the Tanakas down the street recently had their baby there. They said that Kuroda Sensei only deals with cesareans and other irregularities, and they were very happy with his clinic. Kurodain (the name of the clinic) looks like it will be just the right place to bring little Hortense or Hank into the world of air-breathing beings.

"Not only traditional," said Morikawa, cleaning her lenses. "Kurodain is new."

She was right. It's got the benefits of a hospital, like blood and oxygen, without the drawbacks like disease, gloom and an impersonal approach.

Tanahashi confirmed that natural childbirth is the rule in Japan. She said that taking medication for giving birth is not well thought of. "It is a sign of weakness," she said.

Kurodain also has a low 5 percent cesarean rate and is cautious about episiotomies. No one wanted to talk about those topics. They just went "ahhh" and looked down.

Elin and I had not only met with Kuroda Sensei but with his main midwife, Fukiko-san, as well. She was tall, confident, pleasant and had strong arms. She spoke with much greater authority than the doctor. In the course of our discussion she told us that it was important to make love as much as possible during pregnancy. We promised to do our best.

At Kurodain the mother doesn't have to be separated from the baby at all. Kuroda Sensei and Fukiko-san were comfortable with the idea of me being an active partner in the labor and birth. She said that participation by husbands is on the increase in Japan, though it's still practically unheard of.

The members of the MMC were particularly interested in the fact that I would help Elin through her labor and birth.

"My husband didn't even miss work when I gave birth," said Morikawa, the older lady of the group. "I didn't care. My sister was with me."

"My husband was with me, but he waited outside during our daughters' births," said Tanahashi. "I think he's too shy to have been there."

"No, I would not have wanted to see it," said Shimizu, father of three daughters.

"We know a Japanese couple, artists who live over toward the river, who delivered their own baby at home," I said. That was met by gasps. Shimizu said he thought it was illegal.

"We wouldn't do that," I said, "but Elin needs me to be there. It's part of the way our subculture does things."

"You and Elin have no family here and you are very close," said Kubo. "You share the housework. Japanese husband and wife are not so close. They only do things together they have to. But we have other family members. My husband was out of town for both my children's births."

Kubo asked if Elin was sick and I said that so far she's having a pleasant pregnancy.

"Will she work?" asked Etsuko.

"She's planning to work until about a month before the birth. And then she's not going to teach away from home except for one class downtown."

"Maybe she shouldn't work," said Etsuko. "Are American women so strong?"

"I stayed in bed for the whole ten months," said Kubo.

"Ten months?" I asked.

"And for a month after."

"You had a ten-month pregnancy?"

"That's normal, isn't it?"

Everyone nodded.

We went back and forth on that for a while till we discovered that it was just a matter of counting differently. They start with one and we start with zero.

"But aren't you worried about your wife?" asked Morikawa. "She should rest and be careful."

"Thank you, I will," piped in Elin from the kitchen.

Strangely, of the conditions that we were looking for in a place to have a baby, the hardest one to fulfill was permission to leave the clinic after two or three days. Almost every place said that we had to stay for a week. One or two weeks is the custom here. There's nothing wrong with that from our point of view, but it's expensive and unnecessary.

Morikawa seemed surprised and said, "But the mother *has* to stay in the hospital for at least a week." The others nodded.

"And why is that?" I asked.

She stopped as if looking for an answer and then said, "Because she'll need clean towels."

I didn't understand her until I realized that she meant that the mother shouldn't be doing the washing and other chores the first week. Oh, I forgot. The husband has no role at home. The wives have so much responsibility in the house that they need to be somewhere else to rest. That's the way it was with my mother's generation in the States.

I tried them on another challenging detail. Kuroda also agreed the baby doesn't have to be washed for a few days so as not to remove the natural skin cream it's born with, the vernix. That's what we did with Kelly. The blood dries and falls off in no time and the vernix can just be rubbed in. I thought that would freak out the normally squeaky clean Japanese, but both Shimizu and the mothers of the MMC made sounds of interest.

"Kuroda Sensei sounds like a good doctor," said Morikawa.

Kubo said she thought she had the "best" obstetrician in town, though he induced labor in her so that he'd be sure not to miss his Sunday golf.

"But I was afraid of midwife. Doctor is expert."

GOOD FRIDAY
THE THIRTEENTH

MARUYAMA, APRIL 13, 1990

Spring is here and winter is truly gone. We realize now that something in us has relaxed, something that shored us up against the cold, the cold that is omnipresent even in the mild Maruyama winter in these uninsulated buildings without wasteful and dear old central heating.

Today was a good day. It's even Good Friday. And it's not your run of the mill Good Friday either—it's Good Friday the thirteenth. Elin and I had decided in the morning that the combination might be propitious and we were right. For something that had been keeping the brain weevils (as Norman says) fed was cast aside today. I got a call from Miyake at Immigration concerning my request for permission to work. I was, in fact, working at the moment and had left my class to answer the phone. The request was granted and thus I am no longer a criminal—at least in that particular way. Thus ends, for now, a long road to almost complete legitimacy.

Elin already had permission to teach. Over half a year ago Miyake had told her it would be appropriate for her to apply. At that time he said, "The money you saved to study here must be getting low now, and since your husband has the visa to study and you have the spouse visa, they would expect you to be the one working."

"The Osawa Culture Center wants me to work for them," she had said.

"Get a letter from them saying they want to employ you. That should do it," he had said, pulling their brochure from his files. Our eyes bulged. We knew that brochure. Her name was already printed in it as one of their teachers. Miyake had glanced through the pages and set it down without expression. Had he seen it?

When the brochure had first come out I called up Bop in Kyoto and said we're dead for sure. As always, he calmed me down.

"You're on a cultural visa," he said.

"She's on a spouse's visa."

"Same thing. No problem. Teaching without permission on a visa other than tourist is a minor infraction. The worst that could happen is you'd have to write a letter of apology to the minister of culture. And they'd probably make you sit in their office at Uzu all afternoon and listen to a lecture."

"That would be awful. Now they've got proof."

"You know Bob here in Kyoto?"

"Of course."

"He's running classes out of five apartments—it's a major language school and it's got his name on it. He went to Immigration and they asked if he was teaching and he said no. Then they showed him one of his ads from the buses and trains. He said that no one had responded. They just stuck it back in their file and he didn't even have to write a letter of apology. So don't worry, no one's going to bother you."

Therefore we hadn't worried (excessively) about the brochure with Elin's name on it, but I did swallow hard when Miyake brought it out that day half a year ago.

When Elin and I renewed our visas a month ago, Miyake (continuing to compassionately guide us step by step) had suggested that if I wished, I could apply for permission to work.

"I thought you said I should forget about that."

"You've been here long enough. They'll understand. The worst thing you could do now is to teach without permission."

Flashing red light. I applied and got the response. What a relief! Legal at last. Of course, technically I only have permission to teach four hours a week at a local kindergarten where I've been teaching for a year, but once I've got permission to teach somewhere, according to Bop, that's it—that's as close as one can get to perfect compliance while teaching private classes here and there.

After we got that phone call, Elin let out a "yiperoo!" and we danced around and acted silly. Then I returned to the English class with two young, single piano teachers in the living room. They were in hysterics over our celebration.

THE HEARTLESS SUTRA

HŌGOJI, JUNE 4, 1988

In the late hot afternoon I sat baking in the study, collating guest gift packages. Koji was nearby busily preparing food with the assistance of a dozen or so women from Ryūmon and beyond. From the hatto we could hear the muffled ceremony rehearsal punctuated by unexpected halts in the chanting and angry bursts from Dokujiki.

Shuko had tried to get me to go, but I refused, saying that Dokujiki would talk too fast for me to get anything out of it.

"Maybe you will learn where your place is," he said.

"I'm not going to a two-and-a-half-hour rehearsal so I can find out where to stand," I answered adamantly.

Koji sided with me, saying that I could be a guest. Shuko nodded. That was the right word to use. It's the secret to getting by in Japan: remain a guest and all falls in place.

So instead of going to the rehearsal, I had to put eighty gift packs together—the sort of task I can sink my fingers into. The gift packs would be placed next to each guest's setting at the *obentō* lunch and general meeting that would be held before the ceremony. Among the items was a thin book by Nishiki with a photo of Hōgoji on the cover. It was slipped into a custom-made envelope. Also included for each guest was one of his works of calligraphy, protected by a transparent sheet and encased in a thick folded paper that was then wrapped and tied with a red cord. These and a few other items were placed in a white cardboard box that was wrapped in handmade paper and then cloaked in a purple *furoshiki*, a square of cloth with the seal of Suienji emblazoned on it. I veiled and layered, putting tasteful thing in thing. Doubtless, at the same time, in shops, temples, offices and homes, countless others were wrapping objects, slipping bags in boxes and boxes in bags with handles and bows, the presentation not separate from the present in this Pleasure Island of the container industry.

The rapid clicking of knives slicing through vegetables blended with the sound of crickets scraping legs outside. The thump of the wooden fish stopped and again—that voice like a dog barking in the distance. During lunch Dokujiki had talked through his meal while he ate, oblivious that everyone else was silent and unreceptive. At dinner last night when Nishiki and Katagiri were eating with us he was on his toes, mute and grinning like a scared kid.

With the influx of all the older and shorter Japanese, Norman seemed to have grown a half foot. He was busy working on altars and had no time to chat, but once when he got near me he pulled me aside and said, "I'm gonna write a book called 'I was a nigger for the Sōtō-shū.'"

"I hate that word," I said.

"Me too."

Shuko brought a couple of old guys from the village to help me. They looked at me like I was an escaped convict, but then adjusted, smiled, and after a cordial greeting we got to work and didn't say a word. Fine with me—I was wiped out. Shuko was right, if I'd had on samue they would have felt more at ease.

I'd met some of these people just the other night when Koji,

Maku and I had run down the hill and gone from door to door reminding them of the ceremony to come. Koji would open the doors and call out. He'd even walk in. No knocking, no bells. Just slide the door open and announce our presence. I told him he'd better not do that in the States if he ever goes there—unless he's feeling suicidal—we are much more territorial about our front doors. He said that the entryway, the area where shoes are worn and taken off, is still like part of the outside. The private part begins where you step up in socks and put on slippers. He made me do it: open a door, go in and announce our presence. A lady came to the entryway and, ignoring me, talked to Koji. That was easy. I told him he'd come a long way since he was afraid for me to do takuhatsu. He looked embarrassed and then I remembered that Norman had told me not to tell him that. "Never mind," I said.

After dinner there was another ceremony rehearsal. I had been napping in Maku's room in the corner of the hatto and cracked the shoji open to take a peek. Dokujiki started it off by replacing Jakushin as the doan. In front of everyone, Dokujiki said that Jakushin made the bells scream. He put one of his own boys in his place. Jakushin didn't say anything, just got up and stood next to Norman behind everyone else where no one could see his face. It was so painful I couldn't stand it. Norman walked out and I went out on the deck and met him.

"God I hate their racism. I used to get so mad about ours in the States and I couldn't do a thing about it. I can't do anything about it here either. I wanted to go pull Dokujiki's tongue out of his throat but I just stood there. I know that guy that Dokujiki put on the bells in place of Jakushin. He's only been at Suienji a year. His father's got a big temple over in Takamatsu. Dokujiki couldn't stand the thought of a Korean hitting the bells for the ceremony tomorrow. Jakushin's the real nigger here, not me."

I went over to Koji's cabin and sat on the steps. A few people who'd come to help were mulling about in the courtyard. Some women were in the kitchen still working with Koji, Miki-obāsan and Yoshiko. I could see Katagiri across the way sitting on the tatami in the corner of the dining area by himself. He was reading a magazine, which he looked away from as much as he looked at. He was just waiting for all this to get over with. Laughter was coming from Nishiki's room, where he was entertaining some wealthy businessmen patrons from Beppu (big right-wingers, Koji had told me with disgust). I could hear chanting from the hatto, where the rest of my buddies were. In half an hour we'd all be sitting zazen together, the lay folks and the monks. Zazen, the great equalizer—I hoped it worked. I had mixed feelings about hearing the Heart Sutra at the time, especially the bells. Some of the heart had gone out of it for me.

PERIOD THEATER

HŌGOJI, JUNE 5, 1988

Aside from takuhatsu, there's nothing like a high ceremony to bring out the time travel aspect of Zen life in Japan. Here we are dressed like monks of centuries ago, chanting the same lines in the same buildings. It's *jidai-geki,* period theater, these robes and trappings, chants and choreography.

Koji said that since I was wearing robes I should be with the rest of the monks, reversing his opinion that I should be a guest. He had just wanted to help me skip the rehearsal. So there I was seated right behind Dokujiki, who gave me a "what the hell are you doing here?" look and then turned away. The bonsho started ringing and Nishiki was on his way in. With the shoji all down, including the ones separating the zendo, the hatto was now a spacious room that could hold all the monks and the guests. You'd think after the painstaking preparation and much to do that there would be a very solemn atmosphere at this time, but there wasn't. An old lady behind me reached up and straightened my kesa and tucked it in correctly. Nishiki was at the altar. Ladies were still out at the sinks cleaning up after lunch, chattering and washing pots and all those lacquer bowls I'd helped stack. Maku was all over the room snapping pictures. When Nishiki entered, people were still coming up to a table near the altar and adding their white donation envelopes. Men put their cigarettes out. Nishiki wore soft elegant robes of muted hues, a light brown koromo, a purple kesa and a high pointed golden cap.

Then we were off and chanting the Heart Sutra and I felt right at home. When we finished we went right back to the first word of it and started over without missing a beat. There were large wooden boxes right in front of us that I hadn't noticed—the size of foot lockers. Dokujiki reached in front and took off the lid. I then recognized them as the boxes that held the long version of the Prajnā Pāramitā Sūtra that we kept in cabinets behind the altar. That's what the Heart Sutra is the heart of. There were six of these boxes with the tops off and the monks were reaching in and taking out the folding sutra books, so I took one out too. They started fanning them. These aren't books with bindings but are made from one long piece of paper folded back and forth with hard brocade covers on each end. What the monks were doing was to let the sutras rest in their left hand and then to grab the top with the right and pull it way up and around so that it fanned out like an accordion, and when it started falling down on the right side they pulled their left hands over, following the arc into the right hand and closing it. This is the turning of the Prajnā Pāramitā Sūtra. Koji had quickly shown me how to do it before the ceremony. The first time I tried it, it worked just like a slinky going down the steps in my grandmother's house.

It was no normal Heart Sutra chanting anymore, for when

each monk's book would rise and fall, so would his voice. They were shouting at the apex and since the fannings were going on at random, the heavy rhythm of the chanting was being augmented with the arrhythmic punctuation of rising and falling roaring voices. We went through six hundred volumes in about ten minutes. Now what does this sutra say? I thought to myself. Oh, forget it, just throw the next one. The only mistake I made was once I lost control and one side of my sutra book came down on Dokujiki. His growl was covered by the din of the ceremony. He straightened his kesa and we continued unflustered. It was ancient ritual rock and roll and when it ended the room echoed with reverberations. What we had done was to symbolically recite the whole long version of the Perfection of Wisdom.

During the next chant the monks stood up and walked around in a snaking line down toward the altar and away from it. Then we sat down and Nishiki did some special very slow chants. His voice went up and down, wavering like a ghost in an old movie. After that he kindly gave a brief lecture. By that time all the ladies had finished washing the dishes and were sitting in the back of the room.

The whole assembly then got up and followed Nishiki out into the warm, sunny outdoors and we had three brief services at different altars that had been prepared by Norman. One of the services involved Yoshiko and the statue of Avalokiteshvara in her garden. It seemed like a recognition of her practice and maybe a farewell. Following this treasure hunt of incense, flowers and candles, the procession went over to the stupa, where there was a last brief ceremony for all the people on both sides who died in the Pacific War. There was an altar set up for each of the four directions and Nishiki made an offering at each one. We circumambulated the monument, walking inside the low hedge while guests congregated on the outside. Then the chanting stopped. That was it. The ceremony was over.

People talked on the lawn while others offered incense at the altars around the stupa. Shuko was standing with Nishiki and

Akagi and some distinguished-looking visitors. Jakushin seemed
to have recovered from his humiliation and was deep in conversation with some young ladies who'd come with their parents.
They were looking at him with admiration. Norman was talking
with a couple of the Suienji monks he knew. Dokujiki was keeping his eyes on the younger monks. Koji ran back to the kitchen
to get dinner going and Katagiri wandered off by himself up the
road. Maku was still taking pictures, a lot of which were of me.
Songbirds were singing, *mejiro* (the white-eye) in the lead. There
were several mejiro, tiny and yellow-green, drinking nectar from
the camellias between tunes. There was a warm, fresh-smelling
breeze that escorted incense away into the air as I exchanged pleasantries with Miki-obāsan and Yoshiko. We looked down into the
gorgeous green cultivated valley. Miki-obāsan imitated the mejiro:
"Cho bei chu bei cho chu bei." She sounded just like them and she
laughed and said something about its call being a pun on some
men's names—I didn't get it. A pair of black butterflies were
zooming around and she gave them a different name than Koji
had. She called them *ohaguro*—black teeth. In the old days women
used to dye their teeth black.

The ceremony had gone fine. It was simple, direct, almost
casual and not too long. I realized I'd been too negative about it
beforehand. It's my anti-institutional self-programming, my fear
of confinement. But it was no more confining than a bus ride to
town and I could see how much it meant to all the visitors. Even
though I've lived with groups for so many years, I still get claus-
trophobic at the thought of losing myself into the whole when
quite often the opposite of my fears is true. I lose nothing but
gain a lot. It's clear to me that when we function smoothly as a
group, our differences and gripes become irrelevant, but we do
not lose our distinctness. It's transformational. The very substance
that was an irritant becomes a note in a harmonious chord.

. . .

That night Nishiki and Katagiri were in the abbot's quarters getting plowed on sake with Akagi and a few other guests who remained. Norman and I hung out for a while in the dining room with the Suienji monks and Dokujiki, and we all drank sake too.

"Don't stand up," he said to us. "You make me feel short. Stay—sit and drink." The more sake we drank the less he seemed like a jerk. As things got looser I accidentally spilled a cup on his lap. Taking no offense he jovially poured his over my head.

Before Norman and I left for the evening we did a little song and dance for the boys, something that Norman had dreamed up. We danced arm in arm, moving sideways and kicking. The song went thus:

> Do the Sōtō-shū 'cause nothing else will do
> Do the Sōtō-shū just me and you
> A one a two, a doodly-doodly-do

The other monks thought that we were crazy, but applauded appropriately.

On my way to bed I brazenly stuck my head in Nishiki's room and said good night to him and Katagiri. Katagiri asked me to come sit by him. I politely declined, but he insisted so I went in for a minute. I was quickly introduced to the guests, who smiled drunkenly and went back to talking to Nishiki. No sooner had I sat down than Katagiri poured me sake in a small cup and insisted I drink it all at once. This he did several times. I refused on the fourth. Katagiri's guard was all the way down. He looked at me like the old friend he was, threw his arms around me and hugged me with abandon. "I love you, David," he said, and hugged me some more.

"I love you too," I said, hugging him in return.

The others didn't pay any attention.

. . .

The next morning at tea Katagiri reminded Nishiki who I was, where I'd come from and how long I was there for. I thanked Nishiki for the opportunity to practice at his temple and reminded him I'd shown him around Green Gulch a few years back. He asked me a lot of questions about my history with Zen and seemed genuinely interested in my answers. I was touched by his kind manner. The whole time he was there he had been reserved and gracious. I'd had an image of him as being a snobby aristocrat and what I was looking at was more like an elegant old monk who probably spent all his time trying to promote his institution and train priests. He was going to a lot of trouble to get Hōgoji up and running as an international temple. Of course it wasn't being built to Norman's and my specifications, but it was still a noble venture. Nishiki may not be my type of teacher, but he appeared to be a person who had cultivated some wisdom and self-control. I saw him as a sort of public servant and I felt petty for having thought ill of him.

Akagi-san came from Kikuoka to drive Nishiki Roshi out, and waited with Koji in the courtyard while Nishiki finished doing a work of calligraphy for each of us as a parting gift. Nishiki came out on the deck to say goodbye. I nudged Katagiri and asked if he'd brought up the romanized sutra book deal with Nishiki. He said it was up to Shuko. Heck. He'd just been putting me on. I took matters into my own hands.

"Excuse me, Nishiki Roshi," I said as politely as I could.

"Hai," he said, offering me his attention.

"I've been having a lot of trouble chanting here because the books are hard to read. Maybe I could make you a new romanized version for Westerners. I'd be happy to do it."

Nishiki nodded thoughtfully.

Katagiri broke in and suggested that maybe Norman could go to Suienji and do it and they talked about it for a moment. I breathed a sigh of relief that Katagiri had understood where I was coming from. I'd done what I could, but I wouldn't wager that anything would come of it.

We all bunched together on the kuin steps for a group picture, which Maku took. Typically, he didn't want anyone to take another group picture with him in it, but Nishiki insisted. Maku then announced that the film was a gift from me. So that's why he'd taken all those pictures of me at the ceremony. He'd been short and I'd loaned him the money to buy several rolls when he went into town. Later I'd refused to let him pay me back. It was my only donation to the temple up to that point. Nishiki thanked me and I told him I'd give him copies of all the good pictures.

Everyone laughed at me. They had to be laughing at me. I had no idea why. I said, "What's so funny?"

Koji came over and whispered in my ear that when I used the word *agemasu* for "give," even though it was the polite form, it wasn't polite enough. When speaking to Nishiki I should use the very polite term, *sashiagemasu,* meaning to give to someone clearly on a higher level.

"Sashiagemasu," I said, and they all laughed even harder, especially Katagiri. I looked at Koji and he indicated I'd done just fine, though he didn't stop laughing.

After that Nishiki bid farewell to Yoshiko and then the whole group walked down the wood steps under the *sugi* to where the vehicles were parked. There was a moment's wait while Nishiki talked to Katagiri and the monks stood at attention with their hands in *shashu.*

Dokujiki turned to Norman, who was standing next to me, and said, "Poketto wa dame," meaning "the pocket is no good."

Norman looked at him blankly and said, "Nan desu ka?" meaning "What?" and Dokujiki tapped his hand and said again, "Poketto wa dame."

"Poketto? Poketto?" And Norman laughed and took his hands out of his pockets.

As we stood on the road in gassho, Nishiki rode off with Akagi, and the Suienji monks followed in the van driven by Dokujiki.

The sound of the vans disappeared. We were alone again. We

looked at each other happy and relieved and walked back up the steps. There was no schedule and no cleanup. Koji said it could all wait till the next day. Radical. Yea! At the stupa Norman turned to me with a wacky look and shook his finger at me. "Poketto wa dame," he said. "Poketto wa dame!"

ADDRESSING WOMEN

MARUYAMA, APRIL 19, 1990

America is a very wide country," I said, pointing to a map of the United States of America. America—that's what Japanese call it. I usually try to be more considerate of others from our hemisphere and just call it "the States." The other day I was shattered when a Canadian woman said, "The States? Isn't it just like you Yankees to think you're the only 'states.' "

"I was born here," I said, pointing the stick to Texas. "Texas." (Pause for recognition.) "The city where I come from is Fort Worth. It is next to Dallas. You all know Dallas because Kennedy was killed there." (Ahs and ehs.) According to Ishitaki, the first day that Japan was hooked up to receive live American television was November 22, 1963. Like us, the Japanese will not easily forget the Kennedy assassination.

"It was a very sad day." (Nods.) I mentioned the Wild West and oil and made a pun about the word "cowboy" in Japanese and English.

"We don't use chopsticks there. I had a hard time with them at first in Japan, but now I'm gradually getting used to them." I picked up two pencils and exhibited ridiculous hashi style. (Laughter.)

"It gets very hot in Texas in the summer." (Wipe my brow.) "When I was a kid we used to eat a lot of ice cream and water-melons in the summer." (Mmmms, going up in pitch.)

I was giving a talk to a ladies' group in a town way up in the hills. It took an hour and a half to get there by bus and train. There were about eighty women, mostly farmers' wives, not poor or uneducated, but, according to their own president, "not as sophisticated or snobby as Maruyama women," whom Ishitaki called "not as sophisticated or snobby as Kyoto women." My mother goes to The Woman's Club in Fort Worth. I wonder if it's anything like this.

I'd been giving talks to groups for half a year, ever since I recovered from the debacle at the Gifu JCs. Poor Yasushi. He tried to tell me. Everyone tried to tell me. As the old Japanese saying goes, "Open your ears, fathead!" At least that's the gist.

I demonstrated a car whizzing by me so close it made me spin. I had looked to the left instead of the right. "Your streets are backwards!" Laughter.

Every sentence was written large on a piece of typing paper. I could improvise without fear of getting lost. All I had to do was look down and say what was next. I'd gone through these pages a number of times and most of it was from prior talks, so I wasn't really reading. Ishitaki had helped me greatly. The prin-ciple of the talk that we developed was to give them 90 percent what they wanted and expected and to say a little something extra for the other 10. She enthusiastically assisted with that didactic 10 percent and made it as effective as she could for the particular audience. What she wanted me to say was not just the diplomatic nice-nice—I was elated with it. She told me it was what she would like to say in public but never gets to because outspoken women are not appreciated. "I have to say what I think very indirectly. You can be frank. That's what they expect from an American."

I told the ladies about a language problem I had in Tokyo when I was there with Kelly in July of 1988. We were still new to Japan and were trying to figure out if we were at a temple or a shrine. I went up to a bald man in robes and asked, "Is this a temple (*otera*)?"

He pointed to the left. "The rest room (*otearai*) is over there."

"No, I didn't say 'otearai.' I said, 'Is this a temple (*otera*)?' "

"There's a hotel (*hoteru*) over there," he said, pointing to the left. They applauded and laughed.

The best hint I ever got on how to communicate with Japanese was something Bop told me late one night as we walked through the grounds of a temple on a wooded hill near his place in Kyoto. "When Americans get together we exchange information," he said. "When Japanese get together they exchange feeling. They are also exchanging information, but the feeling is primary. I've often seen them go back and forth, starting off with a seasonal or literary comment and then progress. There's an almost infinite body of knowledge, of stories, poems, sayings, observations, a lot of Confucianism and Chinese folk wisdom in there. And the Japanese language with its Chinese and especially pre-Chinese words, is so descriptive of feelings, moods, subtle aesthetic distinctions and stuff like that. Depending on how educated they are, they just go deeper and deeper into it, and that makes them feel better and better. Ideally they don't one-up each other, they build on what the other says. And if someone is good at it they'll make the other person feel good. Making others feel good is important, more important than truth or principle."

He told me about a Japanese harpsichordist who gave a special benefit concert for the environmental group that his ladyfriend Keiks works for. A hundred or so people went to hear the concert, about twenty of them gaijin. The musician had studied in Europe and was well known in Japan as an expert at playing Bach. But that night he played only his own compositions. Bop said that they were musically based on koto music, which Bop likes a lot. But, he said, the man's own music was overly simple and irritating in its lack of melody. To him the compositions were just not good at all. After the concert, the Japanese guests were enthusiastic in their praise. Bop and his gaijin friends were not impressed, but played along with the general mood till they were back at his place and could express to each other how poor they thought the guy's music was and how embarrassed they felt for him. Then Keiks came in with some friends of hers who were Japanese musicians. Bop asked them offhandedly, as they sat down, how they'd liked the concert, and they all nodded and smiled and made general positive comments. Keiks asked Bop how he liked it.

"Sō desu nē," he said with a bit of hesitation in his voice.

"Ah, we wondered if you could tell," she said.

"They wanted the guy to feel good," said Bop to me when relating this story. "Maybe no one will ever tell him what they truly think. There has to be a place for him—that's more important than people's opinions. Everyone needs to feel appreciated. The Japanese can be brutal to each other in their conformity, but there are many kindnesses we could learn from them."

"I like nattō"—the sticky Limburger of soybean products—"but my wife doesn't. Who here likes nattō?" I asked, raising my hand. Just about half the ladies' hands joined mine.

Giving my classes a plug, I told them that teaching English is difficult for me—but I love teaching the women. They learn better, listen better, speak better, express better.

I could keep talking to those ladies forever. They were actually listening—and responding. Senior groups listened well too. But it was hard to get working men to show any interest, even in a prepared talk.

I told some stories about misunderstandings between our cultures. The one about our friend not putting "sama" after the family name on a letter. A story about a Japanese kid doing homestay in Ohio who was kicked out of the house for not being able to eat spaghetti without slurping.

I told them I believed in cultural exchange to promote international understanding. (Serious nods.) That's true, but sometimes the superficiality of the exchange can drive Elin and me batty. We declined to be on a TV show about internationalism, the Japanese buzzword of the decade. Things still weren't straight with Immigration and we didn't want to draw attention to ourselves. Also we didn't trust them not to do something weird. When we sat down in the den to watch the show, our suspicions were confirmed.

Twenty Maruyama residents, foreigners from all over the world, mostly students, sat in chairs on a raised, bleacherlike stage. Before them they each had two buttons, one red and one green—red no, green yes. A moderator introduced them and one by one they said hello and told a little about themselves. Then he asked questions and they would hit one or the other button. Above their heads was a banner with the words INTERNATIONAL HEART on it. Below the banner was a screen upon which would appear the yes/no percentiles of their answers. Some of the questions asked were: Do you like Japanese food better than the food from your country? Is it difficult to eat with hashi? Is the Japanese language difficult or easy? (red for difficult, green for easy). It became clear to Elin and me that to some people, "internationalism" meant gathering people from all over the world to answer the same maddening questions over and over about Japan.

"Japan doesn't seem so small to me when I ride my bicycle. It seems endless," I said and looked around the room. Some of them were taking notes. "I love to visit the shrines and temples in this area." Then I listed them.

It was time. We were cruising together. I could say something special to the women's club.

"There is something that bothers me about U.S.–Japanese relations: we are not yet in true harmony with each other." I took a sip of water. A lot of heads were nodding seriously. "To me, however, there is one area where our governments and businesses are cooperating splendidly. Unfortunately, they are cooperating in the destruction of the earth. I think we could find in our cultures and in our hearts better ways to cooperate. There are ways you can help and things we can offer to keep this earth and her people strong and healthy. Each of us has special talents we could offer to help us live more lightly on the earth. Maybe what we need is the emergence of the feminine side as a cultural and political force to help bring this healing about."

I told them I feared the results of what the men in power were doing. "The earth is their toy to do battle on and to use up with economic games as if no children and grandchildren would follow. The time has come for you to step forward." I suggested that for a hundred years women run the businesses and the governments. Eyes lit up, backs straightened.

"It's like your PTAs. Yes, I know that many of them are run by the few men who come, and you have to go and sit and listen and never get to present your ideas. Maybe the men should have to come to the PTA and listen to you." (Applause.)

"Surely you would nurture the world," I told them, "if we could just keep the men in the kitchens. You can take turns with the kids. I know it's funny that I, a man, am saying this but I think I can explain. My neighbor, Ishitaki-san, who is a housewife and a strong, independent woman, helped me to write this talk and it was my feminine side that worked with her.

"And now it is time for me to sit down and let you take over—unless you have any comments or questions." A few hands were raised amidst the laughter and applause. There were no comments and all the questions were about the earlier parts of the talk, but afterwards a number of women thanked me privately for sharing my unusual thoughts about the role of women. They knew I was just stirring things up and didn't take me too literally. I may have believed it more than any of them.

CUT THE MŌZŌ

In sanzen Hōjō-san said, "Cut, cut, cut!" and "Fresh, fresh, fresh!" Then he elaborated. A lot of it went by me, but I think it went something like: Cut out your tired old thinking and let in the fresh always-new mind that is there waiting to be recognized. Leave behind the world of *mōzō*, of confusion and illusion, for the real world, which is the real me just sitting there waiting.

I nodded.

He said, "You're living in society, where it is difficult to practice. If you lived in the monastery you could be part of the rhythm and there wouldn't be all the confusion and distraction. In your life there is one thing after another tugging away at you. It is hard to concentrate on your koan. But there are times the mind is quiet and you can grab those moments to practice mu. And one day when you return to America, will you be a person without practice? You will have to continue pushing deeper and deeper in the midst of confusing, complicated social life." Something like that.

There's always so much I can't understand and so much I forget. He says not to worry, that my deeper mind is listening and will remember. I asked him if I could tape our sanzen in the future and study it and he said no. I thought of wiring myself, but remembered Brian De Palma's *Blow Out* and pictured the mike crackling or the recorder falling to the floor when I bowed and Hōjō-san hanging me by the light cord that I brush by in the morning.

Sometimes I run home to look up a word or phrase or catch Jessica after zazen and ask her about it. She'll give me a more relevant definition than any of my dictionaries, which might not have what I'm looking for at all. If I'm lucky she may elaborate on it before she has to run off to breakfast or I may walk with her on the diagonal dirt path through the temple grounds and find some gems of the immediate beneath the pines.

GOODBYE TO KATAGIRI

HŌGOJI, JUNE 6, 1988

Koji's brush moved from top to bottom, from right to left. My right hand guided a black felt-tip pen from left to right, top to bottom, while a small fuzzy white moth sat on the back of my left hand. It had been there for at least five minutes and was the delicate mascot of the moment. Breakfast had ended an hour before and we were writing letters, Koji to his parents and I to Elin. Katagiri was packing and we were letting Norman spend time with him alone. The schedule was on hold till Katagiri left. The moth remained.

Three sharp hits, a roll down and a final whack of the clackers sounded from the kuin deck. That was the signal for Katagiri's imminent departure. I got up slowly, keeping my left hand as still as I could. Koji came around and slid open the shoji, which had been closed to keep out the morning chill. I put my left hand out and the moth flew away.

Katagiri was on the deck in a soft brown traveling robe. He had on a brown cotton hat indented from front to back like a sergeant's headpiece. Suzuki used to wear one of those when he traveled. Norman had Katagiri's bag at his side. Shuko and Katagiri spoke a few words quietly. Jakushin and Maku walked up. Katagiri looked at each of us and said, "Thank you very much for your effort. Please take care of your practice." He gasshoed and we responded. Norman picked up his bag and they started down the steps into the sunlit courtyard.

A suzumebachi swooped down just past Katagiri and he looked up, startled and amused at the huge bee. Suddenly I was reminded that we exist in a living universe of infinite beings. Ladybugs were flying between us, small yellow butterflies above and the tiniest winged creatures were everywhere, moving in short spurts. It seemed there were more songbirds than ever that morning singing in the granddaddy oak, and sparrows pecking on the moss. The earth and air were full of spring life.

"Bye, Roshi. Thank you."

He looked at me smiling. "Goodbye, David." And then, reaching behind me to feel, "How's your back?"

"Oh, it's fine. It only bothered me the first week. It's been okay since then."

"Good." He patted my stomach. "Then take care of this."

"Thank you, Roshi, and you take care too," I said, smiling back as best I could.

They went off down the hill, Norman and my dear friend and teacher of so long. I would never see him again.

LSD NO, WHALE MEAT YES

HŌGOJI, JUNE 10, 1988

Have you ever had LSD?" Jakushin asked.

I was taken aback and remembered the evening at Ogawas' country house in the suburbs of Beppu. "Yes, but it's been over twenty years." I had been pleased that he'd wanted to talk. We'd never had a friendly conversation. Our exchanges tended to revolve around my trivial transgressions of temple etiquette. I felt uncomfortable with Jakushin and had never been able to figure out how to extend myself to him. We sat on the deck outside our room. He pulled a couple of cigarettes out of his sleeve—he'd never offered me one before.

"Can you get me any?"

"I don't know where . . ."

"Do you know anyone who could send it from America?"

"No, I don't," I immediately answered, and not in all honesty. It was very interesting that he asked, but no way was I going to get involved in something like that.

"I've taken it several times," he said. "But it's almost impossible to get."

"Yeah, I don't know," I said, wishing he'd talk about something else.

"Too bad."

"Do you have someone to take it with if you find it?"

"Yes. I have a friend at Suienji."

Wow, he has a friend. I was glad to hear it.

He asked me to wait a second, went into his room and came back with a book. "We use this," he said, handing it to me.

I looked at it. It was in Japanese, but seemed familiar. Ahhh. It was a translation of a book that had been big in the late sixties.

"Be Here Now," I said, surprised. "I can't believe it."

"Do you know it?" he asked.

"Oh yes," I said, "Quite well. It's a bit of history. Very interesting. Well, I don't know what to say. When you take it, are you quiet? Do you sit?"

"Yes, we sit and sometimes read from this book."

Nishiki would just die. I couldn't help but laugh.

Just then Koji came out of his cabin looking at his watch and told Jakushin that the bell for evening service was two minutes late. Jakushin excused himself quickly, thanking me, and went in to get his robes on. I told him I'd start it for him. Saved by the bonsho.

There was a three-day sesshin before I left Hōgoji—three days of just sitting, or "mind gathering," as it's sometimes translated. It was a perfect way to conclude my stay there. The calm following the ceremony had been a welcome period of relaxation and was good preparation for three days of doing nothing alertly. The sesshin schedule and positions were discussed at the morning tea the day before. Wake at three and sit all day in the zendo except for services, meals and half-hour breaks after the meals. I was used to forty-minute zazen periods, but, as usual, we could do *kinhin*, walking zazen, anytime. Since there was no senior priest leading the sesshin there would be no lectures or dokusan. Just us chickens.

Ten policemen from Beppu arrived on that day before the sesshin. They were young and strong, with short hair, and walked energetically into the hatto with a precision that made the Suienji monks look like bums. They changed into dark blue jumpsuits and assumed the seiza kneeling position, awaiting instructions like obedient Dobermans. I went out to look for Koji, who was on his way to greet them.

"I've got to give them a lecture. What should I say?"

"Tell them the opposite of what they expect," I said, "like the Sixth Patriarch suggested."

He stopped and looked down. "Hai," he said, and went on.

The sesshin officially began for us with the evening sitting before the three full days. During the sunset bell I walked from my room through the hatto to the zendo and paused to look out the open window into the courtyard. There was diligent Koji in his robes combing the courtyard into a novel scheme of thick parallel lines. He used an instrument I'd not seen before, a wooden rake that relied on fat dowels to divide the gravel into wide, deep valleys and high ridges. Toward the end of the second round of the han he ceased his energetic landscaping, slid the rake under the deck and leaped up the steps and into the hatto where I was. Before entering the zendo—on time—we stood for a final five-second appreciation of his efforts at nest building for the mind gathering to come.

After that evening sitting, the cops all stretched and groaned and rubbed their legs. Koji, playing the tough guy, yelled at them sharply to shut up and keep still. The zendo took on a samurai atmosphere till they were gone. I asked Koji after the sesshin why he had acted that way and he said they would have been disappointed if he were not strict.

"Hey, I told you not to give them what they expected."

"I'm sorry, that's the way we do it."

"Old habits die hard, huh?"

The cops brought whale meat as a donation to the sangha. When they departed after dinner the next evening, they left an envelope with ten separate ten-thousand-yen notes in it as a donation, about eight hundred dollars at the time. Down the hill they went in single file, never having spoken a word to anyone.

The sesshin was a real vacation. Monkey mind slowed down, emotions quieted, and the curtains of consciousness pulled back. I did my best to be a light unto myself and "just sit," as Katagiri had taught, "without trying to do zazen and without expectations." The problems of day-to-day life faded and I was filled with a wonderful feeling.

I guess it may appear out of balance to sit and follow one's breath all day—not exactly a natural daily life sort of practice. But if there's one thing I felt, it was balanced, which shows how out of kilter my daily life gets. During a sesshin the mind's clarity can be experienced as not different from the body. As the clock ticks or the incense burns, time becomes less of a thing, and space not so defined.

Dōgen might say that I had the zazen of demons. I know for sure that I didn't experience the "dropping away of body and mind" that he did one day in China. But he also said that taking the posture and practicing zazen *is* enlightenment. To me it just felt like your ten-cent deluded-student-of-the-Way type of zazen. Maybe I sat therapeutic zazen or not-zazen or just failed zazen. But I didn't sit there going "darn it, darn it, not enlightened yet" or anything like that. I worked that out of my system a while back.

There are a number of experienced teachers of meditation and zazen all over the world with whom one can study. Maybe they're more like guides than teachers. Some of them, like the formative ones I've had, don't say too much. A lot of practitioners say that one can't study zazen without a teacher. The teachers I've known definitely liked to have students and never seemed eager to let them go, but, at the same time, indicated we had to do it for ourselves. Indeed. All the books and teachers in the world can't do it for you. But one thing I *have* picked up from my teachers and fellow students is the joy of continuing this bumbling unseen path of me as I am and us as we are.

PART SEVEN   GOING

EDDY DUCHIN IN THE POST OFFICE

MARUYAMA, JANUARY 12, 1990

It was a cold day in Maruyama. I went into the post office carrying my shoulder bag. The small interior area for the public was crowded with about ten customers. There were two clerks behind the counter wearing thick glasses and methodically taking care of business. The man on the left was weighing letters and packages and selling stamps and the short thin lady on the right was doing cash transactions such as sending money and banking. A housewife was giving her an envelope full of ten-thousand-yen notes for deposit. Ishitaki says that postal savings interest is ridiculously low, but the tax people can't check accounts there, which is surely why they have the most money on deposit of any savings institution in the world. She says the rules aren't likely to be changed because the government depends on the funds.

There were four postcards in my bag. I got them out and stood third in the left line. They were unusual, made of paper-thin slices of cedar. The messages were brief. Even though my penmanship could qualify me for a special parking place, I wrote in *sumi* (black ink) with a thin brush. The cards were addressed to my mother, sister, Kelly and one to Katagiri in Minnesota. He was very sick with cancer.

I never know what to say to someone who is terminally ill, even someone in the mind-beyond-birth-and-death business, but I'd taken a stab at it. On Katagiri's card I'd written a message not rooted in Eastern tradition: Praying for your health, dear friend. Love, and my signature. I looked at it, sighed and hurt. I'd written him a few times since I'd known he had cancer. Mainly short, encouraging notes. He'd written me once. It was a sweet, sad, shakily handwritten letter that began by addressing me just like a lot of friends have: "Dear Chadwick," and the rest was in Japanese.

Thanks for your letter. Is it already warm in Japan where the uguisu calls? Minnesota is full of snow, but right now the weather is good. I feel like I'm getting better little by little. The characters in this letter are really poorly written, aren't they? Sayonara, Dainin Katagiri

I knew from Isabel's calls that he was pretty sick and getting the triple whammy: surgery, radiation and chemotherapy, which caused him to throw up all the time. I feel so bad about it and helpless. Damn. He deserves better.

I learned of his illness last winter. I remember that Isabel had gotten the times confused and had called at two in the morning. She should have known, she said—first about the time and then about Katagiri. The telltale signs were there. The doctors hadn't figured it out either and it had already metastasized. That's why he'd been coughing. From the first his prognosis was poor. I remember standing naked by the phone in the kitchen in below-freezing weather, waking up to Katagiri's cancer. Lots of people recover, I had reasoned to myself. Isabel did. She knows about standard Western treatment, alternative medicine, visualization and when to use what. She's also well versed in the arts of being with the dying and helping them in the last transition.

He'd already had so much grief. He'd had abdominal surgery toward the end of the war without the benefit of anesthetic. The doctor had told him to shut up when he cried in pain. In recent years there had been corrective surgery in that area. I'd thought maybe his illness was related to that old problem—but no. Another theory was that we'd broken his heart by not choosing him as the abbot of Zen Center in San Francisco a few years back. We'd sucked him into a power struggle he couldn't handle and found distasteful. It had been a messy, complicated process—a real demolition derby of cultures and personalities. We never should have talked to him about it before it was decided. We were reminded he had feelings. He was so angry and hurt. Maybe that did it. Who knows—nobody knows why.

An older man with glasses and thinning grey hair rose from his table in the back of the post office and came up to the counter to take care of the overflow. He's the manager—he wore a brown suit and tie instead of the blue postal uniform that the others wore. He doesn't speak as he takes care of people unless it's a point of information. The post office is a quiet place like other public institutions, without all the enthusiastic and customary greetings and farewells of the private sector. The service, however, is no less efficient or pleasant. He stuck his hand out and a short old lady in front of me in a grey kimono moved over and thrust her package up to him. I stared through them.

Katagiri's Buddhist name is Dainin, "great patience," and he shared that intangible quality with us in day-to-day life in the city and at Tassajara. The first time he had a sesshin of his own at Tassajara, while Suzuki Roshi was dying in the city, the scheduled zazen went around the clock. If I hadn't done it I'd never have known I could. We all could. We sat unmoving in silence without going to bed for a week. Every forty minutes there would be a ten-minute kinhin and there were lectures and services followed by meals and short breaks. But most of that week was spent cross-legged, just finding out a hint of what we are beyond our little boxes of unfolding thought. On the fourth night, during an unbroken two-hour period, it seemed to me as if all fifty of us had lifted anchor together and were effortlessly moving in eternity, our luminous sails full of silver wind.

In the back a phone was ringing. A little boy of maybe three who had been in the arms of a woman at the money window started crying and hitting her in the stomach with his fists when she put him down to conduct the transaction. A trembling old man, awkwardly swabbing glue on an envelope at the work table, looked at the kid. The fourth clerk, the only one without glasses or a customer, got up from his seat, went to the manager's desk and answered the phone. I was now second in line. A young woman in front of me was filling out a form with the help of the clerk, who was patiently answering her questions. I looked at the grain in Katagiri's card and polished it with finger oil.

Katagiri and Nishiki had studied with Hashimoto Roshi, a venerable and strict teacher at Eiheiji. Hashimoto was their *zuishin,* the master who cultivates and refines your understanding after you've received transmission from your original teacher. He was known for his emphasis on discipline and monastic rules. Katagiri had the honor of being the man's *anja,* one of his attendants. He said that when Hashimoto would ride in a train he'd sit bolt upright doing zazen for the whole trip. Katagiri deeply admired that example. I'd heard him mention it several times. I guess you had to be there. What I thought was thank goodness he himself wasn't that sort of person at heart—always leaving the world behind for emptiness. He was considerate and warm. I've taken him into coffee shops on the way to Tassajara—he'd catch people's attention because of his robes and someone might ask him a question. He wouldn't sit there like he was a statue in a zendo. He'd loosen up and start talking with the person next to him. There seemed to me to be a conflict between how he was taught he ought to be as a priest and his own natural way. And his original teacher was no good-time Charlie. Katagiri told me the guy never said a nice thing to him, only, "You are very stupid!" Happily, Dainin's soft side, his kind friendly nature, survived all the strict Zen training and the grueling lessons of the war.

A tinny tune came from the post office phone's exterior speaker. The clerk had put the caller on hold and was leafing through a large book. One never gets the pleasure of silence when put on hold. There's always a tune and always the cute toy notes. Usually it's something like "Home on the Range" or "When the Saints Go Marching In." Elin and I liked ours at home—a choice of "A Taste of Honey" or "Take Five." But our local post office had more class. The most compelling of telephone waiting music themes was playing, a classic schmaltzy piece that evoked memories from as far back as my infancy. I think of it as the "Eddy Duchin theme" because I remember it from the movie *The Eddy Duchin Story*. My mother would occasionally play it on the piano or the victrola from the time when I was a baby, but I didn't start being a snob about it until the sixth grade, when it became the movie theme. It was one of those movies that made all the girls cry. One time it had filled the postal air while I was waiting to buy some stamps and talking to one of my English students, a piano teacher.

"There's the Eddy Duchin theme," I said.

"The what?" she said.

"The Eddy Duchin theme," I repeated. "That music, from the phone."

"Is that what you call it in America? We call it Chopin's Nocturne in E flat Major, opus 9, no. 2."

"Oh yes, of course, that's the real name," I said.

I remembered the dark theater on Saturday, the noon matinee, snickering with the other boys at the sad parts of the movie, like when Eddy Duchin's wife dies, and waiting for the girls to stop sobbing so we could go back and try to make out again.

On one of his many visits to the Bay Area from Minneapolis Katagiri came to Green Gulch Farm for a week. Elin was in Taiwan and I had been overwhelmed with missing her. Katagiri and I took a walk and had a couple of friendly visits in his room, but when I saw him in dokusan the social world was left behind. We sat in a small room lit by a candle and fragrant with subtle Japanese incense.

"You have stopped running from your suffering," he said softly. "You know now that we all suffer. You have become more compassionate, which means you are including others in your practice. Now deepen. Buddhism is a two-edged sword, wisdom and compassion. Keep both edges sharp. Take it with you wherever you go and there is nothing you cannot meet with deep joy." There was nothing new or clever or exciting in what he said. I guess it was the timing. In that moment I felt more than friendship, I felt something we don't talk about much, a deep connection between us—love, a love that we all arise out of.

The clerk picked up the phone—the music stopped. The postmaster called to me that it was my turn.

"Oh, excuse me," I said, stepped over and handed him the thin wooden postcards bound for the States. He stuck out his bottom lip and looked them over. "I got them in Kyoto," I told him. "Interesting, aren't they?"

"Interesting, aren't they?" he replied appropriately while accepting my money. He handed me the change and waved me off, signifying that he'd mail them for me. I thanked him quickly and walked out awash in nostalgic associations and emotions I had not asked for.

PRISONER OF PEACE

HŌGOJI, JUNE 15, 1988

Maku was pulling out tiny spring weeds that were popping up in the gravel of the courtyard. He worked with a young Japanese wanderer who had spent the night and was joining us for the morning samu. Koji seemed to have a low opinion of this scruffy, bearded fellow but knew we couldn't refuse him a night's stay. With his long hair and single earring, his appearance certainly differed from ours. Koji went off to work alone so he could keep his huff to himself.

Norman and I were clearing out grass and dirt from a wooden drainage trough. We were talking temple politics again. "I was so fed up I was thinking of leaving after the practice period and going to Shinbōji," he said. "Katagiri said it was up to me. He's had other students go there. The roshi is a good teacher, I hear. But I can't do it. It would embarrass Katagiri—and me too."

This was not the first time Norman had brought up the subject of leaving. "You're gonna stay then?" I asked, as I scooped up a spadeful of mud.

"Yep, another year or two. I think Shuko and I can work this out. They need me—they need a foreigner. They've had two foreigners leave Suienji because they couldn't hack it. There was a Canadian guy who'd been in Japan five years and studied Zen in Tokyo. His Japanese was fluent—he'd studied Soto texts in the original. His teacher sent him to Suienji and even after he'd been there a year they didn't count his seniority when they handed out positions. They always had some excuse, like his Japanese had too strong an accent. All the Japanese moved through the training strictly according to their seniority, regardless of ability. Ask Koji—no, never mind, don't. Or do. But all he'll say is that his

Japanese wasn't good enough. That's what I mean. There's a bamboo ceiling. Finally he left, disgusted. His teacher was furious with them, but didn't complain. Another student of Katagiri's left after a month and went to Shinbōji. He read the writing on the shoji. As for me, I've read it and torn the paper off the frame and stuffed it in my mouth and eaten it and thrown it up and I still haven't left. I've come this far—it's important that I stay."

"I can appreciate why a Westerner would want to practice at Hōgoji for a little while, say, half a year," I said. "The practice here feels good, even though it seems there's not a good teacher for foreigners, at least not after Katagiri leaves. But what about Suienji?"

"Suienji was not the perfect training temple that I had envisioned, with serene monks gliding through the schedule. It was a reality sandwich. The training wasn't what I wanted at all. It was a lot of priestcraft—all geared toward learning ceremonies and how to run a funeral business. Zazen was always being canceled for one reason or another. It's the central practice of Zen, but at Suienji it was like an afterthought. It seemed to me that most of the monks were proud of their position, lazy, stupid, greedy, angry, confused, or some combination. Mainly they were the sons of temple priests putting in their obligatory training time so that they could follow in daddy's footsteps. They listened to radios, drank at night and had pinups on the wall.

"What they were really into, though, was power trips. It's what got them off. You wouldn't believe it. The senior monks were always pushing around the junior monks, who in turn were pushing around the ones that came after them. Sometimes it would seem like everyone was getting pushed around or making somebody else grovel. The ones doing the lording-over would growl and the ones groveling would grunt. I saw them as bears and pigs all growling and grunting at each other. And then one day I heard a growl starting to come out of my throat and I ran and hid in the *tōsu*.

"Curious thing, though, after being here at Hōgoji for two

months I went back to Suienji for a couple of weeks and, what-do-ya-know, I got all excited. I felt like a kid who'd been away at camp and was going home. The train goes right by the temple and I recognized the area and felt all tingly and when I saw the temple rooftops above the trees coming around a corner, I started to cry. It's funny, the things I valued didn't necessarily come wrapped the way I might have expected. I knew the b.s. through and through, but when I returned, I found it didn't bother me. I saw my fellow monks in a different light. Some of the older priests were so wise and kind and many of the younger ones were my friends. They welcomed me back and it was good to see them. They have a system of correcting each other a lot that gets on my nerves, but that time I appreciated it more. It's just a different way of being together. Finally I was happy to take it like it was. Anyone could practice in a dream temple. I had to learn to practice in a real one."

Norman tied his work boots. "But I'm still an American progressive egalitarian at heart and a thorn in their zafu. They need me here to help them figure out how to relate to foreigners, how to include us as equals. They might not listen to me, but my very presence will give them some hints."

"Yeah, like a club over the head. What about when you do go?"

"Others will come to take my place."

I glanced over to make sure no one was listening. "I've got a suggestion in case you keep running into trouble with Shuko," I almost whispered, "or any Japanese monk."

"What is it?"

"I had a geometry teacher in the tenth grade who was in a Japanese POW camp where eighty-five percent of the prisoners died. I learned my first Japanese from him. He used to say, takusan shigoto, lots of work—that's what they always told him in the camp. He said the prisoners were all skinny and weak and that the guards were old guys who would do things like load a giant bag of rice on their backs and if they fell they got bayonetted.

He said that if the guards didn't like someone's attitude they'd cut his head off and hang it on the fence. Why don't you pretend you're in a Japanese prison-of-war camp and that if there is discord, for whatever reason, they will cut your head off."

"Good idea," he said rubbing his chin. "And Shuko can pretend that he's been captured by the CIA in Vietnam and if I get irritated he just might fall out of a helicopter. You might suggest that to him?"

After lunch Norman and I stood on the path in front of the stupa. The sky was blue and full of billowy white clouds. A gentle warm wind wafted up the valley. Yoshiko and Miki-obāsan were weeding not far away. Behind us the wanderer was sitting on the stupa steps reading before taking off with his backpack into the mountains. Across the valley, a huge truck was unloading a bulldozer on the narrow gravel road that cut across the side of the mountain. I followed the power lines from the mountain's distant tower back to the ridge above us. In between, swallows were dancing in the air and a hawk circled. I could hear scrapes from the shoveling of a farmer below us.

Just then Norman tugged at my sleeve. There were two black butterflies on the edge of the lawn. One of them was flying up and down and the other was on the grass making jerking motions. A stretch of spider web was stuck to one of its legs and there was a twig on the other end of the twisted silken thread. The butterfly was dragging this anchor around. Norman motioned me to be still, then very slowly moved in on the hobbled butterfly. I held my breath, knowing that if he touched it he could damage it so that it couldn't fly. He grabbed the string of web. The butterfly was flapping for high heaven and Norman the giant was moving closer. He put his finger just a smidgen below the creature's leg and pinched the burden off. Immediately the butterfly was in the air. It flew around Norman's face and took off with its partner.

A CHAT WITH KOJI

As the day for me to leave approached, Koji and I spent more and more time together. We stayed up late the last couple of nights talking. He helped me mark a map of Japan with all the places I wanted to go. We were serious at times and silly at times, but I couldn't make him fall down anymore, the novelty had worn off.

One good thing we did was to swear off tobacco. We were starting to get hooked on the demon weed. Maybe what did it was the night we were drinking cooking sake from the kitchen. We drank the bottle up and talked and smoked so much that the next day we were coughing and totally disgusted with ourselves and vowed to stop playing around with the world's most dangerous drug. I started to give the rest of the pack to Jakushin, but Koji suggested we throw it away instead. We had a slight altercation when he threw it in the burnable trash and I pointed out that there were synthetics in the filters and the wrapper. We finally compromised by tearing the filters off, throwing them into the unburnable can with the wrapper and dumping the shredded remains in the compost.

One morning after breakfast, while Koji looked through his address book for a few names, I mentioned how content Norman seemed to be recently and attributed this to the soothing effects of the sesshin.

"I don't think that's it," said Koji. "He changed when Katagiri left. For some reason he showed his worst side to Katagiri. I couldn't understand that."

"He sure didn't keep it in like some nationalities I know," I said.

"You Americans and your idea of 'working things out,' " he said, shaking his head.

"Katagiri can deal with it."

"I admire him for that." He stared for a moment and repeated what he had said the first time he'd talked to me about Katagiri. "To me he's a real emptiness teacher."

Koji looked away from his address book. "I wanted to have dokusan with Katagiri."

"Why didn't you ask?"

"I was afraid that Norman would be jealous."

"He would have been happy," I said, irritated.

"You think so?"

"Of course. That's ridiculous, Koji. Why do you keep denying yourself what you want?"

"I guess I was wrong. Next time."

Koji gave me the addresses and phone numbers of three friends of his I should look up in different parts of Japan and I transferred them into my address book and onto the map.

"Well, they've both gone to town," I said, while trying to make out the kanji he used, and then, "Help me romanize this, huh?"

"Who've gone?" he said, reaching for his pen.

"Shuko and Norman."

"Oh yeah, to clear up a problem with Norman's insurance."

"Uh-huh, which Norman says Shuko screwed up in the first place."

"Oh no," Koji shook his head.

"Don't worry. Norman wasn't so concerned about that. He said that he wanted them to talk about their problem in general."

"Japanese would just never speak to each other again."

"Well, Norman wouldn't accept that and Shuko knows they have to live together. Norman is determined," I added. "He said that either they'd work it out or Shuko would come back stuffed in the three-inch pipe that they've got to buy for the kitchen."

THE TYRANT OF NARA

HŌGOJI, JUNE 17, 1988

I was leveling the gravel in the courtyard while Koji carefully raked the delicate moss islands, one with a decaying stump, two with young cherry trees and two islands that are bare but for their soft green mats. I was bringing renegade pebbles from stepping stones and the edge of the moss blankets back into the flock. Then I drew the gathered gravel hills into the valleys, equalizing the distribution. Koji had taught me two verbs for "to level": *taira suru* and *narasu*. I repeated a phrase over a few times. "The tyrant of Nara is on the level."

"What's that?" said Koji.

"The tyrant of Nara is on the level," I repeated.

"What does it mean?" he asked.

"It's how I remember that 'taira' and 'narasu' mean 'to level,' " and I pointed out to him the similarity in the sounds.

"Got any others?"

"Yeah, like I kept forgetting *bessu*." (Bessu are traditional Japanese socks that we wear for ceremonies. I've only seen them in white. They're like *tabi* except without the separate compartment for the toe.) "Ready?"

"Hai."

"Bess and Sue went down the street, with their bessu on their feet." That took a little explaining.

"Do you do this with all the words you learn?" he asked, looking at me as if I were a little peculiar.

"As many as possible."

"Doesn't that give you more to remember?"

"I think the brain likes it that way. The more ways we can tie things together, the better we remember."

"Then we will remember each other well," he said.

. . .

At the tea break Norman was telling me how things went with him and Shuko the day before on their trip to town. It sounded like they'd resolved some sore points. Norman got Shuko to admit to consistent transgressions, a minor miracle, and Norman owned up that he let things get to him too much, that he had a problem with anger. Instead of each attempting to gain an advantage over the other they promised to work together toward harmony.

"That's very noble of you, Norman."

"Noble schmoble. The problem is putting it into practice. But I'm gonna try, I'm really gonna try and I think he will too. It's been a lose-lose situation. We both keep thinking the other guy is wrong, but if we can't live in peace with each other then we're both wrong."

I asked Norman if there was historical precedence for his dilemma in the Buddha's lifetime.

"Oh yeah, everything you can imagine happened within the Buddha's sangha and they had all sorts of ways to deal with it, including dhyana (meditation). It's how the rules developed—one by one in response to real issues that came up." Norman went on to explain that in time the Vinaya, the rules and regulations, became as important as dhyana. That situation is considered a major obstacle in itself. Before Buddha died he told them not to stick too hard to the rules, especially the long list of precepts— just be flexible and recite the short list. "He could already see what the anal retentives could do with guidelines."

Norman laughed.

"What's so funny?"

"Buddha was once asked something like, 'If you're so perfect then why is there discord in the sangha?' and he said that it was because he'd hit a fish on the head in a previous life."

"A fish, huh?"

"Yeah, wonder what Shuko and I did."

"Whatever it was, may I extend my best wishes to both of

you in your endeavor to sever all your ancient twisted karma."
He raised his teacup. "I'll drink to that."

A VISIT AND A CALL

MARUYAMA, MARCH 1, 1990

What shall we have for dinner tonight?" said Norman from the kitchen. He'd been staying with us for a week and had been doing much of the cooking.

"Whatever you want," came my reply from the living room where I was playing with a pocket-sized, computerized Japanese-English translator and sitting in my favorite chair, the high-backed, soft rocker. Norman had been sprawled on the rattan sofa just a moment before, reading some Chinese poetry in English translation. The sofa was obviously not designed with somebody his size in mind, especially in the prone position. Now he was looking in the fridge. This was a good sign. I was getting hungry too.

"How about noodles?" he said.

"Sounds great to me," said Elin, coming in from the garden. She looked at me and winked. Norman always makes noodles for dinner: *soba,* which are buckwheat noodles; *udon,* which are thick white wheat noodles; or *somen,* which are thin white wheat noodles. He cooks them just as they do at Hōgoji, where they always eat noodles for dinner. He prepares little dishes of condiments to go with them, like chopped scallions, a plate of crisp seaweed sheets to crush, raw egg or a special type of raw potato goo that's all whipped up. This week he's our Japanese housewife.

After dinner Elin took a bike over to the convenience store

and got some ice cream. When she got back, I was cleaning the stove top and Norman was doing calligraphy. My calligraphy teacher had flipped over his work when I brought him to class. Every time I go there now she looks at the first thing I do and asks me how Norman is. She said his was the best calligraphy she'd ever seen by a Westerner. He beamed with pride. I bet no one ever praised him in the monastery like she did.

I hadn't seen Norman for almost two years, since I left Hōgoji. We'd been talking about everything that came to mind concerning ourselves, Buddhism and Katagiri. When I was busy he would read, do calligraphy, watch baseball or sumo on TV or take walks in the hills behind the temple. I set aside my studies for the week he was there so we could spend time together. We went cycling and saw the most interesting temples, gardens and shrines in the area, following a public bicycle path that led into the countryside through rice fields and by virgin woods.

The dark cloud over the week was the news that Katagiri's condition had deteriorated. He was on his death bed now. He had given Norman and eleven others transmission in America a few weeks back. "Transmission" is a ceremony that signifies that the teaching has been passed mind to mind, from teacher to student. Katagiri asked Norman to go right back to Japan afterwards so he could go through with a few ceremonies that he needed to have under his belt in order to have the proper credentials to be a teacher and head of his own temple. It wasn't imperative that he do so, because those credentials only apply in Japan, but it was part of maintaining good relations with and further experiencing the source system for better or for worse. He'd just finished off four years of practice at Suienji and Hōgoji by leading the chanting of the Ryaku Fusatsu ceremony at the home temple. He'd had a long, late evening talk with Godō Roshi, the old priest who had been his confidant and adviser. Godō told Norman to go back home, start his own temple and to forget about Japan for ten years.

The next morning, before Norman had left Suienji, he had met with Nishiki. They discussed the future relationship between Soto Zen in Japan and America. Nishiki implied that Katagiri's Minneapolis group wasn't mature enough to run itself without him. Norman made it very clear that if he had anything to do with it, there would be no control at all on it from the Japanese end. He said American Zen students didn't want all the Japanese baggage —they just wanted to sit and live sane lives. Nishiki wouldn't understand this, Norman said, because he just teaches monks the ceremonies and forms that they need to get their certificates. Norman said he got all worked up and was pacing and shaking a pointed finger at Nishiki, who remained seated. Assuming an elevated position over a person of higher status is specifically prohibited in Dōgen's writings, and even without considering Dōgen it's like breaking a taboo. Norman said that Nishiki's attendants were horrified. I wish I'd been a fly on the bull in that china shop.

After a scrumptious noodle dinner we enjoyed a congenial evening, sitting in the living room. Elin left us to our shop talk and retired to the bedroom to read. The conversation returned to Hō-goji and Suienji and the difficulties that he'd had there.

"I know that it hurt Katagiri Roshi to see the way I fought them over here. He just wanted me to look and learn, to absorb how they do things, how the priest and laity relate and to try to live in harmony with others. I did my best and there was a lot of harmony at times, but at other times . . ."

Yes, those "other times." I remembered the day of the big spring *hōyō*. Norman had been energetically preparing the altars for the ceremony. He knew just what to do. But it seemed as though every time he put a vase with flowers on the right side of an altar, there was Shuko moving it to the left. After the ceremony he grabbed me and asked me to take a walk with him. I could tell by his grip that it was imperative. I was happy to get out of there and so we went way up above Hōgoji and stood on a dirt road above a rice field looking down over the marvelous valley below.

"I am so furious and I am tired of being furious. I am a monk, not a psychotic killer. I try meditating on loving kindness. I try letting the anger come and go. And still sometimes I am overcome with rage. What do you think it is like to go to zazen and to have incessant images of smashing someone's brains out with a baseball bat?"

"It must keep you awake," I said.

"Yeah, it does that and a hell of a lot more."

"How about Abhidharma? There are specific practices for overcoming unwholesome passions. What is it you hate? A person is only an aggregate of elements and factors. There's no *being* to hate. Right? There are no bad people, just bad acts."

"I try that too. What is it that I hate? Do I hate his fingernails or his hair, skin, bones and so forth. It works for about two seconds and then I start thinking that yes, I hate his fingernails and his hair and his guts and his . . ."

"Oh, I'm sorry. Maybe a vacation . . ."

"Yes, maybe a permanent vacation. For him."

"No no, Norman, that would interfere with Katagiri's plans for you."

"I know, I know. Don't take me seriously. I just need to blow off steam. Don't worry about me. I've never even hit anyone in my life."

"Have you ever been angry at anyone like this before?"

"Just my ex-wife."

"You see, it proves my theory that you were married to Shuko in a past life. Except I guess it's more like you're married in this life, so to speak."

"Well, I want a divorce. It keeps me awake and it drives me crazy. I want to grab him and scream in his face until his ears are bleeding. I want to scream at him that I am not a baby! I am a man! I am a grown man! I can do things! I can decide things! I can take responsibility! He won't let me hang a picture without him moving it to another place! If I do anything innovative in the kitchen he'll tell me not to make it again. He denies every suggestion. There is nothing I can offer! He is not my teacher! He has no right to do this! I am tired of it and I am tired of wanting to smash his brains out!"

And with this, Norman began to scream at the top of his lungs out over the valley. He screamed with the voice of a giant and with the passion of an angry titan. He screamed until the distant mountains shook and until there was no anger but just pure sound, and then he started crying and he sat down on the ground and grabbed my ankle and sobbed. I'm not so good at comforting people but I put my hand on his shoulder. I hoped no one was rushing up from the temple. After a minute his storm was over and his rain stopped. He groaned. Then he stood up and wiped his eyes.

"Thank you," he said. "Now let's go steal some of that sake the guests are drinking." We walked back down and did just that.

Now Norman walked to the shoji, opened them and looked out on our garden, bare in winter and illuminated by the front porch light. He had been saying how Katagiri must have been disappointed in him.

"We all have trouble, Norman. Katagiri had a lot of grief with the system here too. He wanted you to learn something from it, but I doubt if he expected you to be an angel. We all drag through the muck as best we can."

"But you're not angry. You guys have a pretty harmonious life here and seem to have a good relationship with the temple," he answered.

I laughed. "Yes, but Norman, we have distance. We are living next door. We have each other. We are not trying to be one of them, or should I say, two of them. It's pretty obvious that the extent to which foreigners suffer here is the extent to which they try to belong. Japanese don't even accept their own who have been tainted by the West. Ishitaki-san says that the standards of behavior here are so narrow and demanding that the greatest insecurity of Japanese people is that they're not Japanese enough.

"Poor Shuko. He has it worse than you do. Did you ever consider that? He's been contaminated by too much contact with the West." Japanese who get the smell of the West on them have trouble getting jobs, they get ridiculed in school. The ones that have lived abroad are called "returnees," but "pariahs" might be more accurate from what I've heard. Shuko is like a man without a country. He's a trailblazer in Japan's struggle to be less insular.

"And you know what's funny? You were the only friend he had. His problem was that he dumped on you like he'd been dumped on. It's an old story. Garbage in—garbage out. He was more helpful in the States where he could forget the Japanese roles and rules."

"It was tough for us," Norman said. "Our hassling always brought me face to face with my own defects and it ain't a pretty picture. So much anger. At Shuko and at the system and at . . . who knows? The only redeeming aspect of the anger was to show me what elements of the Japanese system I don't want to see incorporated into American Buddhism. Since I've been away from Hōgoji and Suienji, it's been easier to see the good points. Even though I gripe a lot, if you just look at the faces of the guys who've been around you can see how the practice softens them. I suppose even learning to absorb and deal with the macho b.s. can be helpful. Sort of like meat tenderizer. Brother, if you can come out of one of these places without getting your psyche twisted, the results can be quite desirable. But it's the rare Westerner who can do that. It's going to take me a long time to heal."

.   .   .

Late that evening we got a phone call from the States. It brought the sad and inevitable news that we had been waiting for. Katagiri Roshi had died. A few days before, he had rejected any further treatment. "The body has suffered enough," he had said. Norman and I sat zazen and did a service. Afterwards he cried for a while. I felt callous that I didn't cry. My dear friend and teacher of twenty-three years was dead and I just sat in my easy chair depressed and not knowing what to do.

WE REMEMBER KATAGIRI

MARUYAMA, MARCH 2, 1990

I've come to understand him a lot better since I've been over here in Japan," Norman said to me the day after Katagiri's death as we walked around the pond behind Daianji, its water chilly and still. "Katagiri came from a place where the hallmarks of education are conformity and control and where initiative is discouraged, where the sense of adventure is null, where there's no questioning and you have to follow the teacher to the letter, and where there's only one correct answer for any question. He came to a place where initiative and nonconformity are valued, where people having control over one's life is not ideal. He came to a place where he needed pioneer spirit and he didn't know what it was. It must have been extremely difficult for him to go to the States and to try to do what he wanted to do there, given where he came from. He moved from the predictable to the unpredictable. He left Japan to get away from the rigidity of the inbred Zen scene. It was fresh in America, but we were like a bunch of puppies cavorting around, undisciplined, unencumbered and uncouth."

"Enthusiastic and crazy," I agreed.

"That we were. So I've come to appreciate his troubles there a lot more. Unfortunately he got cancer and died and his death seems to me to have been caused at least in part by the difficulties he had in adjusting. I think that's the inescapable consequence of having your guts wrenched all the time by being ill-prepared for your mission in life and not knowing what to do. But the fact that he didn't know what to do caused him to open up a lot more and to drop away a lot of the crap that goes with being a roshi in Japan. That's why we loved him so much, not only because he was so kind and gentle, but because he was informal and willing to be a true spiritual friend.

"Do you remember when we were at Hōgoji how he'd come out on the porch and have tea with us in his kimono? The Japanese monks wouldn't know what to do with him. Nishiki would never have been so informal. The status distinction between the teacher and the taught was always primary with him. There was no such gap with Katagiri Roshi.

"Before Katagiri Roshi came to Hōgoji, Nishiki Roshi told me he was going to be different over here in Japan. So I said, 'Do you mean he's going to be like a Japanese roshi?' and Nishiki said, 'Yes, he'll have to be.' After his arrival, when I offered him a stick of incense at the hatto altar, he looked at me and smiled and I realized right then that he'd changed too much in his time in America. He would meet people just where they were and love them for who they were, and not for something he could make them into. He would suggest things, but he wouldn't put on any pressure. He knew that to have profound changes come about, you have to willingly do them by yourself."

We had walked around the pond slowly. I hadn't said much of anything. I also had memories of Katagiri, but I let them lie.

Norman was his disciple and needed to talk. I was numb and sad and needed to listen. We sat on a large rock at pond's edge and broke twigs for a while and then walked up to where the local royalty is entombed. We moped around going "duh" and "uh" and kicking the dirt with our zori. Katagiri was gone and we had been left only with ourselves and the practice of being a light unto ourselves, and our batteries were low. His answer to so many questions had been silence, or "I don't know." His teaching was simply to continue practicing and to find things out for ourselves.

Just like when Suzuki Roshi died; some of the little lies and games we played with ourselves were exposed. The myths we perpetuated and nourished without examining: fairy tales about our teachers. As the child makes super beings out of parents, the student of the Way makes an idol of the teacher. If this phase is not grown out of, the disciple suffers, for this idol is not of stone, but of flesh. Flesh that dies and decomposes and leaves you completely.

"I'll tell you a funny story about Katagiri Roshi," said Norman. "Setting up the altar correctly and straight is considered important, and it's the first thing you notice when you're leading service. Katagiri used to say, 'Don't be cricket. Line up straight, don't be cricket.' One day at Tassajara when I was jisha, I couldn't help but notice, as I handed Katagiri Roshi the incense, that the altar had been horribly set up. The *chiden* (who tends to the altar) was an older fellow who wasn't so good at those sorts of details. The side sticks of incense were at forty-five degree angles, the flowers looked like they'd been put together by Attila the Hun, and the ashes were a mess. After service, after he had made his final bows at the altar, Katagiri Roshi stood looking at the altar rather than going to his seat for lunch. He turned around to the students who were standing in gassho to make the final bow of the service and he unexpectedly launched into a stern lecture about the importance of attending to details, going on and on about making things neat and straight, about preciseness and clarity. The sloppy altar had brought it to his mind, but it was more than that, he said. It meant being aware of what you were doing at all times. 'If you can't line up everything straight on the altar then your life won't be straight. Your life comes out of your practice. When we set up the altar, we set up the dharma world. And it is this way with every detail of our lives. If the details of each moment are not attended to then you are not practicing the Buddha's way. What are you here for? Are you here to be careless and mindless?' He went on like that for about five or ten minutes and everybody was standing and waiting to get started with lunch. When he finished talking, the final bell was rung to end service and then he stepped down, turned around and walked out, completely forgetting that it was time to eat lunch. I followed him out and asked him if he intended to eat in his cabin. With an 'Oh,' Katagiri Roshi started to walk back. I suggested that his prior point might have more impact if he let me bring his lunch to him."

At the point when the guru is dead we may try to bring him or her back in one way or another, talking to her, seeing him as watching over us, or whatnot. I suppose it's a way to look for them in ourselves. But I have heard people talk about various situations that came about after a guru's death as if that teacher had known all along exactly what was going to happen. This is a way to try to resurrect the teacher. To talk about how great the teacher was is another way. The "Oh, my teacher was so great" talk puts us in a musty room filled with cobwebs. I too, of course, am guilty of it because my teachers have impressed me, but I know I've got to leave them behind. It's like saying, "I'm great because they were great and I was with them." Innocence by association. But I *am* great and you *are* great. Forget about them.

There's an old warning against confusing the great wonderful Absolute Truth with the teacher, which goes, "Don't confuse the finger pointing to the moon with the moon." It's as if a fellow came along who pointed to the moon and we just stared at this gentle, kind Oriental man in his brown robe and went, "Wow, far out!" and then he fell over dead and we cried and said words of praise about him and walked off talking about him and never noticed the moon. So here we are all walking around in the moonlight, mumbling and grumbling and bumping into each other. We are a silly lot.

Another thing we do, when we go on babbling about how great our teacher's understanding was, is we imply that we are qualified to appraise their understanding. This seems arrogant. When I first met Katagiri and watched him fiddling with his pencil and wondered if an enlightened person would do that and he told me that a teacher was beyond the student's judgment, he wasn't telling me that he and Suzuki were beyond karma or making mistakes. He didn't mean that they could have a burglary ring going that I should ignore because their every act was perfect buddha dharma. To me, what he was saying was, "Don't look at me, look at the moon."

We do not know what their understanding was. There is no reason to say they were enlightened, whatever that means, or that they were anything other than our spiritual friends or good friends.

What Suzuki and Katagiri learned and knew, I do not know. I learned from them to have confidence in zazen while sitting, standing and walking, as it is traditionally said. I am thinking and commenting on these people because that is the subject now, but in my life today, I am just as encouraged by family members and my mutually irritating fellow students and by living peers who have all sorts of ways and practices as by the memory of the Japanese teachers whom I have known and loved.

"Katagiri Roshi used to love to mow the grass at Hokyoji, our monastery in the country," Norman said as we walked back home, "It's one of my fondest memories of him. There were acres of it and he loved to hop up on that tractor and mow it all. I remember that when Nishiki Roshi came to Hokyoji with Shuko-san, Katagiri Roshi was out there mowing the lawn, so I ran out into the field and stopped him and said that they were waiting up at the cabin and Katagiri said, 'Well I'm busy right now, I'll talk to them later.' I was shocked. He revered Nishiki Roshi. But he'd forgotten everything—he'd lost himself in the mowing. That's where he is in my memory—on that tractor, too busy for us now. He's done what he had to do, met whom he had to meet and said what he had to say. He's just mowing away out in those fields and we should let him be."

GETTING WET TOGETHER

HŌGOJI, JUNE 17, 1988

There are moments that cut through the pettiness of day-to-day life and the confusion of social existence. They don't always come during religious rituals or in the elusive depths of meditation. On a clear, warm day after cutting enough firewood for a month of baths, Norman, Shuko, Koji and I, sweaty and invigorated from the day's physical labor, went to the creek in the ravine. Our quartet crossed the road above Hōgoji and took a narrow dirt path that descended to the water's brink. There we walked over two logs that bridged the creek. Shuko and Koji were in *geta*, wooden platform sandals, which are unbelievably impractical when not on level ground. I watched them negotiating the steep dirt path and the rocks and then finally the logs.

"It's like mountain climbing with stilts," I said to Norman.

"Or threading a needle with gloves on," he responded.

We walked down the rocks, gravel and sand on the other side and took off our clothes by a small, clear pool below a short waterfall. The two Japanese monks discreetly held their hands before their genitals as is the custom and bathed themselves from the edge while Norman and I plunged in, sending a tidal wave down their way. It was cold. We bobbed in the deep, rolled over under the surface and sat so the cascade of the falls pounded our heads. We beckoned our comrades to join us from where they waded ankle high, scooping their cupped hands down to bring up splashes of cold water.

A twenty-foot-high stone wall, covered by moss, rose on the side of the creek we were on. I had thought we were in such a remote place. According to Norman, the ground up there once supported a rice paddy, but now there are cedars like the ones planted all over these mountains to be harvested for charcoal and lumber. Above us on the other side are rows of *kunugi* logs. They were a yard long and stacked upright, leaning crisscrossed against each other in a line up the steep hillside. Shiitake mushrooms were growing out of the bark in the shade of the cedars. A small mountain crab ran sideways across a slippery rock. Tiny wild flowers were growing on the embankment.

So there we were, Norman and Shuko who weren't into their squabbling brothers routine, and Koji and me who weren't off to ourselves having an intense conversation. We weren't alone studying, each in his niche, and we weren't following the schedule with the rest. At this unusual moment, the four of us were just having a pleasant time, not talking much and not being entirely quiet either. Shuko pointed out a configuration of lichen on the side of a stone. Norman said that this may have been the spot where Daigyo Zenji washed his face with the stars. It was a complete moment, a time unto itself with no particular meaning or accomplishment—no one-upsmanship or culture wars. The sunlight streaked in through the trees toward the end of the hot afternoon. We forgot our own naked bodies and the futures we had planned for ourselves. A *yamabato* cooed from a high branch.

The distant knell of a deep resonating bell wafted softly through the air. Each of us listened, absorbing the vibrations.

"Mellow," I murmured, while floating in the cold water.

"So clear, even down here," said Norman, squatting on a stone island.

"Mmmmm," intoned Shuko.

"Evening service!" said Koji standing up, reminding us that we had forgotten the meaning in the sound. We quickly dried off with washrag-sized towels, threw on our clothes, ran over the rocks and the logs and leaped up the dirt path and onto the asphalt road down to Hōgoji's entrance steps, which we vaulted in our plastic zori and wooden geta, scrambling back to get our robes on. We arrived at the hatto, panting, just before the third round ended. Koji placed the incense in the smooth ash plain of the large incense pot before the altar. A few gongs of the brass bowl-shaped bell and we were off chanting the Dai Hi Shin Dharani, an invocation whose roots go back to pre-Buddhist Hindu magic incantations. It asks for mercy for all beings. I stood in the room, eyes unfocused, feeling love for my good dharma brothers. We chanted to the thump of the wooden fish and forgot the magic moment in the creek.

A FINAL SURPRISE

HŌGOJI, JUNE 19, 1988

Hey, Norman, thanks for everything." It was after breakfast and he was at his desk, painstakingly writing a letter in textbook-quality kanji. I was out on the deck, all packed. I'd sent two large bags ahead the day before, and I was ready to go with a light load.

"Sure you don't want to stay two more days?" he asked. "A bunch of new monks from Suienji are coming to town tomorrow and Shuko and I are gonna go out on takuhatsu with them."

"Oh no, I'm all raring to go. I'm going to spend the night with the logger, the one I met when I first arrived at Kikuoka. I'll drop a dime in your cup. But don't look at me. It's forbidden."

"Okay. Thank you. You've been a lot of help. I'm sorry to have put you through so much."

"It was great, my pleasure. I hope everything works out. As soon as I know where I'll be living I'll let you know so you can come for R 'n' R."

"Please do. Will Elin be there?"

"Looks like it. Our correspondence has taken a distinctly favorable turn. She's planning to come in the fall."

"Congratulations."

"Well, we'll see."

"She'll be there."

"Whatever."

"Don't give me that bull. You're dying for her to come."

"I can take it or leave it," I said playfully.

"Sure. Better get outa here before your nose starts growing."

"Yeah, well thanks a lot again."

And then before we could hem and haw and say goodbye any more, Norman leaped up. "Oh! I gotta show you something."

"What?"

"Come with me," he said and went out into the hatto. I followed curiously.

He went back to his room and got a flashlight and led me to behind the altar. The grin on his face was illuminated by the light in his hand as he pulled out a large cardboard box.

"Just came in yesterday—a gift from Akagi-san," he said. "I watched Shuko unload it and carry it in."

"What on earth could it be?" I said densely, moving in closer as Norman opened the box, pulling back the flaps. Suddenly he was laughing diabolically as he thrust his hand into the case. He pulled out an A-frame-shaped box. It was something that we had looked at for a long time and that we thought we would never see again. I knew the man on the side of the box, giving the thumbs-up sign and winking. I knew him well. He had come to be like a member of the sangha.

"THANK YOU AND OK!" said Norman, holding it high. "THANK YOU AND OK!"

WORSHIP IN THE RUINS

MARUYAMA, MARCH 3, 1990

I received a call from Isabel, who had been with Katagiri the night before he died. She and another disciple of his, a male nurse, had turned him over the night before. One of his feet was cold. They knew he didn't have long when they felt the cold foot.

"I remember once he said, 'When the time comes to die, just die.' But he didn't want to die," she said. "He hung on and changed his diet and took all the treatments. He didn't think it was going to get him and he didn't give up till the very end. And then he followed his own advice beautifully."

Tomoe-san, his widow, was exhausted and grieving, but surrounded by friends, fellow students and family. Preparations for the funeral were underway. Nishiki would fly over to conduct it. Calls and cards were coming in from all over the Buddhist world.

Norman had left our house early in the morning for Eiheiji to complete the ceremonies that would give him the irrelevant credentials he'd never need and that I wished Katagiri had left behind as he once seemed more prone to do. That day fifteen or more years ago when the plaque came from Eiheiji stating that

Tassajara was an official Soto Zen temple, he had thrown it in the firewood by the cast iron stove in his cabin. Why hadn't he left it there?

All the disciples and both his grown sons gathered around Katagiri's body on the morning of his death. Isabel guided the others in washing the body and preparing it so that fluids would not leak from his orifices. Tomoe-san rubbed his skin with a lotion. Isabel said his body was beautiful, youthful and lovely in color. Chanting at each transition, they dressed him in his best robes, carried him downstairs, put him in his coffin and lit incense.

She said that at the altar in her room she had offered him a tiny bowl of broken incense bits. When Katagiri was five or six, she explained, he had admired the priest who used to come to his house to do services, and decided that he wanted to be a priest too. He started sneaking all the broken and burnt-down stubs of incense sticks. He kept them in his pockets and would snack on them during the day.

For a couple of weeks before he died, people had been flying and driving in from all over and sitting zazen downstairs below his room. His body remained there the standard three days before cremation. Even though the winter was cold, the house was warm, and techniques of preservation were therefore especially important. At that time of year in Minneapolis the demand for ice packs was nil. The stores were out. So Isabel had to improvise. As a result, Katagiri's body, which was covered with flowers and herbs, lay in state in his simple casket on a bed of frozen bags of Birds Eye Tiny Tender Peas.

I left home groaning inside and walked onto the Daianji grounds. I was alone for the first time since we'd received the news. I crossed the back lot where the temple trash is burned, compost dumped on the wild edge without being properly covered, scrap wood stacked and bamboo cured by leaning it up on a frame, the poles punching high into the air. A pile of logs waiting for the chain saw reminded me of cutting firewood with Katagiri at Tassajara and again at Hōgoji, where finally he didn't try too hard.

Walking across the back road, up on a cement footpath behind a row of homes, I looked at their disarrayed backsides and into a *mizo*, deep down to my right, full of mountain runoff and soap bubbles. The air was crisp and smelled of burning oak from a potter's wood kiln. Veering off on a dirt path into the woods, I stepped up through oaks and pines, past brush and high grass to a clearing cultivated into a potato garden, and next to the spuds, persimmon trees with interlocking branches. It was winter. There was no fruit save for some mangled and dried dark carcasses on the ground—skin, stem and seeds.

Katagiri once said people expect a Zen master to be like a perfect piece of ripe fruit hanging from a tree: firm, full, bright with color, ready to eat and looking delicious. But that's not what it is, he said. The fruit gets overripe and squishy and falls to the ground scattering its meat and seeds. That is a Zen master: splattered fruit.

On the edge of a thick and untended bamboo grove, I came to the ruins of an old shrine or temple—some mix of the two. I go by there sometimes and admire it returning to the earth. There are weather-worn stone Buddhist carvings propped up against the hillside. The roof of the crumbling building has fallen to the dirt at one end, the tiles broken and dispersed. I walked up over the rotting boards of a collapsed section, sat on a fallen beam. In the hillside there is a tended niche, a shallow cave with a Jizō, the bodhisattva for those who died as infants or before birth. Someone had recently offered a glass of sake, lit candles and incense, and the pock-marked Jizō wore a fresh red bib to catch the drool of the world's lost children. A tiny brown leaf floated on the sake.

I thought of Katagiri's life, from the five-year-old boy who chewed on bits of incense to the priest who died feeling he hadn't realized his dream of sinking his dharma roots deep in America. He tried in Monterey, in Minneapolis, in San Francisco and in Marin County to have the sort of following and success that he'd seen bloom around Suzuki and Baker.

"How's it going in Minneapolis, Roshi?" I asked him on one of his visits to Green Gulch after he'd given a talk to several hundred people.

"Not so well," he said sadly. "We don't have such a big group. There's not so much interest in Minneapolis. And people are mad at me for being too strict. Ralph stopped wearing his robes. He doesn't like me anymore."

"Oh, I'm sure he likes you, Roshi. But do the numbers really matter? That's not very Zen is it?" I ribbed him. "Wasn't Suzuki Roshi the only one of his dharma brothers who didn't eventually leave *his* teacher?"

He nodded.

"And aren't you the only student who stuck with your teacher?"

"Yes, I was the only one. Though eventually I left him too."

"Not till long after you'd completed your training. You had to move on."

"Yes."

"And what of Suzuki's so-called success? Look what's happened. We've got fine buildings and many students, but we're all a bunch of idiots. Nothing to brag about here. Just a lot of depressed dopes and infighting. Who of us understands anything? So didn't Suzuki fail?"

"He needed more time." Katagiri smiled at the line of thought I was hitting him with.

"And didn't Dōgen say that the life of a Zen master is one continuous mistake?"

"Something like that."

"Congratulations, Roshi, you're right on target."

"I never knew how hard it would be," he said, shaking his head.

. . .

I continued on through the woods till the trail descended down to the farm co-op warehouse, filled with bags of rice. I passed the single dirt tennis court, where we could play for a thousand yen a year each, and continued on the asphalt path by an old farmhouse with black wrinkled walls of charcoaled wood, between gardens of giant cabbages, by a peach orchard and in front of a row of greenhouses to the busy street. The sidewalk took me past a mechanic's shop and a lot with piles of tires, junked cars and parts. Miserable dogs in cages barked at me from the pet shop. From the street I could see the hillside, which revealed the stillness of an ohaka, a thousand white stones amidst dry yellow grass in the winter day's sun.

The post office door swung open before I could reach for it. A departing housewife held it for me deferentially as I entered and she apologized politely in a singsong voice as I in turn held it for her. I sat down, put my shoulder bag in my lap and pulled an envelope out of it. It was neatly addressed to Tomoe-san. She had been with Katagiri over thirty years, most of it in America. She had been his partner, the mother of their two boys, his disciple and his fellow student as well. And she had been a friend to so many of us. I hadn't written the letter yet.

Two nights before when I'd called Suzuki's son in Yaizu and told him of Katagiri's death, he only said that no words came. I knew just how he felt. No words. I also had no tears and I couldn't find my own feeling. Am I callous? Is it me who's dead? I don't know. I just wanted to get something on paper, get it off to Tomoe and then forget it all.

I'd known her for twenty-five years too. She was always cheerful and ready to play around with words in her second language. Once when she and her husband were staying in the guest house at Green Gulch, Kelly and I paid them a visit. We had found a frog carved from green Mexican stone and brought it as a gift for Katagiri. Like Suzuki, he was known to love frogs. Katagiri was eyeing the box I brought, but I wanted to drag the time out some for dramatic effect. So the four of us had a most pleasant visit with the conversation centering around Kelly's school and how their two boys were doing. I looked at them fondly and thought about what a dedicated team they were and how much she supported him. People were always giving gifts to him, but only rarely was she on the receiving end.

"I have a gift," I said, pulled the frog out of the bag and put it on the table.

"Oh, how wonderful, thank you," said Roshi, delighted. He reached for it.

"Now wait a minute," I said, putting my hand on it. "I didn't say it was for you. I just said it was a gift." I paused and looked at them with no further explanation.

He turned to Tomoe and together they said, "Janken!"

They put their right hands in fists and together went "One, two, three!" and threw their right hands down in the air, his ending up flat and hers with two fingers held wide.

"Scissors cut paper," she said in her sweet, high voice and proudly took the frog. Katagiri looked at me with feigned heartbreak.

Selecting from the people doing business at the post office, I asked a kind-looking lady of fifty or so if she would help me write a note in Japanese to convey my sorrow. That way I wouldn't have to be expressive—the phrase would do it for me. She gave me several standard condolences to choose from. We settled on something that could roughly be translated as:

From my heart I feel pain for your husband's death and humbly extend to you these words of mourning.

She said that even if we were close friends it would be enough. "Don't go on and on," she said. "Just say that." She wrote it out and then sat by me and made sure that I copied the kanji and *kana* correctly. I sighed as I wrote the words, thanked her, sealed the envelope and went to the counter where a young lady who had helped me many times before was sitting. As I handed her the letter the phone was ringing in the back. The postmaster answered it. I was seeing Katagiri in his samue, laughing with a group of us twenty years back as we walked through the woods near Tassajara, swinging our arms, feeling free and easy. The clerk put the letter on the scales and asked me if I wanted airmail or sea mail. Just then from the phone in the back came that tune— the Eddy Duchin theme.

Instantly I was flooded with grief.

"Airmail," I stammered as the first low-fi stanza played.

"Eighty yen, please."

I started making low gasping sounds and clutched the counter. She looked up. No, this can't be happening. Get through it quickly. She applied the stamp for me as I sniffed jerkily.

"Do you want to write your return address on it?" she asked, looking down again.

I responded with a cracking grunt. And then I couldn't hold it back. While Chopin in cheap electric notes from a one-square-inch speaker continued building, I stood up in the dark Saturday matinee theater, moved over and sat down with the girls.

My hand could barely write the return address on the envelope. I was sobbing, sobbing and then laughing at myself and then sobbing again as softly as I could manage in the middle of clerks and customers who were carefully pretending nothing was happening. She took my thousand-yen bill and while she was making change I whimpered and wiped my eyes. Then, coins in shaking hand, I walked out of the post office crying for Eddy Duchin and Katagiri Roshi, people who lived their best and left this messy world like I would and like all our loved ones would and everyone would.

VITAL ENERGY

Today I had sanzen with translation by Jessica. It's such a relief to hear it in English as well as Japanese. I never stop enjoying the language study aspect. Of course the words he uses in sanzen are mostly not of any use on the street. Jessica did a dynamite job in her translation. I don't mean that I'm qualified to grade her technical ability, but that her energy is strong. Like Hōjō-san, in sanzen she is really in her element.

As I walked in, I could see the garden at dawn through the open shoji—gravel raked in circles like waves around islands of stone and mounds of grass accented with long green leaves and tall iris leading to the large temple pond.

After I'd bowed in, Hōjō-san started off by asking how my practice was doing. "Here I am," I said. "What do *you* think?"

He said it's up to *me* to determine if it's working for me—it's up to me to bring out the living energy of every instant. Not him. Am I using mu in a creative and dynamic way? The difference between someone who is working on these things and someone who isn't is that to the former there is a sense of the vital energy of every instant, it's not a matter of intellect or memory, but of expressing my own vital inner power, my *ki*.

As always, I can't really remember much of what was said. But I felt I was with an authentic teacher who is not intimidating, but empowering, patiently pointing out my own strength, working with me and waiting for me to break through to the world where there is no idea of a permanent self moving from instant to instant—the world of emptiness, divinity, beyond birth and death, always here and ready to be enjoyed.

As I stepped outside, the sky was becoming light and filled

with swooping bats. Songbirds announced that they were awake. Everything was awake. I took a deep breath and looked around.

BIRTHDAY BOY

MARUYAMA, AUGUST 13, 1990

We have named our boy Clayton Randolph, to be called Clay.

He was born 8/13 at 14:13 in Maruyama.

He weighed 9.26 pounds.

His basic interests are nursing, sleeping, excreting and crying.

Bye

David

P.S. The neighbors can't tell Clay's name from his big brother Kelly's till I say that the new one is Kurei and the older one is Keri. Elin and I had talked about naming this baby Kerry instead so they REALLY wouldn't be able to tell the difference.

(a note I put on TWICS, the Tokyo-based computer network)

Clay, like Kelly, was born by natural childbirth with the inspired guiding hands of a skilled midwife. In Clay's case, the midwife was Fukiko. I had dutifully been doing whatever my spouse told me throughout the labor. I barely had time to pee. I will never forget the incredible effort made by the mothers of both of my children in childbirth. I am convinced that men around the world are not involved in birthing because it would be hard for them to continue believing in their own superiority if they had to witness their wives exerting an effort that was so heroic.

Elin was a week late and was dying to have the baby. We didn't want to induce labor artificially so she did all the things she'd heard would induce labor naturally. She took a three-hour walk in the morning and in the afternoon went to Daianji and helped Jessica move a stack of firewood to the kiln. In the evening we tried erotic stimulation. An hour after we fell asleep, her water broke. The first contractions were irregular and mild. Unable to sleep in the excitement, she lay on her side and read. I dozed between frequent requests for back massage—relief from the discomfort of the initial contractions. Some hours later we took a peaceful walk through our sleeping neighborhood, following another standard procedure to help the process along.

Before returning home we stopped at an all-night store on the main drag and loaded up on wholesome snacks and juices to take with us to the birthing center—apple juice, rice crackers, yogurt, dried squid.

"Let's get out of here," said Elin, breathing heavily. It was coming on harder.

As his polished, scented car idled in the street, the white-gloved taxi driver untypically complained about waiting as we kept remembering things and running back to the house to get them. He was especially dense. I told him a couple of times that Elin was in labor, to be patient and not to bother her. When he again asked her to hurry up, I forcefully directed him to be quiet. That worked for a while. The clinic was thirty minutes away—even on the six A.M. streets. Elin was groaning loudly and holding me for thirty seconds about every four minutes at that point. Now the driver was nervously asking us standard polite questions as if there were nothing unusual happening. "Where are you from? Do you like Japan? What are you doing here?" Having been rude to him once, I answered automatically while keeping all my attention on Elin. Finally he got into a monologue about how Japan is superior to the United States, touching on the laziness of American workers, our unsafe streets, the natural beauty of Japan and how there is only one way to say everything in English whereas in Japanese there are many ways. "You have only one word for 'you' and we have many," he pointed out as Elin sighed and caught her breath from the prior contraction. I vowed never again to generalize about Japan. He continued unchallenged in that vein until we reached our destination. I was glad there was no tipping in Japan as it would have been a dilemma for me when the thirty-five-dollar fare was paid.

At the clinic we got our own room with two beds. It would be eight hours till we moved to the birth room. Fukiko kept in touch and cheered Elin on. While Bach played on the tape deck we brought, I massaged Elin and helped her through contractions as she instructed, by holding her or applying pressure at a particular spot.

"Lower! Harder!" We shut the music off and concentrated our efforts. As the contractions got more and more intense, a wonderfully empathetic female attendant joined us. She held Elin, rubbed her, and moaned with her.

I'd heard that some Japanese doctors scolded women in labor for "vocalizing." Not at Kurodain. Fukiko coached Elin to strongly express *fun* on the exhalations. The word is breathy, pronounced a little like "who" with an initial wisp of an "f" and a closing nasal "n." It was the perfect sound to carry Elin through the contractions, though I couldn't quite forget that it's a homonym for their word for animal poop.

At noon we were each brought a tray with a full lunch. We knew that would happen. In a birthing book, Elin had read that Japan is the only place in the world where women in labor are encouraged to eat large meals—weird. Elin did take a few bites and drank the miso soup. I ate the rest.

. . .

After the birth we spent two and a half more days in that room —marveling at Clay (who slept most of the time), taking it easy and reading Arthur Conan Doyle and P. G. Wodehouse. We kept Clay with us the whole time—except after the first five hours we felt secure enough to let Fukiko take him for five minutes to weigh and measure. There was a modern Japanese couple next to us who also had a private room and kept their baby with them. All the other babies—about a dozen of them—slept on their backs together in the nursery while their mothers doubled and tripled up in other rooms. In a room across from ours there were breast-feeding classes that they would all attend with their infants. There were other types of instruction as well in the motherly arts. Since Elin had read enough books on the subject to write a doctoral thesis, we skipped all that. She'd also talked endlessly with friends and midwives.

While walking around to stretch her legs, Elin saw the lovely line of light brown babies in the nursery and was shocked at how small they were. She asked the nurse if they were preemies, only to learn that they were normal-sized for Japanese babies, about six and a half pounds, and all older than Clay by at least two days. He *was* big but he still seemed tiny to us.

After the birth, when the nurse said, "Are you happy it's a boy?" Elin, having pushed the envelope of exhaustion and elation to the limit, had answered, "After that, I'd be happy with a goat."

When Clay was crowning (top of the head coming out), his head looked about the size of a tennis ball. Everything was so far out at the time that I could hardly think, but I was wondering about how his head could be so small. In my confusion I pictured him as six inches tall. The midwife was giving positive indications in Japanese and English, so I knew everything was fine—but I didn't understand.

What I had forgotten was that the head is soft and malleable and squeezes into a bullet shape so when the tip thrust out, I didn't know what it was.

"Push hard!" said the midwife.

Elin roared like a wild animal fighting for its life and the little hairy tennis ball started to come out. Then it started getting bigger and emerged as an enormous rubbery, hairy, purple form. I watched it with a blank mind, a shocking breathless moment, and had no idea what I was looking at—until it grimaced and I realized it was a face! There's nothing quite like seeing an agonized face, like some creature from a swamp movie, sticking out of your wife's vagina.

"Okay! One more big push!" the midwife said loudly in one language or another and as Elin again wildly bellowed and pushed with the force of the 1985 Chicago defensive line, a wet, bloody form sloshed onto the bed followed by a thick, purple, bloody, twisted cord. Having gone through this almost eighteen years before hadn't prepared me a bit. A birth can be in some respects not unlike that scene from *Alien* where the unfortunate crew member writhes in agony before that little monster pops out of his chest. He certainly didn't go through any more difficulty than most mothers do in childbirth.

I looked down at a terribly wrinkled little quivering mass, saw that it had male genitalia as the sound waves had predicted, and said to Elin, whose hands were fiercely clutching mine, "He's born."

And then everyone waited: the midwife, her assistants, the doctor who was standing back observing, Elin and I. These seconds, waiting for the first breath, must be the longest on earth. Clay was quick. He sucked in a breath that reminded me of the Chinese brother who swallowed the ocean, and then he cried and he did so with more power than I would have thought possible for a little glob like that. The midwife picked him up and started to wipe him off. "Give him to her now," I said firmly. We'd been over that. She did so and Elin held her baby, trailing the thick, wet, twisted umbilical cord still connected to the placenta, and watched the nameless, tiny, slimy, quivering thing in his first intense minute of air-breathing time. The struggle was over. She had transformed from woman warrior to loving, adoring mother and she was soft, gentle and glowing—pure beautiful radiance. Our eyes met.

There is a wide-awake period that babies have in the first two hours when, if things go naturally, they will look quite intently at their mothers and even their fathers, or a bedpost for that matter, if that is what is before them. I remember it with Kelly and now I saw it with Clay. The whole thing is unrehearsed and raw. And when that wee powerful wet fellow looked around, he was doing so in an authentic for-the-first-time way.

Clay's eyes were to me in this period after birth something both helpless and frightening, as in that trembling instant of transformation from one world to another, from the womb to the room, he looked at us with a powerful innocence. One swollen eye opened wide and one peeked out of a slit. I gulped.

I'M OFF

HŌGOJI, JUNE 19, 1988

I guess what it comes down to is choosing one's set of limitations," Shuko said as we sipped our farewell tea.

I nodded.

"Please come back anytime."

"Thanks. You think you'll be here for a long time?"

"Maybe so. I may be useful here to Nishiki Roshi."

"Creating the international monastery, huh?"

"We will try," he said.

"Good luck. It's a tough job."

"I'll do my best," he said with an unsettled but friendly smile.

"I guess I should go." I drank the rest of the tea in my cup.

"Good luck to you too." He got up just as the morning work drum sounded.

Everyone gathered on the steps.

I thanked Maku for the photos of the ceremony with pictures I could send to family, Elin and friends. Jakushin gasshoed and smiled. Norman gave me a big hug. I bowed to them all and turned around. Koji and I were off down the steps. Koji had insisted on carrying the heavier bag (I carried the shoulderbag) because he was concerned about my back. I bowed goodbye to the patriarch oak.

"Do you think that's the tree Daigyo Zenji sat with?"

"Could be," said Koji.

We made a brief stop at Yoshiko's place, where I paid my respects and thanked her for taking care of everyone. I asked her how her condition was, not the standard "Ogenki desu ka?" but a more concerned query that is used for someone who has been ill. She thanked me for asking and said "I've pretty much recovered." And then she added "Okage sama de," which is a wonderful phrase that means "thanks to all that has made it possible." It's a little like "Thanks to the good lord," but without the sense that there's only one paternal superbeing to be grateful to.

Yoshiko didn't ask where I was going and what I was going to do, but just gasshoed with a piercing eye and encouraged me with, "Gambatte." It's like what Katagiri would say to us when we would part, except he'd state it as a request: "Please take care of your practice." Her spirit is more severe. She is the good witch whose cold eye told me, "Don't be a coward and a flake. Throw yourself into the Great Question."

There was water gushing down a ditch on the side of the road before the stupa as we walked past. It had been dry for a week.

Koji explained that a farmer had been irrigating his rice fields but that now they were obviously full and he'd shut his intake, releasing this flow. At a bend of the trough there was a large, deep, clear puddle that had formed from the spill and already it was full of tadpoles swimming to and fro, wagging their tails.

Bulldozers and dump trucks were working on a road across the valley. We stopped for a moment and watched these tiny toys in the distance. Their sound carried strongly across to us.

"I love heavy equipment," I said to Koji.

"I like cranes the best," Koji said, looking down. There was a pause and then he spoke again. "I'm going to leave too. I'm going home a year earlier than I'd planned."

"Is that okay?" I asked.

"Yes, I'm happy to go back to my father's temple. He and my mother can use me. And I've had enough. I think that maybe Dōgen's way is too cold for me."

"Will you get married right away?"

"After one year maybe. And you, will you get married when Elin comes?"

"I don't know. We don't have to. We should live together for a while and see how we feel."

"I envy you having a love marriage and being so free."

"Japanese marriages are much more likely to last though, aren't they? And I'm sure you'll fall in love with each other in time," I said, trying to offer what I could.

"Please come stay with us when she comes."

"Yes, we will come," I said. "Of course. Tell your parents we're married."

"Hai, that would be best," he said.

The Laurie Anderson bird called from the nun's grove as we walked down the road. At Ryūmon we stopped at Miki-obāsan's. She was at home and made us strong instant coffee with Creap and sugar. Koji in his boots and I in my tennis shoes sat on the edge of her tatami with our feet down in the entranceway. She put my coffee on her desk by the phone, located, I noticed, so she could come in from working on her garden and answer it without deshoeing. From where I sat I could see into a couple of small tatami rooms. Everything was in faded colors. Straight ahead was her kitchen, with no room for a table. That was it, I think. Everywhere there were boxes, magazines and various items stacked on the floor. She had lots of Japanese knick-knacks on tables and pictures hanging high on the walls, tilted down from the top— scenes of famous Japanese places: Fuji San, Nikkō, Miyajima. She gave us special Beppu *manjū*—aduki bean paste in *mochi,* the chewy, sweet, gluten rice cake. We reminisced about picking tea together and she teased me for running away from the suzume-bachi, which she just called *hachi*—an ordinary bee. She offered us more coffee but we declined and left after accepting a couple of apples. We tried not to take them, they're so expensive, but she insisted.

From her phone Koji called the logger who had insisted that I come stay with him. He said that he must have been drunk and couldn't remember a thing about it. That was a little embarrassing.

I said goodbye and she gave me three thousand yen. I didn't want to take it, but Koji told me to. As we walked down the road I remarked on how simple and poor her life was.

Koji said, "See that house there?" and indicated a large new home next door, well built, with two new cars in a broad driveway. "That's her daughter's. She likes her run-down old place better, but she has the run of the big one too. She's doing okay."

"You mean she doesn't work at Hōgoji because she needs the money?"

"Of course not."

At the bus stop Koji gave me an envelope. It said "from all Hōgoji monks." Inside was five thousand yen, exactly what I had left on the altar as a gift to the temple. I had little money and I gratefully accepted it. I was afraid that if I said anything my voice would crack.

"And this is from me," said Koji, handing me another envelope. "Look," he insisted. It was ten thousand yen.

"Oh no, I, uh . . ." But I couldn't talk. I couldn't even say "no, you shouldn't have." He's so poor. He'd worked in the family rice fields and gone to night school while I'd played tennis at the country club and driven my three, two-barrel carburetor Pontiac around at night looking for action. Oh, well. I stood there feeling raw, thankful and sad.

"Do you know what the Buddhists said an icchantika was?"

Koji surprised me. It took me a moment to remember. "No —what?"

"Not a being without buddha nature—only someone lacking faith. You are neither." And then he said, "Kipu za feizu."

"Kipu en tachu," I responded.

I'm sure we were both relieved that the bus pulled up then. Koji stepped in, putting my bag in the bus and then stepped back down. I stood inside the bus and he stood just below on the ground. In a nation where what one says at times like this is pretty well set in concrete, the monk and the foreigner exchanged farewells. Several people in the bus looked on.

He put his hands together in gassho. "Boku wa namagomi desu, dōzo umete kudasai."

I answered him in kind, "I am namagomi, please bury me."

The bus took off. Koji stood there bowing till we rounded a bend and he was out of sight. As the bus moved down the road toward Kikuoka, now and then one of the other passengers would turn around and look at me, maybe wondering if they'd heard right.

The next day, after an uneventful and blissful rest in the capsule hotel, I was sitting in the back of a bus waiting for it to leave for

Beppu. The bus was parked in the station lot right next to the intersection and I had a ringside seat on the local action. There were farmers in their minipickup trucks going by; an old lady pushing an old lady's buggy, like a baby buggy but smaller; coming from the other direction was an old man in a kimono walking slowly in geta, pushing a cane; a young woman was carrying a child wrapped in a cloth pack on her back. Meanwhile, people were boarding the bus. They would look at me before they sat down as far away from me as they could.

Suddenly from across the intersection came a familiar sound. It was like approaching cows. "Hō! Hō!" And there, coming down the sidewalk toward the intersection was a line of black-robed monks calling out that the dharma was back in town. I could make out Norman easily as he was a good head higher than any of the others. People on the street stopped and put coins in their begging bowls. From my vantage point high in the bus I could hardly see their chins under the wide conical straw hats but it looked as if there were just Norman, Shuko and those novices from Suienji. The line approached the corner. Then I realized that Norman was leading them. Shuko was letting Norman be in charge. Glory be. Behind Norman were seven young monks. Shuko was pulling up the rear. They were probably coming to catch a bus to somewhere else for the afternoon's begging and were now catty-corner from the station.

After a line of schoolgirls in dark blue uniforms had stopped giggling at me and taken their seats, the bus driver shut the door. I kept looking secretly at my friends out the open window. There was no stop light on the corner so Norman could go either way. He chose to go to the right. Shuko, however, decided to go the other direction and he called softly to the novices to follow him, which they dutifully did.

"Hey!" Shuko then called to Norman, just loud enough for him to hear.

Norman looked around, finding himself alone in the middle of the street. "What!?" he shouted at Shuko.

"Where are you going?" Shuko asked.

"I'm going to the station!" said Norman. "Where are you going?"

"I'm going to the station too," answered Shuko, walking with the puzzled monks behind him.

My bus started to pull away from the intersection.

"You give me a tiny bit of responsibility and then you take it away! You won't even let me decide which way to cross the street!" Norman yelled.

Shuko didn't answer. He was surely getting embarrassed at this public display.

In the roar of the bus heading away, I couldn't hear the rest of their exchange, but I watched the pantomime: Norman jumping up and down and swinging his long sleeves in the air, gesticulating and probably by now cursing at Shuko, who was walking into the station with his little ducks behind him. The scene reduced to miniature and Norman and Shuko disappeared into the past.

The bus to Beppu stopped and an old lady got on. There was only one empty space left and that was the one next to me. Bravely she lowered herself onto the seat, placing a paper shopping bag with handles between us.

I said the equivalent of "It's a nice day, isn't it, ma'am." When she heard these words coming from this alien mouth, and after a moment's thought realized that they indeed weren't English, it was music to her ears, and she sang along to the old song. "Yes, nice weather, isn't it!"

"Ogenki desu ka?" I said.

"Genki desu," she answered, saying she's fine, and then added, "Okage sama de."

Yes, I thought, okage sama de, thanks to all that has made it possible. And I profusely thanked all who had helped me and all that had brought me to that place at that moment. Thanks to parents and ancestors, wives and lovers, children and friends, teachers and fellow travelers. Heartfelt gratitude to all beings and nonbeings on earth and in heaven, in the ten directions, from the past, present and future who have made it possible for me to have been where I've been, done what I've done, known what I've known and to be sitting in this bus seat now, so very happy to be rolling on toward Beppu and beyond, to more adventure and discovery.

The old lady asked me where I was going and what I was doing there. I don't know what's next, I told her. She looked at me puzzled, as if thinking, he must have a plan or he wouldn't be here.

Well, I thought, if I don't have a plan, I'd better have a set phrase. "Tomorrow's wind blows tomorrow," I said.

She laughed and nodded, understanding perfectly. She told me her daughter once went to L.A. and saw Disneyland, and as we glided down the highway together she started jabbering away in dialect like Miki-obāsan and I had no idea what she was talking about.

PART EIGHT

GONE
BEYOND

ASHES TO DUST

KYOTO—TAIZOIN, SEPTEMBER 9, 1990

I stood under a pedestrian bridge in Kyoto at six-thirty in the morning and waited for some friends to pick me up so we could go together to a *nōkotsu,* an ashes ceremony for Katagiri Roshi at his home temple near Tsuruga, about an hour north by express train. It was a warm morning on the northeast side of Kyoto and there was not yet much traffic. It doesn't get busy around there till eight or even eight-thirty.

That morning, eager taxis were out looking for business and I felt like a lone flower in a field, attracting much attention from the bees about. They'd buzz by and slow down, come to a stop and pull open their back doors from the lever by the driver's seat, and they'd bid me to come in. Several taxis started U-turns before I could convey to them that I didn't want a ride. "This flower has no pollen—buzz on." I just wanted to stand there and look at the sky and the mountains that rise up around the outskirts of town, look at the colored clouds and the sparrows on the wires going *chin chin chin chin* as Japanese sparrows do, but my simple morning reverie would continually be interrupted by these eagerly entreating taxis. A raised hand intended to shoo them away would draw them nearer much as our wave goodbye makes people here stop and come back to you. So I tried crossed forearms held before me, which I've seen Japanese use for various negations—"we're out of that," "don't enter." But that just attracted their attention and made them check to be sure. Thumbs down didn't work. A businessman crossed the wide thoroughfare, the traffic being sparse, and a taxi slowed to check him out. He waved his hands, palms downward, in a gesture I immediately recognized as a rebuff. Ah, that's how it's done, I thought. But the taxi only slowed further, the driver craning his neck and looking back. The man continued to give various discouraging signals as he walked on his way and finally the cab pulled off. So then I decided that no signal at all would be best and I looked off at the giant kanji for "great," the Daimonji. It's in a grassy area way up on a mountainside to the east. It looks like the form of a person standing with arms and legs stretched out. Just a few weeks prior, the Daimonji's yearly blaze had lit the mountainside during the Bon festival.

A horn honked, pulling me away from the charred symbol. There was a taxi directly in front of me with its door open and its meticulously clean and sweet-scented interior awaiting. I shook my head and looked away—the taxi went on. Then I tried looking straight ahead as if alert and aware, but made no motions to encourage them and even though this meant that my object of meditation was the pedestrian bridge steps across the street, it worked and I was free as the occasional taxis passed me by.

Another taxi slowed in front of me and I heard my name being called. My old friend Ann, a lay Buddhist who lives in Kyoto, and Ando, a woman priest disciple of Katagiri's, were waving at me from inside. I hopped in.

On the platform at the Kyoto train station, I was surrounded by American and Japanese Zen priests, short and tall, thick and thin, with black robes, shaved heads and big grins. Only Ann, I and the wife and child of Okamoto Sensei, one of the priests, were in Western garb. Okamoto was young, handsome, spoke fair English and had a relaxed and straightforward manner. I'd always wanted to meet him. He has a temple near Kyoto where he translates texts and practices with a few foreigners at a time. Of the two ordained men and three ordained women from the States, disciples of Katagiri, the only one I knew well was Isabel. She's about fifty, a young fifty, holds herself well, solid, bright, discriminating and spirited. I was glad that I'd met everybody else first and had had a chance to talk to them before she got there, because once Isabel and I got together, we couldn't be stopped—at least this time we weren't running up the long-distance bill.

We were about to pass an encyclopedia of words. First she wanted to know all about the birth and the baby. I produced pictures, which temporarily diverted everyone's attention and brought forth a shower of congratulations. But soon Isabel and I were jabbering together of other things. We philosophized, politicized, talked about friends in America, the state of Zen and Buddhism in America and Japan, and what we liked and didn't like about Japan. She'd been there for a month traveling from temple to temple with robes and a shaved head (an orthodox style she was assuming for her pilgrimage).

She had felt quite comfortable both inside temples and out. She said that people accepted her and didn't look at her as if she were weird. I told her she was doing pretty good, because people look at me as if I'm weird when I'm just standing waiting for a train in my Sunday best. I felt sure that her strictly positive attitude was still intact because of how recently she'd arrived and because of the independent nature of her visit—traveling around as a guest and observer. But I didn't rain on her parade. She reminded me of how vast and multidimensional the world of Japanese Buddhism is. It's not all just *furukusai*, stinking of old, as my young English students regarded it. Anyway, even if it is, we're both still interested in rummaging through old trunks to find antiques of interest.

In her travels her strongest focus had been on Jizō Bosatsu. Jizō is the bodhisattva of the underworld whose job is to protect and nurture travelers, including those in transition between life and death. Thus Jizō consoles those who have just died, or have been miscarried, stillborn and aborted. It was a Jizō statue I'd sat with at the crumbling shrine in the Maruyama hills on the way to the post office. Isabel had found that Jizō statues were all over Japan, on street corners as well as in temples, and she was coming to know Jizō as comfort to the guilty and grieving, and as cash flow to those who sell statues of stone, wood and plastic. Like everything of depth, Jizō has two sides and infinite faces.

Isabel told me about the funeral. It had been held six weeks after Katagiri's death. She'd wanted me to come, but it was too far and too expensive. Norman was there. All sorts of high mucky-muck roshi from the Sōtō-shū in brocade robes came and there were endless testimonials to Katagiri's teaching from students and teachers alike. This was in stark contrast to Suzuki's funeral to which no one from the Sōtō-shū came except for his old buddy Niwa Roshi. I almost got the impression Isabel liked it better when they'd written us off. But then she said she was moved by the ceremony—she realized what a bridge Katagiri had been to help bring together two worlds so far apart. She said that Katagiri's body hadn't been left untended for a moment since well before he died until he was cremated. The funeral home was completely responsive and let Katagiri's disciples tend to his body as they saw fit. She took the ashes out of the oven and personally ground the bones as per law and divided them into five equal parts destined for the Minnesota monastery of Hokyoji, the Minnesota Zen Meditation Center, Tassajara, his wife Tomoe, and his home temple of Taizoin in Japan.

Nishiki had given an eloquent and poetic talk at the funeral, which Shuko translated. I'm sure it was moving, but I couldn't help but think how neat it would have been, in addition, to have played some of Katagiri's own talks back.

When the time comes for you to face death, you have to return to the very first moment of death. . . . We should practice this again and again. We have to return to the silent source of our life and stand up there. We have to come back to the realm of oneness and make it alive, with a feeling of togetherness with all sentient beings and a deep understanding of human suffering.

I remember Katagiri's first lectures at Sokoji. Suzuki had asked him to speak, so he did, but we could barely understand him. In fact, I couldn't catch enough of what he was saying to get the point. He was horrified to be in such a position, but we all smiled and nodded, encouraging him on. Little by little he learned how to say what he wanted in lectures and dokusan. Even years after those first talks I used to sit and take notes on his grammatical errors. I'd mark every one so that he'd get a feel for his repeated mistakes. There would sometimes be a hundred article errors. A decade later Norman would do the same thing and he told me that others had done it too. The guy did not learn easy—and he tried so hard. But gradually he came along and developed his own style, full of far-out metaphors and creative new Buddhist technical terms.

> Let your heart become as soft and magnanimous
> as if you were nestled in the bosom
> of the grandeur of nature.

I took him to a junior high school once—he'd been invited to introduce that pubescent audience to Buddhism and Zen. I couldn't believe what he said. "Do you think God is far away? Do you think Zen is far away? Do you think it is hard to understand? It's just toilet paper! That's all it is. You may not think so. But that's what it is! You may think Zen is something wonderful and in some heaven. It is just toilet paper!" And he went on into the stratosphere. In the car on the way back he turned to me and said, "I don't think they understood."

We arrived in remarkably ugly Tsuruga (surrounded by a dozen or so nuclear power plants) at nine in the morning, and our unusual entourage filled three sparkling taxis, which took us to Katagiri's temple, a twenty-minute ride out of town into the country and by the sea. It's a small old temple located up a rich green valley that descends from the forested mountains to the Japan Sea below. A farming and fishing village of a few dozen people lies between the sea and the temple. A narrow two-lane road runs through the village to the main highway. When Elin, Kelly and I had visited there the year before, this road had been bumper-to-bumper in families and gangs of young people in vans, cars, and big-tired four-wheel drives coming home from the beach with snorkels and inner tubes.

In the rice fields that lead to the temple, various types of scarecrows had been put up. There were black silhouettes of big birds dangling and flapping from strings that hung from poles and there were bright shiny balls that bobbed in the wind. In some places, metallic tape, reflecting in various bright colors, was twisted between poles and glittering in the breeze. But on that day there were no smiling old women unbending as best they could to wave at us. For today was the *nōkotsu* of their errant priest.

Almost thirty years before, he had left them and gone first to Zenshuji in L.A. and then in 1965 to help Suzuki Roshi at the San Francisco Zen Center. What they had been told was that he was going to the States for a couple of years to be a priest for Japanese-Americans. That's why Suzuki was sent there too, to minister for a reasonable term to Japanese abroad in the land of the materialistic heathens. They just didn't come back. They didn't come back because they were both priests who were passionately absorbed in the core practice of their religions, and in California they were sought out by hippies, housewives and investors who desperately wanted to do what they did and know what they knew. The traditional Japanese-American Buddhists went to the temple on Sundays to hear a sermon and participate in a brief service and the rest of us newcomers went Monday through Saturday to practice zazen, chant the Heart Sutra and bug those two guys with questions till their English improved considerably. So Katagiri was supposed to come back home, but he had only visited a few times and, since he was never replaced as the head priest of Taizoin, the congregation had to make do with going to another temple further away or having another priest come there once a month. It wouldn't have worked out anyway

—the village couldn't afford full-time help. Taizoin was reduced to an occasional meeting hall for the locals. The two times that I had visited it before, it was dusty, musty and shockingly dilapidated with mouse turds on the old tatami that were rotting and caving-in in places.

The taxis managed the winding, elevated, one-lane road through the soggy rice fields. Admiring the patterned beauty of the stalks rising from the water, I was also silently eyeing the near and sudden drop-off into the paddy.

We unloaded our bags next to the old storage shed, which on one end contained the time-stained outhouse. Its exposed urinals in the entryway emptied into a trough that ran to the outhouse's receiving hole in the ground. Camouflaged by only a few bushes, two men were peeing away as a woman edged by them to get to the squatter. Later I would notice other old country women squatting out behind where the cars were parked, eliminating the morning's green tea unconcerned that I was walking by.

The sliding doors outside the main hall were opened, leaving the front left half of the building exposed. Through this opening the entering priests stepped with clean white tabi and bessu up onto the new fresh-smelling tatami, and prostrated themselves at the immaculately prepared altar and then to each other in greeting. Communication between the Japanese and American priests and lay folk was quiet and consisted mainly of nodding heads and bending bodies. The priests wore similar robes, but were of different worlds—only Okamoto was comfortable with the gaijin outside of the brief forms of convention.

I watched the Japanese priests and lay people greet each other. All over Japan at that very moment others were bowing and apologizing and thanking: businessmen in the office and on the golf course, housewives on the street, athletes on the field and delivery people, vendors, teachers, students, politicians, imperial family members and gangsters. These people have no doubt about what to do or say when they meet. It's all worked out by millennia of culture. Zen groups in America have got to have some sort of culture and many have taken on these "thank you, forgive me" forms to some extent because that's what their teachers did. What is Japanese culture and what is Buddhist, I wondered, and thought we gaijin Zennies should be careful not to perpetuate unnecessarily foreign forms that isolate us from others back in our homelands.

The townsfolk were scattered around, inside the building and out. Women were hurrying, getting things ready, while the men were milling about, smoking and talking. Today their lost beloved priest who had forsaken them for outsiders, outsiders who should have been going to church, was coming home for good. His wife, Tomoe, had brought a share of ashes and bone bits in a cloth-wrapped box. She brought it tense and straining, deep ridges of pain running vertically between her eyes. She carried the box into the temple amidst the respectful and bowing farmers and fishermen and their wives. By her side walked her younger son, born and raised in the States and just as out of place as any other American there.

Tomoe's husband was back in his temple, this meager building with exterior walls of mud and weathered wood and windows with wood-framed panes. There was an addition on the right side of the front of the building made of fake plastic wood. Next to this was a centuries-old, moss-and-lichen-rich rock garden and pool. Surely at one time the water had flowed through thick bamboo, but now there was only a grey four-inch plastic pipe with a trickle coming out of its broken and uneven end. Inside the building hung a photograph of the temple as it used to look—the thick straw-thatched roof not yet covered by sheet metal, and no trace of modern tackiness. But the clay-walled interior is probably about the same as back then. There are some big old earthen wood-burning stoves for cooking and a small iron wood-heated bath.

A breeze from the Japan Sea fanned away the heat that was still stifling further inland. In this salt-scented air and beneath a clear blue sky, I walked around outside and said hello to some of the old folks, which meant anyone not of the gaijin group and the Okamotos. I was not surprised that almost everyone was over sixty. You don't see many younger people in the fields or in the temples. I walked around the building and through it, talking to some farmers smoking out back and some housewives preparing lunch within. I walked to the deck and looked out toward the rice fields. The stalks swayed in synchronized motion past the windbreak cyprus. Rice—it's always in the news. I wondered if the solution to the rice import problem would automatically come about when these elders retired to the hospitals and to the futon in their farmhouses, when their ashes entered the ground by the stones in the ohaka. For when these old folks were gone, who would work in the fields? The kids are in the cities in offices or shops or schools or they're driving trucks or they're anywhere but in the fields. Mr. Shimizu of the MMC says that big business and government destroyed the small farm in America and will soon do so in Japan with no concern for those who till the soil. This may be true, but I wonder if the transition to the mega-farm has not all along been greatly abetted by the flight of the young seeking a better life than that of their bent parents. I circulated and talked to these weathered old parents and grandparents, but not to their kids and grandkids because the younger generations had no use for their elders' dead, tired, useless, old religion or life on the farm or in the fishing boat. The kids were not there.

It must have been a strange day for the old folks. They were getting their priest back in powdered form and they met relatively young Americans, more than half women, who had taken on the clothes and practice of this religion that these old folks had always assumed was strictly a Japanese thing dominated by men. It's integrally tied in with Shinto, Japanese history, Japanese ceremonies, their secret language, and their spirits and ancestors. So how could these pale foreigners have anything to do with it or understand it in the slightest? They don't even speak Japanese—they hardly know how to say hello and goodbye.

The farmers' and fisher folks' kids are out chasing after the toys of the materialistic conquerors and the conquerors' kids are chasing after Japanese Buddhism. Were they thinking this or just putting on a polite show with blank minds? They did seem to appreciate the sincerity of the gaijin. Their own venerable Katagiri had dedicated his life to training foreign priests. The locals were so polite and kind and smiling and they were shaking hands and giving themselves to us that day. But surely they must have been nervously anxious for it to be over and for us all to leave—to leave them alone again to their simple disappearing lives that are hard and make sense and that would make a lot more sense once we had gone.

A half-dozen more Americans had arrived from Kyoto by car—laypeople who had studied with Katagiri at one time or another. I knew them all well and waved to those who caught my eye. No time to talk anymore—a bell was ringing. Nishiki had arrived and was ready to lead the service. I hopped up on the tatami from the side entrance and sat with Okamoto's wife and daughter, whom I'd met at the station. As the ceremony got going I looked across the open and airy room at the various colors of the robes of the priests and kimono and dresses of the country women and suits and ties of the country men—all those wrinkled faces so full of character, each distinct and strong. The foreigners, priest and lay, were in front of me in three rows, chanting with the natives and randomly sucking in air. Everyone was much more comfortable now that we were doing one of the few things we could do together.

With Isabel's camera I caught scenes of the ceremony: of her and the others from back home offering powdered incense, pinching and sprinkling, bowing and moving on. Isabel had already taken pictures of just about everything else—the Jizō out front, the earthen ovens, ladies preparing lunch, and her favorite, a statue of a badger in robes in the memorial-plaque-lined hall behind the altar.

The old folks were watching and chanting or not, bowing or not, sleeping or fidgeting, and the little girl by me was making some delightful contributions of her own in a high, sweet voice while her mother tried to occupy the child's attention with trinkets.

I looked up directly above our heads in the alcove and was chilled by what was there. In the midst of this gathering and recitation, tilting down in their high-hanging frames, were the faded, yellowed photographs of boys in military uniforms: teenagers, scared and fatalistically looking straight ahead into the camera lens, boys whose pictures were adorned recently, probably today, with fresh purple ribbons. These boys were the children of the locals, people who'd seen hard times, very hard—like losing these boys whose sad photos attested to the fact that they had died in the war. After the ceremony, an old-timer shocked me when she said, "Do you know where they died?" "No," I said. "Neither do we," she said. "We only know who killed them— the Emperor Shōwa." She was looking at one picture in particular. "The Emperor Shōwa and the right-wing fanatics who said the Emperor Shōwa was a god killed these boys." She smiled as I tensed up and swallowed. "The Americans only pulled the triggers," she added.

The priests were changing into less formal outer robes and people were dispersing. I got one last picture for Isabel of a man sitting on the tatami in front of the altar and flicking the ashes of his cigarette into an ashtray. He couldn't even wait for the echo of the last gong to fade before he lit up. Nobody noticed or cared, but if it had been an American zendo, the gasps would have blown his match out before the cigarette was even lit.

.   .   .

A procession walked up to the ohaka out back. It's a lovely little ashes yard on the side of a hill overlooking the valley. From there I could see the temple enclosed on three sides by cyprus and hydrangea. The winding path from below entered the ohaka and, on the other side, continued up and disappeared into a thick wood, suggesting that death is not final. Here were the stones and earth of local people who had passed on, fresh flowers offered before their proxies. It didn't seem as though there had been so many of them. This is a tiny village and the diminutive size of this ohaka gave it a cozy quality. It wouldn't frighten children or make adults nervous. It made it look like maybe just important people die.

Katagiri's stone was in the back row with the markers of the prior priests of this temple and was a gleaming light grey marble peppered with black dots. These memorial stones were about two and a half feet tall and looked like bombs on end. They were smooth and round and tapered at the bottom, got wider near the top, then came in to a point like a soft ice cream cone. On Katagiri's stone his Buddhist name was written vertically in black kanji. On those of the prior generations, if the names had been written, they had worn off. Those stones were darker and, as they stood for men of longer and longer ago, their rock was more and more worn and stubby and like the rough earth from which they came.

But today we concentrated on Katagiri's ice-cream-cone-bomb stone, all fresh and new and shiny. There was a hole at the base of it in front. Nishiki's eyebrows looked particularly frosty that day as he gently placed the urn of Katagiri's ashes in the hole. He took herbs that Isabel had brought from Green Gulch Farm and sprinkled them in the hole, put them on top of the stone and around it. Having done so, he filled the opening with dirt. Two metal buckets stood full of water at his side and he picked up one of two bamboo ladles that floated on the surface, dipped it in and poured the water over the stone two times and then with a third ladlefull he sprinkled water over the flowers that were placed in wide bamboo vases on either side of the memorial stone. We all silently watched his every move. From a bowl he took a little ball of white, glutinous mochi and placed it tenderly on the base of the stone. After that we started chanting the Heart Sutra and, one by one, each person did what he had done—including pouring water on the flowers, which he had improvised to freshen them up, not thinking that everyone else would copy him. The flowers became flooded with water and were practically washed away. I wondered if it would catch on and be done that way in future ceremonies at that temple or if some of the younger priests would henceforth include flower drenching in their ceremonies. Esoteric reasons for such a practice might even develop. Whole lectures could evolve: Avalokiteshvara, the bodhisattva who hears the cries of all beings, rains tears of compassion upon the flowers and suffering of the earth.

Then a disturbing thing happened. Something moving at the base of Katagiri's stone caught my eye. The surface appeared to be covered with short squirming white worms. They must be maggots, I thought as a shiver went down me. How could this be? His body isn't rotting down there—they didn't come with his ashes, did they? I stared longer and was sure they were moving. There were lots of people crowded around it taking turns offering water—none of them seemed to notice. Bending over, hoping not to be obvious, I inspected more closely and realized that what I was seeing was some of the Green Gulch herbs Isabel had brought floating on a thin film of water that covered the base of his memorial stone.

I straightened up and shook my head, then looked at Katagiri's wife and his students. They had suffered so much with him during his illness and death and had been mourning his absence for six months already. I looked at his long lost congregation. Today they came together to say goodbye to a memory. Today was just as much their day as his. At last they got to do something with him—sort of. It had been almost half a year since he died. None of us were overwhelmed with grief, but we were all a little down. Gradually the disparate group wandered back to the temple to have a modest feast and drink beer and sake in memory of a departed friend.

The gaijin and the locals were distributed much more equitably at this point around the long table. The unifying ceremony followed by alcohol and a generous spread of sushi, tempura and local dishes loosened us all up considerably. There were a few brief words before we ate. What I remember best is when the tall, thin, reserved caretaker of the temple said, "Katagiri-san was a great priest who took on a big job in America and died twenty years too soon." We toasted Katagiri. How true, I thought, just like Suzuki, twenty years too soon. It's a shame, a real shame, and nothing can be done about it.

TRAIN REFLECTIONS

KYOTO–MARUYAMA, SEPTEMBER 10, 1990

Looking out the window of the Shinkansen as it flew down the unclicking tracks from Kyoto, I stared at the irregular rice fields that led to farmhouses, highways, industry and the sea below. Every once in a while the train would enter a tunnel and my view would change to flashes of Katagiri's disciples pouring water on his granite stone at the ashes ceremony. It was good to have been with them. I hadn't yet seen him off in my mind's eye. Now I felt some satisfaction from the low moaning sadness I heard as the train slowed and pulled into one of the few stations it would stop at before Maruyama.

Maybe Katagiri didn't fail as much as he thought—or I thought. Things could be cooking in subtle ways that we hadn't anticipated. There are indications that he was pleased with the way he left it. Maybe in the end he just sailed over the contradictions.

Take the priests he left behind. For a while some years back he said he wanted his priests to be celibate, even though most Japanese Soto priests get married. That fell by the way along with other expectations. I know that Isabel is really more of a lay priest than what Katagiri originally had in mind as a priest priest. But as she told me, he had come to accept that his priests weren't going to be Nipponistically single-minded and diligent like him. Forget it. He told Isabel there was no one way to be a priest in the States, that the very definition of what it means is in flux and can't be pinned down. He accepted that that's the way it is and it's okay. She said that in that last winter before he died, they were discussing relations between the Minneapolis group and Sōtō-shū headquarters in Japan, and he said that it was fine for U.S. priests to register with headquarters or not to, that there could be a connection or not. Either way, that person could practice as a priest, the dharma was already flowing, already rooted beyond rules and regulations.

Katagiri once told me that Suzuki had never thanked him for his years of selfless service—showing he'd reacted to this typical closed-mouth Zen modus operandi much as I would have, hurt and still waiting for appreciation. So before he died I wrote him a letter in which I said thank you about twenty times. Thank you for coming to America and thank you for being such a good friend and thank you for being such a good teacher and on and on like that. Isabel said that he got hundreds of letters along those lines —people thanking him for touching their lives in such pivotal ways. She said he had no idea he'd affected people so strongly. All us expressive American students left no doubt that he passed on realizing that he was appreciated. And Isabel said it was from receiving this gratitude that he got a sense of how deeply he'd touched people, lots of people, lay and priest, and made a real difference in their lives. And even though she is a priest he gave transmission to, she said that his lay students carry his flame just as brightly.

Transmission is mysterious. I felt that at his ashes ceremony. Maybe his true dharma heir is the whole sangha, everyone he got to—not like the traditional stories with one or more of us realizing the true light, attaining a perfect understanding, and the rest just plodding along. I think we're all just plodding along—and that is the true light.

So did Katagiri fail, and am I a failure because I can't remember what Buddhism is—and are all the rest of us failures, as it seems, when contrasted against our early pure and simple expectations and the clear-cut enlightenment of the story books? The Shimbōji monks would say so. They'd just say we were all wallowing in delusion and that if we were enlightened we'd understand everything completely. A couple of them came to Katagiri's *nōkotsu* and they both mentioned afterward that he was a nice man but not really enlightened like their teacher, Chisei Roshi. The Shimbōji monks said that Zen had not come to America yet and that in Japan it only resided in their master and maybe a couple of others.

Isabel and I laughed and agreed. "That's why we had to use the peas," she said. "I'm sure that Chisei Roshi will not decompose." They had no more idea what she was talking about than those junior high kids who probably still think that Buddhism is some sort of toilet fetish cult.

Anyway, it seems to me that all our endless failures are adding up to a magnificent success. It's just not what we had in mind. It's real.

And Suzuki *did* thank Katagiri. I was there and I remember it well. Maybe Katagiri was expressing himself so completely that there was no room left to remember it, or maybe he just blocked it out. But I admired him for what he did. When the time came to grieve, he just grieved. It was the last formal meeting between

Suzuki and those disciples whom he had ordained as priests. There were about a dozen of us. We were sitting full of sadness around our tiny beloved teacher who had turned dark brown from the cancer and who was so weak. He was encouraging us to practice forever and to let go of the teacher. At one point Suzuki turned to Katagiri and thanked him for all he had done through the years.

Katagiri burst into tears and with a mournful voice he beseeched Suzuki, "Don't die." He started to make his way across the tatami floor on his knees, treading awkwardly on his brown kesa, and repeating, "Don't die, don't die." Throwing his arms around fragile Suzuki, he sobbed, expressing unreservedly the grief and love that the rest of us were trying so hard, like good little Zen soldiers, to keep inside.

A LETTER FROM NORMAN

MARUYAMA, SEPTEMBER 12, 1990

When I arrived home from the ashes ceremony there was a letter waiting for me from Norman. He'd been back in the States for a year and a half and was running his own zendo in Kalamazoo. He brought me up-to-date on what's what with the gang that was at Hōgoji.

Koji is living at his father's temple, helping out there half time. Two days a week he goes to a wealthy temple in Tokyo that can afford to pay him. I knew that much because Elin and I visited him in both places when she first arrived in Japan and we were pretending to be married. I didn't know the rest because he's one of those people who doesn't write. I've written him a number of

letters and he never answered one. I was so hurt—I thought he
was mad at me for some reason, that I'd made some fatal mistake
like not using the proper form of address in my letters. But I
knew everything was okay when he sent his regards to me through
Norman, who had called him on company business. Norman said
Koji wants me to come to Tokyo to teach Torture English. We
are friends forever. He's married and his wife is pregnant. She's
very happy, he says, and living most of the time with her parents
a couple of hundred kilometers away. They are not "separated,"
it's just one of the ways things are done. I sighed and waved to
Koji way up northeast.

Norman said that Maku and Jakushin both left Hōgoji before
their time was up, an anomaly—people are supposed to be dependable in this country and stick to one calling forever. Maku
took a job with the Sumitomo Bank. That's not totally outside
the fold, as the Sumitomo family is the most established *danka*
(member-supporters) of Suienji. Nishiki probably even arranged
it. I can just see Maku, looking respectable in a business suit,
surrounded by fellow employees all waiting late for the boss to
leave first. They'd all be napping and reading newspapers, except
for Maku, who'd be sitting at his desk still plugging away at an
obscure text on how to cultivate magic power.

Jakushin didn't even give notice. He just walked out one day.
Maku told Shuko that Jakushin went off to find Gyūhō, the monk
who'd been busted for LSD. Wonders never cease.

Dokujiki roughed up one too many freshmen and got canned,
though it was apparently handled so as to seem to be a promotion.
He had a temple to go to and so he's there now with his wife and
kids. Hope they can handle him.

Norman has ordained a woman disciple and is sending her to
Hōgoji for a year—"It's the practice place where I learned the
most about myself."

The last one of our old gang hanging on at Hōgoji, Shuko,
will be leaving too—at least for a while. Nishiki Roshi took pity
on Norman all alone in Michigan and asked Shuko to go join

him—to "let him know we love him and that there are no hard feelings"(!). MUTILATED JAPANESE MONK FOUND FLOATING IN LAKE.

What is this? A marriage of minds? or some sort of sadistic plot? The karmic shuffle continues.

I think Nishiki picked something up from Katagiri, something I hadn't thought of—they need us as much as we need them. I mean, they don't need us if they just want to be good Japanese monks and irrelevant to the present tense and the rest of the world. And we don't need them if we just want to be cowboy iconoclasts without regard for tradition and harmony— but we need each other to get out of our ruts and get on with it, get on with creating this diverse unity. Maybe we are each other's secret ingredient—to metamorphose. It's butterfly time.

EPILOGUE

BUILDING A *FUMIDAI*

I was outside making a *fumidai* in the soft presunset light when the call came from Jessica at Daianji. "Hōjō-san wants to see you after dinner."

I gulped and said I'd be there. I slid the aluminum-framed screen door open, stepped back out onto the swept and cleared cement into my zori and walked out from under the corrugated plastic overhang to stand under Maruyama's October sky. The heat was gone and the cold hadn't yet come. What does he want?

Then it was back to work on the fumidai. That's the word Okamura-san next door had used when told that the mess of planks at the edge of her drive was going to be a small platform to step up on before entering the house. I didn't know why on earth I'd waited so long to build the thing. I never liked seeing all the shoes and sandals scattered around. I was constantly straightening them. The fumidai would take care of that, the fumidai and the *getabako*.

Getabako means box for wooden clogs, and that's what Okamura-san called the shoe rack. She thinks it's the neatest thing on earth that we do projects like this around the house. She asked if everyone in America did all their own work on their houses. "Some people do sometimes," I told her.

I was sure that once I got the kitchen door area set up, everything would be in order forever. The idea was to step up on the fumidai from one's foot gear which would then be placed on a shelf. The house would be entered with clean feet and the kitchen entryway would remain tidy with plenty of room for our three bikes and two blue plastic trash cans.

Between the house and the neighbor's garden wall, I looked through a stack for some more appropriate wood, watching for

441

mukade in between the boards. Does Hōjō-san want to see me about the letters for Immigration that I had just asked him for before he went to breakfast? They were to be ready the next day and only he could write them. One letter verifies what studies I'm doing in Japan so I can renew my cultural visa and Elin her spouse's visa. Another letter assures that we are upstanding people, that he will be responsible for us and that, if we do anything reprehensible, he will cover for it and fly us back home. He hadn't checked with me about the specifics of the first letter as he usually did. Maybe he has a question on that. But he knows what to say. He's so used to writing these letters for us and his foreign monks and students who live at the temple. Most of us need new visas every six months. And he keeps copies. Hmm.

I found the board I wanted and took it around to where I was working. It matched its mates just fine. I put it down and started wire-brushing off the dirt and loose bark of a rounded end piece scavenged from the trash heap of an old family-owned lumberyard nearby. It would be the outside vertical piece for the getabako and would add a natural touch. It was the sort of quick and funky job that I'm best at.

Maybe Hōjō-san feels I'm not doing enough, that I gotta shape up or start going to the temple earlier in the morning as I used to, I pondered uncomfortably. It was the first time in three years he had asked to see me. We see each other a lot so there's never been a need to call me up. I turned on the trouble light that hung from the wall—it made everything look more yellow in the fading light of day.

I had the handy inches-and-centimeters tape measure that Kelly had brought me in the summer from the U.S. The blond pine floorboards and the brown weathered lauan shelf pieces were all to be thirty-seven inches and the supports for both structures thirty-three inches. Just two lengths—keep it simple. My finger squeezed the trigger of the skill saw and the first piece was cut, the remainder falling to the cement surface with a smack. I wanted to get the cutting done before dark, mainly so as not to bug the neighbors, but looking into the kitchen at the clock on the wall, I could tell it was time to see the boss. I hopped inside, walked through the kitchen and washed up at the laundry sink. After putting on clean pants and a shirt in the bedroom, I bid farewell to the baby-sitter, a twenty-year-old student of Elin's who lives in the neighborhood. She and baby Clay were playing on the tatami in Elin's study. Then I left by the front door and walked apprehensively over to the temple. Elin was downtown teaching at a culture center. What news would I have to tell her when she got back?

Inside the temple, I made my way in the semidark to the faded landscape on the fusuma outside of Hōjō-san's room. "Shitsurei itashimasu (excuse me)," I called out politely.

"Hai," he returned with oomph. "Go get Jo-san and wait in the ōsetsuma."

Jo-san was in her room.

"Hey, Jessica." I called her by her Christian name.

"Coming!" she answered enthusiastically.

She was as cheery as usual. I was smiling numbly, tapping my fingers on a knee as I sat on my shins in seiza on a flat blue cushion she had slid over to me. Jessica gave no hint as to why we were there and I got the feeling she had no idea. I didn't ask. We made small talk. How's the baby? from her; how's the kiln? from me.

Hōjō-san came in. He was humming. Good. I scanned him quickly. His eyes were clear and intense as usual. The tightness in my chest released and I felt my breath lowering. He seemed in a good mood.

He was wearing a loose light-brown cotton samue and holding a grey set of the same. He had been sewing a patch on one of the elbows. Looking at the patch and the thread that connected it to the worn sleeve, I knew that these materials wouldn't be there if he was angry with me. I watched him finger the patch.

"A true monk," I said in Japanese.

"A true monk," agreed Jessica.

Hōjō-san was still standing. He looked down at me where I sat and, ignoring our light-hearted praise, gave the first hint.

"What did he say?" I said to Jessica. "I didn't catch it."

"He said, 'I hate to tell you what I've got to tell you, when I look at your face.' "

Oh god, what could that mean? He can't write the letters for me for Immigration because he doesn't want to exaggerate anymore. The new head monk insists that I come every morning at four A.M. or not at all. A jealous neighbor has told him lies about us. What? . . . What? . . . I leaned toward him, largely ears, wanting to hear it quick. He complied.

"It's your landlord, Tsuda Sensei. His wife called. They want to sell the house. They want to sell it as soon as possible." He looked at me gravely.

Why hadn't I thought of it? Our wonderful home and garden next to the temple, our irreplaceable castle by the bamboo grove, which we lovingly restored and nurtured, our place to live, love and work is now to be pulled from under us.

"I thought this was going to be something bad," I said. "This is just a . . ." I fished for the word in Japanese. Technical? No. Realistic? No . . . "What is it in Japanese, Jo-san? A . . . yes, this is just a *practical* problem."

He chuckled and then made us the usual—thick, sudsy stimulating macha. We drank it and talked on about the ramifications of the news. The doctor was sick, I knew; lung cancer, I thought. His wife had told me secretly about it. He'd had it for years. Was the home to be sold because of inheritance taxes or what? Anyway, we had to get out if they insisted, because it had been rented to us dirt cheap as a favor to the temple and without the usual exorbitant key money.

Hōjō-san was so kind and concerned. I remembered the paranoid thoughts I'd had of him being tired of us or angry at me or dissatisfied with my participation. Nothing like that. He just wanted to help us get through this smoothly.

He asked me what would we do if we lost the house. "I don't know," I said. "Maybe go back to the States earlier than we'd planned."

Jessica remarked on how well I was taking it and how unattached I was.

Hōjō-san looked up at her. "You don't really think that's how he feels, do you?"

Ananda, the young monk from India, came in to report on the events of the day and to check up on a few things. I gave him the rest of my tea treat as I knew well that chocolate was Ananda's favorite object of desire that was compatible with his vows. I excused myself. Hōjō-san and I agreed to talk the next day after I'd gotten hold of the landlords. He said he'd have the documents ready for me at eight in the morning to take to Immigration. I'd forgotten all about that. I thanked him, standing and bowing in the hall, and was just about to step off when Glen, a tall, good-natured young monk from southern California, walked in with a box of chocolates he'd just received from his mother. He asked me to come back in and have some, but I declined.

Hōjō-san looked at me and said something else I didn't understand.

"Do you know what that means?" asked Jessica.

"No," I said. "Something about leaving early."

"Yes," she said and repeated his quip: " 'They who leave early . . .' It refers to an old saying that goes something like, 'One who leaves early may miss out on something.' "

I headed home, buzzing internally. On the way I looked at the lights of our house shining through the temple bamboo grove— so cozy. We'd just completed a new reorganization to accommodate the fact that Clay would soon be crawling. We'd bought some secondhand cabinets, fixed up the kitchen and prepared a baby room. Oh, change, I thought. I am so attached to all these fleeting things, things I love to collect and build and fix and write about. "And things that will disappear," I said out loud, standing on the darkening temple grounds, looking at the glow of our home.

I walked up the driveway to the side entrance by the kitchen, looked at the materials and tools lying about, sighed and wondered if I should even bother to finish the fumidai and getabako. So much has happened here. It's been a good three years in Maruyama—is it time to move on? Yeah, I guess so—it's time, I thought. I was sad, but also relieved of the burden of various petty thoughts and memories that had been bothering me just hours before. Why do I let such trivia get to me? I wondered. After all these years of Zen. What good is it? What have I learned? I shook my head. Looking into the evening sky, I felt light and imagined my family and me going way, way up there in a balloon, empty and free.

Then I glanced down at the wood before me and smiled. It looked so good I wanted to eat it. And so, returning to the full life I am enslaved by, I picked up a board and went back to work.

ONE DROP

MARUYAMA, APRIL 1, 1992

A week before we left Maruyama to return to the States, Hōjō-san said in sanzen that I had pretty much got the feeling of mu. Almost, huh? He said it just the way he's said things many times before —with a "nice try but no cigar" edge to it, just before he tells me to push harder, go deeper, cut, pierce and completely express the world of emptiness. Except this time he didn't say those things. He said I didn't need to do it anymore. What? I was so into it I didn't know how to respond. I didn't think of it as something I'd graduate from—it was a practice. I hadn't had any breakthrough experience. Is he just being nice to me because I'm leaving?

"No more mu?" I asked.

He elaborated. I listened closely. It was frustrating—I couldn't understand some of the key words. Damn his Japanese, I thought. Why can't he say it in simple terms? I couldn't read my final grade.

The next day I had sanzen with Jessica translating.

Watanabe told me that when people depart the temple, too often they leave their practice behind them. "Your way is not only in the temples and zendo but in your own everyday life. You don't have to be with a group or sit in a big zendo to practice. You can sit in the One Drop Zendo, walk and stand in the One Drop Zendo—and that of course is you. It will be wherever you are."

I thanked him for that teaching and then asked him if he could clarify everything he'd said to me about mu the day before. He laughed and said he had no idea what he'd said the day before.

"Well, what do you think my practice should be?" I asked, "If I don't do mu, what should I do?"

He looked at me fiercely. "Open your ears!" he yelled. "I already told you!"

GLOSSARY

Brief definitions of some Japanese and Buddhist terms, as used in this book (Skt. means Sanskrit)

Avalokiteshvara   Skt., the bodhisattva of compassion who hears the cries of the world.

bodhisattva   Skt., enlightening being, one who vows to enter Nirvana after all others, who vows to save all beings.

Bodhidharma   An Indian monk who became the first ancestor of Zen in China.

bonshō   Large brass hanging temple bell.

daikon   Giant white Japanese radish.

dhāranī   Skt., chants or incantations the sounds of which have beneficial effects, encouraging compassion or longevity.

dharma   Skt., Buddhist law, teaching.

dhyāna   Skt., Buddhist meditation.

Dōgen Zenji   The founder of Soto Zen in Japan.

dōjō   Practice hall.

dokusan   Soto Zen term for *sanzen,* private interview with the teacher.

eightfold path   The way to Nirvana: right meditation, right wisdom, right livelihood, etc.

Eiheiji	One of the two head temples of Soto Zen.
fusuma	Sliding door or partition, often covered by thick paper.
futon	Bedding.
gaijin	Foreigner (literally, "outside person").
gambatte	Go for it, make a strong effort.
gasshō	Buddhist gesture of greeting, with the palms of the hands placed together.
gāthā	Skt., originally a song, a short verse used to remind one of fundamental intention in the midst of everyday activities.
genmai cha	Green tea with some brown rice in it.
geta	Wooden platform sandals.
hai	Yes.
han	Wooden plaque struck with a mallet to call monks to the zendō.
hashi	Chopsticks.
hattō	Dharma hall, often the main temple building.
Heart Sutra	The core text of the Prajñā Pāramitā Sūtras, the Perfection of Wisdom, teaching on emptiness.
hinoki	Japanese cypress, temple carpenters' favorite.
Hōjō-san	Title for the head priest of a temple.
hōmu sutōru	A home store.
hondō	The main hall, or building, of a temple.
hōyō	A Buddhist memorial service.
ino	Soto Zen term for the officer in charge of ceremony and zendo discipline.
jinja	Shinto shrine.
Jōdo Shin-shū	"The true school of the Pure Land," a faith-oriented sect of Buddhism, the largest in Japan.
kama	A short-handled sickle.

kami	Spirits; gods associated with Shinto. Also used to mean God the creator.
kana	The Japanese syllabaries, hiragana and katakana.
kanji	Chinese characters (ideographs) used in Japanese writing.
kesa	Outer monk's robe of ordination (*okesa*, more respectfully).
ki	Vital, dynamic energy of body, mind and spirit; *chi* in Chinese.
kinhin	Walking zazen.
kōan	Literally, "public case," an exemplary story or dialogue used as a meditation object and worked on with a teacher.
koromo	The long-sleeved monk's robe worn over the kimono and under the *kesa*.
kuin	The temple kitchen.
kunugi	A kind of oak.
kyōsaku	Soto Zen term for the stick used to hit drowsy monks on the shoulder in order to bring them back to alertness.
mamushi	Japan's main poisonous snake.
mizo	A water run-off ditch, from curb to canal size.
Mountain Seat Ceremony	A rite in which the abbotship of a temple is passed on to the successor.
mukade	A kind of poisonous centipede.
namagomi	Organic garbage.
nani	What.
nine clay balls	Reference to a very old Soto Zen method of wiping the behind.
obentō	Boxed meal, compartmentalized meal, from cheap to fancy.
obi	A sash wrapped around the waist over the kimono.

ofuro	Bathtub (respectful form of *furo*).
ohaka	Grave, tomb, graveyard (respectful form of *haka*).
omedetō	Congratulations.
ōryōki	Monks' stacked and cloth-wrapped eating bowls.
ōsetsuma	Parlor.
rakusu	Monk or lay biblike vestment.
ramen	A type of Chinese noodle very popular in Japan.
Rinzai Zen	One of the two main sects of Zen, emphasizing vigorous dynamic style and systematic koan study.
rōshi	Venerable old teacher; respectful title for priest, especially in the U.S., where it is used as a title to mean Zen master.
sama	Polite form of address used after the name of another (never of oneself).
samādhi	Skt., a deep meditative state.
samu	Temple work practice.
samue	Temple work clothes.
sangha	Skt., the Buddhist community.
sanmon	The entrance gate to a temple, often a substantial building.
sanzen	Private interview with the Zen master concerning koan, breathing, Zen practice. Usually a Rinzai term.
seiza	Traditional Japanese position for sitting on floor wherein one rests on the knees and shins.
sensei	Title of respect, used especially for teachers, doctors and other professionals.
sesshin	A concentrated zazen retreat of one or more days, usually five or seven.

shashu	A formal position wherein the hands are held together at the solar plexus.
shiku nichi	Days for attending to private tasks in temple life (literally, four-nine days).
Shinto	Japan's native animist religion.
shōji	Sliding door of latticework and translucent rice paper.
shū	Sect, as in Sōtō-shū.
soba	Buckwheat noodles.
sodai gomi	Coarse trash, big useless stuff; often used as a term for retired husbands (who are also called "wet leaves").
Sōtō Zen	(In Eng., Soto Zen) One of the two main sects of Zen, emphasizing "just sitting" or silent illumination meditation, and its application to everyday activity.
stūpa	Skt., memorial monuments, originally built for the historical Buddha, pagoda being a type of stupa.
sugi	Japanese cedar.
sumi	Traditional black ink.
sumimasen	Something like "excuse me."
sunakku	Night club or bar (literally, "snack").
sūtra	Skt., discourses of the Buddha, used more loosely for old Buddhist scriptures or scriptures to be chanted.
suzumebachi	"Sparrow" bee.
tabi	Socks with a separate pocket for the big toe.
takuhatsu	Formal monk's begging (literally, to entrust the bowl).
tenzo	The head of the temple kitchen.
tōsu	Temple toilet.
uguisu	Japanese nightingale.

ushigaeru	Bullfrog.
yakitori	Japanese shish kebab (literally, grilled chicken) and the restaurants that specialize in such.
yakuseki	Monk's informal supper.
yakuza	The Japanese crime syndicates.
yamabato	Turtledove.
zabuton	Flat square cushion to kneel or sit on.
zafu	Zazen cushion, usually black and round.
zagu	The monk's bowing cloth.
zazen	Zen meditation, sitting meditation.
zazenkai	Zazen group or meeting.
zendō	Zen meditation hall, zazen hall.
zōri	Traditional straw sandals, now usually plastic thongs.